Rank-and-File Rebellion

Rank-and-File Rebellion

Teamsters for a Democratic Union

D A N   L A   B O T Z

V
VERSO
London · New York

First published by Verso 1990
© 1990 Dan La Botz
All rights reserved

Verso
UK: 6 Meard Street, London W1V 3HR
US: 29 West 35th Street, New York, NY 10001-2291

Verso is the imprint of New Left Books

British Library Cataloguing in Publication Data
La Botz, Dan
    Rank and file rebellion : Teamsters for a democratic union.
    1.   United States. Road freight transport services. Trade unions: International
    Brotherhood of Teamsters, Chauffeurs, Warehousemen, and Helpers of America.
    Leaders. Disputes with members, history
    I.   Title
    331.87

    ISBN   0-86091-289-2
    ISBN   0-86091-505-0 pbk

US Library of Congress Cataloguing in Publication Data
La Botz, Dan
    Rank and file rebellion : Teamsters for a Democratic Union / by Dan La Botz
        p.   cm. — (Haymarket series on North American politics and culture)
    Includes bibliographical references (p.) and index.
    ISBN   0-86091-289-2. —ISBN   0-86091-505-0 (pbk.)
    1.   International Brotherhood of Teamsters, Chauffeurs, Warehousemen, and Helpers of
    America—History. 2.   Teamsters for a Democratic Union—History. I. Title. 2. Series.
    HD6515.T3L3   1990
    331.88'11388324'0973—dc20

Typeset by NorthStar,
San Francisco, California
Printed in USA by The Alpine Press Inc.

To the men and women of the
International Brotherhood of Teamsters

The Haymarket Series

Editors: Mike Davis and Michael Sprinker

The Haymarket Series is a new publishing venture initiated by Verso offering original studies of politics, history and culture focused on North America. The series presents innovative but representative views from across the American left on a wide range of topics of current and continuing interest to socialists in North America and throughout the world. A century after the first May Day, the American left remains in the shadow of those martyrs whom this series honors and commemorates. The studies in the Haymarket Series testify to the living legacy of activism and political commitment for which they gave up their lives.

Already Published

THE FINAL FRONTIER: The Rise and Fall of the American Rocket State
by Dale Carter

POSTMODERNISM AND ITS DISCONTENTS: Theories, Practices
Edited by E. Ann Kaplan

AN INJURY TO ALL: The Decline of American Unionism
by Kim Moody

THE SOCIAL ORIGINS OF PRIVATE LIFE: A History of American Families,
1600–1900 *by Stephanie Coontz*

OUR OWN TIME: A History of American Labor and the Working Day
by David Roediger and Philip Foner

YOUTH, IDENTITY, POWER: The Chicano Movement
by Carlos Muñoz, Jr.

Forthcoming

FIRE IN THE HEARTH – THE RADICAL POLITICS OF PLACE IN
AMERICA: *The Year Left 4*

CITY OF QUARTZ: Excavating the Future in L.A.
by Mike Davis

THE MERCURY THEATER: Orson Welles and the Popular Front
by Michael Denning

THE POLITICS OF SOLIDARITY: Central America and the US Left
by Van Gosse

THE HISTORY OF BLACK POLITICAL THOUGHT *by Manning Marable*

Foreword

by Victor Reuther

The past decade, the Reagan years, have been among the most difficult that the labor movement has faced. Beginning with the Chrysler bailout of 1979, the employers began demanding and winning contract concessions from labor unions, cutting wages, taking away health benefits, and changing work rules. Contract concessions spread throughout the economy, and as a result workers' real wages declined and the standard of living of working people fell.

The employers began hiring law firms that specialized in defeating union organizing drives and in decertifying and removing labor unions from their companies. And when strikes occurred, employers began replacing union workers with strikebreakers in an attempt to destroy the union. The employers were successful in many of these efforts, and today only 16 percent of the workforce belongs to labor unions, the lowest level since World War II.

At the same time there has been an anti-union political climate, and the National Labor Relations Board and the courts have made many decisions that have limited the rights of workers and reduced the power of unions. The government itself acted as strikebreaker and union buster when Ronald Reagan destroyed the Professional Air Traffic Controllers (PATCO) in 1981.

During these years the unions were challenged as they had not been for decades, and, unfortunately, in many cases the union leadership proved unprepared to meet the challenge. But when the leaders failed to develop a strategy to deal with these new and threatening developments, rank-and-file union members began to become more active, and this has given rise to one of the most exciting and important developments in the labor movement in many years: the growth of union reform organizations that are revitalizing and reinvigorating the labor movement.

I have been most involved with New Directions, the rank-and-file movement that has been fighting for democracy and advocating a more militant policy in the United Auto Workers Union (UAW), the union in which I have been involved for more than fifty years. New Directions has been fighting for an end to union collaboration with management in the name of 'jointness' and the 'team concept', and demanding that the union fight to put the workers' interests before the company's profits. In doing so, New Directions is challenging the Administration Caucus, which had become a one-party state ruling the UAW.

I have also had the privilege of being associated with what I consider to be one of the most important developments in the labor movement today, Teamsters for a Democratic Union. TDU has invited me to its meetings and conventions, and I have met many of its activists. They remind me of the UAW activists I have known over the years – dedicated, committed union members – 'good hell-raisers' we called them in the UAW.

It was thirteen years ago that about 200 rank-and-file Teamsters formed an organization called Teamsters for a Democratic Union and took on the task of ousting the mob and reforming the Teamsters. At the time it seemed impossible. The Teamsters union was notorious for its ties to the mob, and Teamster President Jimmy Hoffa had only recently been abducted and was presumed to have been assassinated by the Mafia. Acting Teamster President Frank Fitzsimmons had made an alliance with President Richard Nixon, and government investigations into Mafia involvement in the Teamsters and its pension funds seemed to stall. Only 1 delegate out of 2,000 had the courage to stand up and speak out at the 1976 Teamsters convention, and shortly afterwards that delegate, TDU member Pete Camarata, was beaten by a goon squad right in the convention hotel.

When it began its fight for democracy TDU had only modest resources: little money, a tiny staff, a storefront office. It had only one thing going for it, but that one thing was the most important: the involvement and initiative of the rank and file. For thirteen years TDU organized and educated, opposing concession contracts, running candidates for local office, and putting forward a program for reform at the Teamster conventions. Over the years the group grew from 200 to 2,000, and from 2,000 to 10,000. By the mid-1980s, a majority and frequently two-thirds of the Teamsters were following TDU's lead in opposing concession contracts. TDU was no longer merely a gadfly engaged in constructive criticism of the Teamsters, it was no longer merely a small group of dissidents on the fringe of the union. TDU had become, as the author of this book puts it, 'the party of reform in the union'.

In 1989, largely as a result of the pressure brought by the TDU and the Teamster rank and file, two tremendous victories have been won. First, the Teamsters membership has won the right to majority rule on contract votes.

The idea of majority rule might seem a well-grounded, fundamental principle of democracy. But the principles of democracy did not prevail in the Teamsters union during the administrations of Frank Fitzsimmons, Roy Williams and Jackie Presser, when it took a two-thirds majority to reject a contract.

Second, under the pressure of the growing rank-and-file movement, in March 1989 the US Justice Department and the Teamsters union settled the Racketeer Influenced and Corrupt Organizations Act civil suit in basically the way that TDU had suggested. The government will not take over the union, but it has demanded that the Teamsters constitution be amended so that convention delegates and the union's top officers are directly elected by the members. The fight for democracy in the Teamsters union is far from over, and much remains to be done, but these two victories are enormously important not only for the Teamster rank and file, but for activists in other unions as well.

Dan La Botz's book, *Rank-and-File Rebellion: Teamsters for a Democratic Union*, should be read by every Teamster, by every labor union member, and by every citizen who is concerned about the future of democracy in our unions and in our nation. Most other books on the Teamsters have concentrated on the Mafia and on the union's top leadership; they have focused on corruption and scandal in the union. This is one of the few books on the modern Teamsters union that puts the ordinary worker, the honest and hard-working rank-and-file union member at the center of attention. The men and women described in the pages of this book, the men and women who drive trucks, work in warehouses, and cut vegetables in frozen food plants, have begun to build a movement not only to take back their union but to make it a force for progressive social change in America.

We're at a historic crossroads, and I'm going to be so bold as to make a prediction: the next decade will see changes on the trade union and political front far more sweeping than those of the 1930s. They will take a different form, but their impact and their direction will be far more profound, for this moment in history is pregnant with change. The nature of that change is not only in the hands of men like William McCarthy and Owen Bieber, or Ronald Reagan and George Bush – it is even more in the hands of the rank and file. For the rank and file is working at the level where change will take place; the rank and file is in a position to shape the future of the labor movement and this great nation of ours.

The age of one-party states is coming to an end. The one-party state is being overthrown in Poland and in China, in Mexico and in South Korea. And it is also coming to an end in our labor unions, in the Teamsters and in the UAW. The future is with democracy, with trade union democracy, with greater political and economic democracy. The future is with the rank and file.

Acknowledgements

I owe thanks to many people for their help in writing this book. First to my family. I was raised in a family where unions were important. My father's father, John Cornelius La Botz, was a Dutch immigrant and worked in Chicago's European bakeries, where he stood up for the rights of the bakers and was fired more than once for doing so. For most of her working life, my mother, Betty Buchanan, was a member of the Retail Clerks, a union steward for a while, and always the first person to call the union hall if someone was treated unfairly. My stepfather, Buck Buchanan, was a Teamster and a truck driver for Safeway in the late 1940s and early 1950s, and he has shared with me his memories of that experience.

In 1974 I went to work as a truck driver at F. Landon Cartage Co. in Chicago and became a member of the Chicago Truck Drivers Union Independent Local 705 (CTDU). The union was a dictatorship run by Executive Director Ed Fenner, and just before I became a member, a group of rank and filers had begun to fight for democracy. The group was made up of Bill and Mary Sullivan, Ray and Marcie Lopez, Bob and Mary Grant and Jim Benston, and I soon joined them.

Later, others from the city's Teamster locals joined the group as well, including Laura Hodge and Aaron Kesner of Local 705 and Danny Charleston of Local 710. Those were the founders in Chicago of Teamsters for a Decent Contract and later Teamsters for a Democratic Union. I learned much from all of them, but most from my friend Bob Grant. After TDC and TDU were organized, I worked as a volunteer with TDU leaders from other parts of the country and learned a great deal from them: Ken Paff, Carole Paff, Steve Kindred, Mel Packer, Mike Friedman and Steve Burks.

I left the trucking industry and TDU in 1980 but remained interested in the movement, and in 1986 wrote the text for a short picture history for the TDU's tenth anniversary. At the end of 1987 I asked the International Steering Committee of TDU for cooperation in writing a book about TDU. They agreed and so beginning in 1988 I traveled around the United States talking with TDU activists. Altogether I interviewed about seventy TDU members in the United States and Canada, visiting many in their homes, talking to some at TDU meetings, and interviewing a few by telephone. To each of them I owe the greatest thanks: Frances Adcock, Doug Allan, Mary Allan, Scott Askey, Sarah Bequette, Richard Black, John Braxton, Pete Camarata, Paul Castillo, Bilal Chaka, Niambi Chaka, Dennis Carlson, Jim Carothers, Sharon Cotrell, Roland "R.C." Davis, Joe Day, Bob Ellerman, Wanda Ellerman, Joe Fahey, Sam Fenn, Mike Friedman, Gerald Gallagher, Keith Gallagher, Milly Grant, Sam Grant, Frank Greco, Linda Gregg, Charlie Helton, Neal Henderson, H.C. Hulett, Eileen Janadia, Joel Jordan, Diana Kilmury, George Kirby, Don Landis, William Calvin Lawson, Sally Lynch, Cheryl Marquis, Vince Meredith, Doug Mims, Joyce Mims, Nick Montalvo, Jim Moody, Dennis Nagle, Tom O'Keefe, Don Paddock, Jim Petroff, Konstantine Petros, O.L. Pinson, Tom Pizzuto, George Ragland, Bob Richardson, Mildred Riley, Mike Ruscigno, Michael Savwoir, Don Scott, Bill Slater, John Smallman, Harold Smith, Jessica Soffer, Joe Stabilito, Linda Strom, Bill Stromatt, Waymon Stroud, Gail Sullivan, Esperanza Torres, Joe Urman, Patricia Wade, Rodger Whitehead. I also interviewed James Bender and Pat Lauer, who are not TDU members.

I am particularly grateful to the TDU staff: Chris Allamanno, Peter Cole, Myra Cordona, Frank DePirro, Susan Jennik, Steve Kindred, Ken Paff, Rick Smith, Marilyn Penttinen and former staff member Dave Pratt. I am also indebted to *Labor Notes* staff members Kim Moody, Jim Woodward, Jane Slaughter and Phill Kwik.

Mike Davis and Michael Sprinker of Verso saw this project through some difficult spots, and I appreciate their support. Thanks also to Steve Hiatt for his conscientious copyediting and production work. Barbara Garson got me in touch with my agent Frances Goldin, and I thank her for that. Frances read and made helpful comments on the entire book. A number of other people read and commented on part or all of the book, including Ken Blum, Peter Cole, Frank DePirro, Russel Durst, Sam Farber, Rusty Gilbert, Steve Kindred, Nelson Lichtenstein, Kim Moody, Ken Paff, Mike Parker, Rick Smith and Dave Staiger. I thank them for their comments and suggestions. The views and opinions expressed here are, however, my own.

My wife and partner, Sherry Baron, has been especially helpful. She supported me while I traveled, interviewed and wrote. She read every page and made me throw away nine out of ten of them. Our son, Traven, who is nearly two years old, has just learned how to pull off a sit-down strike and seems destined to be a militant.

1

The Revolution in Local 138

On 22 October 1986, Frank 'Butch' Ribustello, the president of Teamster Local 138 in Long Island City, New York, stormed into the Key Food warehouse. Followed by a couple of his men, he swept through the aisles until he found a warehouse worker named Mike Ruscigno. Ribustello started shouting at Ruscigno and cursing him, then punched Ruscigno again and again until he drew blood.

When his fury had subsided, Ribustello summoned the Key Food supervisor and ordered him to call the employees to the spot where he had beaten Mike Ruscigno. Once the workers were gathered around, Ribustello made a fifteen-minute speech filled with obscenities, attacking Ruscigno and other union members. He ended his diatribe with the words, 'The guy responsible for me blowing my job, he better f — ing watch out and watch his f — ing back.' Followed by his men, Butch Ribustello stormed out of the warehouse, got into his big car, and drove away.

Back in 1986, Teamster Local 138 in Long Island City was run just like most people think the whole Teamsters union is run. The 2,200 warehouse workers in Local 138 were dominated by a little dictator, Frank Ribustello, who was reputed to have ties to the Colombo Mafia family. As he had for years, Ribustello ran the union more or less as he saw fit, deciding who worked, who got fired, who got paid, and how much. Ribustello didn't like conflict with the employers, so he gave the grocery companies just about whatever they wanted. To keep the peace, he usually didn't accept grievances from the workers. And he told some workers at companies where he had contracts that they couldn't join the union at all, so they didn't get union wages or benefits. Local 138 was just a small cog in the big, corrupt machine that was the New York and New Jersey Teamsters union. It had been that way for years.

In September 1986, however, a group of rank-and-file union members decided to challenge Ribustello and the rest of his executive board in the local union elections. They began to put out literature criticizing Ribustello and his administration for stifling union democracy and negotiating substandard contracts. Mike Ruscigno, the man Ribustello attacked that day, was one of the challengers.

At one time violence might have worked, but, as Ribustello was to learn, it didn't work anymore. On 7 December 1986 Butch Ribustello and his buddies on the local's executive board were thrown out of office. They were not removed by higher officials of the Teamsters union, or by the US government. Despite firings and physical attacks, a group of rank-and-file Teamster members had undertaken to clean up their own union – and they had won. Overcoming fear and apathy, the union membership voted overwhelmingly against Ribustello and his cronies and replaced them with a group of union reformers.

When Butch Ribustello punched Mike Ruscigno, he hit the wrong man. Ruscigno was born in 1952 in Brooklyn and grew up there. He wanted to travel after finishing high school, so he became a merchant seaman and spent four years at sea, making port in Russia, India, various ports-of-call in Africa, and up and down the east coast of South America. 'It was quite an education', he says in his heavy Brooklyn accent. 'I thought I should have paid *them* when I got home. I was nineteen when I left, and I tell you after you leave this country and see somewhere else, you're glad to be back home.'

After four years at sea, Mike still had the urge to travel and began hitchhiking around the United States, eventually settling down for six or seven years in Louisiana. He worked at a variety of jobs there, including building fiberglass boats, working in a toy warehouse, and doing auto-body work. After a time he tired of Louisiana, sold the house he had bought there, and eventually came home to Brooklyn.

After visiting with the family and friends he had not seen for years, Mike went out to find a job. 'First I worked at a casket company, South Brooklyn Casket Company. When I got the job I thought the guy said *gasket*. Then I went there and found out it was *caskets* they bury people in. They were metal boxes – which is the latest – so I was knocking the dents out of them and priming them with primer paint – body shop work again.' He was laid off at the casket company, and in October 1984 he got a job at Key Food, a grocery warehouse, one of the workplaces in Butch Ribustello's Local 138.

Mike was hired at Key Food as a 'selector': his job was to pick grocery cases to be loaded on pallets, which were then loaded on trucks for delivery to grocery stores. Mike is a big man, six feet tall, about 180 pounds, and in pretty good shape, and at the time he was younger, just thirty-two years old. Still, 'It was rough', he says. 'You're supposed to pick over nine hundred cases an hour. I said, "give it three weeks, a month, and I'm out of here." I don't think I've ever worked that hard in my life. I didn't think I'd make it.' But he did make it, and after a ninety-day probationary period, he became a member of the union. It was not something he was particularly proud of: 'To me the union was just something you pay your dues to, and you keep your mouth shut, and you keep the job.'

Then one day at work a friend drove up on his forklift and asked Ruscigno if he would be interested in becoming a member of an organization called Teamsters for a Democratic Union – TDU – which was trying to reform the union. 'He asked me, "Would you like to know what your rights are? What the union is supposed to do for you, and learn your rights as a working person?" And I asked him if he belonged to it, and he said he did. And I said, "Okay, if I have any problems or questions, I'll ask you." He drove away, then he came back and looked at me, and he said, "Wouldn't you like to know for yourself?" And it kind of hit me like a brick wall, you know.' Mike Ruscigno joined the reformers.

A few months later there was a problem at work. The company had assigned a man to a job in violation of the seniority rules. At another company, in another union, the matter would have been routine, but in Teamster Local 138 it was a big problem. The union steward was John Smallman, a 41-year-old Vietnam vet who had been working at Key Food since 1979 and, like Ruscigno, had recently joined Teamsters for a Democratic Union. For weeks Smallman had been wanting to file the grievance, but local president Ribustello had refused to give him the official grievance form. 'I got tired of asking for grievance sheets', says Smallman, 'so I copied a TDU fact-gathering grievance sheet and started using it.' Smallman wrote up the grievance, then went round and asked Ruscigno to join in signing it. A few days after he filed it, Smallman was fired for use of an unauthorized grievance form and conducting union business on company time.

It happened that the company fired Smallman on Memorial Day. 'That really hit me', says Ruscigno. 'It was really dirty. I mean here he is a Vietnam vet, and they fired him on Memorial Day. And they fired him for using an unauthorized form. It caused quite an uprising and a stir in the workplace, because here's a man was out of work now after he's been there eight years.'

Others had been fired at Key Food in the past, and the men who worked there knew that it was pointless to go to the union. They knew that it was in fact quite likely that the union had asked the company to fire Smallman because he had had the audacity to file a grievance and had been involved in TDU. In the past, the warehouse workers probably would not have done anything about a firing, but this time things were different. 'We had somewhere to turn to', says Ruscigno.

With the help of TDU, the Key Food workers organized an informational picket line and began picketing the company in the morning. And not only did the Key Food workers picket, but TDU even got Teamsters from other locals to join the picket line to protest Smallman's firing. 'We had one demonstration', remembers Smallman, 'with people from other shops in Local 138, and even Teamsters from Long Island TDU. Altogether about two hundred people showed up.' The workers were amazed. No one in Local 138 had ever seen such a thing before. It was a new experience: solidarity.

Because of pressure from the workers at Key Food and because publicity about the incident had gone beyond the local union, Ribustello was forced to grieve Smallman's case, taking it to arbitration. 'But he lost the arbitration', says Ruscigno. 'We've always lost every arbitration we've ever had, so for Smallman to lose his arbitration was nothing new.'

However, with TDU's help Smallman took the case before the National Labor Relations Board (NLRB). 'I was involved as a witness and testifying, and so were the other workers', says Mike. 'I was going into this thing hook, line and sinker. In the process I was learning a lot about my rights, about organizations, about organizing, about what it really takes, *and that we are the union.*' The TDU attorneys succeeded in proving bias on the part of the arbitrator, and John Smallman won his case before the National Labor Relations Board, although the company of course appealed and it was more than a year later that the appeal was denied and Smallman was finally vindicated.

Meanwhile, the situation at Key Food had really changed. 'I call it the revolution', says Ruscigno. 'The uprising against the union was caused by your second and third shifters, your new people. The old timers wouldn't get too involved. We were fighting for our rights, for some representation. We thought that if you had a problem the union should come down and back you up.' A couple of Key Food workers even started putting out their own newsletter, with articles about the shop and the union written by the workers themselves. 'It was the *Free Key Press*, and it really had Key Food jumping and hopping.'

Teamsters for a Democratic Union had been the catalyst of what Ruscigno called the 'revolution'. Throughout these events, a few of the Key Food workers had been meeting with the New York–area TDU organizer, Susan Jennik. Jennik, herself an experienced labor union activist and an attorney, had advised them on their legal rights as union members and had helped them think through problems as they arose. Jennik also helped set up meetings between the Key Food workers and other workers in Local 138. 'The law cannot solve your problems, and no lawyer and no judge is going to reform the Teamsters union', she told Ruscigno and the others. 'That's something that can only be done by the members. In order to have democracy you have to have the members actually running the union, and in order for the members to run it they have to be active in it. And in order to do that they have to organize themselves.'

The workers began to organize, and within the empty shell of the old union, a new union was born. 'We formed a Local 138 committee from all the different shops', Mike recalls. 'TDU helped us get in touch with other people from different shops – White Rose, Schreier Groceries, Schaeffer, Captain's Post, Krasdale's, Modern Maid – these were all Local 138 shops. We never realized that Local 138 had all these shops, until we got to digging and talking to other people and asking, "What shop do you belong to?"

'And we found out the consensus – if that's the right word – everybody was disgruntled with the Local 138 executive board, and they wanted changes but they never had anywhere to go. You had the union, and you had the company. And you couldn't get the union to do anything for you, and the company wasn't going to do anything for you. So the worker was lost in the middle. After contacting these other shops we all got together, and we started meeting together on Sundays. There weren't huge turnouts at the meetings, but the people that came were the active people.'

Nick Montalvo was one of the other Local 138 workers at those meetings, and a man who was destined to become another crusader in the union. Montalvo had been born in Puerto Rico, grew up on a farm there, and came to the United States in 1952. After he first arrived, Montalvo worked on farms in New Jersey in the summer harvesting everything from asparagus to peaches, while during the winter he worked in restaurants and became a fry cook. Later he moved to New York, and in 1960 he got a job at the H. Schreier grocery warehouse and became a member of Local 138.

From the beginning Montalvo wanted to know more about the union. 'Through the years I sort of educated myself', says Montalvo, 'because I didn't get any kind of help from anybody. I kept educating myself about the rights of a union man in this country.' The other workers came to Montalvo for help and advice, and sometimes he served as the union steward. But with Butch Ribustello running Local 138, the union didn't do much for the members. 'Every time an employee had to deal with some kind of legal demand we used to go to the Labor Board rather than going to the union.' Montalvo didn't become a vocal critic of the Ribustello regime until 1984, when, he says, 'They sold us.'

What happened was this: in the 1980s employers in many industries began demanding take-aways or concessions from the union. 'In 1984', explains Nick Montalvo, 'the Greater New York Wholesale Association, of which my employer was a part, demanded that the starting time be moved to seven o'clock in the morning instead of eight o'clock.' Under the old contract, which had been in force for twenty-five years, the workers who started work at seven o'clock, as most of them did, were paid overtime at time and a half for the hour between seven and eight.

Under the new contract, work would officially begin at seven, so the workers would lose that one hour of overtime per day, which amounted to

$85 a week, about $365 a month, or more than $4,420 a year, out of the paycheck of a warehouse worker with a family to support. 'We were counting on that money as part of the salary', says Montalvo.

Nor was money the only issue. The union also gave concessions on work rules that affected warehousemen and drivers and helpers. And the union gave it all away without a fight. 'We had no say in the agreement', insists Montalvo. 'We had no say in the signing. We were put out on strike for three days without votes; and then we were told to go back to work without votes. The democracy of the worker was taken away by the union officials. The membership became very unhappy with the local.'

Montalvo, angry about being sold out, began going to the Sunday TDU meetings with Mike Ruscigno and other workers from other grocery warehouses in Local 138. The group met for several weeks, discussing union issues, and in April 1986 began to publish a newsletter called *The Bottom Line*, circulating it throughout the warehouses in the local. The first article in the newsletter was titled 'A Call To Arms':

> We are Teamsters! We should be proud of our union, but most of us are not. Why? ... We see our [Teamster] National President on television pleading the Fifth Amendment to sidestep questions that decent union members expect him to answer. We see our local officials around the country being indicted by organized crime commissions. In the eyes of the public we bear the embarrassment that Mr. Presser [then president of the Teamsters] refuses to acknowledge. We live in the shadow of shame blanketing the Teamsters because our leaders have led us here.
>
> No one on the tube tells America what kind of people work as Teamsters. All America sees are hoodlums and flunkies going to jail and squirming to make deals.
>
> Well, I am a Teamster. I work hard. I feed and care for my family and I obey the law. The only compromise I make is when I ignore the kind of people who run my union. This brings me to a pair of questions:
>
> DO YOU BELONG TO LOCAL 138?
> DOES LOCAL 138 BELONG TO YOU?
>
> It's 1986, an election year in Local 138. It's time to open our eyes to the future. It's time to establish our pride.

In September 1986 the disaffected members of Local 138 put up an entire slate to challenge the Ribustello regime. They chose John Georgopoulos, a 39-year-old warehouse worker from White Rose to head the New Beginning slate, as they called themselves; among the other candidates for the executive board were Mike Ruscigno and Nick Montalvo. The slate represented most of the major workplaces in the local; one member of the slate was Puerto Rican, and one was Black. Six of the seven were members of Teamsters for a Democratic Union. Their platform called for regular union meetings, enforcement of the contract, election of stewards and respectful representation of the members.

Ribustello and his cronies couldn't debate the issues with the members: they didn't have a leg to stand on. So they did something else. When Nick Montalvo talks about it, he seems as hurt as he is angry. 'They did something that was very unfair, calling me, branding me as a Communist', says Montalvo. They went to warehouses where he wasn't known, and told workers who had never met him that Montalvo was a Communist. 'That was the only kind of campaign they could put up against me – and they used it, to no avail, but they used it.'

Ribustello's slate spread the word throughout the warehouses that the men on the New Beginning ticket were a bunch of Communists, but the ploy didn't work. The workers saw through the red-baiting. The New Beginning slate didn't respond to the attacks but instead focused on the issues, talking about union democracy and contract concessions. In addition to *The Bottom Line*, they put out buttons, palm cards and direct mailings to the entire union membership, all paid for out of voluntary contributions from union member supporters. But Ribustello and the other incumbent officers retained considerable power: they had the simple advantage of incumbency; they had the use of the union office, the phones, the mails; they could visit all the workplaces, supposedly on union business, but actually campaigning.

It would have been a close race, and Ribustello might have won – if he hadn't proven to be as big a fool as he was a thug. When Ribustello visited the Key Food warehouse, attacked Mike Ruscigno, and gave his threatening speech to the assembled warehouse workers he made a big mistake. Ruscigno had turned on the tape recorder he carried at work to protect himself from company setups, and he had every foul word on tape. TDU took the tape to court and sought an injunction against Local 138 President Frank Ribustello. In November 1986 Judge Glasser of the United States District Court for the Eastern District of New York enjoined Ribustello 'from infringing the free speech rights of Michael Ruscigno ... and any other candidate for union office in Local 138 of the International Brotherhood of Teamsters by attacking, harassing, or threatening these individuals, or by interfering in free speech and assembly during the pendency of this action.'

Ribustello had turned the tide for the New Beginning slate. The attack and the injunction were discussed throughout the local, and on election day busloads of members came to the polls wearing New Beginning slate buttons. Georgopoulos defeated Ribustello by a vote of 528 to 200, and others on the New Beginning slate won by margins of as much as three to one.

In a sense, the election victory was only the beginning, for, when they took possession of the Local 138, Georgopoulos and the other members of the New Beginning group discovered that things were worse than they had expected. 'Ribustello had a lot of contracts with two people in the union', explains TDU organizer Susan Jennik, 'the boss and his son. The workers didn't know anything about the union. The contract had none of the standard benefits. But the boss and his son had a health and pension plan.'

'The records that they kept weren't in good order, and it took us a whole year to try to straighten out the membership records', says Montalvo. Not only were the records poorly kept, but in some cases the outgoing officials had shuffled and scrambled the file drawers. The new Local 138 reform leadership was faced with problems from the employers who had gotten such a good deal from Ribustello over the years. No sooner were the reformers elected than there was a lockout at one company and a decertification petition to remove the union at another. And nineteen contracts came up for expiration on 31 January, a little over a month after the election.

'We had a couple of strikes', says Montalvo. Both of them were over important issues like fringe benefits and wages. When the union was forced out on strike, 'We tried to get others involved. We let everybody know that we were on strike, and that we wanted the help and cooperation of everybody else.' Such solidarity was unknown in Local 138 during the Ribustello years, when each group of warehouse workers, if they struck, struck on their own. 'In the end', says Montalvo, 'we came out all right.'

I talked with the reformers more than a year after the election in the union offices on Jackson Avenue in Long Island City, near Queens. There was a lot of history in the office: old charters from the United Hebrew Trades dating from November 1913, and Teamster charters dating back to 1915 and 1940 signed by Teamster President Daniel Tobin and Secretary-Treasurer Thomas L. Hughes. And tacked on one of the bulletin boards was, in a sense, the latest charter, a newspaper clipping dated 8 December 1986 with the headline 'Dissident Teamsters Win Local'.

The union officers were busy. President Georgopoulos was on the phone discussing a contract negotiation. Paul Auriemma, the secretary-treasurer, was working on the local's financial records. Others were dealing with grievances. The office was a little disorderly and a little hectic, the way a busy union office ought to be. 'A lot of things have changed', says Ruscigno. 'There's more traffic, more communication. We follow through with the workers' problems. If they have a grievance to file, or if something's wrong at work, we go down there and try to get it cleared up for them.

'We've given them representation, which is one thing they never had. We're down at the shops. We're making ourselves available to everybody. We're also conducting union meetings. We're making their contracts available to them. We're giving them a voice in their union. We've conducted seminars for shop steward education. We want the union to work for them, and we're trying to educate them that *they* are the union, that we work for them now.' As Mike Ruscigno says, it was a kind of 'revolution'.

2

The Fight for the Teamsters Union

What happened in Local 138 was a microcosm of a fight for union democracy that is taking place throughout the Teamsters union. A tremendous struggle for control of the union is taking place between the Mafia and the federal government, the top Teamster officials and some of the country's largest employers. But also fighting for control of the union are those to whom it rightfully belongs: its grass-roots membership, its rank and file. This book is the story of TDU – Teamsters for a Democratic Union – the rank-and-file movement leading the fight to reform the International Brotherhood of Teamsters, the largest and most powerful union in North America.

For decades the government had been investigating corruption and mob influence in the Teamsters. Finally, in late June 1988, the Justice Department filed suit in US District Court in Washington, DC to throw the top Teamster officials out of office because they were controlled by the Mafia. In its brief the Justice Department charged: 'The IBT leadership has made a devil's pact with La Cosa Nostra – La Cosa Nostra figures have insured the elections of the IBT's top officers, including the union's last two presidents.' The Justice Department claimed that Mafia control of the union was 'so pervasive that for decades the IBT's leadership has permitted La Cosa Nostra figures to dominate and corrupt important teamster locals, joint councils and benefit funds.' The criminals, the brief alleged, had carried out a 'campaign of fear' that included twenty murders and dozens of bombings.

Working with the Mafia, several Teamster officers and employees had engaged in an orgy of plunder. They sacked the Teamster pension funds, taking millions of dollars; they put ghost employees on the union payroll who received large salaries but who never showed up for work; and they took pay-offs from the employers to prevent strikes and forestall organizing drives. They ignored labor laws and bullied the members.

9

This corrupt regime was perfectly symbolized by former Teamster President Jackie Presser's appearance at the 1986 Teamsters convention in Las Vegas. It was like a scene from ancient Rome in its days of decline and depravity, as Presser, an enormously fat man of some 300 or 400 pounds – looking like some decadent emperor, some Nero or Caligula – was carried into the hall on a sedan chair on the shoulders of four husky weightlifters dressed in the sandals and tunics of Roman centurions.

The men lugged Presser's palanquin into a great hall where hundreds of guests were gathered around tables straining under the weight of a cornucopia of caviar and lobster, ham and beef, cheese and pâté, and vast quantities of alcohol. Cheers and applause went up from the crowd, hailing the chief who had provided this bounty. Jackie Presser, President of the International Brotherhood of Teamsters, Chauffeurs, Warehousemen and Helpers of America had arrived! Let the orgy begin!

That party was hosted by 'Joe T.' Trerotola, head of the Eastern Conference of Teamsters; it cost $675,000 and was only one of several such affairs for union officials, with the total cost of Teamster entertainment at that one convention exceeding a million dollars. Delegates were given 'I Love Jackie' buttons the size of a saucer, and for $35 delegates and guests could purchase wrist watches adorned with Presser's face. Throughout the convention Presser was surrounded not only by the usual collection of Teamster toadies and timeservers, and his praetorian guard, BLAST, the Brotherhood of Loyal Americans and Strong Teamsters, but also by trucking company officers and employers association representatives bedecked with 'I Love Jackie' buttons and sporting their new Presser timepieces. At moments like these Jackie Presser seemed to have become his own caricature, a larger-than-life cartoon of himself. It was to this scene that the Teamsters union had arrived, this comic opera, this circus sideshow, this Marx Brothers movie.

The process had begun long before: in the early days, President Daniel J. Tobin turned a blind eye to corruption in the big city locals like New York and Chicago. Later, in the 1950s, President Dave Beck enriched himself at the expense of the union and the members. Jimmy Hoffa, the idol of the dock workers and truck drivers and the man who negotiated their freight contract, betrayed their trust when he brought the Mafia into the union.

By the 1970s, when Frank Fitzsimmons took over, the union had become a dictatorship of the general president. He controlled it all: the five Regional Conferences, the several Joint Councils made up of Teamster organizations in major cities or states, the negotiation of the major contracts, the important grievance panels, and the union representatives on the boards of the billion-dollar pension and health and welfare funds. The union had passed from the control of its members to the control of a president who had been handpicked by the Mafia.

The union became infamous for murders, bombings, embezzlement and bribes, and the public came to identify the Teamsters with the mobsters, and the Mafia with the members. The notoriety weakened not only the Teamsters, but the entire labor movement, and it became more difficult to organize, tougher to negotiate contracts, and harder to win strikes. The Teamster = mobster equation was unfortunate, because, of course, few Teamsters are criminals. The 1.6 million Teamsters in the United States, Canada and Puerto Rico drive trucks and work in warehouses, handle heavy equipment and drive schoolbuses, process frozen food and work in nursing homes. At the heart of the union are the dock workers and truck drivers in the motor freight industry who load and drive the trucks that carry goods across the continent. The vast majority of these Teamsters are honest, hard-working men and women who want a better life for their families.

If these workers did not stand up and speak out against the union leadership, it was not because they were apathetic, but because they knew that the union had reached an accommodation with the employers, and that those who called for reform might be fired or blacklisted – or perhaps worse. It is all the more impressive, then, that in 1976 nearly 200 Teamsters met at Kent State University in Ohio and formed Teamsters for a Democratic Union to fight the influence of the Mafia, to end the dictatorship of the general president, and to win the union back for its members.

TDU has survived and grown because of the members' increasing disappointment with the union's inability to negotiate decent contracts. During the period from the 1940s to the 1960s, the Teamsters were perceived to be a union that delivered the goods for its members, and there was much truth in that perception, particularly for freight workers, who got higher wages and more generous benefits throughout those years.

But beginning in the 1970s, the union became less effective in winning higher wages and benefits from the employers, and this led to increasing dissatisfaction. The members began to vote in ever larger numbers against proposed contracts. In 1987 and 1988, an overwhelming majority of Teamster members rejected the contracts proposed by their leaders with the freight companies, carhaul companies, and with United Parcel Service (UPS), the largest Teamster employer. Those contract votes were a rank-and-file referendum on the government of the Teamsters, and the members cast a vote of no confidence in their leaders.

Behind these votes is an attack by both the government and the employers that is virtually indistinguishable in its effects from old-fashioned union busting. The government deregulation of the freight industry in 1980 resulted in hundreds of union carriers going bankrupt as new, non-union companies entered the industry. At the same time, union companies began 'double-breasting', that is, opening non-union subsidiaries and shifting work to them.

As result, the Teamsters' largest and most important contract, the National Master Freight Agreement (NMFA), which in the 1970s covered nearly 500,000 workers, today covers only 200,000. The decline of the NMFA was the result of union busting on an enormous scale, not by frontal assault, but rather by a shift in terrain of employer-worker struggle. Although the public still thinks of the Teamsters as a powerful union, the employers have decimated the union during the past ten years, and the Teamsters have nearly lost control of the motor freight industry they once dominated.

Where the union has not been eliminated, the contract has been weakened. The intense competition caused by deregulation has led trucking industry employers to demand take-away or concession contracts that cut wages and benefits and attacked working conditions. At the heart of the contract are the issues of working conditions, productivity, and control of the workplace. In the last fifteen years the Teamster employers have introduced new methods that have pushed their employees to work harder and faster, risking their health and taking a toll on their family life.

Other Teamsters never even got a permanent, full-time job. Perhaps the greatest disgrace to the industry and the union is the growth in the use of 'casuals' – throw-away workers who not only receive lower wages and fewer benefits, but who also suffer the added indignity of being treated like second-class citizens in their own union.

For Teamsters union members, these trends have together meant a decline in their standard of living for the first time since the 1920s. Many union members have been forced to deny their families many of the things they once hoped to afford – college educations, new homes and automobiles, better quality clothing, food and entertainment – all of the things we call 'the American way of life'. Unable or unwilling to defend its strongest and highest paid members in the trucking industry, the union has done little to improve the situation for the hundreds of thousands of members, many of them Black, Latin and female, who labor in the manufacturing, food processing and service industries.

The union leadership has not resisted this employers' offensive. As the employers bullied the union, taking away and tearing up one clause of the contract after another, the union leadership organized no show of strength, no work stoppages, no Teamster strikes. Quite the contrary; throughout the 1980s Teamster officials collaborated with management in foisting concession contracts on the union's members. Adding insult to injury, many Teamsters were asked to lend or give money to their employes, and to participate in employee stock ownership plans (ESOPs), many of them utterly fraudulent, while at the same time accepting further pay cuts. It is the crisis in the union – in the relations between the union and management, and between the union leadership and the rank and file – that led to the growth and expansion of the reform movement.

The Mafia dons, US government attorneys, trucking industry employers, and, most recently, rival cliques on the IBT General Executive Board have tremendous political power and vast economic resources. They are accustomed to wielding power and are prepared to fight for it. As individuals, the rank-and-file members of the Teamsters have no political power and few economic resources. Yet collectively they are potentially the most important force in the struggle for the Teamsters today.

Over the past two decades these ordinary men and women have by extraordinary effort succeeded in building a movement and creating an organization to reform the Teamsters union. Their organization, Teamsters for a Democratic Union, has become more than a union reform caucus. It has become a crusade involving tens of thousands of Teamsters across the country who demand democracy in their union and justice from their employers.

During the last fourteen years TDU has aided individual workers in dealing with grievances and firings, and has helped groups of workers fight for democratic local union by-laws. It has taught workers their legal rights and has helped fight for them before the National Labor Relations Board, at the Department of Labor, and in the courts. TDU has helped reformers run for local union office and has put forward candidates for the top offices of the International union. And TDU has helped freight workers, carhaulers, UPS employees, grocery warehouse workers, and cannery workers battle for decent contracts.

There have been struggles to control union pension funds, to improve health benefits and safety conditions, and for civil rights and equal opportunity. And TDU has fought for over a decade to reform the IBT's General Executive Board and the International Convention, and to win the right of union members to elect their convention delegates and International officers. Teamsters for a Democratic Union has given rank-and-file union members a voice with which to express their needs, desires and ideals. It has given women and men who were beaten down by the system the courage to stand up and demand their rights from their union officials, their employers and their government.

While fighting against corruption, Teamsters for a Democratic Union has also tried to redeem and revive the best traditions, the really heroic traditions of the Teamsters. Like other union members, Teamsters risked their lives – and sometimes lost them – to fight for their union. In the great Chicago Teamster strike of 1905, shortly after the union was founded, 21 workers were killed and 415 injured, and the union was broken – but not for long. In the Minneapolis Teamsters strike of 1934 two Teamster pickets – John Belor and Henry Ness – were killed, while scores of others were wounded by police, some shot in the back, in a fight for union recognition. One of the leaders of the campaign to organize over-the-road drivers, Pat Corcoran, was assassinated in 1937, probably by the employers, though no one was ever charged with his murder.

Over the years many other members have made sacrifices, been fired from their jobs, been blacklisted and driven from the industry, or have walked the picket lines so that workers today might have the right to belong to a union, be protected by a contract, and enjoy a better life. TDU believes that the rank and file did not make those sacrifices in order to see their union handed over to the employers, taken over by the mob or run by the government. The Teamsters who were capable of building the union, they argue, are capable of reforming it and running it.

The reform movement's fight for democracy, combined with government legal action against the corrupt union leadership, has now begun to bring about some really significant changes. On 13 March 1989 the US government and the Teamsters settled the lawsuit filed by the government against the union under the Racketeer Influenced and Corrupt Organizations Act, with the court appointing officers to oversee many activities and the union agreeing to conduct direct elections of convention delegates and International officers. That historic agreement marks the beginning of a new era in the Teamsters, and has the potential of breaking the Mafia's stranglehold on the union.

In September 1989 Ron Carey, the president of Teamster Local 804 in New York, declared his candidacy for the office of general president of the Teamsters. Two months later, TDU endorsed Carey's candidacy. For the first time in decades, not only are there to be democratic elections in the Teamsters, but there is also a candidate who calls for an end to corruption, for union democracy, and for a militant stand against the employers. And standing behind him is a movement determined to win his election and prepared to see that he keeps his promises. This remarkable development could not have happened without the fourteen-year-long struggle of TDU. More than a dozen years ago, when TDU began its fight for union reform, it was a David and Goliath struggle. It isn't any more. Today the Teamsters reform movement is an increasingly powerful force within the Teamsters, a reform party vying for leadership of the union.

The struggle for control of the Teamsters union is not merely of interest to Teamsters. The fight for union democracy, to end mob control, weed out bureaucratic dictators, and give the members a vote on their own affairs, is an issue in which all who believe in democracy, in workers' rights and in social justice have a stake. A victory for union democracy in the Teamsters union would be a victory as well for those who suffer under gangster domination in other unions, and for all union members who spend their work lives in labor unions that are one-party regimes.

Moreover, if the Teamsters union becomes a strong, healthy force in the labor movement, fighting to improve the wages, benefits and working conditions of its members, that too will be an example to other unionists who are fighting against concessions and against union collaboration with management. A democratic and militant Teamsters union led by men and women with a vision of improving the lives of all working people would be a beacon in the land.

I have tried to explain how over the last fourteen years TDU has worked to reform the union, the positions it has taken, the campaigns it has organized, the defeats it has suffered, and the victories it has won. Mostly, however, this book is about the men and women of the Teamsters and of Teamsters for a Democratic Union, that righteous, raucous, rebellious group we call the rank and file. This book is for them.

PART I

THE ORIGINS OF THE TEAMSTER REFORM MOVEMENT

3

Militancy, Democracy, Secession and the Founding of FASH

Bob Ellerman, today a TDU member in Los Angeles, was a freight driver and a member of Akron Local 24 in the 1950s and early 1960s. 'At that time', Bob remembers, 'if something happened we didn't like, if management came out and started anything, we'd just sit down where we was at till they got off our back and got out of there. Or if it was a serious problem, something we had to deal with that we figured took strike action, we'd just walk off the job and put up a picket line. Usually it was a major beef when you did something like that, and it only happened maybe a couple of times a year.'

Ellerman's story is typical of the men of his generation who worked in the trucking companies of the Midwest. He grew up in Columbus, Ohio, where he went to school until the ninth grade. When his father died, leaving his mother with four sons, Bob dropped out of school to go to work to help support his family. Soon, however, the truant officers found him and told him he would have to return to school or he would be sent to the reformatory. So when he was thirteen he packed up and left home.

'I ended up on an island in Put-in Bay out in Lake Erie working in a bowling alley. In them days you could work anywhere, it was during the Second World War.' When he was about sixteen, Bob returned to Columbus and got a job in a shoe factory, but he was too restless to settle down. A year later he joined the Army. Ellerman was in the service for seven years, between 1948 and 1954, making the rank of sergeant more than once – 'up and down a few times', he says. While home on leave in Akron, Bob met his future wife, Wanda while staying at her mother's boarding house. When he got out of the Army, they married and settled in Akron. Wanda's father was in the Bricklayers Union, and he helped Ellerman find a job in construction as a laborer. After a couple of years, he got tired of going from site to site looking for jobs and took a job with a trucking company, Freight Incorporated. 'First I worked on the dock, but they didn't really have permanent dock workers. In them days they'd let you start hostling in the yard and get some experience, and then they'd turn you loose on the streets – and you'd end up as a driver.'

At that time, in the late 1950s, the American labor movement was at its peak in terms of membership and political influence. The Teamsters union, under the leadership of Dave Beck and Jimmy Hoffa, was still growing and in 1956 reached 1,368,082 members. The power of the labor unions was tangible.

'Well, it was great', says Ellerman, 'especially in that section of the country. You take Ohio, especially the Akron area, it's strictly union country. I'd say ninety percent of the people that worked in that section of the country were all either Teamsters or members of the Rubber Workers or the Steel Workers. They dominated the local politics. For example, the sheriffs, all the deputy sheriffs were elected positions.' Since the Teamsters union membership helped elect the sheriffs, Bob explains, it was harder to use the sheriffs against strikers.

In those days the contract still contained the 24-hour strike clause, and workers used that clause to take care of grievances. 'We had the right to strike anytime we wanted for twenty-four hours before they could even start to get a court injunction against us or anything like that. So we'd just go out and start up the fire barrels and shut the place down. Management saw it as a real hazard, because the union officials themselves didn't usually have any control of it. Nobody ever would call a union hall in them days and say, "We're going to set up a picket line." We just went and did it.'

Though the strikes were unauthorized, rarely was anyone fired for organizing or participating in them. As Ellerman explains, 'That would be the death of any union leader that allowed his people to get fired on a wildcat strike. They'd never get us back to work until we had a hundred percent amnesty.'

The employers put pressure on the union officials to stop wildcat strikes, and higher union officials from the Joint Council or the International would sometimes come in to break them up. 'There was one strike there that went on for three weeks, with pictures in the paper of lines of trucks winding out of Akron, Ohio three or four miles long. In them days, Roadway was always the toughest trucking company in the system. So we'd always set up strike headquarters in a bar down the street from Roadway. Because if you could hold Roadway, and CF and in them days Motor Cargo, then you could pretty much hold the industry.

'We had communications set up, and we got word down there one day that they had taken control of our hall. William Presser had snuck in a bunch of goons while everybody was out manning the picket lines. They'd taken control of the union hall, Local 24. Well, within three or four minutes Wanda was calling friends of hers, and it was on the radio – we had the disc jockeys already set up – and the news was all over the radio. The men poured out of there in nothing flat, and charged to the union hall.

'A second call went to Sheriff Campbell and told him there was going to be a damned blood bath. Of course, he was marshalling forces to come down there, and he had Bill Presser on the phone up there threatening him. Anyhow, we had a lot of guys there, and they were on daisy chains and them doors were buckling on the front of the hall. Then the call came through from Presser, and these guys filed out of the doors in a column of twos, and got in their cars, and they were followed out of Summit County by everybody else. Presser never sent his people back into Summit County again while I lived there.'

There was militancy on the job, and there was also militancy in the union, though the members were not as effective in creating a democratic union organization as they were in building a wildcat strike. At times, says Bob, the union could be 'pretty rough'.

'You'd go in there and there'd be twenty, thirty sergeants-at-arms standing around the hall. And if you got out of line, if you got in a debate with them, they didn't like it, and every other word was "Out of order!" and then they started pitching you out the door. That didn't last long, though, because then we just organized ourselves and voted the turkeys out of office and reintroduced democratic controls of the union.'

In the 1950s and 1960s many Teamsters were part of such local networks, organizations able to organize quickie job actions or wildcat strikes, to turn out members for union meetings or rally behind candidates for local office. They were effective in organizing at a particular barn, or in a local union, or perhaps even among several barns or several local unions in one region or state. They were not, however, well enough organized to lead a rank-and-file movement that could actually take control out of the hands of powerful International Teamster leaders like William Presser.

Traditions of Teamster Democracy

Another important element of the rank-and-file Teamster movement has been the tradition of union democracy. Despite domination by the Mafia and the increasing centralization of the union, there have always been a number of democratic Teamster locals. St. Louis Local 688, formerly headed by Harold Gibbons, was frequently cited as a model of union democracy, rank-and-file involvement, and social activism.[1] New York Local 804, headed by Ron Carey, has a similar reputation.

The story of Los Angeles Local 208 is particularly interesting because it was once a dictatorship and became a democratic union as the result of a long struggle by the union's rank and file. Dave Beck, head of the Seattle Teamsters and later president of the International, had originally organized the Los Angeles freight industry in the late 1930s. Beck had appointed John Filipoff to the top office of secretary-treasurer of Local 208 in 1948, and Filipoff held that position until 1959, running the union like a virtual dictator. Mauricio Terrazas, a rank-and-file member of Local 208, remembers the local during those years: 'There was no democracy at all. They ruled it from the top. One guy I worked with was paid ten dollars each meeting to work over anyone who raised stuff from the floor.'[2]

Under the Filipoff regime, the workers had no union stewards, but in the mid-1950s, a rank-and-file movement for elected union stewards began to grow. In 1955 the workers at Pacific Intermountain Express (PIE) got together, elected union stewards and forced the company to accept them. Then at Pacific Motor Transport (PMT), the trucking subsidiary of the Southern Pacific Railroad, workers began to organize and started to go to the union meetings in a group, challenging Filipoff's policies and putting forward their own. The drivers from PIE and PMT were supported by the workers without regular jobs who worked out of the union's hiring hall.

As the rank and file gained power, one of the business agents, Sid Cohen, broke from Filipoff and challenged him for the office of secretary-treasurer in the 1959 election. He ran on a platform of rank-and-file democracy and called for the creation of democratic union bylaws. Cohen won the election, but once in office he not only failed to carry out his promise to institute democratic bylaws but became an opponent of the local reformers. Faced with Cohen's betrayal, hundreds of rank-and-file members showed up at a union meeting, and – over Cohen's protests – carried a motion for the creation of a local bylaws committee.

The committee was headed by John T. Williams, perhaps the man most responsible for the democratic revolution in Local 208. Williams grew up in a poor, Black neighborhood 'adjacent to the railroad tracks' of Charleston, South Carolina. After serving in the Navy, he settled in the Los Angeles area, got a job as a driver in the Los Angeles produce market, and became a member of the Teamsters, studying law in his off hours. His first experience in the union was in a committee opposing an employer-sponsored 'right-to-work law' that would have abolished the union shop. That experience led him to involvement in the union reform movement.

'There was at that time', says Williams, 'a surge for rank-and-file participation and control. The bylaws were a way to get it – bylaws the rank and file had a say in. During this same time, there was a demand for rank-and-file contract committees, and BAs [business agents] elected by the rank and file.'[3] Williams's idea was to involve as many members as possible in writing the bylaws, discussing them, and later voting them through. Teamsters were asked to collect union bylaws from their friends in other Teamster locals and other labor unions. At meetings involving scores of Teamsters, these bylaws were compared, discussed and debated until the best language was agreed on. Eventually, Local 208 adopted bylaws that were among the most democratic in the country, providing for elected stewards and business agents, elected negotiating committees, and a stewards' council empowered to discuss not only grievances, but also issues of union policy and strategy. Hundreds of rank and filers turned out for the local's meeting, and the bylaws were passed by a huge majority.[4]

The democratic bylaws passed by Local 208 were a tremendous achievement, removing all obstacles to full membership participation in the union, and creating structures such as the stewards' council that had the potential to broaden power beyond the top officer and the executive board.

The Testing of Reform Strategies

Locals like those in Akron and Los Angeles soon came into conflict with International General President Jimmy Hoffa. Local union officials and members frequently felt that they were paying dues to an International union that used its power thwart them, not support them. Only a few decades before, locals had been, at least in theory, virtually autonomous organizations, running their own affairs and making their own contracts. By the mid-1960s, however, the International laid down all the rules and negotiated all the important agreements.

Many local unions simply wanted to get out from under the power of the International, and the first strategy of union reform was simply to leave the Teamsters. In 1961, Philadelphia Teamsters Local 107 attempted to secede and join the AFL-CIO, and came close to doing so until Hoffa personally took charge of the campaign to defeat the decertification movement. A secession movement also arose in 1961 in Chicago's Teamster Local 777, then run by the gangster Joey Glimco. The Democratic Union Organizing Committee (DUOC), headed by Dominic Abata, led a successful movement to decertify the Teamsters, and then became Local 777 of the Seafarers International Union.

The Steelhaulers Rebellion

One group of Teamsters that began as reformers was virtually driven to dual unionism and secession by the Teamster leadership. The Fraternal Association of Steel Haulers, or FASH, was formed in 1967 following a long and violent strike. Steelhaulers, most of whom were owner-operators, had particular problems that the Teamsters union had ignored for years. Although the union negotiated their wages, it refused to negotiate the fee the owner-operators were paid for the lease of their tractors and trailers. Consequently, their wages had gone up but their total income had not increased much or had even declined. In addition, drivers were often detained at the steel mills waiting to be unloaded for hours or even days, and they wanted to be paid detention pay for the lost time. The union had neglected this issue as well.

In the late 1960s it seemed as if Teamster President Jimmy Hoffa had adopted what was virtually a policy of not representing owner-operators. Under Hoffa's successor Frank Fitzsimmons, the situation deteriorated further. Union officials began to make disparaging remarks, lumping the working drivers together with small businessmen and referring to them all derisively as 'brokers'.

Whether it was a matter of policy or negligence, the failure to represent the owner-operators and the tendency to disparage them was a mistake. When the union had represented and negotiated for the owner-operators they had been among the most loyal and militant union members. When they were neglected or unfairly treated, they were among the first to rebel.

Long-time steelhauler George Sullivan explains, 'There were strong feelings of discontent throughout the steelhauling industry, but most drivers felt that they either had to learn to live under the present conditions or else go into some other line of work.' In 1967 a group of steelhaulers made up of Jim Leavitt of Detroit, Tom Gwilt and John Hack from East Gary, Indiana and William Kusley of Hobart, Indiana went to the Local 142 union hall in Gary to get a copy of the new contract and ask the officers what improvements had been made under the new agreement. At that time Don Sawochka was the secretary-treasurer of the local. According to Sullivan, 'Don Sawochka inherited his position from his father, Mike Sawochka, after his death in 1964. He had not been elected to his position. Instead he had been crowned king, almost like a feudal overlord.' Not only did the Local 142 officers refuse to give the men a copy of their contract, but business agent Jacob Abshere threatened the men with a blackjack and ordered them out of the hall.

Used and abused by the employers and ignored or berated by their union, the steelhaulers were forced to attempt to represent themselves. They decided to organize a picket line protest at the steelhaulers local union halls on 21 August 1967. Jim Leavitt went back to Detroit to try to organize a picket line at Local 299, but the union simply ignored him and he and his group went home. In Gary, Tom Gwilt and twenty-five other men put up a picket line, and Don Sawochka came out and told them, 'You men can walk until you wear your legs off, and it won't do you any good.'

'I was fighting mad', says Gwilt, 'and I was determined to so something to make them listen to us.' Gwilt and seven other steelhaulers went to the US Steel Corporation in Gary and set up a picket line: eight men were attacking the world's biggest steel corporation. Soon the big flat-bed trucks that haul the steel began to pull up at the gate. When the drivers saw the picket signs, they turned away with comments like 'It was about time something was done.' The drivers parked their trucks and began to join the picket line, and soon Tom Gwilt was dispatching pickets to other mills. By the morning of the second day, according to George Sullivan, 'Steel shipments in the Gary area were nearly halted.'

The Teamsters union told the steelhaulers to take down the picket line, but they refused. The Lake County Sheriff's Department started arresting pickets, but still more pickets showed up. Tom Gwilt and Paul Dietsch of Wisconsin took responsibility for the organization of the strike, which was still confined to Gary. They received some help from Mike Parkhurst's *Overdrive* magazine and his organization of truck drivers, called the Roadmasters, which provided legal help.

The strike went on two weeks, and neither side budged. 'Men who found picket duty too boring', says Sullivan, 'took to the highways and started shooting at steelhaulers who were trying to take advantage of the situation to make some extra money.' They were out on the picket lines for three weeks before the strike began to spread. In Middletown, Ohio the wife of a steelhauler organized a picket line at ARMCO Steel. In Youngstown, a fellow named Mike Boanao organized a picket line that stopped steel shipments. The strike became increasingly violent, with the strikers not only shooting at the scab steelhaulers, but also at the police who were escorting them. One driver in Detroit was badly burned when a fire bomb was thrown into his cab. But as Sullivan explained, 'The Teamster attempts to negotiate with strikers were unsuccessful, as the Teamsters wanted them to return to work without any gains.'

In the eighth week of the strike, Governor Raymond Shafer of Pennsylvania called a conference of governor's representatives from eight states, shippers, carriers, Teamster officials, and the strike leaders. Still nothing came out of the meeting, and that night the Pennsylvania lieutenant governor's summer home was destroyed by an explosion. The strike resumed, and finally the Teamsters agreed to negotiate the strikers' demands with the carriers and shippers. In the end the strikers won pay increases of 11 percent over the next three years and, most important, pay for detention time.

Immediately after the strike the Fraternal Association of Steel Haulers was organized. Tom Gwilt was elected president of the Indiana chapter, Paul Dietsch president of the Wisconsin chapter, and William J. Hill chairman of the National Committee. The steelhaulers' deep distrust of the Teamsters union was evident in a resolution adopted at the founding meeting; it stated that FASH would stay in the Teamsters only as long as that union served their needs.[5]

The steelhaulers had won a real victory in the form of detention pay. And in response to the strike, the Teamsters union created steelworker local unions or craft sections in local unions in Pittsburgh, Youngstown, Canton, Detroit and Gary. The Teamsters even offered Gwilt, Dietsch and Hill jobs with the union in an attempt to coopt and end the steelhaulers movement, but the FASH leaders refused the offer. Only Mike Boanao went over to the other side, first provoking a split in FASH and then accepting a job with the Teamsters – a demoralizing blow to the steelhaulers movement.

In 1969 a second FASH strike occurred, and this time the Teamsters union decided to try to destroy it rather than ignore it. According to one source, John Angelo, president of Teamster Local 337 in Youngstown, put together an army of 120 union officials and hired thugs and sent them out in a fleet of fifty cars to attack a group of FASH strikers. Both sides were armed, there was some shooting, and when the smoke cleared eight men were wounded and one had been killed.[6] In Gary, Tom Gwilt's home was bombed and badly damaged.[7]

'We knew then', says FASH leader Bill Hill, 'that there was absolutely no reason for us to stay in the Teamsters any longer. Three months later we announced that we were going to form our own union.'[8] FASH had not started out with a dual union strategy. As unhappy with the Teamsters as they were back in 1967, the steelhaulers had not necessarily intended to leave the union. It was the Teamster leadership that made FASH a dual union and then drove it to secede.

Whether chosen by the dissidents, as in Philadelphia, or forced on them, as in the case of FASH, secession was not a viable strategy for union reform, at least for most Teamsters, as the rank and file soon realized. The Teamsters union could be counted on to use all its power to stop any local that attempted to secede, and any group that left the Teamsters would be in a much weaker position in dealing with the employers. And finally, secession was a selfish strategy, not a solidarity strategy. One local union, such as the Chicago taxicab drivers, might solve its problems by leaving – but what about all the other Teamsters?

Reform could not be achieved by each of the local unions simply going its own way: it would take cooperation. But to bring that cooperation about would take a national event to bring the local activists from different parts of the country into contact with each other. That development was not long in coming.

Notes

1. Steven Brill, *The Teamsters*, New York 1978, p. 358.

2. Samuel R. Friedman, *Teamster Rank and File: Power, Bureaucracy, and Rebellion at Work in a Union*, New York 1982, p. 60.

3. Ibid., p. 76.

4. Highly regarded by his fellow members for his role in the democratic reorganization of the union, and for his conscientious representation, Williams was elected to six consecutive terms as business agent totaling seventeen years, and served as vice-president of the local as well. He was also a leader of the Black community in Los Angeles.

5. This account is taken from George Sullivan, 'Rank-and-file Rebellion in the International Brotherhood of Teamsters', *Liberation*, May 1971.

6. Dan Moldea, *The Hoffa Wars: Teamsters, Rebels, Politicians and the Mob*, New York 1978, pp. 234–37.

7. George Sullivan, 'Working for Survival', in Staughton Lynd and Alice Lynd, eds, *Rank and File: Personal Histories by Working-Class Organizers,* Boston 1973, p. 218.

8. Moldea, *Hoffa Wars*, p. 337.

4

The 1970 Wildcat and TURF

The contemporary Teamster reform movement actually began with the 1970 wildcat strike. On one level, the strike was a fight about wages, but on another it was a struggle over leadership between Teamster acting General President Frank Fitzsimmons, local union officials, dissident groups, and rank-and-file members. It was a strike that can only be fully understood in the context of the tremendous upheaval then taking place in American society and throughout the labor movement.

Rank-and-File Rebellion

In the 1960s and 1970s the US was swept by a rank-and-file rebellion involving hundreds of thousands of workers in a variety of unions, and eventually stirring up the Teamsters' ranks as well. The reasons for the rebellion were many. With the maturing of the postwar baby boom generation, millions of young workers entered the work force. Then the civil rights movement, the student movement, and the anti–Vietnam War movement made protest an everyday experience. Soon protests began to spread to the labor unions.

In the 1960s the United Farm Workers Organizing Committee (UFWOC) led by César Chávez was both a labor union and a crusade for social justice for the Filipino, Mexican, and Mexican American workers toiling in the fields of California. UFWOC (later the United Farm Workers, UFW) adopted the tactics of the civil rights movement to fight for the traditional demands of labor unions for recognition and a contract. The union's pilgrimages and hunger strikes won the sympathy of much of the country, and millions supported the UFWOC boycotts of non-union grapes and lettuce.

In those same years the previously unorganized public school teachers and other public employees began to organize unions, demand contracts and engage in strikes. Strikes by teachers and public employees were still illegal in many states, and photographs of teachers union officials being thrown in jail for leading a strike became a common sight on the front page of the morning newspaper. The American Federation of State, County and Municipal Employees (AFSCME) grew from 100,000 in the early 1950s to 350,000 in the late 1960s, and by 1967 was growing at a rate of 1,000 new members a week.

The new labor movement spread among industrial workers as well. A disaster at the Consol No. 9 mine of the Mountaineer Coal Company in Farmington, West Virginia on 20 November 1968 touched off a rank-and-file rebellion in the United Mine Workers (UMW). Seventy-eight miners were killed in the explosion, and miners were outraged when UMW President Tony Boyle immediately spoke out, not in sympathy with the workers and their families, but in sympathy with the company.

That was a turning point in the union, leading Joseph A. 'Jock' Yablonski, a member of the UMW executive board, to run against Boyle for the office of president in 1969. Using the traditional fear, favors, and fraud, Boyle and his machine won the election by almost two to one. Yablonski appealed the election results to the US Labor Department, and not long thereafter Yablonski, his wife and daughter were found murdered in their home in Pennsylvania. The presumption was that Boyle had ordered them killed.

After Yablonski's murder, some of his supporters joined with other miners from the Black Lung Association and created the Miners for Democracy (MFD) to fight for reform in the United Mine Workers. In December 1972, in a rerun of the contested 1969 election, MFD leader Arnold Miller defeated Boyle, and the UMW began a long process of democratization. Later Boyle was convicted and sent to prison for Yablonski's murder.

Black autoworkers in the Detroit Dodge Main plant were also caught up in the new union movement. In 1968 they formed DRUM, the Dodge Revolutionary Union Movement, challenging racism in the company and the United Auto Workers (UAW) and fighting management on the shopfloor with slowdowns and wildcat strikes. The Revolutionary Union Movement soon spread, first to other plants in Detroit and then to other parts of the country. At about this same time the predominantly white work force at the General Motors plant in Lordstown, Ohio became famous for its militancy, which erupted in a bitter three-week strike in 1972.

The new labor movement later spread to the United Steel Workers of America (USWA), where in 1974 union staffer Ed Sadlowski defeated the corrupt Joe Germano for the directorship of important Chicago-Gary District 31. Shortly thereafter, dissident union officials and rank-and-file activists came together to create a reform organization in the steelworkers union, Steel Workers Fight Back. Fight Back became Sadlowski's campaign organization in his unsuccessful bid for the USWA presidency in February 1977. Such was the climate of militancy and reform at the beginning of the 1970s when Frank Fitzsimmons prepared to negotiate his first contract.

The 1970 Wildcat Strike

When the 1 April 1970 deadline for the expiration of the Teamster contract approached, the nation was already in the midst of a tremendous labor upheaval. On 17 March New York postal workers had voted to strike in defiance of federal law and had set up picket lines, and the postal strike had quickly spread to New Jersey and Connecticut.

Union officials asked workers to return to their jobs, but instead on 20 March some 6,000 postal workers at the system's center in Chicago walked out. They were joined the next day by striking postal workers in Detroit, Philadelphia, Cleveland, Pittsburgh, San Francisco, Minneapolis, Denver, Boston, and some 200 other cities and towns. President Nixon sent US Army and National Guard troops to break the strike in New York and move the mail. Nevertheless, the strike brought about both a reorganization and reform of the Post Office and improved bargaining with the various postal workers unions. About the same time the Professional Air Traffic Controllers (PATCO) began a 'sick-in' that would last for weeks, and railroad workers threatened a national walkout. Almost all of these struggles were the result of workers' demands for wage gains large enough to keep up with the high rate of inflation.

The Teamsters union, representing about 450,000 workers covered by the National Master Freight Agreement, was negotiating with Trucking Employers, Incorporated (TEI), which represented some 12,000 trucking companies. In January 1970, acting General President Frank Fitzsimmons, posturing to prove that he was as tough a Teamster leader as his predecessor Jimmy Hoffa, asked for total wage increases of $3.00 an hour. At the time truck drivers were earning about $4.00 an hour, and Fitzsimmons's initial wage demand raised the freight workers' expectations that they would get a big raise.

But when midnight on 31 March 1970 arrived no agreement had been reached. Frank Fitzsimmons did not call a strike, but thousands of Teamsters around the country followed the old slogan 'No contract, no work' and walked off the job. By 2 April wildcat strikers had shut down seventy-two trucking companies in thirty-seven cities including Buffalo, Atlanta, Milwaukee and Oakland. That same day Frank Fitzsimmons announced that the Teamsters had reached a tentative agreement to settle for raises totaling $1.10 over three years, and the striking Teamsters were told to return to work. After the talk of a $3.00 raise, the figure of $1.10 was a disappoint-

AP/Wide World

1 April 1970: Teamsters from Local 600 in St. Louis strike after the expiration of the National Master Freight Agreement.

ment. Nevertheless, many Teamsters started to go back to their jobs.

However, the next day Chicago Teamster Local 705 and the independent Chicago Truck Drivers Union, which had never been brought into the National Master Freight Agreement and still negotiated separately from the International, announced that they had rejected Fitzsimmons's tentative agreement and were sticking with their demand for $1.70 over three years. Fitzsimmons flew from Teamster headquarters in Washington to Chicago to plead for their agreement to a settlement of $1.10, but Ed Fenner, executive director of the Chicago Truck Drivers Union, and Louis Peick, head of Teamster Local 705, held out for $1.70.[1]

The announcement of Chicago's rejection of the tentative settlement reversed the return-to-work movement, and the wildcat strikes spread to several other cities, including Cleveland, St. Louis and St. Paul. By 6 April the strike had spread to San Francisco, and Oakland Teamsters imitated the air traffic controllers by organizing a massive sick-in. The epidemic of 'blue flu' among the Bay Area Teamsters brought the trucking industry there to a halt. Also joining the strike were thousands of strikers in Columbus and Akron. The strike in New Jersey began when seventy Teamsters set up picket lines in Carlstadt, while forty Teamsters put up a picket that began the strike in Charleston, West Virginia.

The Lee Way Trucking Company, headquartered in Oklahoma City, shut down and laid off 2,000 employees in fourteen states. Sidney Upsher, Lee Way's executive vice-president, explained that the company had suspended operations because of 'union obstruction'. Though the Teamsters in Oklahoma City were not on strike, Lee Way could not get its trucks out of the region because Teamster pickets from St. Louis would not allow them to cross the Mississippi River.[2] The St. Louis strikers had also shut down Railway Express Agency.

At the same time, on 7 April Teamster Local 705 and the Chicago Truck Drivers Union had called a selective strike against sixteen companies, and because Chicago was the hub of national freight movements, the strike in Chicago threatened to stop freight shipments to many other cities, resulting in the layoff of tens of thousands of Teamsters across the country. The official strike in Chicago gave encouragement to the wildcat strikes going on in other areas, which ebbed and flowed as workers were convinced to return to work briefly, only to walk out again a few days later. The strike was strongest in Los Angeles, St. Louis and the Akron-Cleveland area, with an estimated 32,500 Teamsters on strike in those three areas forming the center of the wildcat for almost three months.

To complicate matters, on 6 April the Fraternal Association of Steel Haulers called a strike against both the employers and the Teamsters union, seeking both an independent contract and an independent union for the steelhaulers. By 8 April there were 1,500 steelhaulers on strike in Chicago, 1,000 on strike in Gary, and thousands of others joining the strike in Canton, Youngstown, Detroit and Pittsburgh. FASH must have been having some success, for the strike soon got a response, presumably from officials in the Teamsters: on 15 April the home of Jim Leavitt, a FASH leader in Detroit, was bombed.

The freight strike was almost completely based on local rank-and-file initiative. With some exceptions, local union officials repudiated the wildcat, either to avoid legal liability or to curry favor with the International officers. Don Fink, the secretary-treasurer of Columbus Local 413, said that 'outside goons' had caused the strike. 'We've been telling our guys to go back to work', said Fink, 'but since they've talked with these outsiders, they also want more money.'[3] But the officials of St. Louis Local 600, Los Angeles Local 208, and Oakland Local 70 came out in support of their striking members.

The truth was that, as in most strikes, the leadership came from a small core of militants, but the strike could not have spread so far and lasted so long had it not had both active and passive support from a majority of Teamster rank and filers. That's why Fitzsimmons and the local officials failed completely when they tried to get the wildcatters back to work. In

Toledo on 10 April, for example, 2,000 Teamsters shouted down their officers and refused to go back to work. When William Presser ordered the 16,000 wildcat strikers in the Cleveland and Akron areas to return to work, they not only refused but in mid-April some 500 of them marched through downtown Cleveland in a public demonstration in defiance of the Teamster leadership.[4]

Fitzsimmons, who had been determined to prove he could be a powerful leader like Hoffa, had completely lost the initiative to the Chicago unions, the FASH dissidents and the wildcatters in the Midwest and Los Angeles. On 9 April the Chicago unions signed an agreement with 500 local cartage companies employing 15,000 Chicago Teamsters; it called for a raise of $1.65 over three years. The contract was also signed by two large food chains. The Chicago contracts proved that the $1.65 figure could be won, strengthening the wildcat movement. On that same day even Fitzsimmons's home local, Detroit Local 299, joined the strike, making it clear that his leadership had been completely repudiated by the rank and file.

On 10 April the 1,200 Chicago companies that had not signed the new contract locked out their 35,000 employees. The lockout caused other terminals and companies across the country to close and lay off still more Teamsters. On 13 April the Chicago unions retaliated by striking the companies that had locked them out. Oddly enough, the Chicago employers' lockout fed into the national wildcat strike, since it permitted some wildcatters to return to work to be laid off so they could collect unemployment. Throughout the second week of the strike some wildcatters voted to go back to work, while other cities erupted in new wildcat strikes. In Columbus 2,500 wildcat strikers returned to work and 3,500 returned in Harrisburg, but in Detroit only a few companies were able to operate because of what one company official called 'large numbers of roving dissidents'.

Some companies attempted to move convoys of trucks under the protection of armed guards or the police. Pacific Intermountain Express attempted to move two convoys of thirty trucks each, but the first convoy was stopped at Richfield, Ohio by 150 men throwing bricks and bottles that destroyed every windshield in every truck. The second convoy attempted to proceed, but the lead truck was hit by bricks and the driver lost control and smashed into a car. The other trucks then turned back.

By the end of the second week hundreds of thousands of workers had been laid off in manufacturing plants that had shut down because of lack of parts. For example, the St. Louis wildcat forced Chevrolet, Fisher Body and Chrysler truck plants to lay off 12,300 workers. The St. Paul-Minneapolis strike forced Whirlpool to lay off 1,200 workers. The official Chicago strike and the Milwaukee wildcat forced Motorola to lay off 3,000 workers. And so it went around the country. Eventually it was estimated that half a million workers had been laid off. And still more locals voted to join the movement;

for example, on 10 April the 1,800 members of Local 701 in New Jersey authorized their local leaders to call a strike.

Perhaps because he could not get a hearing in any assembly of Teamsters, Frank Fitzsimmons spoke before the United Auto Workers union convention in Atlantic City on 14 April. Unable to accept the fact that the rank and file had repudiated his policies, Fitzsimmons blamed Communists for the wildcat strikes taking place.[5] The claim that Communists were behind the strike was utterly preposterous, because it was clear that the strike was a spontaneous rebellion supported by tens of thousands of Teamsters and a number of local officials. This slanderous red-baiting was a tactic Fitzsimmons would use again and again over the next several years.

The strike was rapidly becoming a political issue. In Chicago, Republican Senator Percy tried to break the strike, urging all truckers to return to work because, he said, the strike was a threat to the community. Similarly, Cleveland Democratic Mayor Carl Stokes asked President Nixon to intervene because, he said, the 8,000 striking Teamsters in Cleveland were having 'a very serious impact'. The steelhaulers continued their strike throughout the Midwest, where they clashed with shippers, carriers and Teamster officials. In Middletown, Ohio some 400 steelhaulers stopped trucks and forced drivers to drop their trailers and return home in their tractors. The pickets were concentrated around ARMCO Steel, and FASH loyalists found themselves confronting members of Cincinnati Teamster Local 100. On 29 April a firebomb went off at the ARMCO offices in Middletown, while a stick of dynamite blew up part of Local 100's union hall.

The news media barraged the striking Teamsters with hostile criticism. Labor writer Victor Riesel repeatedly criticized the strikers in his column. On 26 April he compared the striking Teamsters to campus radicals: 'Apparently teamster wildcatters reckoned that if it's done at some of the best universities, why should the proletariat restrain itself? These rebel teamsters needed no radicalization. They waved no flags – just rocks, bottles, bricks, some dynamite, rifles – and spewed language as unrefined as any ever heard at Berkeley or Columbia University.' While the columnists excoriated the strikers, the editorialists condemned them. The *New York Times* criticized Chicago Teamster leaders for destroying any hope of controlling inflation, and lesser newspapers across the country joined in the condemnation.[6]

On 29 April Governor Rhodes of Ohio declared a state of emergency in that state and ordered 3,700 Ohio national guardsmen into action. He deployed 3,200 in the Akron-Cleveland area and 500 in the Cincinnati-Dayton region. 'There are hoodlums roaming our highways and city streets, armed with shotguns and rifles with intent to kill, and we're going to put a stop to it', said Rhodes. On 2 May, Pennsylvania Attorney General William Sennett put three National Guard units of 380 men on alert in western Pennsylvania.

Most of the country's military might was still deployed in Vietnam, and the weekend warriors, even those who had trained by putting down ghetto riots, proved unequal to the task of smashing the strike. The guardsmen patrolled the highways in military vehicles and protected trucking company terminals, but when fifty state troopers and guardsmen attempted to move a three-truck convoy out of a Yellow Freight Line terminal in Ohio they were driven back by 200 rock-throwing strikers.

Fitzsimmons attempted to regain control of the situation by calling a meeting in Chicago on 30 April of 700 local union officials to approve the freight contract, which they dutifully did despite the rebellion in their ranks. But if Fitz thought the officials would be able to go home and get everybody back to work while awaiting the ratification vote he was sorely mistaken. Some 3,000 angry Teamsters meeting in Cleveland on 2 May accused their union leaders of trying 'to ram the contract down our throats', and vowed to stay out on strike. And in Cincinnati road drivers voted against accepting the contract despite the best efforts of Local 100 President Ira Farmer. Akron was intermittently on strike, while St. Louis and Los Angeles stayed out. At the beginning of May, Teamsters in Massachusetts and New Hampshire joined the national Teamster strike.

The federal government might have interceded in the strike at the beginning of May, but another series of events intervened. First Nixon ordered the invasion of Cambodia, expanding the unpopular Vietnam War into yet another country. This was followed immediately by student strikes at over 200 college campuses across the country protesting the invasion. The National Guard in Ohio was taken from the highways and sent to the campuses, where at Kent State the exhausted guardsmen overreacted to a peaceful protest and shot five students, killing four and paralyzing a fifth. This led to a further expansion of the student strikes and protest demonstrations, further diverting attention from the striking Teamsters.

The Teamster strike continued through the first two weeks of May, and on the West Coast it expanded. The strike in Los Angeles had had the support of Local 208's top officer, Ed Blackmarr. However, Blackmarr believed that he would endanger the local union if he personally took charge of the wildcat, leading to lawsuits by the employers or a trusteeship by the International, so he left responsibility for the organization of the strike to the stewards. It was the stewards of the biggest barns in Local 208 such as PMT and WesCar who called the strike and brought together a strike committee under the leadership of Archie Murrietta, a close associate of Blackmarr.

The local leaders expected the strike to be short, a day or two, perhaps a week, like other wildcat strikes they had been involved in. But events proved otherwise. The 1970 wildcat in Local 208 went on for two months, with the rank and file and the local officials fighting both the employers and their own union. Los Angeles–area Teamster Joint Council 42 had come out in opposition to the strike on 6 April, cutting Local 208 off from any official Teamster support. At the same time the trucking companies sent telegrams to their employees firing somewhere between 10,000 and 14,000 Teamsters, and while no one expected all of them to stay fired, the firings put an enormous burden of responsibility on the stewards and the strike committee.

The strike committee responded by taking some daring initiatives. Local 208 strike leaders sent roving pickets to the San Francisco Bay Area to try to stop the trucks from rolling there. In mid-May several hundred wildcat strikers from Los Angeles arrived in San Francisco to spread the strike. For a few days the Teamsters stopped not only trucking services, but newspaper deliveries, and even buses and cabs. Tom O'Donnell, a business agent of Teamster Local 85, said that the union had no control over the strikers: 'They're running wild on the streets right now. They're going to close the whole town down.' And so they were. The trucking industry was paralyzed. Doctors and editors in town for conventions had to hitchhike into the city. Mayor Joseph Alioto called it 'the most anarchical situation we've ever faced'.

The Los Angeles strikers also invited the local college students – who were already on strike against the war and the shootings at Kent State in Ohio and Jackson State in Mississippi – to join the Teamster picket lines. Some did join, though their participation never became an important factor in the strike. During the first two weeks of May the Teamsters union conducted a mail ballot vote on the contract, and on 18 May Fitzsimmons announced that, with 71 percent of those eligible voting, the membership had voted seven to five to approve the contract calling for a $1.10 increase over thirty-nine months. He called it the best contract in Teamster history. Nobody cared what he called it, and still the strike went on in Los Angeles, St. Louis and Akron.

While the freight strike continued, the steelhaulers strike came to an end. On 23 May the local representatives of the Fraternal Association of Steel Haulers met in Pittsburgh and voted 300 to 194 to return to work. The strike had been hit by an injunction, and the steelhaulers had lost their appeal in the US Court of Appeals. Having ended the strike, FASH President Bill Hill said that the group would attempt to work through the National Labor Relations Board to 'get the hell out of the Teamsters'.[7]

In Los Angeles the wildcat ended on 1 June. Despite its daring attempt to strengthen the strike by using roving pickets and student supporters, the wildcat strike had failed. The wildcat strikers had been strong enough to get the big interstate carriers and some California carriers to sign amnesty agreements, but most of the California carriers saw the wildcat as an opportunity to break the back of the militants in Local 208, and refused to sign a contract with an amnesty provision.

Blackmarr called a meeting and asked Local 208 to declare the California carriers action a lockout, which the local did. This allowed Blackmarr to send out the business agents to organize official strikes at nonsigning companies. But at that point, Frank Fitzsimmons ordered Blackmarr to call off the strike, and the courts ordered the Teamsters back to work. Meanwhile, the Chicago Teamsters voted on the national agreement calling for $1.10 and rejected it by a vote of 23,813 to 6,478. The *New York Times* editorialized that President Nixon's attempt to hold down wages had collapsed with the vote by the Chicago Teamsters.[8]

Finally, after three months of both official and wildcat strikes, the struggle ended during the first week of July. The Chicago Teamsters won their wage demand of $1.65 over thirty-six months on 3 July. As a result, the Teamsters agreement was revised to $1.85 over thirty-nine months. Ray Schoessling, president of the Chicago Joint Council of Teamsters and an International vice-president, called the settlement 'a complete victory. ... That settlement came only with the Chicago teamsters in the drivers' seat once again'.[9] The contract was approved by the 89-member executive board of Trucking Employers, Inc. on 7 July, thus ending the strike.

The 1970 wildcat strike had been a remarkable event. In reality it was three interrelated strike movements unfolding at once: the rank-and-file wildcat strike, which was strongest among the 30,000 Teamsters in Los Angeles, St. Louis and Akron but also involved thousands of other Teamsters from coast to coast; the FASH strike involving an estimated 12,000 steelhaulers; and the official Chicago strike involving as many as 50,000 Teamsters at first and about 10,000 toward the end.

This historic strike had revealed several things. It proved what many had believed, that Frank Fitzsimmons was a weak and ineffective leader. It demonstrated great dissatisfaction with the International union's leadership, both among powerful local Teamster officials like those in Chicago, and among the rank and file. Perhaps most important, it showed both the tremendous power of a rank-and-file rebellion in the form of a wildcat strike movement but also the limitations of such a movement in terms of exercising rank-and-file control over the union.

The point was made most painfully in Los Angeles, where, after a tremendous show of militancy, several hundred Teamsters were fired and blacklisted. In the end, Local 208 leader Ed Blackmarr signed an agreement that allowed the companies to fire 500 workers on a case-by-case basis to be decided by a joint union-employer panel. Apparently he signed in the hope that the local would not be thrown into trusteeship by the International, and because he believed Teamster officials on the panel would protect the members' jobs.

But Blackmarr proved to be wrong on both counts. Union officials agreed to the firing of 500 workers, many of whom were blacklisted, and the International put Local 208 into trusteeship anyway. When the trusteeship ended, Alex Meharis was elected the secretary-treasurer of the local, while Archie Murrietta, organizer of the wildcat, became president. Both had been Blackmarr associates and Hoffa supporters.

In Oakland and St. Louis, Teamster locals suffered huge financial judgments as a result of the lawsuits that flowed from the strike, and the Teamsters International – happy to see the dissidents punished – did nothing to bargain away those employer judgments. In sum, a big wage gain had been won and other improvements had been made in the contract, but the union remained in the hands of Fitzsimmons and other officials without the desire, will power, or ability to enforce the contract.

The Founding of TURF

It was in this atmosphere of mingled feelings of victory and defeat, of success and frustration following the national wildcat strike, that eighty Teamsters from sixteen states met in Toledo, Ohio on 25 July 1971 to form the first national reform organization within the Teamsters: the Teamsters United Rank and File, or TURF.[10] The gathering in Toledo was made up of rank-and-file activists, would-be union officials, and a few idealistic young socialists. There were Teamsters who had been local leaders of the 1970 wildcat strike, and there were several groups of pension reformers, including 'Curly' Best's '500 at 50' Clubs.

Some of the most important groups represented at that first TURF meeting were the Unity Committees. The first Unity Committee had been started in the late 1960s by Andrew Provenzino, a rank-and-file Teamster in Detroit Local 299. The idea of local rank-and-file dissident groups became popular among Teamsters, and the name Unity Committee spread, so that by 1970 there were several Unity Committees in the Midwest. Provenzino was at the Toledo meeting, as were representatives of the Unity Committee of Teamster Local 407.[11]

There were also the followers of Don Vestal, the controversial former president of Nashville, Tennessee Local 327. Vestal had been a close associate of Jimmy Hoffa in the 1940s and 1950s, and Hoffa had appointed him head of Tennessee Joint Council 87 and had made him a trustee of the Central States Pension Fund. However, in 1958 Hoffa and Vestal had had a falling out, and in 1960 Hoffa supported a challenger for president in Local 327. When that effort failed, Hoffa tried to put Vestal's local into trusteeship, though Vestal successfully fought the move in court.

After Hoffa went to prison, Fitzsimmons also tried to throw Local 327 into trusteeship, and like Hoffa, he also lost in court. Unsuccessful before a judge, Fitzsimmons tried a more direct approach. According to writer Dan Moldea, Local 327's secretary-treasurer, a Fitzsimmons supporter, had his gunmen shoot up Vestal's office and then led them in an armed attack on Vestal's home.

The contest continued when Vestal announced that he would be a candidate for the presidency of the Teamsters union against Frank Fitzsimmons at the 1971 International convention. At the convention, however, Vestal withdrew in favor of Theodore Daley, secretary-treasurer of New York Local 445 and a Hoffa supporter. Fitzsimmons was, of course, elected general president, and a week after the convention, Fitz finally succeeded in putting Vestal's local into trusteeship. It was this defeat that brought Vestal to the TURF founding convention.[12]

The dissidents' meeting in Toledo formed TURF, proclaimed their intention to reform the union, and elected Curly Best their president. They also called for a national founding convention to be held in September in Denver, Colorado. The group adjourned with promises to return home, recruit new members and build a powerful national reform movement.

Even before the group was formally launched, Fitzsimmons attacked. On 25 August 1971 Fitzsimmons sent a letter 'To All Affiliates' telling them that TURF literature 'has no place on union bulletin boards. TURF has no official Teamster status'. TURF, wrote Fitzsimmons, 'is merely an attempt by Don Vestal, formerly president of Local 327 in Nashville, to recoup his fortunes. Local 327 is in trusteeship largely because of Vestal's mismanagement'. Fitzsimmons accused Vestal of 'financial malpractices, as well as failure to represent the Local's membership or to negotiate or administer several bargaining agreements'. Vestal denied all of Fitzsimmons's accusations. Fitzsimmons, said Vestal, 'is attempting to make this a personal thing with Vestal when in truth he, like all other dictators, is afraid of the people. He is afraid that the rank and file membership is going to tear down the International officers' playhouse. The truth of the matter is that is exactly what we are going to do!'[13]

Despite, or perhaps in part because of this vicious attack on Vestal, TURF chapters sprang up across the country, in many cases founded by local activists who had little or no contact with Best, Vestal or the TURF newspaper, which was being published in Downey, California. TURF had caught the imagination of the Teamster rank and file, who wanted reform, democracy, and a union that would stand up to the employers. Unfortunately, TURF proved to be a disappointment. No sooner was TURF founded than its leadership began to fall apart. Some TURF founders or leaders simply used TURF as a stepping stone into union office. For example, Andy Suckart, on probation after pleading guilty to possession of ninety bars of stolen nickel, left TURF and took a job working for Jackie Presser and Frank Fitzsimmons.[14]

More important, within a year Don Vestal and Curly Best, TURF's two best-known leaders, had a falling out. Associates of Vestal brought a lawsuit against Best, while at the same time Best charged that 'Don Vestal promised everything and did nothing'.[15] Curly Best, whom everyone describes as nice guy and a well-intentioned reformer, simply was not an effective leader. Best and Vestal, the two most prominent leaders of TURF, each accused the other of attempting to destroy the organization.

The problem with TURF was that it never had a unified leadership or political program for the union. TURF was a coalition or federation of various local leaders and organizations, rather than a unified national organization with a common program and a national leadership. And while some of its leaders were dedicated reformers, others were opportunists who had no commitment to the rank and file, men who just wanted to use TURF to run for office or get an appointed job in the union. Personalities, particularly the personalities of Curly Best and Don Vestal, loomed too large in TURF.

While the TURF newspaper published beautiful programs calling for union reform, in fact TURF had no agreed-upon goals or means to achieve them, and by 1973 the national TURF organization was a shambles. Some local TURF chapters continued to thrive for a few more years, either as campaign organizations for one or another would-be union politician, or, in some cases, as genuine rank-and-file groups, but the national organization was dead by 1974. Despite all its weaknesses, however, TURF was an important milestone for the rank-and-file movement, because it was the first attempt to create a national rank-and-file reform organization embracing all Teamsters. Its failure demonstrated the need for any future reform organization to have a clear program for the union and a leadership capable of putting principles above personalities. Several TURF members learned those lessons and went on to play an important role in organizing Teamsters for a Decent Contract (TDC) and later in founding Teamsters for a Democratic Union. In many ways the TURF experience made TDU possible.

Notes

1. There were a number of other important issues in the contract, perhaps the most important of which was the maintenance or improvement of the cost of living allowance (COLA) formula.

2. Associated Press, 7 April 1970.

3. Christopher Lydon, 'Teamster Chiefs Meet on Strategy', *New York Times*, 9 April 1970.

4. Associated Press, 17 April, 1970.

5. 'Teamsters to Vote on National Contract', *New York Times*, 5 April 1970.

6. 'Fight for Wage Stability', *New York Times*, 7 May 1970.

7. 'Steel Haulers Vote to Return to Work After 7-Week Strike', *New York Times*, 24 May 1970.

8. 'A Blow to Wage Stability', *New York Times*, 29 June 1970.

9. Seth S. King, 'Chicago Teamster Pact Brings New National Rise', *New York Times*, 4 July 1970.

10. 'New Rank and File Organization Sets Goals for Union Reforms', *Overdrive*, September 1971.

11. Dan Moldea, *The Hoffa Wars*, New York 1978, pp. 218–33.

12. Moldea, *Hoffa Wars*, pp. 65–66, 141–44, 282–89, 310.

13. 'Fitzsimmons Bungles Attack on TURF', *TURF: Teamsters United Rank and File*, 25 September 1971. The article contains the text of Fitzsimmons's letter and Vestal's reply.

14. Moldea, *Hoffa Wars*, p. 289.

15. 'President Tells It ... Like It Is!!!' *TURF: Teamsters United Rank and File*, 25 March 1972.

5

Health, Safety and PROD

Even as TURF was fading from the scene, another reform organization was being created, this one through the impact of Ralph Nader, the consumer advocate and safety watchdog. Nader had conducted a survey about truck safety, and the drivers had expressed so much concern about the employers' unsafe practices and the union's failure to do anything about them that Nader had organized a Professional Drivers Conference on Truck and Bus Safety, held in Washington, DC on 2 October 1971.

The conference adopted a series of resolutions dealing with health and safety issues and called upon the Department of Transportation to take action. Typical was Resolution 1: '*Whereas* design of the shape, room, and equipment of the truck cab and the operating conditions within it, such as noise, fumes and exhaust, and comfort of ride, have been disregarded by vehicle manufacturers and resulted in harming the health, safety, and comfort of the driver, *Be It Resolved* that the Department of Transportation should set requirements for cab design and performance which medical research and driving experience demonstrate to be essential to decent working conditions.'[1] Most of the resolutions called upon the Department of Transportation (DOT) or some other government agency to take action.

However, another resolution by the conference was perhaps most important. Resolution 11 read, '*Whereas* the Teamsters seldom represent the best interests of the drivers in safety rulemaking actions in the Department of Transportation, or in consideration of legislation about driving, vehicle and highway safety, *Be It Resolved* that President Fitzsimmons, who turned down the invitation to join us here today, should establish an office in IBT headquarters devoted to technical evaluation of all such government proposals and to lobbying the Department of Transportation and the Congress to improve motor vehicle driver safety conditions.'[2]

That resolution, criticizing Fitzsimmons and calling upon the union to take action on behalf of its members, adopted by a conference of professional truck drivers, had the effect of creating not only a health and safety group, but also a reform organization within the Teamsters. PROD, the Professional Drivers Council, Inc., was formed shortly thereafter, and Arthur Fox II, a talented labor lawyer, became its executive director.

While the Teamsters union continued to ignore the safety issue, PROD opened an office in Washington to lobby for improved health and safety. In 1974 PROD won an important legal victory when it helped James Banyard win back his job and six years' back pay after he had been fired for refusing to drive an overweight truck because it was unsafe. It was a precedent-setting case that has since been cited hundreds of times. As a result, PROD soon attracted a number of dedicated and conscientious Teamsters who were interested in pursuing not only health and safety issues but also the reform of the union. PROD members tended to be road drivers concentrated along the eastern seaboard and in the South.

Frank Greco

In 1974 Frank Greco, a New Jersey truck driver, was concerned about some health and safety problems at Consolidated Freightways, the shipper for which he worked. CF frequently asked its drivers to pull overweight trucks, and Greco didn't think this was right because an overweight truck was a danger, both to the driver and the public. In addition, truck drivers lost work when the company overloaded trucks.

The union wouldn't take up the issue, but Greco and some of his coworkers tried to deal with the problem. Soon most of the other drivers became discouraged, but Greco continued on the company's case. He went to the National Labor Relations Board, the state police, the Interstate Commerce Commission – anywhere he could think of. None of them helped. But Greco was a persistent man, and finally in frustration he sat down and wrote a letter to Ralph Nader. That letter was the beginning of Frank Greco's long career in the Teamster reform movement.

Nader responded, suggesting that Greco contact PROD. Greco drove down to Washington, DC and met with several PROD staff members, including attorney Arthur Fox and researcher John Sikorski. It was after his discussions with the PROD staff, Greco says, that he realized that what he and his coworkers at CF faced was not an isolated problem. There were many other Teamsters who couldn't get their union to process grievances dealing with health and safety issues. 'I found out', says Greco, 'that the union just didn't pursue things like this, they just sat back and let them happen.' While the issue of overweight trucks and contact with Ralph Nader were directly responsible for bringing Greco into the reform movement, perhaps it would be more correct to say that the accumulated frustrations and aggravations of the truck driver's life were really responsible for his becoming an activist.

Frank Greco was born on Staten Island in 1926. He quit high school at sixteen and joined the Navy in 1944, and at the age of seventeen he was assigned to a gun crew on a merchant ship. He spent eight months sailing around the world, and then, like many ex-GIs, he went back to school, taking courses in television repair. He worked at the television repair business for a while, but then gave it up and went to work on the East Coast docks. During the Korean War he was a marine carpenter, securing tanks, armaments, and construction equipment on ships bound for Korea.

'I got into trucking in 1953, I guess it was', he remembers, 'hauling livestock. Another friend and myself, we had a couple of trucks, and we used to run livestock out of the Midwest into New Jersey. We ran a sleeper operation in and out to Michigan three times a week out of New Jersey. That's when the Pennsylvania turnpike was only halfway through. There was no excuse to stop; if there was ice and snow, you just put the chains on – though at that time when the weather was bad the roads would just shut down overnight. Once the trucks blocked it off, that's it, you sat there to the next morning when the state sand trucks come and got you out. We were hauling mainly hogs. Livestock was all non-union. I did that for ten years.

'We moved to Ohio, and I went to work for Consolidated Freightways, out of Akron in 1965. That's when I first became a member of the Teamsters Union, Akron Local 24. I was on call a lot because I had a double-bottom card, a license to pull double trailers on the Ohio Turnpike. When you had that double-bottom card you were always on call for the long trips. You were always on the road, you didn't have a chance to participate in the union in any way, shape or form. Let's say that you ran a short trip, you come back, and you had ten hours and then you had to go back to work. If you were on a long trip, say two or three days, then you would come back and have ten hours off again. Once a week you were allowed twenty-four hours off.

'You had to have six days to get twenty-four hours off, and in that twenty-four hours off you had to do everything that you had to do. You had to be the family man, the father to your children, the husband to your wife, your social life – all of that was jammed into one day. You do not have a family life when you work on the road. When I was in Local 24, I never attended any union meetings or anything because you never had any time. Then we moved back to the East, bought a house in New Jersey, and I started driving a truck locally, city work. I went to work for Cooper-Jarrett, and I was with them for about a year, and I was a member of Local 701. As soon as I could get back with Consolidated Freightways I went back with them, that was in 1968, and I've been with them ever since. At the present time I'm in Local 478.'

It was after he moved to New Jersey that Frank became active in PROD. Greco began studying PROD's literature dealing with the structure and finances of the Teamsters Union and the power and personal wealth of the Teamster officials. 'When I saw all those things', he says, 'I realized the rank and file were very uneducated as to the internal structure of the union, and how and why people had their power. The rank and file was unaware of what was really going on in their unions, as far as salaries went, the multiple pensions, the lack of democracy within the union meetings. What PROD was doing was trying to expose the whole thing and fight it at the same time in order to change it.' Soon Frank was making frequent trips to the PROD office in Washington, and in 1975 he joined the organization. For years the New Jersey Teamsters had been dominated by the notorious Provenzano family and controlled by the Mafia, and it took courage to stand up as Frank Greco did. And, 'because of fear of economic and physical reprisal', he was not particularly successful in winning a following for PROD in New Jersey.

Nevertheless, he was willing to take on responsibility, and Greco became a national PROD leader and one of its foremost public spokespersons. 'I was handing out literature locally, appearing on radio and television here in New Jersey and down in Washington, testifying before congressional committees in Washington on truck safety and pensions.' One of the things that Greco did from time to time was throw a copy or two of the PROD newspaper, *The Dispatch,* into a trailer heading west.

Charlie Helton

Charlie Helton almost literally stumbled across PROD. 'I picked up one of the PROD papers in the floor of a trailer I was working', he remembers. 'It had their Washington address on it, and I joined right away.' Perhaps it was Frank Greco back in New Jersey who had tossed that paper in the trailer. In any case, Charlie had been hoping that something like PROD would come along: he had gotten tired of the bombings and the thugs.

Charlie Helton is a fifty-year-old truck driver from Ringgold, Georgia. Charlie likes kids, and he and his wife have a large family; their eight children range in age from thirty years to eleven months. The last three were adopted. 'Just got to have 'em around', he says of the children. The Heltons are active in the Baptist Church, and Charlie used to be involved in the 'bus ministry', picking up underprivileged children in the church bus and bringing them to Sunday school.

Charlie was born in 1938 in Bristol, Tennessee and raised in Oak Ridge, Tennessee, where his dad was a bus driver and a local leader of the Amalgamated Transportation Workers. Charlie dropped out of high school in his senior year to get married, and about the same time the bus company his father worked for folded, so all the Heltons picked up and moved to Southern California.

Out on the West Coast, both Charlie and his dad got jobs working in a furniture factory represented by the Teamsters union, and Charlie's dad was elected the shop steward in the spray paint department. In the 1960s Charlie left the factory and took a job as a truck driver hauling construction materials in Orange, California. He was a Teamster, a member of Local 235, and he had no complaints. He worked piece rate and made as much as $35,000 or $40,000 a year, and that was a lot of money in those days.

Then, in 1968, the Helton family decided to move back down South. 'We just got burned out with big city life, and we wanted to move back here in the South where it was a little slower paced.' They moved to Ringgold, Georgia, just across the state line from Chattanooga, Tennessee. His wife's uncle put in a word for him, and Charlie got a job at Roadway, one of the country's biggest trucking companies. Charlie has worked there ever since, sometimes as a dock worker and sometimes as a driver, but mostly as a 'switcher' or hostler shuttling trailers from the yard to the dock.

When Charlie Helton first came to Chattanooga Local 515, the local had been thrown into trusteeship because of corruption, and the International had appointed David Halpenny as trustee. Halpenny, says Helton, 'was a likeable guy', and after serving as trustee, Halpenny was elected president and business manager of the local. As head of the union, Halpenny was an aggressive organizer. The local, which had 1,200 members when he took over in 1969, grew to 4,200 members by the end of 1974. 'He organized places all over town', says Charlie. 'though he wouldn't take care of the members he had. He represented us pretty good for a few months. Then he just kind of relaxed, and you'd never see him, there wasn't any representation. The companies just had their way, and if they chose not to go by the contract, they just didn't go by it.'

Charlie worried about the situation at Roadway, where he felt the company walked all over the employees. 'Roadway', says Charlie, 'is not like an employer – it's like an incarceration. A shift over there is like a day in a penitentiary. They've got supervisors that tail you on the docks. They just stand around and look, like a guard at a prison. They issue warning letters for drinking too much water between breaks, and going to the bathroom too many times on a shift. You're not allowed to speak to the people working on each side of you in trailers. They don't want any conversation. They just want continuous work. They want you picking up boxes the whole time you're there.'

With an employer like Roadway, the workers wanted the union to be present and protect them right there in the barn. But the stewards were not doing their jobs, the contract was not being enforced, and, most important, the company paid no attention to seniority. 'In talking to the men, I guess some of them thought I might be the answer, so they had a little election on the dock there one day, and got the business agent over there, and chose me as their job steward', says Helton. He called a meeting between the company and the union to go over the issues. 'I thought, it's just a lack of communication, so we just need to sit down and take a look at the rules and see if both sides agree to it.' They held the meeting, and both sides seemed to agree on the contract provisions and their interpretation.

'So we go back to work – and right back to the same thing.' No matter what the workers did, the company wouldn't abide by the contract. 'And', Helton says, 'the union wouldn't process the grievances. We'd go to a lot of trouble to investigate and file grievances, and then a few months later, if you asked them about it, they'd say it's been postponed, and then next month, it's been postponed again. And if you really persisted and demanded to know what happened to it, they'd give you a little scribbled note saying "denied".'

In 1975 Helton, other workers from Roadway, and other disgruntled members from other shops went down to the union hall and staged a protest demonstration, but it brought no results. Charlie Helton finally threw up his hands in disgust and frustration and resigned as steward. But about that time one of Helton's coworkers who was also fed up with the situation decided to challenge President Halpenny for the top office. Paul Reyher had originally come from the Chicago area to Chattanooga to go to college, and after graduation had taught school for a couple of years. He settled down on a farm in north Georgia with his wife and five kids, joined the Trinity Baptist Church, and, like Charlie Helton, got a job as a truck driver for Roadway. He had been a Teamster for about fifteen years and a member of Local 515 for six. He was a serious contender.

Charlie Helton was glad that somebody was going to try to change things, and he worked hard on Reyher's campaign. 'The companies wouldn't cooperate – they wouldn't let us on the premises to campaign', Charlie remembers. 'We contacted the Labor Department, and it just wasn't serious enough for them to get involved.

'Right before the election Paul Reyher's house was firebombed. They just blew the front right off of his house. It was never determined who did it. He filed a Labor Department complaint that they harassed him throughout his campaign. Nobody took it seriously. He got twenty-five percent of the vote. The biggest problem with the election, though, was that people wouldn't vote. People were afraid to go near the place.'

Meanwhile, Halpenny was undergoing a transformation. 'Power took him over or something. He just felt like he could force companies to sign contracts. He got involved with some shady characters. They were trying to organize a Buick dealership here in Chattanooga, the service department, a bunch of mechanics. They couldn't get a contract, so they had a few explosions around the building there. Blowed the top off the building.

Dynamite or gas bombs or something. He was indicted, convicted, and went to prison down in Alabama, federal prison down there. I think he served four years.'[3]

Halpenny wanted to leave his friend Bobby Logan in charge of the local when he went to prison, but Logan was on probation after pleading no contest to a bombing in Tennessee and was therefore ineligible to hold union office. Halpenny decided to leave the local in the hands of Paul Smith. When Smith's term of office was up, Halpenny still had a year to serve in prison, and Smith had come to like being the boss. But Bobby Logan was now eligible and ran against Smith in a heated contest and defeated him. Logan has run the local ever since.

But Charlie Helton didn't give up, and he continued to try to reform the local. Attending local meetings, handing out literature, trying to organize in spite of the difficulties. 'They don't have meetings – they have lectures. If you'll sit there and be quiet, everything goes smooth. I've been ruled out of order every meeting I've ever went to. He will not let me speak.

'You can hand out literature if you want to risk it. His goons, they just surround you, interfere with you, cuss you, intimidate you in general until there's very little of it goes on. I do some of it, but ... it really takes some guts. Members, just run-of-the-mill members, won't go near it. They even serve a buffet lunch there to try to get people to come and make it look good for them. People won't go, they just won't go. Well, really nothing happens. There's no old business, there's no new business, there's no organizing. Nothing's going on.'

Several years ago, Charlie ran for office against Logan, even though he was well aware of the danger. 'I had a constant stream of phone calls from people that would like to help. They wanted me to understand they'd like to help, but they would say, "We just can't get involved" because their jobs were at stake. They've got a method of retaliation, you know. The companies cooperate with them – you mess with the union leaders, and the companies mess with you.' Charlie Helton and Frank Greco were perhaps exemplary PROD members, but there were many more like them who wanted safe and healthy jobs and good union representation, and were getting no help from their union. Moreover, they were honest people, and they wanted a union run by honest people, and they were fed up with the crooks.

PROD had decided it would take the fight to the 1976 Teamsters convention in Las Vegas, and in May, just a month before the convention, PROD released a report written by Arthur Fox and John Sikorski, *Teamster Democracy and Financial Responsibility*.[4] The PROD report argued that the Teamsters union was a dictatorship 'in the firm grip of a single solitary individual – Frank E. Fitzsimmons.' Using the union's reports to the federal government, the 177-page PROD book detailed criminal connections and financial abuses and listed some seventeen union officials who made over

$100,000 a year in salaries and expenses.

Having explained the problem, PROD called on the union members to end the dictatorship of the general president and reform the union. 'The principal responsibility for reforming the International Brotherhood of Teamsters must lie with the Union's rank and file', said the report, and it urged the ranks to use the federal courts to accomplish their goals. PROD's *Teamster Democracy and Financial Responsibility* was the first full-scale critique of the Teamster bureaucracy's power and corruption written from the point of view of the Teamster membership. With the publication of that report, PROD established itself not only as a lobbying group for driver health and safety, but also as an important reform group within the union.

Notes

1. 'Resolutions Adopted October 2, 1971 at the Professional Drivers' Conference on Truck and Bus Safety, Mayflower Hotel, Washington, D.C.', mimeo, p. 1.

2. 'Resolutions', p. 4.

3. Dick Kopper, 'Halpenny Given Four Years for Role in Bomb Conspiracy; Others Lighter', *Chattanooga Times*, 19 July 1974.

4. Arthur L. Fox, II, and John Sikorski, *Teamster Democracy and Financial Responsibility: A Factual and Structural Analysis*, Washington, DC, 1976.

6

'Ready to Strike!': TDC
and the 1976 Contract

The 1970 wildcat had been an impressive demonstration of the potential power of a rank-and-file movement, but the ranks had not yet found a way to channel such an outburst of energy into an organizational form. Teamsters United Rank and File had failed to create a national reform organization because it had never developed a united leadership or a program. PROD, the Professional Drivers Council, was primarily concerned with health and safety issues and had been organizing only among road drivers. There was no national rank-and-file organization of all Teamsters concerned not only about particular issues, but about the future of the entire union.

The members, unable to control their own union, soon saw it falling under the control of others. The first to intrude was Republican President Richard Nixon. Nixon, who would be running for reelection in 1972, was eager to have the support of the Teamsters, particularly because no other labor unions would support him. So, despite strong political opposition, Nixon commuted Jimmy Hoffa's sentence on 23 December 1971 and Hoffa emerged from prison. However, as the result of an arrangement between Nixon and Frank Fitzsimmons, the commutation also required that Hoffa 'not engage in the direct or indirect management of any labor organization prior to March 6, 1980, and if the ... condition is not fulfilled this commutation will be null and void in its entirety.'

The conditions of Hoffa's release established a close political partnership between Nixon and Fitzsimmons that lasted until 1974, when a committee of the House of Representatives recommended Nixon's impeachment, leading to his resignation. While the partnership lasted, Fitzsimmons had Nixon's blessing despite evidence of Mafia involvement in the union and its pension funds. At the same time, Nixon could count on Fitzsimmons to support him throughout the Watergate scandal. They were the perfect couple, Nixon as busy undermining democracy in the republic as Fitzsimmons was active in demolishing it in the Teamsters union.

Of direct importance to the economic well-being of the Teamster rank and file, Nixon counted on Fitzsimmons to back the government's anti-inflation program. In 1973 the Teamsters had negotiated a poor contract, because, as one professor of labor relations noted, 'Fitzsimmons was constrained by his political support of Nixon to abide by the Administration's "pay restraint" program.'[1]

Nixon could keep Hoffa out of the union and thus help Fitzsimmons keep his hold on the Teamsters presidency, but, as everyone knew, Fitzsimmons was no Hoffa. Hoffa, a powerful personality and an organizational genius, was able to dominate all the centrifugal forces in the union: employers, Mafia chiefs, regional Teamster leaders, rank-and-file oppositionists. Fitzsimmons had no such organizational talent nor such strength of personality. So under Fitzsimmons, the International gradually gave up power to regional Teamster leaders, men like Roy Williams in Kansas City, Jackie Presser in Ohio, and the Provenzano brothers in New Jersey, many of whom were both corrupt themselves and had ties with organized crime. The breakdown of the union had begun.

The trucking companies and other employers now began to approach these regional leaders seeking concessions, and the Teamster barons began making separate deals, usually granting the employers concessions on working conditions. The regional officials had various motives. As subsequent trials and convictions revealed, union officials were in many cases receiving direct payments from the employers, literally selling out the members. In some cases, regional Teamster leaders believed that by granting concessions they would attract more employers to their area, thus increasing their membership and their dues income so that they could increase their own salaries, expense accounts and pensions.

While they were granting concessions, Fitzsimmons and the Teamster barons neglected organizing, and the result was an increase in non-union trucking. Naturally, increased competition with non-union companies led unionized employers to seek more concessions. This dynamic – the failure to organize and the growth of non-union competition, leading in turn to demands for concessions from union companies – came to dominate the industry and the union.

In a study of the trucking industry done in the late 1970s, Harold M. Levinson of the University of Michigan wrote: 'A final impact of the growing nonunion threat has been the spread of various "under the table" agreements made by local unions with many individual companies or groups of smaller companies under which the officially negotiated wage and fringe benefit standards are being quietly undercut. Technically, such concessions can properly be negotiated only as riders to the major agreements and only with the approval of the international union; for obvious reasons, such riders are rarely approved. As a result, local union officials – with the consent of the employees affected – have simply done so without official approval (though often with official knowledge).'[2] It was in this way that the erosion of the National Master Freight Agreement took place.

As the NMFA's expiration date approached – 1 April 1976 – it was clear that Fitzsimmons would not be a hard bargainer. There was a vacuum in leadership, and no local union president or leader of a joint council or Teamster conference stepped forward. If there was going to be a movement to defend the National Master Freight Agreement and to win a decent contract in 1976, it was going to have to come from the rank and file.

Teamsters for a Decent Contract Organizes

There were various rank-and-file groups active in the Teamsters in the 1970s, as we have seen. Los Angeles Local 208 continued to have a strong tradition of union democracy. Some big trucking companies like Interstate Systems (IS) had networks of active union stewards and were busy fighting the company over working conditions. In Detroit, rank and filers left in the lurch by the disappearance of Jimmy Hoffa had formed an organization called Action Rank and File (ARF) and were trying to find a way to organize themselves into an effective force to fight Fitzsimmons.

In addition, rank and filers throughout the country had organized local union caucuses and newspapers. In the San Francisco Bay Area a rank and filer named Dennis Dalton put out a paper called *The Fifth Wheel*. Lester Williams, a former president of Cleveland TURF, and Ken and Carole Paff and Mike Friedman put out the *Membership Voice* in Cleveland. In Pittsburgh, Mel Packer, Rita Drapkin, Joe Stabilito and Dave Gaibis organized a group called Concerned Rank and File Teamsters and put out a paper called *From the Horse's Mouth*. In Chicago, Bob and Mary Grant and Ray Lopez had helped to organize the Concerned Truckers for a Democratic Union. In addition to these groups, local unions throughout the country had loose networks of active union members, who, though they had no group or newspaper, had informal organizations among their coworkers and fellow union members.[3] Beginning in early 1975 some of the better organized groups had gotten in touch with each other, began to exchange their local newspapers, and in the Midwest began to travel and visit one another, holding small, informal meetings to exchange ideas about the state of the union and the contract. These contacts led to a meeting of about thirty-five rank-and-file Teamsters from fourteen different cities in Chicago in August 1975 to discuss the 1976 negotiations.

In the course of an all-day meeting the group drew up a list of twelve contract demands and established Teamsters for a Decent Contract (TDC). Ken Paff was elected the group's secretary, and his home in Cleveland became TDC's nerve center. Paralleling the growth of TDC, and closely tied to it, was that of UPSurge, an organization for decent contracts for workers at United Parcel Service (UPS) that had organized about this same time. Its leader was Anne Mackie, a Cleveland package car driver.

A brochure outlining TDC's contract demands was quickly drawn up, 20,000 copies were printed and thrown in tractor cabs and truck trailers, and word of TDC soon spread throughout the United States. Soon it was necessary to print another 100,000 brochures. Tens of thousands of UPSurge leaflets were also distributed throughout the UPS system. The response was impressive: rank-and-file Teamsters from more than 100 local unions all over the country began to write and call requesting more brochures and more information about TDC and UPSurge. The initial TDC and UPSurge brochures had fallen on fertile ground, and the harvest was a remarkable collection of union activists. Among those who picked up TDC leaflets on picket lines, bulletin boards, or the floors of trucks were Pete Camarata, Wanda Ellerman, Keith Gallagher and Vince Meredith.

Pete Camarata

At the time Pete Camarata was a steward in Local 299 at the Earl C. Smith barn, and he was a Hoffa man. Camarata had grown up on Detroit's East Side, where he still lives, and went to Catholic elementary and high schools. He attended McComb County Community College for a year and enrolled at Detroit's Wayne State University in 1967. When Pete found he needed some work in order to pay for tuition and room and board, a fraternity brother got him a part-time job at the Earl C. Smith Trucking Company working on the dock.

While going to college and working at the trucking company, Pete also began to take an interest in St. Margaret Mary's Catholic Church, where he had gone to school. 'It was a dying church, I guess you'd say. It was on its last legs. I think it was about one of the last churches in the city that the Catholic Church still kept open. It had changed from being a white church, after the great "white flight" from Detroit, and it was mostly Black, though a few of the white parishioners still kept coming.'

Pete liked working with the teenagers at St. Margaret Mary's, and in order to help them get funds and facilities he ran for the parish council. He was elected, and for a couple of years he spent his spare time going to church meetings and playing ball with the kids. Always an idealist, in those days Pete's ideals came from the Catholic church, and they were ideals of Christian love and service to his community. Those ideals would evolve, and when I met Pete Camarata in 1975 he had become a kind of Christian socialist.

After going to Wayne State for a year, Camarata became a part-time student while working full-time on the dock at Earl C. Smith. Like most of the young guys, he ended up on the afternoon shift. The other fellows he worked with admired Camarata because he was working his way through college, thought he seemed like a pretty smart guy, and in 1970 elected him their union steward. Soon Camarata began to think of himself not as a Wayne State student, but as a Teamster.

It was a great time to be a Teamster in Detroit. 'There was a real cockiness on the part of most of the people that were in the union', says Camarata. 'The guys just had the feeling that you almost couldn't get fired, no matter what you did. They really felt their strength. You couldn't discount the fact that you could walk down the street and get hired just about any place in the city. I mean when I got hired at Earl C. Smith I could have gone into an auto plant, I could have gone into construction, I could have gone into a steel mill. There were any number of different industries that you could just walk in off the street and get hired. This created a real cockiness among those guys.' Nobody was afraid of being fired.

But mostly, the Teamsters' confidence came from being in the union. 'There was a real pride in the union in those days. Everybody really was proud of being a member of Local 299. We had a strong local then. We were up to about twenty thousand members. In the whole city, there wasn't a truck driver that wasn't organized.' The guys on the afternoon shift at the dock at Earl C. Smith company shared that spirit: 'When I think back on it now, I think we really had some pretty good shopfloor organization.' And he tells the story of a little dispute with the company one cold night back in 1970.

'It's a cement dock, one of those docks where, when the temperature reaches freezing, or just above freezing, it will just get like walking in heavy mud. The company was supposed to spread a drying agent on the dock to keep it from becoming slushy and slippery, but the company had run out of the chemical. So the whole place was just like a total slop house – it was awful.'

Camarata was the union committeeman, and he remembers all the dock men came to him, saying, 'You go up and tell 'im, you go up and tell 'im.' So Camarata went to the afternoon shift supervisor to tell him, while the other dock men listened. 'Hey', Camarata told the supervisor, 'we've got to get some drying agent, and we've got to get this dock cleaned up, or somebody's going to fall down and break their leg.'

'That's why we've got workmen's comp insurance', the supervisor told him, 'in case somebody breaks their leg. You just get your ass back to work.' At lunch Camarata and the guys sat down and read the union contract, which at that time said that if there were a work stoppage the company could discipline employees, but it could not fire them as long as they were willing to come back to work within twenty-four hours. 'Well, we all decided we weren't going to work in that shit. And we just came back after lunch, and punched out, and left.

'So the next morning bright and early about a dozen of us went back to the work place.' They went into the office, and the terminal manager was there with the union business agent. The business agent turned to them and asked, 'What the hell do you guys think you're doing?'

'I could see', Camarata remembers, 'that I wasn't going to get too much support from him.' Then the terminal manager turned to Camarata and said, 'There ain't no sense in even coming back here. You guys are all fired.'

'So I got the contract book, and I handed it to the boss. And I said, "You read this." And I told the business agent, "I want to talk to *you* out in the hall." So the business agent got up and came outside, and I said, "Now you see this section of the contract? It says if we're willing to come back to work within twenty-four hours we can't be fired." And I said, "We're ready to come back to work. Now you go back in there and tell him to put us back to work or we're going to break you in half." He just kind of looked at me in a real stare.'

While Pete was talking to the business agent, the other workers who had been fired went out on the dock and took the keys out of all the hi-lo forklift trucks and threw them away. Then they made sure the day-shift workers would give them their support. The day shift was down in the basement having lunch, and the only way in and out of that basement was a steep, narrow stairway. So the fired dockworkers quickly filled the stairway with handtrucks and other equipment.

Camarata meanwhile had convinced the business agent. 'He went back inside and told the boss, "What the hell do you guys think you're doing?" He was one of those guys who had a one-liner that applied to both sides of the fence.'

The next day the company took back the entire afternoon shift except for Pete Camarata and four other employees who had absenteeism problems. 'Well, I think I was off for ten days and finally got my job back with full back pay, plus all the overtime that everybody worked. So that really put me at odds with management from early on. It was my first experience with shopfloor organizing and activism on the job. It was a pretty interesting experience.'

After that, the dock was run from the shopfloor. The supervisor would come out and give the dock workers the work for the night, but he never dared assign work to the men individually. The workers organized the job themselves. And when they got a bad load, like bundles of steel tubing, they would stop everything and put the whole crew on that load, so that no one worker or team would get stuck with it.

However, at about the same time that Camarata had become a steward and one of those cocky Detroit Teamsters, Local 299 had gone into crisis. When Hoffa, who was in prison, had been forced in 1970 to give up the presidency of Local 299, he had chosen Dave Johnson to succeed him. 'Dave was really a good president', says Camarata. 'He really stuck with the rank and file. In 1973 Hoffa was out of jail, and he was coming back. They used to have these dinners called "How Old Friends Feel Active", an acronym for HOFFA. Hoffa was coming back, and Johnson was just going to hand it over to him. There was no doubt about it that Hoffa could just walk right in and take over Local 299. If there was an election, he would have been elected in a minute.'

But Frank Fitzsimmons was determined to prevent Hoffa from coming back, and so Fitzsimmons had Michigan Teamster Roland McMaster attempt to drive Johnson out of office. McMaster, says Camarata, represented the 'crooked, gangster element in the union'. McMaster and his man in Local 299, Ralph Proctor, began threatening and intimidating Johnson. This struggle between Johnson and McMaster was not simply a political struggle for control of the local. It was also about the union's attitude toward the employer. Johnson and the other Hoffa supporters wanted to negotiate good contracts and enforce them. McMaster wanted to give the companies concessions. Some Hoffa supporters suspected that McMaster's attitude toward the employers might be motivated by more than generosity, especially since McMaster had been convicted of taking employer payoffs back in 1966.

In the fight for the local, there was no doubt where Pete Camarata stood: he was with Dave Johnson and Jimmy Hoffa. In 1971 Camarata had been an alternate delegate to the Teamsters convention on the Hoffa slate. And Camarata was one of the Local 299 members actively working for Hoffa's return. After Hoffa was released, his supporters held regular events every month, such as $25-a-plate dinners to build up a campaign war chest for Hoffa's election. Pete Camarata went to the dinners and met Jimmy Hoffa. 'Hoffa was a real charismatic-type character', says Pete. Soon some of the organizers approached Camarata and asked him to get involved in putting together the dinners.

But then Hoffa suddenly disappeared. 'When Hoffa disappeared', says Camarata, 'it just really left a vacuum, they didn't know what to do then.' Things began to get rough. At one point McMaster and his goons came into the Local 299 hall and attacked Johnson, breaking his leg. Johnson, fearing for his life, began to spend almost all his time in Florida and returned to Detroit only once every three or four months to chair one of the monthly union meetings. But somebody, presumably one of McMaster's cronies, followed Johnson to Florida and blew up his boat.

While the leadership factions fought for control of the presidency of Local 299, the rank-and-file Teamsters created their own organizations.

Meetings of Hoffa supporters would take place about once a month. There were no leaflets: from 150 to 200 Teamsters would show up by word-of-mouth. They would mostly discuss job grievances, collect money and elect officers. 'We started a thing called ARF, Action Rank and File', Camarata remembers, 'and that organization would last a little bit. Then we decided that our name should be ACT, Action Committee of Teamsters. We were trying to figure out what the hell we were.'

But the meetings went nowhere. 'The Hoffa faction would be there organizing, and then a few of the McMaster people would show up to the meetings, and the next meeting all the Hoffa people would run away.' And so they went on for several months, meeting, choosing a name, electing officers, dissolving and starting over. The Detroit Teamsters were looking for a way to turn their strong shopfloor organizations into political power in the union, and they did not know where to turn.

At about that time a wildcat strike broke out at Interstate trucking, and Steve Kindred, who had stopped by the Interstate picket line, ran into Pete Camarata and gave him a Teamsters for a Decent Contract brochure. 'I got a hold of one of those brochures, and I brought it to one of those meetings that we had. And everybody said, "Yeah, that's a good idea, why don't you mail away, try to get two or three hundred of them. Let's start distributing them, and maybe we can get something organized around this master freight agreement next year."' In November the group took up a collection to send Pete and another fellow to the next TDC meeting, to be held in Cleveland. They returned home to Detroit and began organizing the old Hoffa supporters into TDC.

Wanda Ellerman

Wanda Ellerman, a clerical worker at a Yellow Freight terminal in Los Angeles, found a TDC leaflet on a bulletin board at work. She picked it up and brought it home to show to her husband, Bob, and they both went to one of the first TDC meetings in Los Angeles.

Wanda Ellerman was born Wanda Cooper and raised in a suburb of Akron, Ohio. She finished high school toward the end of World War II and got a job with Ohio Bell as a telephone operator. It was a turbulent time at the phone company. The American Telephone and Telegraph Company and the Bell Telephone System were strongly opposed to labor unions, and for decades had fought legitimate unions while organizing their own company unions. Nevertheless, during the 1930s and 1940s telephone workers organized independent unions and attempted to unite into one national union of telephone workers. When Wanda went to work at Ohio Bell in Akron, she remembers, 'It was already organized, and we had what you call a closed shop, everybody had to belong. In other words, everybody had to be represented. I was elected steward.'

In the immediate postwar period, when she began working for Ma Bell, the telephone workers' unions were preparing to strike for higher wages. During the war most unions had pledged not to strike, and while profits and prices had risen, workers' wages had lagged far behind. The pent up frustrations of four years of sacrifice burst out in the fall of 1945 and 1946 as more than 4 million workers struck, the biggest strike wave in American history. Telephone workers struck in 1945 and threatened a national strike in 1946, as a result of which they succeeded in winning big wage gains from the telephone company, amounting to an 18 percent increase in wages in two years. Threatened by the rising militance of the work force, AT&T and the Bell companies decided to try to stop the union in 1947. That year some 350,000 telephone workers carried out the first national strike of the Bell System, effective in all but nine states. Among the strikers was Wanda Ellerman.

The big strike began on 7 April 1947 and didn't end until 20 May, six weeks later. 'The supervisors took over the work', she remembers, 'and we all decided that if we were going to be on strike, we were going to keep them busy. So we'd go out to the public telephone and make phone calls into the operator, and the boards would light up till they just about went crazy.'

Out of that 1947 telephone workers strike came the founding of the Communication Workers of America (CWA), the first viable national union of telephone workers. Wanda continued to work at Ohio Bell for twelve years, serving as steward much of the time and playing a role in several smaller strikes.

In 1959 she quit work at Ohio Bell and went to work for Allstates Freight, a trucking company that was later absorbed by PIE. 'I ran the switchboard, I did all the office work, government bills of lading, tracing, and OS&D, that is, "over, short and damaged freight". I did a lot of IBM, this is computer work, and cashiering.' At the time Wanda went to work at Allstates the office workers were not organized and had no union representation, so as a union woman she naturally got in touch with Teamster Local 497, which represented trucking company office workers as well as drivers and dock workers. 'We were a breakbulk, and there were fifty-five workers in our office, and fifty of them were women. It's hard to make office union members into good union members because the company takes them in and talks to them, and says, "Now you people are the ones that run this office. We're your bosses, but you are the company. In other words, you are not dock workers, you're not drivers. When we leave here, you can take care of this place and you run it." So some office workers think they're like management.'

Allstates and later Pacific Intermountain Express spent a great deal of money on dinners and parties for the office workers in downtown restaurants and hotels, all to convince them not to vote union. 'Two times', Wanda recalls, 'we had union representation elections and lost. The final organizing drive came after PIE had purchased Allstates, and PIE tried to stop the Teamsters by bringing in another union. The company got a hold of this other union's representative, and I received a phone call. He asked to meet us in a hotel room in downtown Akron. So several office people got together and we went down to the meeting, and we found out that it wasn't all it was cracked up to be. They wanted us to consider going into that union instead of the Teamsters. Well, we didn't want that, because we knew that all of our people on the dock and all the drivers were all Teamsters, and we wanted to belong to the Teamsters, too. 'The third election we won.'

It had taken Wanda over six years, but she finally brought the union in. They now had to negotiate a contract. PIE brought in its top labor relations man from Oakland, and William Presser sent in a Teamster official from the Cleveland Joint Council, and both tried to get the office workers to accept a contract with a ten-cent-an-hour raise. But the office workers held out for months until finally Jimmy Hoffa authorized strike sanction for the PIE Akron-Cleveland breakbulk, contingent on the approval of William Presser. A strike at that terminal would have severely crippled PIE in the Midwest, so the office workers just had to hold out a little longer and they would win.

'There were four or five of us on the negotiating committee', says Wanda 'and I was one of them. Some of them were very weak. They were elected to this committee because they were people's friends. They didn't elect them because of their knowledge, they just elected them because they liked them. We had quite a bit of fighting trying to get a contract together, this person and that person just wanted to settle it and get out of there. They were ready to settle for ten cents an hour on the money package.

'I had worked for six years and a half to organize these people, and I wasn't about to let them be sold out for ten cents an hour. I went home and I just started crying, I was so mad. I told Bob how I felt, and he said, "Well, it's your people, and you don't want them to settle for ten cents an hour, and if you feel it's wrong, tell them what's going on." So I got on the phone and I called every person in our office, and I told them that these people were going to sell them out for ten cents an hour. The business agent for the local got upset about it. He didn't think I should be telling people this. And I said, "That's too bad. I'm just not going to go for it." We ended up getting fifty cents an hour, and some people got as much as a dollar-an-hour raise in different departments, depending on the different jobs they did. We ended up with the best contract in the whole city, even health and welfare was paid in the first contract, and we got dental coverage and we got eyeglasses.'

At the end of the 1960s Bob and Wanda Ellerman moved to California, where Bob eventually got a job at Yellow Freight, while Wanda was hired at the main Los Angeles Yellow Freight terminal and became a member of Teamster Local 357. It was there that Wanda came across that TDC leaflet.

Keith Gallagher

Another Teamster hooked by the TDC brochure was Keith Gallagher. 'Back in 1975', Keith recalls, 'I rode back and forth to work with a friend of mine; his name was Jim McCloud. One day he found a leaflet at the bottom of a trailer. As we were driving home that night he handed it to me. It happened to be one of the earliest TDC brochures. We were all excited about it, because even during the short period of time between when I hired on in 1971 and when we found the leaflet in 1975, we had seen Roadway start to change, where the harassment had picked up and people were being treated differently.'

Keith was born in Harrisburg, Pennsylvania in 1947 and raised in Middletown, near Three Mile Island. His mother was a housewife, and his father worked for over thirty years at Bethlehem Steel. Keith remembers that his father went through several strikes at the mill, and that there was some hardship in the family: 'I can remember as a youngster standing with him when the steelworkers were on strike, waiting to get our basketful of bread and powdered milk.'

Keith went to college for two years in the Harrisburg area, and in the summers he worked in the steel plant along with his father, becoming a member of the United Steel Workers. 'I paid my dues, but it meant nothing to me. At that time I had my sights set on being a social worker.' But then, right in the middle of his college education, the Vietnam War came along. 'My closest friend who had graduated with me from high school and was going to college had let his draft deferment drop, and he got drafted and went to Vietnam. He came back alive – but in bits and pieces. He stepped on a land mine, and he was almost killed. I decided I had better do something, so I enlisted in the Coast Guard Reserves.' Keith went to basic training at Cape May, New Jersey and then was stationed in Virginia.

When his time in the Coast Guard was up, Keith returned to school and in his third year met and married Pam Winn. Keith was going to school, his wife was working full-time, and he had applied to the Dauphin County Board of Assistance for a job as a social worker. But then his wife became pregnant, and he had to go to work. The position as a social worker with the county still had not come through, so he took any labor job he could get. Through a temp agency he got a job at the Capital Storage Warehouse in Harrisburg and was working there when a friend suggested he could make more money working at Roadway. So in 1971 Keith went to work as a dock worker at the Roadway Express terminal in Harrisburg.

When Keith started at Roadway the union was strong. When the company violated the contract or put pressure on the dock workers, they pushed back. 'I worked on the midnight shift for about a year, and I can remember one instance, where something had happened on the dock, and the guys were extremely angry about it. They called a slowdown, and everyone on the midnight crew participated.' Keith became friends with a fellow named Don Engle, who was the union steward. 'Because of Don I got involved further. We went out on strikes at other smaller companies that didn't have enough people to hold a picket line. Learning from them what a union was, how it backed up everyone, no matter what they did, is probably one of the main reasons I'm in TDU today.'

In 1973 Keith transferred to Stroudsburg and became a member of Teamster Local 229. He found the situation very different from what it had been in Harrisburg. 'I think my first impression of that local union was that it was a dictatorship. The principal officer, Edward Harrington, was one of the conegotiators of the Eight Cities Supplement, the worst supplement under the Master Freight Agreement. He and my business agent, Peter Fiore, pretty much ruled Local 229 with an iron hand. They were the people in power; what they said went. I don't think I was intimidated by them, but maybe I was in awe of them, at the power they wielded over people.'

Edward Harrington was the leader in negotiating givebacks to the company, and the Teamsters union in the Eight Cities area was becoming weaker. At the same time, Keith remembers, the company was becoming more aggressive. 'They were getting different kinds of supervisors in there who didn't respect people as human beings. All they were concerned about were the numbers they could put down on their pad. Though they didn't use the word at the time, production was all they were concerned about.'

So when McCloud and Gallagher read the TDC leaflet they were excited about it. They took it back to work and passed it around among the other dock workers and drivers. Everybody else was interested, too. They called a phone number on the leaflet and learned that there was going to be a TDC meeting in Sandusky, Ohio. 'As a body, on the dock, we decided we had better send some people, and we took up a collection. We had enough money to send four people, including Jim McCloud and P.K. Henry. We sent them out, and they came back and told us what TDC was about, and everybody was excited. I mean, they were all set to go.'

Vince Meredith

Like TDC, UPSurge put out leaflets around the country that attracted Teamsters working for UPS. Perhaps the most outstanding early leader of UPSurge was Vince Meredith, a UPS driver and chief steward from Louisville, Kentucky. One anecdote he tells explains the kind of organization he and his coworkers had created.

One day in the late 1960s a United Parcel Service supervisor in Louisville fired Meredith. When Vince got home, his wife, Chiyo, asked him what he was going to do about being fired. Vince recalls that he told her, 'Listen, I've been chief steward over there all these years, and if the guys don't know what to do, that's tough.' The guys knew just what to do. 'The next morning about seven o'clock my phone starts ringing, and the business agent says, "Vince, come over here, goddamn, everybody's on the picket line." I said, "I can't come over there. I'm fired, man. You've got to be kidding. I ain't getting in that mess."'

The business agent continued to implore him, and finally Vince went down to the terminal. However, when he got there UPS management came out and told him and all of the others on the picket line that they were fired. A quick meeting was called, and UPS workers began to pile into cars and drive away. The company flew in its chief negotiators from Chicago, and later in the afternoon they met with Vince Meredith. At first they told him he would not be put back to work, and that his case would be heard through the grievance procedure, a process that at the time took between two and four months.

But as they sat there talking, the phones began to ring. Each time the phone rang one of the management people would leave the table to take the message, returning with what Meredith describes as a 'very solemn' expression. They were receiving word from all over Kentucky, from Lexington and Bowling Green, from Campbellsville and London, that the picket lines were up and that the terminals were closing down.

Finally, one of the UPS negotiators turned to Meredith and asked him, 'What will it take to get you back to work?' To which he replied, 'All it takes is no action against anybody, and we'll go back to work in the morning.' And that's what happened.

'We were the first ones in UPS to ever use the roving picket line', Meredith says proudly. That was one of a half-dozen wildcat strikes by the Louisville UPS workers in the late 1960s and early 1970s, and, says Meredith, not one worker was fired.

Vince Meredith was born in Louisville in 1931. His father was a self-employed carpenter and a farmer, and his mother was a housewife. After the ninth grade Vince dropped out of school and worked on the farm until he was sixteen; then he got a job at a company that manufactured truck trailers. When he was nineteen he joined the Air Force, where he would eventually spend 'nine years, one month, and twenty-one days'.

In the Air Force he was an airframe repairman, working on the metal surfaces of the airplanes, including fuselages, wings and gas tanks. Then for a while he supervised the crew that maintained the officers' barracks. He was mostly stationed in Japan, where he came to love the country, learned to speak the language, and fell in love with a Japanese woman named Chiyo and decided he wanted to marry her. The chaplain warned him against marrying a Japanese woman, telling him that they would never be accepted in the United States. In some Southern states they would not even be considered legally married because they were of different races. The chaplain succeeded in putting obstacles in Vince's path until his tour of duty expired and he was sent home.

But as soon as he got home Meredith made a trip to the Pentagon to see a colonel who owed him a favor, then reenlisted; with the colonel's help he was soon back in Japan. After more discussions with the chaplain and more hassles with the bureaucracy he finally succeeded in marrying Chiyo. 'It took me about thirty-eight months all together to get married: two tours', remembers Vince.

After he left the service Vince returned to Louisville and got a job at Donaldson Baking as a route salesman. After less than a year he became a supervisor. A friend who was working at UPS suggested he go to work there, and Vince went for an interview. UPS told him that with his experience he would be quickly promoted to supervisor, but that he would have to work as a truck driver for two months first. So on 29 June 1964 Vince Meredith went to work for UPS.

It took a little longer than the two months the company had promised before Vince was offered a job as a supervisor, but by then, says Vince, 'I'd seen too much.' Meredith felt that he could not in good conscience work for UPS management because 'they don't show respect for a person.' Within about five months after being hired, Meredith was elected steward, a position he has held ever since. 'I'd never been involved in unions per se, but I was always in favor of the underdog and tried to help them.' When Vince was first hired the UPS uniform included a bow tie, which employees were expected to wear regardless of the temperature, which frequently reached 100 degrees in the Kentucky summer. Vince and his coworkers decided that the bow tie had to go.

'That bow tie was the hardest thing to get out of that first contract I negotiated', Vince remembers. 'They give us a dollar-an-hour raise, in three years, a dollar an hour, and didn't want to take the bow tie off. It was a strike issue, and we voted ninety-nine percent across the state of Kentucky to strike if we didn't lose the bow tie. Finally the division manager of the state of Kentucky came into the negotiations and said, "Take off the goddamned bow tie", and he walked out. And after that, in the next contract, across the whole United States the bow tie was gone.'

The local union asked Meredith to take a job as a union official but he declined. 'The president of Local 89 asked me over as a business agent – they appoint the business agents, they don't elect them. So I asked him,

"Now, Paul, if you ask me to do something that I consider morally wrong, would I have to do it?" And he said, "Yes." And I said, "Well, I don't need your job."' Vince considered running for office, but rejected the idea. 'When I could have probably ran and got the office of president of the local, then I don't think I could have been effective because of the International union.' Given the situation in the International at the time, he believed he was more effective and more powerful as a union steward than he would have been as a union official.

Ever since being elected steward, Vince Meredith had been in contact with UPS workers in other cities around the country, and some had come to Louisville to sit around his kitchen table and try to put together a national UPS workers network, but 'it just wouldn't jell'. So when UPSurge appeared, says Vince, 'I thought it was a godsend.' Vince Meredith brought to UPSurge what was probably the best organized, strongest and most militant group of UPS workers in the country.

TDC Organizes

The tremendous rank-and-file response to the contract brochure and the recruitment of men and women like Pete Camarata, Wanda Ellerman, Keith Gallagher and Vince Meredith made it possible for TDC to call its first national meeting in Cleveland on 22 November 1975. Over 100 Teamsters from around the country attended and planned a series of petitions and demonstrations for the period from January to March 1976 to force the Teamster leadership to stand up to the employers. Later TDC also began to put out its own newspaper, *Convoy*, to publicize the contract demands and activities of the movement.

In order to gain national publicity, TDC took its demands to Teamster headquarters in Washington, DC, where on 10 January 1976, some 130 Teamsters and their spouses and children from thirty-six cities demonstrated in front of the 'marble palace'. The speakers at the rally included Bob Grant, leader of a reform movement in the Chicago Truck Drivers Union (Independent); James Speciero, hiring hall steward from Los Angeles Local 208; and Pete Camarata of Detroit Local 299.

'We are organizing our power to demand a decent contract', Camarata told the crowd and the press, and 15,000 petition signatures in support of TDC's demands were handed to a guard when no Teamster official would take them. On that same date TDC organized a large picket line and marched in front of Local 299 in Detroit while TDC meetings were being held in other cities across the country. On 31 January 1976 UPSurge organizers called a meeting in Indianapolis, and the organizers themselves were amazed when over 500 UPS workers showed up.

What had begun with a brochure had become a movement, and the young movement was having an effect. The *New York Times* wrote on 18 January that Teamsters for a Decent Contract was 'creating a tremendous pressure on Mr. Fitzsimmons to bring home a contract that he can sell to the membership and then survive with at the convention.' Throughout February TDC held organizing meetings across the country, in Boston, Cincinnati, Cleveland, Dubois, Harrisburg, St. Louis, Charleston, Philadelphia, Akron, Los Angeles and San Francisco. Teamster local unions began to come out for some or all of the TDC program. Support was especially strong in California, where TDC's program was endorsed by San Jose Local 287, Oakland Local 70, and Los Angeles Local 357. Los Angeles Local 208 came out for the TDC demands as President Archie Murrieta told the members, 'Anyone who isn't for a decent contract is a fool.'[4] Local 878 in Little Rock, Arkansas supported parts of the TDC program. Particularly popular was TDC's demand that workers have the right to vote on their local contract supplements.

In early March, a month before the contract expired, TDC put forward the slogans 'Ready to Strike' and 'No Contract, No Work'. These slogans, based on long traditions in the labor movement, were intended to stop the employers and Fitzsimmons from trying to keep the rank and file working while negotiations continued indefinitely under a contract extension. As the movement grew, so did the opposition to it within the Teamster leadership, and those who organized for TDC's program often confronted criticism from local union officials, and sometimes faced violent goon squads. Lorrin Robbins, the president of Local 135, turned out a goon squad to break up a TDC meeting in Indianapolis on 31 January 1976; goons tried to keep union members from speaking at the Local 407 meeting in Cleveland; in Local 407 and in Akron Local 24 hate literature was distributed; while in Local 70 in Oakland Teamster officials made the rounds of the trucking barns telling drivers and dock workers that TDC was made up of 'outsiders' who wanted to destroy the union. Throughout the country the charge was made that TDC was a Communist conspiracy.

TDC responded to these attacks in *Convoy* no. 5, explaining that 'TDC is not an "outside" or "communist" group. The TDC is a grassroots movement involving thousands of Teamsters.'[5] And a week later TDC proved it. On 13 March 1976 over 2,000 Teamsters demonstrated at trucking companies and Teamster union halls around the country. The largest demonstration involved hundreds of Teamsters at the Local 299 hall in Detroit, but there were also large protests in Los Angeles and in Pittsburgh and Harrisburg-York, Pennsylvania.

Two weeks later, on 27 and 28 March 1976, there were union meetings in Teamster halls across the country at which the membership voted to strike if management's final offer was not acceptable. NBC-TV reported that motions to strike passed by ten to one. In some cities the strike vote was absolutely overwhelming: in Louisville, the motion to strike passed 670 to 5; in Detroit it was 898 to 24; in Philadelphia it was 1,487 to 7.

Nevertheless, TDC did not trust the Teamster leadership to carry out the will of the members. *Convoy* warned in an article banner-headlined 'Teamster Officials Talking Strike-Planning Sellout!' that 'it will take the power of direct rank-and-file action to win anything this year and that is what must happen come April 1.'

The First National Teamster Strike and the Detroit Wildcat

Under the pressure of the mass movement of rank-and-file Teamsters, which TDC had organized, on 1 April 1976 General President Frank Fitzsimmons called the first national strike in the history of the Teamsters union. With the exception of Chicago, where Locals 705, 710 and the independent Chicago Truck Drivers Union negotiated separately, the wheels stopped turning and the freight stopped moving. Management greed and a desperate strikebreaker gave the movement its first martyr: in Los Angeles Dominick Ailleo, a union steward at the Big Pine trucking company was run down and killed by a scab driver. Two days later, with a somewhat better offer from the employers, Fitzsimmons called off the strike, confident that TDC could not muster the two-thirds vote needed at that time under the Teamster constitution to reject a contract offer.

But in Detroit Local 299 the rank and file was too strong and independent to be ordered back to work, and the strike continued as a wildcat. Local union officials called a meeting for 5 April in Cobo Hall, and some 4,000 Local 299 members turned out. President Dave Johnson and International Vice-President Bobby Holmes tried to sell the contract Fitz had negotiated, but they were met with boos and catcalls. By a show of hands Local 299 voted to continue the strike until they had a better offer. Even after Judge Ralph Freeman issued an injunction against TDC and twenty-two individual Teamsters, the strike still went on. TDC leader Gene Fleszar replied to the judge, 'The strike is still on, pickets are still out, and the trucks will not roll.' And they didn't.

But as *Convoy* wrote, 'Detroit could not crack the National Agreement alone.'[6] The Detroit strikers met with Dave Johnson and agreed to return to work provided that the employers granted an amnesty. An agreement was reached, and the strike was ended. However, Earl C. Smith trucking failed to honor the amnesty and fired Pete Camarata, who had been one of the leaders of the Detroit wildcat. In response to Camarata's firing, the workers at Earl C. Smith started to walk off the job, and they were soon joined by Teamsters from other freight barns. Both Local 299 officials and management could see that unless Camarata was quickly returned to work the entire strike might begin again. Earl C. Smith rehired Camarata, and work finally resumed.

Meanwhile, voting began on Fitzsimmons's new proposal, and TDC urged the members to turn the contract down. Not trusting the Teamster officials, TDC demanded that 'a representative group of IBT rank and filers oversee the voting procedure', a demand that Fitzsimmons never even considered. In the end the contract was accepted, and as a result of TDC's efforts Teamsters working in freight won a big wage increase. The strike had also saved the contract's cost of living allowance.

Wildcat Strikes at UPS and in Carhaul

But the Teamster rebellion that TDC had started was not dying down. On 1 May, under pressure from the UPSurge movement, the Teamsters union struck United Parcel Service in the Midwest. A few days later the union called off the strike, but in several cities it continued for a few more days as a wildcat led by UPSurge. Only after Roy Williams promised that nobody would be fired did the strikers return to work.

The next group to stand up was the carhaulers. When their contract expired on 1 June, the union agreed to an extension, but in Cincinnati 450 drivers struck in spite of the agreement. They sent roving pickets to other cities, and carhaulers in Flint and Detroit also wildcatted. The Cincinnati wildcat continued for eight days until a federal judge granted the companies an injunction, while the union removed eleven stewards and committeemen from their posts. The companies fired fifty-two carhaulers in the three cities where the wildcats took place, but they could not break the back of the growing TDU movement. Carhaulers actually voted their contract down by a vote of 6,400 to 3,718 (with 10,118 voting out of 18,000 eligible), but the Teamster leadership imposed the contract on the membership by using the 'two-thirds rule'.

One TDC issue had greater support than perhaps any other, and that was the demand that the members have the right to vote separately on their own supplemental agreements. Six Teamsters, including TDC secretary Ken Paff, filed suit against the Teamsters union for this right, and appeared before Judge William Bryant in federal court in Washington, DC on 20 April 1976. The Teamster rank and filers who wanted the right to vote on their own contract were opposed by the Teamsters union, Trucking Employers, Incorporated, and US Secretary of Labor William Usery of the Republican Ford administration. After hearing the arguments, Judge Bryant ruled against the rank and file.

Writing about the case in *Convoy*, Ken Paff said, 'The most important point is this: You can't win rank-and-file power by relying on the courts, federal judges, politicians or union officials. We will win our right to vote by continuing to organize the rank and file until we have our own power. That's how our union was built in the first place. That's how it will be rebuilt now. ... The only way to win is to be so well organized they have to deal with us.'[7]

Notes

1. Harold M. Levinson, 'Trucking', in Gerald G. Somers, ed., *Collective Bargaining: Contemporary American Experience*, Madison 1980, p. 137.

2. Levinson, 'Trucking', p. 139.

3. Dan Moldea, *The Hoffa Wars: Teamsters, Rebels, Politicians and the Mob*, New York 1978, pp. 395–96.

4. *Convoy,* no. 4.

5. *Convoy,* no. 5.

6. *Convoy,* no. 8.

7. *Convoy,* no. 9.

7

The Founding of TDU and the 1976 Teamster Convention

TDC and UPSurge had created an impressive movement among freight workers, carhaulers and UPS employees. In the course of fighting for better contracts, other issues had been thrust upon them, particularly issues of union democracy: the right of workers to distribute literature, to speak up at union meetings without intimidation, and to vote on their contracts. The fight for a better contract tended inevitably to become a broader fight for union reform, and the time had come to turn a contract movement into a union reform organization.

On 5 June 1976 in Cleveland, thirty-five TDC and UPSurge members from various cities met and decided to transform TDC into TDU, Teamsters for a Democratic Union, and to hold a founding convention in the fall. TDC had existed solely to fight for a better contract; TDU would take up the task of building a rank-and-file movement and a national organization to reform the Teamsters union. Its first opportunity to challenge the Teamster leadership would come less than two weeks later at the Teamster convention.

The 1976 Teamster Convention

The convention opened on 14 June on the Las Vegas strip, many of its hotels and casinos built with the pension funds that aging Teamsters were so often denied, a glittering monument to the financial irresponsibility of the trustees of the Central States Pension Fund and a symbol of their ties to the mob. TDU adopted a twofold strategy for the Teamster convention: inside on the convention floor TDU would present the PROD resolutions for reforming the union; outside the convention TDU would organize a small protest demonstration. In this way TDU would appeal both to the officials in the hall and to the ranks across the country who would see the demonstration on television or read about it in the newspaper.

The person designated to speak on the floor of the convention was Pete Camarata, while the man who would be the spokesperson for the movement outside was Doug Allan, a member of Los Angeles Local 208 who had a long history of involvement in his local union.

Doug Allan

Doug Allan was born in February 1928 in Toronto, Ontario and attended school through the eighth grade. From the first, he says, he wanted to be a truck driver, and after a series of odd jobs he was hired driving a truck for a plumbing company, and later drove a dump truck for Dual Mix Concrete in Toronto. But he still wanted to drive a semi. 'While working for Dual Mix, I got close to the fellow that drove the semi-trailer, a flatbed, and if I was off a day and he was going some place to pick up a load, I'd go with him on my own time, and he taught me how to drive semi.'

Sometime later Allan went on a trip to Florida, met his wife Mary, and then went back to Canada to be married. In 1956 he and Mary moved to Los Angeles. 'I was here in California two days, and I went to work for Acme Fast Freight, a car-loading company, as a local cartage driver.' Things went along fine for a while, but a couple of years later the laws governing car-loading companies were changed. Acme Fast Freight divested itself of its local cartage subsidiary and created a new company called West Coast Cartage. The workers were promised that their employment would not be affected by the name change. But only two years later, West Coast Cartage went out of business and was replaced by another new company called Great Western. Management then notified Allan and his coworkers that they would be considered new hires; they would lose their seniority and vacations, and their wages and benefits would be cut and working conditions changed. The drivers still worked out of the same barns, drove the same equipment, dealt with the same customers and handled the same freight. The workers felt that they were still working for Acme, and that the name change was just a scam to steal their benefits.

'So we got together', Doug remembers. 'There were probably thirty or forty drivers and possibly thirty dock people at that time, and the union backed us and we went on strike, and eventually we won.' That was Doug Allan's first strike, and though he had been a Teamster for several years, it was that strike that awakened his interest in the union. Doug was disturbed that the union had not anticipated the developments in the car-loading industry and had not gotten all of the car-loading companies and their local cartage divisions to sign some sort of agreement to protect the rights of the workers. 'I thought: "The union itself must have known something about what was happening, why didn't they do something about it?" It didn't seem right to me. I said to myself, "Well, I'm going to see what this union's all about", and I decided to go to a union meeting.

'Like most people I had to find out where the union was. I found the union building, and I'll remember this to my dying day, since I didn't know where it was, naturally I was late, and there was a guy walking out of the union building at Ninth and Union streets in Los Angeles, and I said to him, "Is the meeting over already?" He said, "No, there is no meeting." I said, "There is no meeting?" He said, "No, *but if you had been there*, perhaps we would have had a quorum, and we would have had a meeting." That made me realize how important I am to the union, that if I had been there, there might have been a quorum.' Doug has not been late for a meeting since.

After he became interested in the union, Allan was elected steward at Acme. As a steward, he felt he had a greater responsibility to be involved in the local union, so now he not only went to the Local 208 meetings, but sometimes stood up and spoke his mind. 'Local 208 was democratic. They had an order of the day, and if you get up at the time where you're supposed to speak, they let you talk', Allan remembers. 'But when I got up and complained about something, they would say, "Well, you know, the IBT or the Western Conference." I thought, "What the hell is this IBT and Western Conference?"' The local *was* the union as far as Allan was concerned, and he did not know anything about the higher Teamster bodies. 'Then I found out that they had a constitution, an IBT constitution. I said, "Well, the problem doesn't seem to be here in the local union." I could see things that maybe weren't exactly as they should be, but to me they didn't seem to be that bad in the local.'

Perhaps the problem was in the higher echelons. 'So I went and got the IBT constitution and took it home and studied it, and it just struck me just as clear as a bell what was wrong. The International union president was controlling the entire union. And that's wrong. If you and I, the workers, don't have any say, then we've got a lost cause.' Until this point in his life, Doug Allan had been an admirer of Jimmy Hoffa, who had been president of the Teamsters since 1957. 'One of my favorite sayings back then – because I wasn't as unionized as I am today – was, "Ah, so what if he stole five bucks from me, he got me fifteen, so am I going to complain?" Many other people, I think, felt the same way. We saw him doing something wrong, and we didn't say nothing about it, 'cause we thought we were being treated right.'

But now, after studying the constitution, Doug changed his mind about Hoffa. 'Jimmy Hoffa changed the IBT constitution, giving himself almost complete authority to run the union. And I believe a lot of the people that were more active than I was at that time, must have said, "Well, so what if he runs it, he's doing a great job, why shouldn't he run it?" And that's where I and the rest of the people made the mistake. We – I have to include myself – we allowed them to change the constitution and give the International president the power he has today.'

Allan, who had been a member of TURF, TDC and then TDU, led the picket line of fifty rank and filers in front of the Teamster convention that greeted the arriving delegates.

The Convention Floor

Once inside the hall, the 2,300 Teamster delegates heard a furious Fitzsimmons deliver a red-baiting tirade. Fitzsimmons called the TDU 'infiltrators' and told them they could 'go to hell', and both Fitzsimmons and former Teamster General President Dave Beck attacked Arthur Fox of PROD as a Communist. For Beck, who had made a career out of calling people Communists, it must have been like old times.

Those reformers in TDC or PROD who had held out some hope that the Ford administration would aid them in cleaning up the union saw their hopes dashed when Secretary of Labor Usery praised Fitzsimmons and other Teamster leaders as outstanding representatives of their members – this despite the fact that the Department of Labor was at that very moment investigating the Teamster Central States Pension Fund. Clearly President Ford was embracing the Teamsters, just as Nixon had done before him. Support for corrupt union officials was, however, clearly a bipartisan issue, and the Republican cabinet member was joined by the Democratic Party kingmaker, Chicago Mayor Richard J. Daley, who had come to sit with and speak before his friends among the Teamster elite.

TDU's only delegate, Pete Camarata, presented to the convention the resolutions PROD had drawn up calling for direct election of all international officers, election of all local business agents, a limit on officers' salaries, and separate ratification votes for contract supplements. As was expected, the Teamster leadership and the convention ignored PROD's analysis and TDU's resolutions. When Camarata tried to propose an amendment to limit the general president's salary he was not allowed to finish his statement. Later Fitzsimmons's goons caught Camarata and beat him up in public in front of the Alladin Hotel.

The most dramatic moment of the 1976 convention came when Pete Camarata rose to dissent from the unanimous election of Frank Fitzsimmons as Teamster president. For a moment the hall grew quiet as Camarata, speaking softly, said that he had to dissent, 'for a friend of mine who's been gone for about a year.' Everyone knew Camarata was referring to Hoffa, and everyone knew that Hoffa's murderers were probably there in the auditorium and possibly presiding on the platform.

AP/Wide World

Frank Fitzsimmons confers with Roy Williams.

In the end Fitzsimmons was reelected 'unanimously', and his salary was increased by 25 percent to $156,250 a year. The constitution was amended, and the general president was given the power to name an unlimited number of International organizers and to determine their duties, salaries and expenses. The general president was also empowered to increase the salaries of other union officers by 25 percent and to raise dues. In addition to Fitzsimmons, all the other members of the official slate were elected, including those like William Presser, Salvatore Provenzano and Roy Williams whose underworld connections or criminal convictions were well-known. There was one departure from the past in a union frequently criticized for its practice of racial discrimination: John H. Cleveland was elected the union's first Black International vice-president.

A number of other issues were also dealt with by the convention.[1] Fitzsimmons reiterated the union's 'determination to maintain [its] position to organize farmworkers in the West', a reference to the union's violent raid on the United Farm Workers (AFL-CIO). The convention adopted a resolution supporting Fitzsimmons's raiding policy. A resolution was also passed against the proposed deregulation of the trucking industry, a matter of vital importance to the members, and about which, after the passage of the resolution, Fitzsimmons did virtually nothing.

The Teamster leaders may have satisfied themselves, but they were alone. A *New York Times* editorial described the union's convention as having an 'aura of moral squalor' and criticized Secretary of Labor Usery for having attended. Many Teamster members found the convention grotesque and repugnant; Arthur Fox of PROD called the IBT convention a 'rubber stamp circus'.

Frank Fitzsimmons had told the rank and file to 'go to hell'. But TDU leader Doug Allan responded that TDU activists were prepared 'to go to hell and back to reform the union'. The convention ended and the TDU protestors returned to their homes, wondering if Pete Camarata's speech had had any affect on the delegates. Were all the union officers who had doubled as delegates corrupt? Why had they sat there while Camarata was interrupted and booed and later beaten? What were they thinking?

Sam Fenn

Among the delegates to the 1976 Teamster convention in Las Vegas was Sam Fenn, a trustee of Los Angeles Local 224. Fenn had been a Teamster then for over twenty years, and a union officer for six. He was proud of the union, and proud to be a member of it. However, things happened at that 1976 IBT convention that made Fenn begin to wonder if something wasn't seriously wrong.

At the opening of the convention, Fenn recalls, 'Frank Fitzsimmons told the delegates that people outside were trying to break into the convention, and infiltrate – infiltrate – our organization. And he said, "Look next to you to make sure the guy sitting there is really a delegate", and we had to check each other. They put that fear and intimidation there. I thought, "God, what the heck's going on."'

After that, business went on without incident until the session dealing with constitutional changes. 'I got the feeling that everything was cut and dried. You know, everything come out of the committee. It was just like the routine stuff that come out of the Joint Council meetings that I went to. Everything is just routine, you know, committee this, committee that – and nobody gets up and takes exception to nothing.'

Then someone began to speak. Sam could not see Camarata from where he was sitting, but he could hear his voice. Camarata was talking about the rank and file and union democracy, about motions that he was putting forward to make the union more democratic, and to lower the officers' salaries. There were some boos and catcalls, and some men stood up and then he couldn't see anything, but Fenn heard Camarata and he took it all in: 'I said to myself, "Boy, that guy is going to get it." Cause, man, he's standing up there for the rank and file and making all these motions.'

Fenn wears a big ring on his finger with four diamonds on it. The ring is for twenty years of safe driving, 'without accident or incident', and each diamond is for another additional safe driving year. Sam is cautious, and perhaps that is why he didn't jump up and speak out at the convention, or rush out to join TDU. Perhaps like many other Teamster convention delegates, Sam just didn't know what to make of it at the time. He didn't know who Pete Camarata was or what Teamsters for a Democratic Union stood for. Still, something struck him: the contrast between the motions coming out of committee, 'all cut and dried', and the voice of the fellow on the floor 'making motions for the rank and file'. It struck him, and it stuck with him for almost three years before he did anything about it.

Sam Fenn had been born in Houston, Texas in 1930, and before he had finished high school he went into the Navy, where he served as a radar man on several ships. He was stationed in Southern California, liked it a lot, and decided to settle down in Long Beach. He had met a woman in the church, married her, and they began to raise a family. Sam got a job at Dewey and Bob's Mixed Concrete driving a cement mixer and became a member of the rock, sand and gravel craft in Teamster Local 692. 'I started going to the union meetings, and I was quite impressed by the people that came and the union officers. I liked what I saw and I made a habit of attending union meetings regularly. I felt good in it.'

There were only six drivers at the company where Sam worked, not enough to warrant having a steward, but the business agent asked Sam if he would be willing to be the committeeman and keep an eye on things. So Sam did, and one day there was a problem: a salaried employee was driving a truck while union members were laid off. Sam got on the phone, called the business agent, and explained the situation. 'The B.A. got on the phone and told the company, no way was they going to allow this salary man to do hourly work and our people, our union people, not working. He said the company had better put a stop to it or else he would lock up the barn. And so that really impressed me that, gee, they had enough power that they could shut a company down for the workers.'

In Southern California those were good times for Teamsters. 'In those years you could switch a job. If you didn't like your job or your company, you could go to another union company and just go right to work – of course, times have changed now. But in them days qualified drivers had no problem at all going from one company to another. If they didn't like who they worked for or whatever, they'd just quit and go someplace else.'

The work in rock, sand and gravel was seasonal, and Sam and the other mixer drivers were usually laid off in the winter when it rained and construction slowed up. Several of the drivers from Dewey and Bob's had gone to work at a car-hauling outfit where they could work six days a week twelve months of the year, and they were making much more money. In September 1960 Sam joined them, becoming a driver for Hadley's Auto-Transport and a member of Teamster line drivers Local 224.

When Sam became a member of Local 224 some changes were taking place. The secretary-treasurer of the local had gone to prison, and other members of the executive board were under indictment, accused of taking money out of the local treasury. Consequently there was an election for new officers, and while Sam found the campaign interesting, he was disappointed in the campaign literature of the candidates. 'Their literature only said, "I worked for this company and I worked that company, and I been a Teamster for twenty years or thirty years, and vote for me", and that was it.'

Fenn himself thought about running for office, but he felt that candidates should be better qualified. So, being the kind of person he is, Fenn went back to school and got his high school diploma, and then enrolled in the labor studies program of the Industrial Relations Department at the University of California at Los Angeles, completing the course a couple of years later. In the meantime Fenn was elected the chief steward at Hadley Auto-Transport, and in 1965 he ran on a slate for local union office – and lost.

Nevertheless, he stayed involved in the local union. 'I got more active and became more or less recognized as an activist. When the union officers tried to say certain things and do certain things, I stood up in the membership meeting and questioned them on it. They didn't like it too much, and they'd say, "Where are you getting your information?"And I'd have my 1959 Landrum-Griffin Act paper put out by the Labor Department that I picked up in school defining the rights of a union member to take part in anything that goes on at your union meetings. We members are the backbone of the union, the union belongs to us, and these officers work for us. They forget that sometimes.'

Others on the slate he had run with became discouraged and dropped out of union politics, but Sam stuck with it. 'We got together a rank-and-file slate the next time, and I ran again for trustee, and made it.' Eventually he was elected to two terms as trustee and then two terms as recording secretary of Local 224, a total of twelve years in elected union office.

However, each time he was elected, the men he had run with would give in to pressure from the higher-ups in the union. 'I ran with a different rank-and-file slate every time. We'd lay down a platform, we'd win the election, and then the old Teamster pressure would come down on the new officers that don't know anything, that come off a truck. You got the Joint Council: a big wheel comes over to the local union executive board for your first meeting, and they start telling you how to run things. They tell you what attorneys you use, the Council 42 attorneys, and you do this and you do that. They tell you, don't make waves, this is the way it's done.

'It puts an awful lot of pressure on the new people and they melt, and you have your first disagreement. I take my position that the membership elected us to do something, and then you turn around and don't want to do it. So we have a big break on the executive board, and I tell them, "Well, three years from now you're not going to be here." They all got voted out of office each time, and I always got reelected with another rank-and-file slate.

'This is about the middle of the 1970s when there were wildcat strikes that was put on by the rank and filers around the country. There would be wildcat strikes, but the rank and file had no organization. Leaders, it seemed to me, would just fade out. And the rank and file had no communications among themselves about what's going on around the country other than reading about it in the newspaper.' It was in the midst of these experiences in trying to represent the rank and file in his local union that Sam Fenn went to the Teamster convention in Las Vegas in 1976 and heard Pete Camarata get up and talk about the democratic rights of the rank-and-file member.

A couple of years later TDU organized a carhaulers meeting in Los Angeles, and Sam decided to go. There was a big turnout, and he recognized two of the TDU speakers as fellows who had once worked with him at Hadley. 'They explained about the TDU organization, and who we are and what we are and what we stand for, that we're for elected stewards and elected business agents. I said to myself, "Well, boy, this is for me", and I signed up and joined then and there with the rest of the people at work.'

In late 1978 Sam Fenn, recording secretary of Local 224, became one of the first union officials to join TDU. Sam became a member of the Car-haulers Coordinating Committee, and later a member of the TDU International Steering Committee, and in 1984, 1985 and 1987 Sam Fenn was TDU's outstanding membership recruiter.

The First TDU Rank-and-File Convention

TDU held its founding convention on 18 September at Kent State University in Ohio. When the delegates arrived at the university hall where the meeting was being held, they found a rare sight indeed: Jackie Presser, head of the Ohio Teamsters, on a picket line. The picket line protesting the TDU convention was made up of paid union officials, retirees, union goons, public relations people and some ordinary union members, most of whom were unaware of the purpose of their protest. In the past such a collection of goons and gofers might have stopped a rank-and-file meeting, but it wasn't going to work that day.

The TDU convention brought together some 200 rank-and-file Teamsters from forty-four local unions in fifteen states. The workers at the Roadway terminal in Stroudsburg had taken up a collection to send three men to the TDU convention, and one of those delegates was Keith Gallagher. 'It was a real big up', he recalls. 'It was exciting, it was new, it was dynamic. People were actually trying to say something that I had felt for several years, that the union belonged to the members, not to the officials. I had seen in Local 229 that the officials felt that the union belonged to them and the membership was subservient to them, and that's not the way it should be, and that's not the way it will be.' Most of the other Teamsters there felt as Gallagher did. They were thrilled to find that they were not alone, that there were hundreds of other Teamsters across the country who wanted to reform the union.

The convention began with a debate over the issue of what kind of an organization TDU should be. A group called Teamsters for Democracy from Madison, Wisconsin Local 695, favored a loose network of Teamster reformers coordinated by a national office that would simply be a clearing house for information and contacts between local groups. However, the majority, feeling that such loose networks had proved unsuccessful in the past, voted instead for a national organization with strong local chapters.

The goal of TDU was stated in Article Two of its new constitution: 'The object of this organization is to build a national, unified movement of rank-and-file Teamsters that is organized to fight for rank-and-file rights on the job and in the union. We aim to bring the Teamsters union back to the membership. We do not advocate secession from the Teamsters Union, or "Dual Unionism" in any form whatsoever.' It was important to make that statement at the time because one of the other important dissident groups among Teamsters, the Fraternal Association of Steel Haulers, did call for secession from the IBT and did operate as a 'dual union'.

The founding convention decided that although the organization was based among freight, carhauling and UPS workers, it should not confine itself to the trucking industry, and that it had an obligation to other Teamsters and would attempt to draw them into its movement to reform the union. As the resolution stated, 'We will seek to unify all jurisdictions behind the struggle of any one section, operating under the general principle: An Injury to One Is an Injury to All; A Victory for One Is a Victory for All!' This resolution distinguished TDU from PROD, the Professional Drivers Council, which, as its name implied, concentrated its efforts among drivers, particularly among road drivers.

It was also decided that so far as it was able, TDU would attempt to overcome discrimination against racial minorities and women in industries represented by the Teamsters. 'Most contracts covering women Teamsters are sweetheart agreements where the company comes out on top. TDU will work to bring these contracts up to the highest standard', read the resolution. 'The Teamster Union must be held to its job of equally representing all union members ... men and women.'

The resolution on race relations stated that 'racial discrimination and the division which results from it have long been used by employers and unscrupulous officials to divide and weaken the rank and file. To be successful, we must be united. To win the participation and loyalty of the hundreds of thousands of minority Teamsters, TDU must pursue and support vigorous policies to overcome discrimination.'

The make-up of the first TDU Steering Committee reflected the discussions that had taken place. The majority were freight workers, but it also included carhaulers, UPSers and beer and beverage workers. The majority of members were concentrated in the Midwest, but it also had representatives from both coasts. There were long-time Teamsters like Al Ferdnance and Doug Allan, who had each spent twenty years in the union, but also young Teamsters with only a few years of involvement. There were members from some of the biggest freight companies, McLean, Time-DC, Consolidated Freightways, and UPS, but also representatives from smaller companies. Its fifteen members included two Blacks and two women, a demonstration that TDU was committed from the beginning to leadership by Black and women Teamsters. In a show of its respect for minority opinions, the steering committee included a member of Teamsters for Democracy from Madison, the group that had proposed a looser form of organization. The first convention also launched TDU's first national campaign, a program to pass democratic bylaws in local unions. At the top of the list of bylaw reforms was the right to elect union stewards and business agents, who in many locals were appointed.

Most of those at the TDU convention were rank-and-file Teamsters, but the organizers had also invited a few lawyers who had volunteered their time to help Teamster rank and filers. A resolution was passed calling on TDU to establish a network of lawyers to help TDU members fight for their rights. 'We will use the courts when necessary', the resolution read, 'but we understand that our success will be based on the size, strength and awareness of our movement.'

The 1976 TDU convention began a tradition of annual rank-and-file conventions at which TDU members from all over the country met together to discuss and debate the next step for the movement. TDU's staying power and successes over the last dozen years are largely due to the principles embodied in the constitution, the resolutions adopted at that founding convention, and the work of that first steering committee.

As Lester Velie wrote in his 1977 book *Desperate Bargain: Why Jimmy Hoffa Had to Die*, with the founding of TDU, 'The possibility arose that, for the first time, the little men at the bottom of the Teamster pile could topple those at the top and do what Senate investigators, crime busters, and courts had failed to do: make the Teamsters go straight.'[2]

Notes

1. Frances E. Kanterman, 'Dissidents Criticized, Leadership Strengthened at Teamster Convention', *Monthly Labor Report*, September 1976, pp. 41–43.
2. Lester Velie, *Desperate Bargain: Why Jimmy Hoffa Had to Die*, New York 1977, p. 221.

PART II

THE RISE AND FALL OF THE TEAMSTER BUREAUCRACY

8

The Rise of the Teamsters

The Teamsters who had pledged themselves to reform their union at that founding TDU convention in 1976 were taking on an institution that had become thoroughly corrupt. It had become a dictatorship of the general president, Frank Fitzsimmons, and was heavily influenced by the Mafia. In order to keep himself out of prison, Fitz had made the union a virtual hostage of Republican President Richard Nixon. Meanwhile, top union officials colluded with employers, granting concessions that undermined contracts. How had all of this come about? How had the union created by team drivers in the early 1900s become so perverted? How did the workers who had made so many sacrifices in the 1930s lose control of their union? How had the crooked bureaucracy developed? The answers can be found in the union's complex history.

For almost fifty years the Teamsters union was synonymous with its president, Daniel J. Tobin. Tobin was from the old school, a labor leader from another era, almost from another world. Born in County Clare, Ireland on 3 April 1875, Tobin emigrated to the United States in 1889 and settled in Cambridge, Massachusetts. He got his first job in a sheet metal factory, then took a job on the Boston street railway. A few years later, Tobin bought a horse and wagon and began peddling butter and cheese, and in 1900 he signed up with Boston Local 25 of the newly organized Team Drivers International Union.[1]

The Chicago Beef Strike of 1902

It was a tough time for labor, and the drivers' union was forged in battles like the 1902 Chicago strike against the Beef Trust.[2] In the spring of that year the 526 Teamsters in Packing House Teamsters' Union, Local 10, who worked at the Union Stockyards in Chicago wanted a raise. They were working sixteen to eighteen hours a day, reporting to work before 6 a.m. and sometimes working until after 9 p.m. For this exhausting day's work they received sixteen to twenty-five cents an hour, depending on the number of horses they drove – with no extra pay for overtime. Some drivers earned as little as $13.50 for over one hundred hours per week. The drivers were asking for five to seven cents an hour more in wages and twenty-five cents an hour for overtime. They also wanted recognition of the union and a union shop. But the meat packers refused to negotiate with the drivers, and so on 25 May a strike began.

The strikers posted pickets at the ten entrances to the stockyards, forcing non-union drivers back into the packing house yards and shutting down the beef business. When the packers tried to get the express companies to move the meat, the members of the Commission Drivers Union refused, announcing that they would not touch non-union meat. Then the packers tried to get the railroads to move the meat, but the Wabash and Erie workers would not handle it, nor would switchmen on the Belt Line. Luggers at the Fulton Market balked at unloading wagons from the big packing companies. Workers at the National Box Company refused to make boxes for the packing houses and then struck in solidarity. Ice wagon drivers told local butchers they would stop deliveries of ice to any butcher shop that carried scab goods. Coal drivers warned that they would not deliver coal to the ice-making and other refrigeration plants that dealt with the beef industry.

Chicagoans hated the Beef Trust because they believed that the monopolies had unfairly raised the price of meat, and a Teamster call for a consumer boycott of beef in support of the strike met a favorable response. The Machinists and Carpenters unions called on their members and other workers to stop all purchases of meat from the packing companies. The 1,200 small butcher shops in the city run by Poles, Bohemians, Jews and other nationalities also closed in support of the Teamster strikers.

The Chicago Federation of Labor sent an open letter to Mayor Carter Harrison, accusing the packers of conspiring against the public, stealing the city's water supply, and poisoning soldiers by selling rotten meat to the Army during the Spanish-American War. The letter led to more militant demonstrations. 'The waiting sympathizers of the striking teamsters seemed to spring from the ground', wrote the *Chicago Record Herald*.

Day after day the streets in the stockyards district were lined with strikers and their supporters. Coal and iron drivers used their wagons to block the streets wherever deliveries were attempted. When packers tried to move a convoy of thirty-five wagons downtown, it was followed along the route by thousands of Teamsters and other workers. At Clark and Harrison the crowd tried to overturn the wagons, and was stopped only when fifty policemen attacked with clubs. At the same time several thousand strike sympathizers fought the police at Halstead and Division streets. Downtown in the Loop the police attempted to clear a path for wagons in a crowd of 50,000 strike supporters. Union hatmakers came out on to a fire escape on Fifth Avenue to throw objects at the scab drivers. 'We are union men', said one hatmaker, 'and we have no sympathy with these non-union fellows.'

'The women are the most dangerous persons with whom the police have to deal', said Police Chief O'Neill. 'They gather at the windows along the line of march and throw anything at the drivers or patrolmen.' A woman named Lizzie Molloy was arrested for throwing a brick at a cop. 'Men', she said, 'I just had to do it.'

The Chicago Federation of Labor criticized the police for supporting the Beef Trust against the strikers and the consumers. But even with police support it was difficult to move the wagons. One caravan protected by 200 policemen was stopped at sixteen different points on its route by strikers and crowds of sympathizers. During the first few days of June there were pitched battles throughout the city between scabs and police on the one hand and strikers and sympathizers on the other. After nearly two weeks, the strike finally ended on 5 June 1902. The union did not win formal recognition or the union shop, but the companies did grant a pay raise to eighteen to thirty cents per hour or between $12.60 and $21.00 for seventy hours per week, a very considerable increase.

So the Teamsters union was built in the early days in cities throughout the country, through militant strikes and broad working-class solidarity, as other labor unions and the public joined to back the drivers in the fight for a decent living.

A Wage Earners' Union

But there was a problem. When Tobin first joined the Team Drivers' International Union in 1900, the union included not only wage earners and owner-operators, but also employers of up to five teams. Such a union was a contradiction in terms. A raise for the worker members was often opposed by employer members, and changes in work rules sought by employer members were frequently opposed by worker members. Inevitably these conflicts threatened to tear the organization apart.

The center of the struggle between team owners and wage earners was Chicago, where in 1902 the wage earners joined with the owner-operators, and, in defiance of the Team Drivers' International Union, expelled the employer members, thus creating the first real Teamsters union. The Chicago Teamsters then organized themselves along craft lines into milk, coal, and ice drivers and so on. With what was at the time a dynamic new form of organization – wage earner craft unionism – they succeeded with less than half a dozen strikes in organizing 5,000 members into forty locals.[3]

The movement to expel employers from the union soon spread across the country, destroying the old Team Drivers' International Union and resulting in several rival factions. In August 1903 a meeting was held at Niagara Falls, New York to bring the various Teamster unions together, and Daniel Tobin attended representing the Teamsters in Boston Local 25. It was at that meeting that the International Brotherhood of Teamsters was founded and Cornelius 'Con' Shea was elected its first general president.

The new IBT was soon tested. In 1905 the Chicago garment workers struck, and the Chicago Teamsters employed by Montgomery Ward struck in sympathy. Montgomery Ward and other Chicago employers decided to try to break the new Teamsters union, and a bitter confrontation ensued. The Chicago Teamsters appealed for help to the new International Brotherhood, but Shea failed to come to their aid. The strike was violent in the extreme, with 21 killed and 415 wounded. The union, reported one historian, 'was utterly defeated and crushed.'[4]

Not only was the strike defeated, but Con Shea and several leaders of the Chicago Teamsters were indicted for extortion. Supposedly Shea had taken $10,000 from a rival mail order house in exchange for encouraging the strike against Montgomery Ward. The members of the new Teamsters union were outraged. The San Francisco Joint Council of Teamsters declared Shea to be 'utterly unfit to hold the high office by which he has been honored. He is a disgrace to himself, a dishonor to the teamsters of the country and a stain to the labor movement.' The San Francisco Teamsters asked the American Federation of Labor to remove Shea from the Teamster presidency, but the AFL declined on the grounds that the Teamsters were an autonomous union.[5]

Meanwhile, furious at Shea and the union for what they felt was betrayal, Teamsters in Chicago, St. Louis and New York seceded from the IBT in 1906 and formed a new rival union, the United Teamsters of America with 10,000 members. The International Brotherhood of Teamsters proved stronger, however, and eventually the United Teamsters disappeared, except for a few independent unions in Chicago.[6]

The 1907 Teamster convention was held in Boston, and Tobin, who had become president of Boston Joint Council 10, presided. The delegates succeeded in ousting Con Shea, and elected Tobin to the office of general president by a mere twelve-vote margin.[7] Labor historian Warren R. Van Tine suggests that the delegates voted for Tobin because they wanted 'someone they felt would maintain an honest but weak administration.'[8] But Tobin proved to be stronger than they expected.

The International, then headquartered in Indianapolis, had little strength; power resided in the local unions and joint councils. The local leaders opposed Tobin, and in 1908 those in New York even tried to drive him out of office. Things were so serious that in 1909 Tobin was beaten by a business agent, knocked unconscious, and left for dead. 'Eventually, however', writes Van Tine, 'Tobin reached an accommodation with powerful local leaders; they supported his management of the national office and he did not interfere in their affairs. Thus by overlooking corruption at the local level, he ensured the permanence of the international body.'[9]

Tobin was not completely powerless. While the local leaders had control of collective bargaining and the contracts, Tobin had the power to bestow, deny or withdraw Teamster union charters, and to grant or deny strike benefits. After the experiences of the early years of the century, Tobin's main concerns were to avoid strikes and prevent splits and secession. Ensconced in Indianapolis, Tobin hoarded the union's money like a miser. Farrell Dobbs described the Teamsters as 'little more than a loose federation of city formations over which Tobin presided much like a feudal monarch.'[10]

Corruption increased enormously during the prohibition era of the 1920s, as organized crime moved in to take complete control of many Teamster unions, particularly in Chicago. Bootleggers needed control of trucks in order to move their contraband booze. They also found that the unions could be used to extort money from legitimate businessmen.

The qualifications for seeking union office were reduced to the possession of a gun. Gangsters would show up at a union hall, shoot the old business agents and officers, and declare themselves the new officials. In this way many Chicago locals, both IBT and independent, fell under the control of the Al Capone mob.[11] Feeling themselves outgunned by the Capone mob, some Teamster officials turned to other mobsters, like Tommy and Roger Touhy, and paid them to eliminate the Capone outfit. This only resulted in greater mob involvement in the union and greater violence. IBT Vice-President Patrick 'Paddy' Berrell, who was from Chicago, invited the Touhy mob into the union. Berrell was killed during a fight between rival Teamster-gangster factions. A year later Henry Burger, an International organizer working out of Chicago, was shot and seriously wounded.

In 1933, Chicago business interests, finally tired of the chaos, forced the politicians to do something. In that first government cleanup of the Teamsters, Chicago Mayor Edward J. Kelly, Illinois State's Attorney Thomas J. Courtney, John Fitzpatrick and Edward Nockels, top officers of the Chicago Federation of Labor and, reluctantly, Teamster President Dan Tobin launched a campaign to remove the gangsters from the IBT and independent Chicago Teamsters. Under the agreement reached, all Chicago Teamsters were to go into the IBT. Only drivers who belonged to the craft and had no record of illegal liquor trafficking were to be admitted to the Teamsters, with the Cook County State's Attorney having a veto over the admission of any individual to union membership. In the end, all of the independent Chicago Teamster locals thus returned to the IBT except for the Chicago Truck Drivers Union (CTDU), Local 705 (Independent).[12]

As head of the Teamsters, Tobin played an important role in the American Federation of Labor and became a close ally of its president, Samuel Gompers. Tobin used his clout in the Federation to make his one contribution to expanding the membership of the Teamsters – by cannibalizing other unions. With the approval of the AFL, over several years he was able to get seven unions – the Bakery Workers, Laundry Workers, Retail Clerks, Bridge and Structural Iron Workers, Longshoremen, Railway and Steamship Clerks, and Street and Electric Railway Employees – to 'voluntarily' turn over their team or truck driving members to the Teamsters. The AFL also backed Tobin and Seattle Teamster leader Dave Beck in their war on the Brewery Workers after 1933.

The AFL leaders were highly paid bureaucrats who worried about their stock portfolios, not about unorganized industrial workers. Tobin was typical. He was content to organize only the craft drivers – meat, milk, bread, ice, coal, and local cartage – and wanted nothing to do with the organization of the outcast warehouse workers and highway drivers, whom he considered 'rubbish'.

Cautious and complacent at best, the AFL was at the peak of its power in the 1920s but had succeeded in organizing only 5 percent of the American labor force. The AFL showed little concern for immigrants and for Black and female workers who worked in basic industry. Nor had the AFL been successful on the political front. The employers had prevented the passage of labor legislation and social insurance laws, and, perhaps most important, had created a political climate in which businesses could safely assume that unions and workers had no rights. The AFL Council, a smug club of labor aristocrats, was hardly prepared to deal with the disaster which befell the nation on Black Thursday, 24 October 1929 – the day the stock market crashed, touching off the Great Depression. The day before the crash all stocks listed on the New York Stock Exchange were valued at $87 billion; by 1933 they were worth only $19 billion. Tens of thousands of investors were ruined. The entire financial system broke down, with some 3,750 banks failing in 1930 and 1931 alone. Many big corporations and hundreds of smaller companies went bankrupt, and thousands of small businesses were destroyed.

Production collapsed, with steel production, the heart of American industry, falling by 80 percent, and all other industrial production falling by 60 percent. As plants closed or cut back, the number of unemployed climbed: from 4 million in 1930 to a high of 13 million in 1933. One worker in four was out of a job, and in some industrial cities like Detroit as many as a third or even a half of all workers were jobless. The total wages earned by all workers fell from $50 billion to $30 billion.

Employers cut pay and increased hours for workers in all kinds of jobs. The Teamsters' situation was pathetic. In Haverhill, Massachusetts, for example, 'drivers worked 80–98 hours a week for as little as 15 cents an hour. The average wage per hour was 40 cents.'[13] It was deplorable, but Dan Tobin had no idea of what to do. He guarded the money in the union treasury. He tried to keep troublemakers out of the union. He waited and hoped things would get better.

When the Depression had first begun in 1929, American workers were fearful and cautious. Those who had jobs were careful to keep them, even if hours and wages had been cut. Those who had lost jobs were often devastated and despondent. Workers waited to see what the employers and the government would do. But as the crisis grew worse from 1929 to 1933, workers came to feel that something had to be done, and that if no one else was going to do anything for them, they would have to do something for themselves. It was time for a change, and change, when it came, seethed up in anger from below, from the poor, tired, abused, wretched workers, employed and unemployed.

It began with demonstrations of the jobless demanding something to eat for their children. Hundreds of thousands marched in New York and in Detroit, where Henry Ford's gunmen shot into the crowd and killed four people. Communists, Socialists and other radicals helped organize unemployed councils to demand relief for jobless workers and their families.

Soon workers began to strike for union recognition, higher wages and job security. In 1932 some 243,000 workers went on strike. With the passage of the National Industrial Recovery Act (NIRA) Section 7(a), which for the first time declared 'that employees shall have the right to organize and bargain collectively through representatives of their own choosing', labor unions grew rapidly and the number of strikers rose to 812,000 in 1933.

Farrell Dobbs

In the fall of 1933, Farrell Dobbs was working at the Pittsburgh Coal Company in Minneapolis. One day the foreman told Dobbs to take his shovel and help a driver from another company load his truck. As the two men worked together, Grant Dunne, the truck driver, explained to Dobbs that he and some other fellows were trying to organize the city's coal workers into Teamsters Local 574. Dunne invited Dobbs to a Teamster organizing meeting, and Dobbs accepted. Farrell Dobbs was to become one of the Teamsters' greatest organizers.

Born in Queen City, Missouri on 25 July 1907, Dobbs was raised in Minneapolis, Minnesota. He graduated from high school in 1925 and then worked at a number of odd jobs. In 1927 Dobbs got a job with Western Electric installing telephone equipment and married his high school sweetheart, Marvel Scholl. Dobbs rose quickly at Western Electric, becoming a planning engineer in 1931 and transferring to Omaha, Nebraska. He and his wife now had two daughters, and prospects looked pretty good; in 1932 Dobbs voted for the Republican Herbert Hoover for president.

But when Western Electric expected Dobbs to cooperate in firing a friend, Dobbs was 'filled with revulsion'. Rather than fire his friend, he quit the job and headed back home to Minneapolis, planning to study law, become a judge, and try to bring some justice into the world. It didn't work out that way. The Dobbs family was soon broke, and he was forced to take a job in the coalyard. He worked sixty hours a week for $18 until he was cut to forty hours for $16, hardly enough to provide for his family. When Grant Dunne asked Dobbs if he wanted to come to a Teamsters meeting, he was talking to a man who hungered after justice.

But the Teamsters union was in sad shape. In 1933 the entire Teamsters union had only 75,206 members, the Minneapolis Joint Council had less than 1,000, and Local 574 had only 75 dues-paying members on its books. There had not been a successful Teamster strike in Minneapolis in twenty-five years. Labor had just about hit rock bottom.

The Coal Strike

Dunne and some other rank-and-file coal workers had convinced Local 574 President William S. Brown to launch an organizing drive among coalyard workers. But the coal employers, backed by the Citizens Alliance, the employers' organization that dominated the city of Minneapolis, refused to negotiate with the union. It would take a strike to win recognition and a contract. Farrell Dobbs joined the Teamsters and threw himself into organizing the strike.[14]

In January, as the thermometer fell, Local 574 voted to strike, supported by the Teamster Joint Council. The tight-fisted Tobin refused strike benefits, but nevertheless, on 4 February 1934 700 workers struck sixty-five of the city's coalyards. The strike was led by a rank-and-file organizing committee using mass picket lines and cruising picket squads, and the coalyards were shut down tight, just as the city was hit by a terrible cold wave. In only three days the strike was over, and the Teamsters had won. The strategic timing of the coal strike in the depths of winter and the workers' radical picketing tactics had defeated the Citizens Alliance. The employers agreed to small improvements in wages and conditions, but most important, they agreed to recognize the union. The Local 574 victory gave new confidence to the city's workers.

In the course of his involvement with the organizing drive and strike, Dobbs learned that at the center of Local 754's rank-and-file organizing committee were several long-time labor radicals, among them three brothers,

Miles, Grant and Raymond Vincent Dunne, and a fellow named Carl Skoglund. In the 1920s they had all been in the Communist Party but had been expelled by the Communists for being followers of Leon Trotsky, one of the leaders of the Russian Revolution. Kicked out of the Communist Party, the Trotskyists founded their own group, the Communist League of America.

It was the Minneapolis branch of the Communist League that had planned the coal strike, and Dobbs was so impressed with their organizing work that in March 1934 he joined the group. 'I reasoned', wrote Dobbs, 'that if I joined a communist organization, I might be able to learn some of the things they knew.'[15]

The First Trucking Strike

Having successfully organized the coal workers, Local 574 now set about the more ambitious task of organizing the trucking industry in Minneapolis. 'For the first time', according to Dobbs, 'a Teamsters local was about to move toward the industrial form of organization, taking all the workers in a given enterprise into a single union.'[16] The campaign was launched by sending teams of organizers to trucking barns, warehouses and markets, where they held meetings with different groups of workers to formulate contract demands.

On 15 April 1934, a mass meeting of thousands of workers was held at the Shubert Theater, and a letter of support was read from Governor Floyd B. Olson of the Farmer-Labor Party. 'It is my counsel', wrote Olson, 'if you wish to accept it, that you should follow the sensible course and band together for your own protection and welfare.' Some 3,000 new members signed up, and the assembly voted to strike if the bosses refused to meet their demands. They elected a rank-and-file strike committee and set a strike deadline.

The Citizens Alliance also carried on its own organizing drive among the employers, forming the Minneapolis Employers of Drivers and Helpers. The employers refused to recognize, negotiate with, or even talk to the union, and would only communicate indirectly through the Labor Board.

A battle was taking shape, and Dobbs and the other leaders of Local 574 realized that they could not win if the Teamsters alone were pitted against the Citizens Alliance. They sought allies. First, they won the support of the Minneapolis AFL Central Labor Union. Then they established relations with the Minnesota Farmers Holiday Association, a militant group fighting farm foreclosures. And, finally, Local 574 made a pact with the unemployed workers organization to help with the picketing.

On 13 May 1934 at a mass meeting at the Eagles Hall, the membership of Teamster Local 574 voted to strike the trucking industry of Minneapolis.

Local President Brown announced that 'every wheel in the city' would stop. When the strike began on 15 May 1934, the union almost immediately doubled its membership, reaching a total of 6,000 members.

The union had rented a large building on Chicago Avenue, where it established offices, a garage, a field hospital and a commissary. Union carpenters and plumbers installed sinks and stoves, and the Cooks and Waiters Union organized 100 volunteers who served meals to 4,000 to 5,000 people daily. A women's auxiliary took responsibility for the commissary and first aid work. Every night 2,000 Teamsters assembled for information on the strike, heard guest speakers and enjoyed entertainment by local talent. A security force kept order, while on the roof four men with submachine guns protected the headquarters from attack.

Other unions contributed several thousand dollars to support the strike, and the Farmers Holiday Association and local grocers provided food for the commissary. The unemployed, other union members and even some college students walked the Teamster picket lines. Doctors and interns from the University of Minnesota provided the medical staff, while lawyers were found to bail arrested pickets out of jail.

The strike was run like a military operation: sentries were posted on fifty roads leading into the city, with orders to stop all trucks not authorized by the union. Scouts called headquarters to report barns trying to open, or trucks on the street. Teenagers on motorcycles acted as a courier service. At headquarters, Ray Dunne and Farrell Dobbs dispatched carloads of pickets from the thousands of strikers who waited for the call to action. To carry the pickets the union had collected 100 cars and trucks serviced by fifteen mechanics.

This amazing organization was soon tested. On 19 May a few trucks from the central market were moved under the protection of cops and thugs who gave a beating to union pickets. That evening James O'Hara, an agent of the employers who had infiltrated the strikers, dispatched pickets to an ambush in Newspaper Alley. The pickets, including five women, were beaten so badly that several had broken bones. City Hall took the side of the employers, and in the first few days of the strike the police arrested 151 pickets. They were sentenced to the workhouse for periods of ten to forty-five days. After the violent confrontations on 19 May police power was expanded, with over 540 men, mostly businessmen, professionals and salesmen, deputized to be used as a strike-breaking force.

On Monday morning, under the protection of as many as 1,000 police and deputized strikebreakers, the employers attempted to move trucks from a downtown store. A battle of military proportions ensued. The union deployed 600 men armed with clubs who had been waiting at the AFL hall. When the police countered by calling in reinforcements, the union sent in another 900 men from the Teamster headquarters. One truckload of 25 pickets drove right into the middle of the police lines to force them into hand-to-hand combat and prevent them from using their guns. As the men fought it out downtown, 700 members of the women's auxiliary marched on City Hall, demanding that the mayor fire the police chief and withdraw the deputies. The battle finally ended after about four hours – and still not a truck had rolled.

The conflict polarized the entire population. The Building Trades Council recommended a sympathy strike, and one by one the building trades unions voted to strike until the Teamsters strike was settled. The electrical workers marched to Teamster headquarters and put themselves at the disposal of the strike committee.

At the same time the police recruited new deputies, and, when the struggle resumed on Tuesday, there were over 1,500 police and deputies in the market, and 20,000 spectators on hand to watch the fight. Again the employers attempted to move trucks from the produce market, but this time the battle was brief and bloody. Two special deputies were killed, including Arthur C. Lyman, a member of the board of the Citizens Alliance. In less than an hour the police and deputies had been vanquished and Teamster pickets controlled the market. Leaders of the AFL Central Labor Union, the Building Trades Council and the Teamsters Joint Council appealed to Governor Olson to help settle the strike. Olson intervened, telling both sides to agree to a truce during which no trucks would move and enter into negotiations to resolve the conflict, or he would bring in the National Guard.

The truce was accepted, and the Teamsters and trucking employers negotiated through the Labor Board. The negotiations dragged on for several days, but finally, on 25 May, an agreement was reached and work resumed the next day.

The Second Trucking Strike

The employers had made a tactical retreat, but they had never really accepted the union or the Labor Board agreement. They quickly set about subverting the agreement, refusing to pay union wages and firing workers. But worst of all, the employers refused to recognize the union's right to represent inside workers. The union appealed the issue to the Labor Board, but the board upheld the employers, effectively denying the union half its membership. Local 574 prepared for another strike.

The Teamsters and the AFL organized a march and rally on 6 July 1934 with contingents from the Farmer-Labor Party, the AFL labor unions, farmers' organizations and students from the University of Minnesota. Six thousand spectators had lined the march route, and two airplanes emblazoned with '574' on their fuselages flew overhead. Some 12,000 people gathered in an auditorium for the rally, and thousands more stood outside.

Union speakers told the crowd that the employers were breaking their earlier agreement and asked for support. The huge assembly voted to adopt a resolution supporting the union's demand to represent all the trucking industry workers and its call for retroactive wage increases.

The enemy was not idle either. Like the Teamsters, the Citizens Alliance had been perfecting its organization. 'In July 1934', wrote Charles Walker, 'it possessed central committee control, a disciplined membership, a permanent staff of highly paid functionaries, the backing of the Minneapolis banks, the cooperation of the police, and one of the most thoroughgoing labor spy organizations in the country. It was a redoubtable antagonist for any rank and file rebellion.'[17] The Citizens Alliance also raised $50,000 for propaganda in the newspapers and on the radio. A federal mediator, E.H. Dunnigan, was sent by the US Department of Labor, but he accomplished nothing. Finally the union voted to strike, supported by both the Central Labor Council and the Building Trades Council.

Teamster President Tobin was not happy about these developments. Tobin loathed all radicals, despised the unskilled workers, and feared that militant strikes would destroy the organization over which he had presided for so many years. He now wrote an editorial in the *International Teamster* magazine attacking the leaders of Local 574 as 'semi-monsters who are creeping into our midst and getting into some of our newly organized local unions, creating distrust, discontent, bloodshed and rebellion. ... If you love the union which you have worked to build up, get busy and stifle such radicals, because they do not belong in the union.' Tobin's editorial delighted the Citizens Alliance and the trucking employers. Local 574 responded: 'We say plainly to D.J. Tobin: If you can't act like a Union man, and help us, instead of helping the bosses, then at least have the decency to stand aside and let us fight our battle alone.'

The next day the strike began under the leadership of Grant, Miles and Raymond Vincent Dunne, Carl Skoglund, Farrell Dobbs and an elected strike committee of 100 members. The union had rented a new headquarters on South Eighth Street. The commissary was stocked for forty days, and medical and legal facilities had been expanded. The women's auxiliary continued to staff committees at headquarters while men served on the picket lines. Nightly meetings were again held for the strikers. Local 574 started its own newspaper, *The Organizer*, which soon expanded from a weekly to a daily – the nation's first labor union daily – with a circulation reaching 10,000 copies.

Police Chief Michael J. Johannes, who had been bested in the spring, was determined to beat the union in the summer. He told his officers, 'We're going to start moving goods. Don't take a beating. You have shotguns, and you know how to use them. When we are finished with this convoy there will be other goods to move.' On Friday, 20 July, the employers notified strikers that they had three days to return to work or lose their jobs. The bosses placed ads in the local papers asking: 'How do you like having our Minneapolis streets in the control of communists?' That same Friday, rumor had it that the employers would attempt to move a truck from the wholesale grocery market. The union deployed 5,000 unarmed pickets, while the police sent in fifty patrolmen on foot and 100 cops in riot gear in squad cars.

When a truck pulled away from the Slocum-Bergren grocery house, it was immediately followed by an open truck filled with nine or ten unarmed union pickets. As soon as they saw the pickets, the police shot to kill, hitting several strikers. Other pickets rushed to aid their brothers, and the police fired again and several more strikers were hit. In a frenzy, the police began shooting strikers in the back and beating the wounded. In the excitement one police officer shot his sergeant. Sixty-seven people were wounded, many of them with multiple wounds. The majority had been shot in the back. Fifty of the wounded were pickets and the rest bystanders. Two of those shot eventually died, Henry Ness that same day and John Belor shortly thereafter. *The Organizer* now asked, 'How do you like having our Minneapolis streets in the control of murderers?'

The people of Minneapolis were horrified by the slaughter perpetrated by the employers and the police. At a protest rally held on 20 July some 15,000 workers adopted a resolution condemning Mayor Bainbridge and Chief Johannes, who was forever after known as 'Bloody Mike'. The funeral for Henry Ness was held on Tuesday, 24 July, and over 40,000 workers participated in the funeral march and services. Angry workers showed up at Teamster strike headquarters armed with rifles, shotguns, pistols and knives, but the union's leaders convinced them that an escalation of firepower would be a mistake.

The employers next attempted to move a few trucks with a police convoy protecting each vehicle. But since it took dozens of police cars and scores of cops to move even one truck, surrounded as they were by hundreds of Teamster pickets, it was impossible to resume operations. Once again, despite bloody murder, the union had stopped the wheels from turning.

Governor Olson increased the number of National Guardsmen in Minneapolis to 4,000 and threatened to take military control of the city if the violence continued. The union wrote in *The Organizer*: 'We never called for the troops. The employers did. We call for their withdrawal. ... We don't need the guard to stop scab trucks. But the employers need it to convoy them through.'

The day after the Ness funeral, federal mediators proposed a 'fair settlement' of the strike. They called for a return to work, a Labor Board election to see if workers wanted a union, and a wage award of fifty-two and a half cents for drivers and forty-two and a half cents for helpers. The proposal excluded some inside workers organized by the union. Olson, who was soon up for reelection, was anxious to settle the strike, and immediately endorsed the federal proposal. If either side rejected it, said Olson, he would use troops to impose it.

The union strike committee found the proposal acceptable in principle, and on the morning of 26 July a Local 574 general membership meeting voted 1,866 to 147 to accept it. The onus was now clearly on the employers, but they told the federal mediators, 'We cannot deal with this Communist leadership.' In the face of the employers' defiance, Olson declared martial law. National Guard troops marched through the streets of Minneapolis and took command of the city market and major thoroughfares.

While Olson gave the impression that his sympathies were with the strikers, it was the union that suffered under martial law. The union was not allowed to picket or hold open air meetings at its strike headquarters, while the National Guard granted permits authorizing trucking companies to operate and permitted unauthorized trucks to move as well. Truck traffic reached 65 percent of normal by 29 July. To protest Olson's strikebreaking, the union held a rally at the Parade Ground on 31 July, which was attended by over 25,000 workers. All supporters were asked to show up at strike headquarters the following morning at 4 a.m. to resume picketing. Everyone wondered if the National Guard would fire on the pickets.

Governor Olson did not intend to let the union put its pickets back on the streets and ordered National Guard commander General Ellard Walsh to close the union. At precisely 4 a.m. in the morning, as the pickets were assembling at the union hall, Colonel Elmer McDevitt led a battery of light artillery, a detachment of machine gunners, a shock battalion of 300, and a total of 1,000 troops to surround the union headquarters. The strikers guarding the headquarters were disarmed, Ray and Miles Dunne and Bill Brown were arrested, and warrants were issued for the arrest of strike leaders who had escaped. The National Guard also occupied Local 574's union hall, AFL headquarters, and the Cooks and Waiters Union.

If the governor thought the Teamsters were going to give up because of what they called 'a few tin soldiers', he was mistaken. The pickets now engaged in a kind of guerrilla warfare. Small bands of strikers spread out through the city, engaging in hit-and-run attacks and putting trucks out of commission. The Teamster paper, *The Organizer*, called for a 'general protest strike' against 'military tyranny'.

Under this pressure, Olson released the union leaders, returned the union headquarters, and even ordered the National Guard to carry out a token raid on the Citizens Alliance. On 6 August the governor announced that all permits to move trucks were being revoked and that new permits would only be issued to companies that signed the federal mediators' proposal, with exceptions for emergencies.

Local 574 kept the pressure on the vacillating Olson. Another mass rally was called for the evening of 6 August on the parade grounds; it was attended by 40,000 workers. The union continued to demand the freeing of its pickets from the stockade and the removal of the militia so that normal picketing operations could resume. At this point, as Farrell Dobbs puts it, the strike became a 'war of attrition'. Some 800 strikebreakers had been hired, and a few strikers began to return to work. At the same time the union continued its guerrilla warfare.

The Minneapolis Teamster strike had become a national issue, and Democratic President Franklin Delano Roosevelt, who was supported by the Farmer-Labor Party, feared that if the strike continued it might hurt the Democrats in the fall elections. Roosevelt wanted the conflict ended before November, and sent a new federal mediator, P.A. Donoghue, to settle the strike. Under the combined pressure of the strikers and the federal government, the Citizens Alliance was forced to yield.

The employers accepted a new pact calling for all workers to be reinstated without discrimination and in order of seniority. There was to be a Labor Board–supervised union representation election in which no scabs would be allowed to vote. Where Local 574 won a majority, the employers would have to recognize and negotiate with the union. Wages were to be fifty cents an hour for drivers and forty cents for helpers, platform and inside workers. Governor Olson consented to release all pickets from the stockade. The strike committee of 100 voted to recommend the proposal, and a general membership meeting on 21 August voted for it overwhelmingly. The strike was over.

The union won the elections at 50 of the 166 companies, accounting for 61 percent of all trucking industry workers. At all the large companies, the workers voted three to one for the union, and workers at all twenty-two market companies voted for the Teamsters. Local 574 bargained for workers at all 166 firms, and within two years had contracts with 500 Minneapolis companies. The union generally signed one-year contracts and retained the right to strike over grievances or for any other reason during the life of the contract.

The new Teamster contracts meant dramatic improvements in the lives of trucking industry workers. To take just one example, within two years the wages of the market workers doubled, and their work week was reduced from ninety to forty-eight hours. A few years later Oscar Halverson, a rank-and-file Teamster, wrote, 'My kids have been eating meat, along with good food, ever since the 1934 strike, so with them the sun rises and sets on 574.'[18]

Nevertheless, Tobin still opposed the leaders of the Minneapolis Teamsters despite the victory. On 15 April 1935 he revoked Local 574's charter and created a new Minneapolis Teamster Local 500 headed by a Tobin loyalist. A group of Teamsters from Rockford, Illinois was sent up to

Minneapolis to try to strongarm Local 574 members into joining Local 500. Tobin also passed a resolution at the Teamster convention barring Communists from membership in the union. But the radicals had too much support to be dislodged, and in a couple of years Local 574 and Local 500 were merged as a new Local 544, still led by Dobbs and the other socialists.

Detroit and Jimmy Hoffa

While the Minneapolis Teamsters were engaged in their struggle, other militant strikes were breaking out around the country. In the spring of 1931 a young man only sixteen years old, hardly more than a boy, went to work in the Kroger warehouse in Detroit. The work at Kroger's was grueling. The shift began at 5 p.m. and ended at 5 a.m., but the workers were not paid for their 'waiting time', only for the hours they actually worked unloading refrigerator cars and boxcars and loading trucks. The pay was 32 cents an hour, or $15.36 for a forty-eight hour week. There were no regular work rules, there was no job security, and the foreman was a tyrant whom the workers referred to only as 'The Little Bastard'. The conditions cried out for justice. The oldest worker in the crew was a radical named Sam Calhoun, who discretely spoke to the workers on the night shift, urging them to unionize in order to do something about their conditions. One of his first recruits was that sixteen-year-old boy. His name was Jimmy Hoffa.

Calhoun and Hoffa began to organize a union and prepare a strike among the 175 night-shift dock workers in order to force management to recognize their union and deal with them. They started to recruit workers in ones and twos, waiting for the right moment to strike. Their chance came in April or May 1931, when a boxcar load of strawberries arrived at warehouse. The workers half-loaded the trucks with the ripe, perishable fruit, and then, led by Hoffa, they struck. Faced with the loss of the strawberry shipment, management agreed to meet and negotiate with the workers.

'When we were finished', wrote Hoffa, 'we had formed an agreement with management that permitted us to live like human beings while on the jobs.' The contract was brought back to the warehousemen for their consideration, and they cheered Calhoun, Hoffa and the rest of the committee. 'In that moment, I realized what my life's goal was to be. I would work for labor.'[19]

James R. Hoffa was born on Valentine's Day, 1916, in Brazil, Indiana. Hoffa's father was employed by a coal prospector to drill for coal in southern Indiana, and his mother, Viola Riddle Hoffa, was a housewife, caring for Jimmy, his brother Billy and sister Jennetta. When her husband died in 1920, Viola moved the family to Clinton, Indiana and took a job as a laundress. 'I never thought of us as being poor', Hoffa later wrote. 'If things seemed different from life in other families, it was because our father had died, and we were without a father to earn money. We had to do it ourselves. It was a harsh but simple fact of life.'[20] In 1924 Viola Hoffa moved her family to Detroit. She took a job polishing radiator caps at Fisher Body's Fleetwood Plant, and at the age of eleven Jimmy Hoffa began working at odd jobs, turning the money over to his mother. After the ninth grade Hoffa quit school and at fourteen he went to work as a stockboy making $12 for a six-day week until he went to work at the Kroger warehouse in 1930.

Having led a strike, created a union and won a contract, the workers decided to elect officers. Sam Calhoun was elected president, and Jimmy Hoffa, at the age of sixteen, was elected vice-president. Bobby Holmes, later to be an important Detroit Teamster official, was elected secretary-treasurer. Having formed their own organization, they affiliated with the American Federation of Labor as Federal Local 19341. Later, a Teamster organizer persuaded them to join that union because they worked with trucks. Constantly harassed by 'The Little Bastard', Hoffa finally quit his job at Kroger's and was immediately hired by Ray Bennett as an organizer for Detroit Teamster Joint Council 43.

In *The Hoffa Wars*, Dan Moldea asserts that in 1934 Hoffa had an affair with a woman named Sylvia Pigano, who associated with various crime syndicate figures. According to Moldea, Hoffa's 'adopted son', Chuckie O'Brien, was really Hoffa's child by Sylvia Pigano. Moldea argues that Hoffa's later involvement with the Mafia had its origins in this relationship.[21] Another theory has been advanced by Lester Velie, who claims that in the course of organizing activities Hoffa killed a mobster. The Mafia then put Hoffa on trial, and, in order to save himself, Hoffa agreed to bring the Mafia into the Teamsters union.[22] These are interesting stories, but, however it came about, Hoffa's involvement with the Mafia began in the mid-1930s and was not fundamentally the result of a romance or an accidental killing, but a moral choice consistent with the business union philosophy that he had adopted.

In 1935 Bennett appointed Hoffa, then twenty-one, as business agent of Local 299 in Detroit. The debt-ridden local had only 250 members, many of them unemployed, and Hoffa was paid only $5 or $10 a week. Under Bennett's direction, Hoffa began work on various organizing drives. 'We were hated and resisted by management', Hoffa wrote, 'shadowed, hounded and dispersed by the police, and viewed with suspicion as some variety of shakedown artists or confidence men by those whom we sought to bring into the fold.'[23]

Detroit was an open shop town, and the employers were determined to keep it that way. Public opinion, businessmen, the newspapers, politicians, ministers all condemned labor union organizers. 'In 1935', wrote Hoffa, 'the labor activist was a "radical", a "Red", an "anarchist". With or without such a label, he was regarded as an enemy of the accepted system and a plotter against the status quo.'[24] In the course of his organizing work, Hoffa was beaten up dozens of times by strikebreakers or the police, sometimes beaten badly enough to require stitches in his scalp. His brother, Billy Hoffa, was shot in the stomach by an employer, and a business agent of Local 299 was shot and killed by a hired strikebreaker. Jimmy Hoffa was frequently thrown in jail, once being jailed and released eighteen times in a 24-hour period by police trying to keep him away from a picket line.

It was during this period that Hoffa met Josephine Poszywak, a striking laundry worker, on a picket line. They began seeing each other and were married in September 1936 in Bowling Green, Ohio. They would eventually have two children, James, Jr. and Barbara, and Chuckie O'Brien, the son of Sylvia Pigano O'Brien, Hoffa's 'adopted son', was a frequent guest in their home.

Despite employer resistance the union grew in strength until R.J. Bennett led a city-wide Teamster strike in Detroit that lasted three days in April 1937. Dan Moldea asserts that Hoffa, taking advantage of people he met through Silvia Pigano a few years before, contacted Detroit underworld figures Santo Perrone and Vincent A. Meli, who, among other things, were professional strikebreakers, and persuaded them to not become involved in the strike on the side of the employers.[25] The strike was a success that Bennett attributed to Hoffa, saying, 'It never would have come off without him.'

The strike raised city drivers' wages to 60 cents an hour and won road drivers $5 for a trip to Chicago. Hoffa now began to organize the carhaulers who delivered automobiles from the Detroit factories to dealers throughout the United States and Canada. The employers were extremely hostile to the union, and the drivers could only be approached when they stopped by the side of the road. So Hoffa began to travel up and down Canada Route 2 between Detroit and Buffalo, US 6 to Cleveland, and US 112 to Chicago, or US 10 to Ludington Ferry, talking to carhaulers and organizing them into the union. In response, the employers hired thugs who waited in the trucks for Teamster organizers like Hoffa to approach, and then beat them. The police cooperated with the companies by stopping and ticketing Teamster organizers. Nevertheless, over time Hoffa succeeded in organizing the Detroit carhaulers into Local 299.

Organizing the Over-the-Road Drivers

Meanwhile, the Minneapolis Teamsters decided to launch an even more ambitious campaign to organize the over-the-road drivers. They aimed to organize the entire Midwest by creating an area-wide structure involving many local unions. It was a plan that would radically change the Teamsters and the labor movement. Farrell Dobbs and his coworkers reached out to other Teamster locals, explaining their idea, and winning their support.

A Teamster conference was called in Minneapolis for 10 January 1937, and the North Central District Drivers Council (NCDDC) was created, made up of representatives from North and South Dakota, Iowa, Minnesota, Wisconsin and Michigan. The NCDDC was a radical innovation, the potential power of which was demonstrated when the Gable-Robinson wholesale produce chain was struck simultaneously by the NCDDC and Teamster locals in Duluth and Hibbing, Minnesota and Eau Claire, Wisconsin. In one week the company capitulated, signing a contract that nearly doubled its workers' wages in all terminals in the NCDDC area.

The response to this new organizing drive was not long in coming. On 17 November 1937 Pat Corcoran, the chairman of Local 544 and a leader of the NCDDC, was murdered. The Teamsters believed that he had been assassinated by the employers, though his murder remained unsolved. 'If assassination of teaming craft leaders is the answer of the employers', wrote *The Northwest Organizer*, 'then Local 544 says, you may kill who you think are the leaders. But we have trained people who will go forward with the fight.'[26] Others did go forward with the fight, and the NCDDC organizing drive continued. More Teamster locals throughout the Midwest became involved, several new locals were organized, and thousands of new members were recruited. Tobin, ever fearful of any novelty, ordered the NCDDC to disband. But the NCDDC then sent a delegation to Indianapolis to tell him that they refused. Tobin was stunned.

Dobbs wrote that 'a couple of facts seemed to percolate through to Tobin. Things were changing within the industry and inside the union faster than he had realized. Unless some readjustments in policy were made, he could have a major revolt on his hands. So he decided to be a bit more flexible.'[27] Tobin gave the NCDDC official status as a Teamster body, endorsed NCDDC strikes, and even doled out strike benefits.

Having won Tobin's endorsement, it was possible to reach out to other areas. The most important was Chicago where Sandy O'Brien, the head of Teamster meat drivers Local 710, had brought all of the road drivers in the city under his jurisdiction. O'Brien immediately appreciated the importance of the NCDDC and brought Local 710 into the organization. Detroit Local 299, which had been organizing the carhaulers, also joined, and Jimmy Hoffa was assigned to work under Farrell Dobbs. Hoffa found Dobbs 'a crackerjack organizer' and a 'brilliant strategist'.[28]

The NCDDC now struck two notoriously anti-union companies in Iowa: Holdcroft Transportation of Sioux City and Brady Transfer of Fort Dodge, beating them both in a matter of weeks. The time had come to demand a contract, but it was unclear with whom to negotiate. The recently formed American Trucking Association's Labor Relations Committee refused to talk to the NCDDC leaders.

Finally the Teamsters simply sent an ultimatum to 1,200 employers telling them that the union would no longer accept the 'chaotic conditions' in the industry and would not 'be sidetracked into a maze of regional and individual city negotiations.' The NCDDC demanded one contract for over-the-road drivers throughout the Midwest. The Teamsters threatened a trucking strike that would shut down terminals in Minneapolis, Detroit and Chicago, and every little town in between, with support from Teamster locals as far away as Colorado, Texas, and Kentucky. That brought the employers to the table.

Eventually the employers and the Teamsters agreed to a closed shop in which all trucking industry employees had to be members of the union, a wage of two and three-fourths cents a mile, or seventy-five cents an hour for road drivers on through runs, and comparable wages for other runs. The union reserved the right to strike over grievances and to honor the picket lines of any striking union. The contract covered directly and indirectly some 125,000 workers, making it the biggest contract in Teamster history.

Agreed to by employers throughout the Midwest, the contract was not accepted in Omaha, where a bitter battle broke out involving over 3,000 workers. Nebraska state laws prohibited most picketing, and so most strike activities were illegal. Nonetheless, the Teamster strikers succeeded in shutting down most terminals and keeping most trucks off the road. The employers used armed strikebreakers, and the police threw Teamster pickets in jail. It was a real test for the NCDDC and the freight contract: if the union could be stopped in Nebraska, its accomplishments could be undone in the rest of the Midwest.

The NCDDC stood the test. Tobin actually provided benefits for the strikers, while Detroit Local 299 assigned Hoffa to help out in Nebraska. Meanwhile, Dobbs masterminded a strategy of strangling the Nebraska companies by organizing the major terminals in the surrounding states. Soon, the flow of freight was completely cut off and the Nebraska employers were brought to their knees. The organization of the Midwestern over-the-road drivers was secure.

Sullivan and the Boston Teamsters

Similar developments were also taking place in the Northeast, where Boston Local 25 was the spark plug. In 1933 Local 25 had only 335 paid-up members, contracts with a mere sixteen employers, and was $1,700 in debt. Then John M. Sullivan and a new group of more militant leaders were elected to lead the local. Sullivan launched an ambitious organizing campaign. The first mass meeting held in April 1933, and over 1,000 workers attended and

800 applied for membership. Between April 1933 and November 1938 at least 35 new members were initiated at every meeting, and sometimes as many as 600.[29] Having built up his power base in Boston, Sullivan sent organizers to other Teamster locals and began to organize new locals throughout New England. Eventually he succeeded in creating a network covering the states of Massachusetts, Connecticut, Vermont, New Hampshire, Rhode Island and Maine, and in 1938 presented demands to the employers for a common contract for the entire area. When the employers refused to agree to the Teamsters' demands, the union called the first general strike of New England Teamsters in thirty years.

The walkout was completely effective: Teamsters shut down the terminals and swept the highways clean. Mass picket lines kept trucking terminals, warehouses and other businesses closed. After an eleven-day strike a compromise settlement was reached providing for a small improvement in wages. The union called a second strike in March 1939, which ended in a complete victory. 'The principal result of the strike was the signing of a uniform contract covering all locals in southern New England.'[30]

Dave Beck

What Dobbs did in the Midwest and what Sullivan achieved in the East was accomplished in the West by Dave Beck, the leader of the Seattle Teamsters. Dave Beck was born in Stockton, California on 16 June 1894. His father, Lemuel Beck, was a poor provider and the family depended on Mary Beck's wages as a laundry worker. From the time Dave Beck was a small boy he worked to add to the family's income, selling newspapers, and on occasion even trapping rats and selling them to the Health Department.[31]

Beck later got a job in the laundry where his mother worked and became a member of Local 24 of the Laundry Workers International Union. In 1917 he became a laundry-wagon driver and a charter member of Seattle Teamster Local 566. When the union struck for recognition, Beck played an active part. After World War I broke out Beck joined the Naval Aviation Service and served in England as a machinist for a navy bombing squadron. After the war he returned home and took up his job as a driver on the eve of Seattle General Strike.

The years 1918 and 1919 were years of revolution around the world, and tremendous strike waves swept Europe and the United States. This international strike wave broke over Seattle in 1919 in the form of a city-wide general strike. The 30,000 shipyard workers represented by the twenty-one unions in the Metal Trades Council demanded higher wages, but the employers refused their demands. The shipyard workers voted to strike.

Seattle had a militant labor movement led by radicals and Socialists, and there was a strong tradition of labor solidarity. When the Metal Trades voted to strike, the Seattle Central Labor Council voted to strike in sympathy. In February 1919 Teamster Laundry Drivers Local 566 met to decide whether to join the general strike in support of the shipyard workers. Still wearing his Navy uniform, Dave Beck was called on to speak. He rose and passionately pleaded with his fellow members, urging them *not* to strike. Beck's speech may have been effective, for Local 566 was the only Teamster local, and one of the few labor unions of any kind, that voted not to strike in support of the shipyard workers.[32]

The general strike brought Seattle to a standstill, and Mayor Ole Hanson, known as 'Holy Ole', declared the strike a 'rebellion' and called upon Governor Lister to send in the National Guard. The strike lasted four days, and, if it was not victorious, neither was it crushed. 'For the majority of Seattle unions, there was no sense of defeat as the strike ended', remembers Seattle labor union activist Harvey O'Connor. 'They had demonstrated their solidarity with their brothers in the yards, and the memory of the great days when labor had shown its strength glowed in their minds.'[33]

Ironically, this demonstration of workers' power only made Dave Beck an outspoken opponent of militant unionism. 'Those Wobblies were nuts', said Beck. 'You can't beat the bosses by trying to destroy them. I have no use for class warfare.' At the laundry, Beck worked hard and built up his run until he was earning a good wage, making it possible for him to marry Dorothy Lesehander. He was also more active in the Teamsters union, winning election as business agent in Local 566, president of Washington Joint Council 28 in 1923, and secretary-treasurer of Local 566 in 1924. In 1925 Seattle was the site of the Teamster International convention, and Beck was secretary of the arrangements and credentials committees and spoke at the convention, bringing himself to the attention of President Tobin, who quickly recognized Beck's talent.

A laundry chain offered Beck the job of general manager, and Beck was tempted. He let it be known he would stay on with the Teamsters only if he were paid more. Valuing him highly, Tobin promoted Beck to part-time general organizer for the International, a post that would mean both more money and more power. In 1926 Beck was promoted again, to full-time organizer in charge of the Pacific Northwest and British Columbia. Beck did not forget his family; his sister was employed on the switchboard at the Seattle Teamster hall.

Stabilizing the Laundry Industry

As a union leader Beck viewed the union exactly like any other business. 'What is good for business in selling its product is good for labor in selling the only thing that it has to sell – labor – exactly that, no difference', argued

Beck.[34] In the 1920s there was virtually no government regulation of industry, and cutthroat competition was the rule. The vicious competition between employers led to wage cuts, driving down the workers' standard of living. In this situation Beck opposed strikes and joined with the employers to try to stabilize prices and wages in the industry. In 1927, for example, Beck won a contract in which the laundry drivers' commissions were based on a uniform price list.

The union even used its power to drive some companies out of business to reduce the competition. 'When I was the secretary of the Laundry Drivers Local in Seattle way back in 1925', Beck recalled, 'I started a program that eliminated 146 out of a membership of 380 individual owners.'[35] Beck's 'stabilization' program led to the Teamsters being sued for price-fixing in 1928, but Beck beat the rap because the agreement with the laundry companies was not signed, and so the charge of conspiracy to fix prices could not be proven. As Beck later explained to Bay Area employers, 'You don't sign the contract, you enforce it.'

From the rank and file's point of view there was a bigger issue at stake. Stabilization and price-fixing led to collusion between management and labor; they joined together in a kind of cartel, and the union became responsible for policing the industry. This led the union officials to view the employers as collaborators, rather than as adversaries. The union officials came to identify with the boss and his problems, rather than with the worker and his problems. Guided by this philosophy of collaboration, Beck visited all the Teamster union halls urging wage cuts in 1929 when the Crash occurred and the Great Depression began.

The Bureaucratization of Seattle Labor

As head of the Seattle Teamsters, Beck was the most powerful figure in the American Federation of Labor in the Pacific Northwest. In 1935 Rose Pesotta, an organizer for the International Ladies Garment Workers Union (ILGWU), visited Seattle and saw for herself Beck's impact on the labor movement. It was, she said, a 'union ghost town. ... Union officers, quartered in the Labor Temple, were largely of the type portrayed by cartoonists in the capitalist press – chair-warmers and cigar-smokers. I learned that rank-and-file members were not encouraged to hang around the union offices. At meetings of locals the officers would take up routine matters – reading of the local's minutes, CLC minutes, the local's correspondence, then adjournment. Dull proceedings, no new faces.'[36]

Dave Beck was not interested in rank-and-file participation, but he was interested in expanding his own power. With the help of Frank Brewster, secretary-treasurer of drivers Local 174, Beck was able to organize many other jurisdictions in Seattle and throughout Washington state: warehousemen, flour mill workers, service station employees, cannery workers, and dairy and bakery workers. When Local 174 drivers cut off pick-up and delivery service, employers who had resisted union organization were forced to yield. Retail clerks were usually organized by the AFL's Retail Clerks union, but not in Seattle. Beck made a deal with a department store manager, who encouraged his employees to join Beck's Retail Clerks. Beck installed the Retail Clerks in the Teamsters' building, chose their officers, controlled their union and signed their sweetheart contracts.

The Seattle Teamsters also built a political organization in Settle. In February 1936, Beck organized the Joint Council of Teamsters Promotion League and got out 15,000 voters in King County to elect John F. Dore as mayor. Returning the favor, Dore supported Beck's Teamsters union against all its adversaries.[37]

As Beck became a big shot in the Teamsters he came to spend more and more of his time with businessmen, industrialists and politicians. 'Some of the finest men I know are employers', he said. The feeling among businessmen was mutual. 'Beck is a top labor statesman and an outstanding civic leader', said Franklin McLaughlin, president of the Northwest's largest private utility. 'He is absolutely tops. With him we've had peace when it might have been hell.'

So Beck was welcomed into the businessmen's clubs: he joined the Chamber of Commerce, became an Eagle, an officer of the American Legion, and an Honorary Deputy Grand Exalted Ruler of the Elks. He raised funds for the Episcopal Church, the congregation of the upper crust, and for the Associated Boys' Clubs. He was Seattle boxing commissioner, sat on the Washington State Parole Board, and the Seattle Civil Service Commission, and became president of the Board of Regents of the University of Washington.

One of Seattle's biggest social events was 'Dave Beck's Round-Up' held each year just before Christmas at the elite Washington Athletic Club. 'It is attended by bankers, senators, state supreme court justices, congressmen, industrialists, and newspaper editors', wrote Richard L. Neuberger. 'Beck's liberal adversaries jestingly say, 'Oh! Everyone is at Dave's "Round-Up" – that is, everyone except working people.'[38]

Beck: A Genius for Organization

Beck began to expand his influence, first to Oregon, then to California and finally to all the Western states. In the early 1930s, Beck sent Charles M. 'Whitey' Dahlager to Portland to strengthen cartage drivers Local 162. Dahlager succeeded in building up Local 162 and then began organizing workers in other jurisdictions and creating new locals. That made it possible to carry out an organizing campaign throughout Oregon in the mid-1930s. Thereafter

Beck began to hold joint meetings of Washington Joint Council 28 and Oregon Joint Council 37 to coordinate organizing and bargaining efforts. Beck next turned his attention to the organization of the over-the-road or line-haul drivers with the objective of organizing Los Angeles. Other Teamster leaders had ignored the road drivers, but Beck believed that if the road drivers were organized the union would be able to organize 'not only Los Angeles but all of the little towns and cities' that were dependent for deliveries on the long-haul carriers.[39]

A meeting of seventy-six California Teamster locals was called by Mike Casey in January 1935, nominally to prepare for the Teamster convention but actually to launch an organizing drive among California highway drivers. The locals that became involved were grouped together in the Highway Drivers Council (HDC) of California. Bay Area Joint Council 7 refused to fund the organizing drive, but both Local 85 and Local 70 backed the campaign with organizers and several thousand dollars.

The organizers went to the trucking barns, the docks and the railroad yards, and by August 1935 had signed up hundreds of new members who were eager to join the union in the hope of shorter hours, higher wages and some job security. At the same time, militant tactics were used to prevent non-union drivers from entering San Francisco, trucks were destroyed and scabs were beaten.[40] The new Teamster recruits were distributed among the local unions on the basis of the driver's domicile, and while San Francisco Local 85 and Oakland Local 70 grew rapidly, other locals such as San Jose, Bakersfield, Vallejo and Sacramento grew even faster. As the union became stronger, it took action farther from its home base in the Bay Area. In May 1935 there was a strike by Local 431 in Fresno, a key city halfway between San Francisco and Los Angeles. The HDC also organized California-based drivers who went into Oregon and Washington; by 1937 almost all of them were union.

Organizing from Above

There was a good deal of rank-and-file participation in the early stages of the line-haul drivers organizing campaign. Some city drivers were hired as organizers, and others worked at the checkpoints on the roads into town, or with the flying squads, or 'goon squads', that chased down scab trucks.[41] But gradually organizing tactics changed, and the ranks became less involved. The Teamsters turned from organizing from below, by convincing the workers to join the union, to 'organizing from above', by convincing the employers to accept the union.[42]

The union would not allow trucks of non-union employers to come into San Francisco or Oakland until they had signed an agreement with the Teamster local in their areas. In many cases workers became members of the union without ever having been convinced by a union organizer that it was beneficial to them.

The first contract, signed in September 1935, did not win great gains for the road drivers and was ignored by some employers. Nevertheless, it was an important step for the union to establish some basis of collective bargaining, even if at a low wage level. Over time the union would force the employers to honor the terms of the contract.

Beck now began to lay plans for organizing Los Angeles, but he would never have been successful had it not been for the San Francisco General Strike of 1934. Under the leadership of Harry Bridges, the International Longshoremen's Association (ILA) had gone on strike for union recognition in all the Pacific ports on 9 May 1934. The key demand was a union-run hiring hall. The system in force at the time was 'the shape', where employers hired for each shift from among the many men who showed up at the docks; it was a system rampant with favoritism, discrimination and corruption, and hated by the workers.

Mike Casey, the leader of San Francisco Teamster Local 85, was reluctant to strike in support of the Longshoremen because the Teamster contract with the Draymen's Association discouraged sympathy strikes. But on 13 May the Teamster rank and file voted unanimously to stop hauling freight to or from the docks, and a large group of Teamsters marched from that meeting to the Embarcadero to join the Longshoremen's picket line. Shortly thereafter the maritime workers also struck: sailors, firemen, cooks, stewards, mates and pilots and marine engineers.

The strike went on for almost two months with mass picket lines and frequently violent battles between strikers and scabs and police. Then on 5 July 1934 the police and the National Guard, using tear gas, pistols and shotguns, broke through the picket lines in an assault on the strikers that also caught up many citizens who happened to find themselves in the midst of the police onslaught. According to the newspapers there were two dead and at least sixty-seven injured. The day became known as 'Bloody Thursday'.

The workers of San Francisco were enraged, and one union after another voted for a general strike. Again Casey did everything he could to try to stop the Teamsters from supporting the general strike, but despite his pleas, Teamster Local 85 voted to strike and walked out on 12 July. The Oakland Teamsters also struck. The strike paralyzed the city and lasted until ended by government arbitration a week later.

On 12 October 1934 the Longshoremen got a contract that included a six-hour day, a thirty-hour week, a wage raise, overtime pay, and most important, union dispatchers for the hiring halls. It was a spectacular victory for the Longshoremen and gave impetus to the organizing efforts of all the other unions. Without the 1934 Longshoremen's strike in San Francisco the Teamster organizing drive in Los Angeles would have been impossible.

Organizing Los Angeles

In May 1937, Beck took over as head of the Highway Drivers Council, expanding the HDC to include locals in Denver, Phoenix and Salt Lake City. He now had the organization needed to conquer Los Angeles. L.A. was an open shop town that had been dominated for over twenty-five years by the Merchants and Manufacturers Association (M&M), and conditions for workers in Los Angeles were poor indeed. In 1936 city drivers made thirty-five to fifty-five cents per hour, while road drivers made as little as fifteen to twenty cents per hour. There was no limit on the hours that road drivers were expected to drive; they often drove on for days at a time, taking short naps by the side of the road. The Teamsters union was weak, with only 800 members in Los Angeles in 1932, though after the passage of NIRA Section 7(a) granting workers the right to organize, the union had grown to 2,000 members in 1936, most of them in Los Angeles Local 208 and Los Angeles Harbor Local 692.

After studying the Los Angeles freight industry, Beck decided to make the Pacific Freight Lines (PFL) his target. With some 700 workers, PFL was the biggest for-hire trucking company in the region and dominated the Motor Truck Association of California (MTA). Because it shipped freight up and down the coast from Southern California to Washington, PFL was suscep-tible to secondary boycotts by the Teamsters in Fresno, San Francisco, Portland and Seattle. 'While they could lick us without question in the Los Angeles area, the minute that freight started moving north of Bakersfield and on into the Bay Area, we were absolutely in a position of greater economic strength than they were', said Beck.[43]

Beck began the campaign in the Los Angeles harbor, first making an agreement with the International Longshoremen's Association to honor each other's picket lines. In November 1936 the Teamsters blockaded the harbor area, demanding that all trucks serving the harbor carry a Teamster swamper (helper). Teamster swampers would, of course, work only with Teamster drivers. Trucks crossing the blockade were violently attacked. Once the point had been made, the union contacted the trucking companies and reached agreements with some of them.

The Merchants and Manufacturers Association meanwhile organized the employers. It raised money to fight the unions, opened its own hiring hall to provide non-union swampers, and organized boycotts against employers who recognized the union. The Motor Truck Association hired the Glen Bodell Industrial Detective Agency, which provided armed men to attack union organizers and detectives to spy on the workers. The city and state mobilized as many as 600 policemen to break the picket lines. Nevertheless, the union succeeding in organizing many new members; Local 692 alone had grown to 1,200 members by the spring of 1937.

Now the Teamsters began to organize Los Angeles itself. Organizers were put on the roads leading into the city. Drivers who could not be convinced to join the union often found their trucks immobilized, usually by breaking the windshield or shooting out the gas tanks as the trucks slowly climbed the steep hills. Finally the strike against PFL itself was called at 3 a.m. on 31 March 1937, but, fearing reprisal by the company, only 120 of the 700 PFL workers walked out of the Los Angeles barn. They formed a picket line around the terminal and were joined by a couple of hundred Longshoremen. At the same time strikes were called against PFL operations in Bakersfield and Fresno.

The Merchants and Manufacturers Association supplied PFL with $67,000 to fight the union, much of it used to hire 175 armed guards from Bodell. The strikers were replaced with scabs, and all PFL workers were given a 10 percent wage increase. The company got an injunction against union use of intimidation or violence, but it could not be enforced. In 'one of the bloodiest strikes in Teamster history', there were constant clashes between strikers, scabs, armed guards and the police, with many on both sides wounded by clubs, knives and guns.[44]

The Teamsters counted on their economic power, exerted through the boycott of 'hot cargo', to win the strike. Teamster dock workers at all freight terminals in California, Oregon and Washington were alerted to watch for PFL freight and to tie it up. Other trucking companies delivering freight to PFL were warned that their deliveries would be stopped if they continued to interline cargo. Longshoremen refused to handle any PFL freight on the docks. As the strike and boycott continued, the Southern Pacific's subsidiary Pacific Motor Transport (PMT) took more and more business away from PFL. As PFL's losses mounted it was clear that it would either go out of business or recognize the union.

After nine weeks of strike and boycott, PFL finally gave up on 2 June 1937. Owner George Duntley signed an agreement with George Shultz, the secretary of Local 208, providing for substantial economic gains for the workers, including a rate of seventy-five cents an hour for road drivers. The contract also contained a union shop clause. A few months later, on 2 November 1937, the Motor Truck Association reached agreement with the Teamsters for a master contract, thus bringing all of the truck drivers in Southern California into the union at once. By the end of 1937, 95 percent of all truck drivers in Los Angeles worked in union shops and 75 percent were actually signed up. By 1938 all the Southern California truckers were signed up.

The success of Beck's organizing drive was not a complete victory for the rank and file, however. Once in the union, workers frequently found that their local was in trusteeship, sometimes for ten years or more. Dave Beck had no use for union democracy. As he said, 'We did just exactly what business would do. The stockholders wouldn't hold an election to see who the hell was going in if they opened a new plant. The top company officials would pick out the best man they could get their hands on and they'd put him in there as manager.'[45] In addition, the first two contracts signed were each five-year contracts with yearly reopeners, though with binding arbitration. No doubt the employers and Beck wanted stability after the upheaval of the 1930s, but such agreements tended to keep the rank and file in a contractual cage. Such terms meant that for ten years the rank and file could not test its own strength in a strike.

A New Structure

Having organized the over-the-road trucking industry and drivers in the city of Los Angeles, Beck turned to reorganizing the Teamsters. In June 1937 he called the first meeting of the Western Conference of Teamsters, a new structure encompassing all the joint councils and Teamster local unions in the West. At this meeting he also created trade divisions for highway trucking, general trucking, dairy, construction and other industries. The creation of the trade divisions was a natural outgrowth of changes in the economy to which the union was responding. The growth of regional and national chains required that the union create regional and later national structures to deal with them. While these new structures made the union more effective, they also concentrated more power in the hands of Dave Beck.

The industrial union approach initiated by Dobbs and used by Beck brought hundreds of thousands of new members into the union, which reached a membership of over half a million in 1941. However, at the same time that the Teamsters union was making such great strides, a struggle for the future of the organization was developing, essentially a struggle between Farrell Dobbs's brand of radical, democratic unionism from-the-bottom-up, and Dave Beck's conservative, authoritarian unionism-from-the-top-down. The future of the Teamsters union would be determined by the outcome of that struggle.

Notes

1. Warren R. Van Tine, 'Daniel Joseph Tobin', in *Dictionary of American Biography*, Supplement V, p. 690.

2. My account of this strike comes entirely from Steven L. Plott, 'The Chicago Teamsters' Strike of 1902: A Community Confronts the Beef Trust', *Labor History,* vol. 26, no. 2 (Spring 1985), pp. 250–67.

3. J.R. Commons, 'Types of American Labor Organization: The Teamsters of Chicago', *Quarterly Journal of Economics*, vol. 19 (May 1905).

4. Robert D. Leiter, *The Teamsters Union: A Study of Its Economic Impact*, New York 1957, p. 25.

5. Philip Taft, *The A.F. of L. in the Time of Gompers*, New York 1970, p. 112. See also Harold Seidman, *Labor Czars: A History of Racketeering*, New York 1938.

6. Barbara Warne Newell, *Chicago and the Labor Movement: Metropolitan Unionism in the 1930s*, Urbana 1961, pp. 94–95.

7. Shea's career in the Teamsters was not over, however; he went on to serve as the secretary of the New York Teamsters District Council until 1909, when he was sent to Sing Sing prison for six years for stabbing his girlfriend, Alice Walsh, thirty-eight times and nearly killing her. After he got out of jail Shea returned to Chicago and went to work for the notoriously corrupt building trades unions there.

8. Van Tine, 'Daniel Joseph Tobin', *DAB*, p. 690.

9. Ibid.

10. Farrell Dobbs, *Teamster Power*, New York 1973, p. 171.

11. Newell, *Chicago and the Labor Movement*, passim.

12. It is still in existence. There is also an IBT Local 705.

13. Samuel E. Hill, *Teamsters and Transportation: Employee-Employer Relationship in New England*, Washington, D.C. 1942, p. 99.

14. The account of the Minneapolis Teamster strikes that follows is drawn from three sources: Farrell Dobbs's *Teamster Rebellion*, Charles Walker's *American City* and Irving Bernstein's *Turbulent Years*. See the bibliography.

15. Dobbs, *Teamster Rebellion*, p. 25.

16. Ibid., p. 61.

17. Charles Walker, *American City: A Rank and File History*, New York 1971, p. 191.

18. Dobbs, *Teamster Power*, p. 122.

19. James R. Hoffa, *The Trials of Jimmy Hoffa: An Autobiography*, Chicago 1970, pp. 53–54.

20. Ibid., p. 8.

21. Dan Moldea, *The Hoffa Wars: Teamsters, Rebels, Politicians and the Mob*, New York 1978, p. 25.

22. Lester Velie, *Desperate Bargain: Why Jimmy Hoffa Had to Die*, New York 1977, pp. 3–4.

23. Hoffa, *Trials*, p. 70.

24. Ibid., p. 79.

25. Moldea, *Hoffa Wars*, p. 25.

26. Dobbs, *Teamster Power*, p. 158.

27. Ibid., p. 176.

28. Hoffa, *Trials*, p. 105.

29. Samuel E. Hill, *Teamsters and Transportation*, pp. 86–89.

30. Ibid., p. 202.

31. Nard Jones, *Seattle*, Garden City, N.Y. 1972, p. 77.

32. Jones, *Seattle*, p. 179.

33. Harvey O'Connor, *Revolution in Seattle: A Memoir*, New York 1964, p. 141.

34. Donald Garnel, *The Rise of Teamster Power in the West*, Berkeley 1972, p. 72.

35. Ibid., p. 69.

36. Rose Pesotta, *Bread Upon the Waters*, New York 1945, pp. 148–49.

37. Calvin F. Schmid, *Social Trends in Seattle*, Seattle 1944, p. 269 and fn 6. Dore's remark originally appeared in the *Seattle Star*, 16 July 1936.

38. Richard L. Neuberger, *Our Promised Land*, New York 1938, p. 194.

39. Garnel, *The Rise of Teamster Power*, p. 103.

40. Roy B. Thompson, *The Trucking Industry, 1930–1950, As Told by Roy B. Thompson* (an interview tape-recorded by Corinne L. Gilb, June–August 1958, in Berkeley, California), Berkeley 1958, pp. 311–12.

41. The word *goon* appears to have entered the English language in 1938 or 1939 and was derived from the character Alice the Goon, who first appeared in Elvie Segar's 'Popeye' cartoon strip in 1919, according to Eric Partridge, editor of the *Dictionary of Slang and Unconventional English*, New York, 1984. Richard L. Neuberger writes in *Our Promised Land*, p. 213, footnote, that 'the origin of the term "goon" is obscure, although from Puget Sound to Mexico it is the common description of teamster picket patrols. The Oregon City *Enterprise* thinks the term is really 'goop'. Another newspaper contends it is a corruption of 'gooney'. The word was first used in Seattle by Beck's left-wing and Communist adversaries. They took it from the *Popeye the*

Sailor comic strip, in which the 'goon' is a weird and terrible monster from another planet. During World War II the word *goon* was applied to German prison camp guards. The word *gooney* means 'simpleton'.

42. Garnel, *The Rise of Teamster Power*, p. 115.
43. Ibid., pp. 148–49.
44. Ibid., p. 159.
45. Ibid., p. 165.

9

The Fall of the Teamsters

The organization of the over-the-road drivers by Dobbs, Hoffa, Sullivan and Beck was only one expression of an even bigger industrial union movement taking place throughout the country. Hundreds of thousands of industrial workers were being organized, and most were joining the new Congress of Industrial Organizations. The CIO had first been formed in 1935 at the AFL convention. John L. Lewis, the head of the United Mine Workers, had proposed that the AFL begin to organize industrial workers. In the course of the debate, Lewis got into an argument with and then punched Bill Hutcheson, the leader of the Carpenters union, a symbolic blow for industrial workers against the bureaucrats of the craft unions. The AFL delegates voted against the proposal, but immediately after the convention, on 9 November 1935, Lewis brought together a number of AFL union leaders to form the Committee for Industrial Organization, as the CIO was first called.

Encouraged by the formation of the new CIO, industrial workers began to strike, engaging in sit-down strikes in which they occupied the factory, sometimes welding themselves inside, until they won union recognition. The event that really made the CIO was the Flint sit-down strike by autoworkers at General Motors in the winter of 1936 and 1937. After weeks in the plants surrounded by soldiers, the workers of the United Auto Workers (CIO) won recognition from GM on 11 February 1937.

Shortly thereafter, on 2 March 1937, the United States Steel Corporation recognized the United Steel Workers (CIO). In that same month the unions making up the Committee for Industrial Organization were expelled from the American Federation of Labor, at which point they changed their name to the Congress for Industrial Organization and became a full-fledged rival to the old AFL. The growth of the Teamsters in the 1930s through a form of industry-wide organizing was thus really part of the same phenomenon that produced the growth of the CIO.

When the CIO was formed, Tobin and the Teamsters naturally stuck with the AFL. Beck was particularly vicious, joining with the employers in condemning the CIO and the strategies that were succeeding in bringing millions of workers into the labor movement. Speaking at the Seattle Real Estate Board in 1937, he said, 'I stand unalterably opposed to the sit-down strike. It is illegal seizure of property and will breed revolution.' He told a meeting of the Seattle Junior Chamber of Commerce in 1937, 'There is no place in our union for Communists or Bolshevists. I am for the capitalistic system!' The real purpose of Beck's anti-Communist oratory was to make clear to the employers that his more friendly Teamsters union should be chosen over the more militant CIO unions, particularly over Harry Bridges's Longshoremen, who had gone over to the CIO. 'This town is going to be organized', Beck told the bosses. 'Choose me or Bridges.'[1] The employers chose Beck. It was in this way that a new Teamster bureaucracy began to take shape, growing up in opposition to the militant CIO and to the radicals within the Teamsters union itself.

Tobin and Roosevelt Destroy the Movement

When World War II broke out in Europe in 1939, it became increasingly clear that Roosevelt would bring the United States into the war on the side of Great Britain and France. Tobin, an ardent supporter of Roosevelt, would back him and his war policy. But the Teamster chief was aware that the Minneapolis Teamster leaders had altogether different ideas. As socialists, Dobbs and the other Minneapolis Teamster leaders opposed what they considered an imperialist war to divide the world among various capitalist powers, Germany and Italy on the one hand, and Great Britain and France on the other. The Trotskyist Teamster activists in Minneapolis felt that working people had nothing to gain from supporting such a war, and should instead work to bring about a socialist society. At the same time, the Minneapolis Teamsters refused to relinquish the right to strike, even during wartime.

These differences not only put the socialist Teamster leaders at odds with Tobin but also led the Roosevelt administration to consider them dangerous political opponents. By early 1941 Tobin decided that the time had come in eliminate the Minneapolis radicals. In the May issue of the *International Teamster*, Tobin launched an attack on unnamed Trotskyists in the Min-neapolis Teamsters and called for the expulsion from the union of members of the Socialist Workers Party.[2] 'It was', says Farrell Dobbs, 'a declaration of war'.

Armed with information from the Federal Bureau of Investigation to document their political affiliations and views, Tobin summoned the Minneapolis Teamsters to a meeting of the International Executive Board in Washington, DC. Ray Dunne, Kelly Postal and Ray Rainbolt were sent to the meeting, at which Tobin read from FBI files on the Minneapolis leadership, the Socialist Workers Party and Trotskyism. Tobin then told the Local 544 representatives that he wanted their union to ask him to appoint a receiver for the local. He demanded an immediate answer.

The Local 544 leaders refused to give an immediate answer, arguing that the issue would have to be presented to their local executive board and general membership for discussion. After the Local 544 representatives left, the International Executive Board passed a resolution stating that the Socialist Workers Party was a 'subversive, revolutionary party' and that its members were barred from the union.

The Minneapolis Teamsters Join the CIO

Local 544's leaders had no intention of letting Tobin appoint a dictator to run their union. They went directly to the Washington office of the Congress of Industrial Organizations to see about the possibility of joining the CIO. A few days later, on 9 June 1941, they were granted a CIO charter as Motor Transport and Allied Workers Industrial Union, Local 544-CIO. At a general membership meeting of Local 544 that was quickly held in Minneapolis and attended by 4,000 members, the local voted to leave the IBT-AFL, and become Local 544-CIO. Several other Teamster locals in the North Central District Drivers Council also seceded from the Teamsters and the AFL and joined the CIO.

In 1941 the CIO had grown to 2.8 million members while the AFL had 4.5 million, and the two unions were engaged in a bitter struggle over control of various industries and groups of workers. In these circumstances, Tobin could not accept the secession of the Minneapolis Teamsters, which might have led to a full-scale rebellion. Tobin sent Dave Beck to deal with the Minneapolis Teamsters. He told them that Tobin would not expel the Trotskyists from the union if Local 544 would accept trusteeship of the local. The Local 544 leaders refused, and Beck left.

Now Tobin used force. He sent Joseph M. Casey of the San Francisco Teamsters with an army of more than 300 Teamster organizers and business agents, hoodlums and out-of-town Teamster members up to Minneapolis. Ironically, Jimmy Hoffa was one of those sent to destroy the union built by his teacher Farrell Dobbs. Supported by the local police and employers, Casey's army of thugs went on the streets and into the trucking terminals and warehouses. They demanded that workers sign up with and pay dues to Local 544 IBT-AFL, and those workers who would not were beaten unmercifully.

Unable to defend themselves against such an onslaught, Local 544-CIO decided to seek a representation election to determine which union the workers wanted. The election was never held, and a National Labor Relations Board hearing ruled that 544 IBT-AFL was the legitimate bargaining agent. The fight, however, was not only on the economic front. On 13 June 1940, Tobin sent a telegram about Local 544-CIO to President Roosevelt. 'The officers of this local union ... were requested to disassociate themselves from the radical Trotsky organization. ... We feel that while our country is in a dangerous position, those disturbers who believe in the politics of foreign, radical governments, must be in some way prevented from pursuing this dangerous course.'³

Roosevelt shared Tobin's concern about the leadership of the Minneapolis Teamsters, who, he feared, might attempt to organize broader labor union opposition to his pro-war policy. So in response to his friend Tobin's plea, Roosevelt had the FBI raid the Minneapolis headquarters of the Socialist Workers Party, while the Justice Department prepared to indict the Trotskyist Teamster leaders. Henry A. Schweinhaut, a special assistant attorney general sent to Minneapolis from Washington, DC, told the newspapers that the US government intended to prosecute 'leaders of the Socialist Workers Party who have gained control of a legitimate labor union to use it for illegitimate purposes' and for 'seditious conspiracy to advocate the overthrow of the government of the United States by force and violence.'⁴

A month later, in July 1941, the government indicted twenty-eight individuals under a Civil War statute and the new Smith Act, though charges against five were later dropped. All those indicted were leaders of the Socialist Workers Party or of Local 544, including the Dunne brothers and Farrell Dobbs. Carl Skoglund, who was not a US citizen, was arrested on a deportation warrant issued by the US Immigration and Naturalization Service and jailed. In addition, four other Local 544 leaders, including Miles Dunne and Kelly Postal, were indicted in a separate case on charges of grand larceny and embezzlement, basically for having transferred the assets of Local 544-IBT to Local 544-CIO.

Local 544-CIO was virtually destroyed. It was under physical attack by an army of thugs. It had lost its legal right to represent workers in negotiations with employers, who were busy negotiating new contracts with Tobin's Teamsters. The union's officers were under indictment on serious criminal and political charges. Besieged, the leaders made the difficult decision to urge most members to attempt to get their jobs back and rejoin Teamster Local 544, while keeping Local 544-CIO alive as a skeleton operation.

The radicals waged a spirited political defense, supported by the Congress of Industrial Organizations, Labor's Non-Partisan League and the American Civil Liberties Union, but they were unable to build a movement strong enough to stop their prosecution. The sedition trial began on 27 October

1941, and the verdict was brought in on 1 December. Of the twenty-three individuals on trial, eighteen were found guilty of advocating armed revolution – that is, they were found guilty because of their ideas and because they expressed those ideas in free speech, not for any act of violence. Twelve received sixteen-month jail terms, and six were sentenced to prison for a year and a day. Most of the officers of Local 544 were actually acquitted. The verdict was appealed to the US Court of Appeals for the Eighth Circuit, which upheld their conviction. The eighteen petitioned the US Supreme Court, arguing that their right to freely express their views had been denied, but the Supreme Court refused to hear the case.[5]

The government attempted to deport Carl Skoglund to Sweden, but that proved impossible because of the war, so he was held prisoner on Ellis Island or in prisons on shore. Kelly Postal was convicted in the larceny and embezzlement trial on 24 April 1942, and sentenced to a term of five years. And in the midst of this depressing situation Grant Dunne, the man who had originally recruited Farrell Dobbs to the Teamsters union in the coalyards in 1934, committed suicide.

On 31 December 1943 Farrell Dobbs went to prison, together with his comrades. Had they acted contrary to their principles, he wrote, ' ... they might conceivably have degenerated into business agents of the ordinary type found in the labor movement.' Instead they had maintained their socialist principles, their opposition to the war, and their belief in 'rank and file control over the trade unions, in keeping with basic democratic principles.'[6]

The legacy of this attack on the Minneapolis Teamsters was to be the corruption of one of America's largest and most important unions. Once the radicals in Minneapolis were out of the way, the leadership of the International Brotherhood of Teamsters was destined to pass to Dave Beck.

Businessman Beck

Over the years Beck's belief in the 'sanctity of the contract', his opposition to strikes and his attacks on the CIO had won him many friends among the employers. He was a good friend of William Short, the head of the Cleaners and Dryers Association (and former president of the Washington State Federation of Labor). He palled around with Emil Sick, the owner of Sick's Brewery. And he was a buddy of Eric A. Johnston, head of the Columbia Electric and Manufacturing Co. and for many years president of the US Chamber of Commerce.

Even as Beck rose in power and prestige within the Teamsters union, the business activities of Beck and his family continued to expand. Beck owned Northwest Securities Corp. Inc., which provided financing and insurance for auto sales companies whose mechanics were usually organized by the Teamsters union. His KellerBlock Corporation owned a local landmark, Grosvenor House. Beck was involved in the real estate business, owning a parking lot and a gas station near the Seattle Teamsters building. Beck's B. and B. Investment Co. did business with Occidental Life Insurance, Co., which at one time bid for and won 75 percent of the Western Conference Teamster's health and welfare coverage. Beverage and beer distribution was another Beck family business, also organized by the Teamsters. While others argued that there was a conflict of interest between Beck's role as Teamster leader and his businesses that employed Teamsters, Beck himself denied any conflict: 'What the hell? If I believed in free enterprise, isn't it natural that I should try to use it for my own financial advantage?'

Beck the Union Buster

In the 1940s, Beck began to engage in strikebreaking and raiding on such a scale that he won the ignominious reputation as the labor movement's union buster. One of the most notable incidents occurred during the Oakland General Strike of 1946. The strike began when workers saw police guarding scab trucks taking goods to the Kahn's and Hastings department stores, which had been struck by the mostly women clerks of Department Store and Specialty Employees Union, Local 1265. The incident led to a spontaneous strike spreading from one group of workers to another and becoming a general strike in the city of Oakland.

The idea of a sympathy strike to support the women retail clerks appalled Dave Beck, who sent a telegram ordering Teamsters back to work in order 'to break the strike', which he characterized as a revolutionary attempt 'to overthrow the government'. Several local Teamster leaders ignored Beck's telegram because the rank and file supported the strike. Nevertheless, the strike collapsed after the third day without any concessions from the management of the Kahn's and Hastings department stores. At the same time, Beck ordered Teamsters to cross the AFL Retail Clerks picket lines in Los Angeles and break a strike there.

Breaking the Oakland General Strike was perhaps the most flagrant of Beck's union-busting activities, but there were many others. During the 1930s and 1940s, California cannery workers, many of them Mexican women, had succeeded in organizing a cannery workers union, the United Cannery, Agricultural, Packing and Allied Workers of America (UCAPAWA/FTA). In 1945 Beck decided to smash that union and replace it with the Teamsters. He reportedly said, 'You'd better see that you come in with us or otherwise there won't be any cannery union.'[7]

When 15,000 machinists struck Boeing in 1948, Beck ordered Teamster scabs through the picket lines and broke the strike. John C. Cort, writer for the liberal Catholic newspaper *Commonweal*, referred to him as 'Beck the Strikebreaker' and told his readers that Beck was a 'good subject for prayer'. During the same period Beck raided the CIO-organized Honeywell Corporation in Minneapolis. The Minnesota State CIO published a pamphlet entitled 'Dave Beck ... Strike Breaker and Traitor to Trade Unionism'. In the late 1940s and early 1950s Beck helped Sears, Roebuck get rid of a militant ILWU local, only part of a long Teamster fight with the Longshoremen that continued from 1947 until 1953.

When the National Farm Labor Union called a strike in the Imperial Valley of California on 25 May 1951, the Teamsters broke the strike in order to get the support of Charles Gibbs of the Associated Farmers to stop an anti-labor bill in the legislature. Newspaper columnist Murray Kempton wrote at the time, 'It is hard to imagine a more popular strike: Associated Farmers has a long-standing reputation as slavers and starvers. If anyone needs a union, it's the pickers who work for them.' Yet Beck had 'kicked a struggling and altogether worthy union in the stomach for his own small advancement.'[8]

Beck's good reputation among businessmen was based on his record of enforcing the contract and his reluctance to strike. A study by J.B. Gillingham in the 1950s found that since Beck had organized them or taken them over there had been no strikes by his laundry and dry cleaning workers, dairy workers, bakery workers, beer and beverage distributors, or local or over-the-road drivers. And of course Beck never engaged in sympathy strikes.[9] Gillingham believed there were so few strikes because the Teamsters did not make demands beyond the industry's ability to pay, were reasonable in bargaining, and because the employers respected the Teamsters' power to strike. However, the employers and Beck both recognized that as long as no strikes were called the rank and file of the union could not feel its economic power and was unlikely to challenge the union bureaucracy or the bosses.

President Beck

By the mid-1940s Tobin had begun a long, slow process of retirement. In 1942 the Teamster Executive Board bought Tobin a luxurious home in Miami Beach, and in 1945 another in a Boston suburb. In addition, the union provided Tobin with a Cadillac, a chauffeur, a handyman, and a full-time maid, and paid all the expenses for the maintenance of his homes. By then Tobin was old, sick and tired, and gradually Dave Beck began to take over the affairs of the union. In 1947 Tobin appointed Beck to a special new post, the executive vice-president of the International Brotherhood of Teamsters. Finally, at the 1952 convention, Tobin declined to run again for president, and Beck, supported by Jimmy Hoffa, was elected International general president. Tobin was elected president emeritus, and his salary was raised from $30,000 to $50,000 a year.[10] At the same time the number of vice-presidents was increased from nine to eleven, dues were raised, and the president's salary was increased from $30,000 to $50,000 a year, though Beck told the convention delegates, 'I don't need the money. I've been very successful in business investments.'

Modernizing the Teamsters

As soon as he became International general president, Beck set about modernizing the structure of the Teamsters. First, Beck moved the IBT headquarters from Indianapolis to Washington, where he built a $5 million headquarters known as 'the marble palace'. Speaking at the dedication of the building, at the high point of his career, Beck vowed, 'We're not going to get fat and lazy.'[11]

Tobin had been a lifelong Democrat, but Beck moved the union in a more conservative direction, supporting Republican candidates for president in 1948 and 1952 and backing Republican candidate Dwight Eisenhower in 1956.[12] Eventually, the Teamsters became the only major union to consistently support the Republican Party at the national level.

Beck also revamped the organization. He created Eastern and Southern conferences and established trade divisions such as dairy, grocery, and warehouse divisions and a dozen others to rationalize the union's organizational work and its contract bargaining. These measures centralized power in the hands of the International union's Executive Board and its president and the union's paid staff. This was all the more true because so many scores of locals were in trusteeship at one time or another, while elected local leaders lived in fear that if they did not toe the line Beck might throw them out and put one of his lieutenants in charge.

Beck was utterly contemptuous of the men and women he had been so successful in organizing into the Teamsters. He considered them ignorant and not entitled to any voice in the union. 'I'm paid $25,000 a year to run this outfit', he said. 'Unions are big business. Why should truck drivers and bottle washers be allowed to make big decisions affecting union policy? Would any corporation allow it?' Quite consistently, Beck viewed union office as property to be inherited; he argued that union leaders ought to be able to pass their jobs on to their sons: 'If a business executive can do this, why can't a labor leader?'[13]

Beck brought to the IBT the same business methods he pursued in his private dealings. He took the $39 million Teamster treasury out of government bonds, bank deposits, and savings and loans and hired an investment counselor to buy corporate stocks and bonds. Many labor union members

AP/Wide World

Dave Beck (left) receives a congratulatory pat on the head from Daniel J. Tobin at the IBT convention in October 1952 after succeeding Tobin as general president.

considered these investments wrong because it meant that the union became an employer, and the Teamster constitution expressly forbade the owning of corporate stocks and bonds. But Beck was not bothered by such scruples. Sometimes Beck used the union treasury as a bank for the employers, such as when he made a $1.5 million loan to Fruehauf Trailer Company.

Despite anti-union labor legislation such as the Taft-Hartley Act, the union continued to grow. One of the most significant developments of the 1950s was the organization of Montgomery Ward by Don Peters of Teamster Local 743 with the help of Teamster leader Harold Gibbons in St. Louis and Jimmy Hoffa in Detroit. The organization of Wards brought several thousand new members into the Teamsters union, which had by then over 1 million members, making it the largest union in the country.

In the early 1950s discussions began that eventually led to the merger in 1955 of the American Federation of Labor and the Congress of Industrial Organizations under the leadership of George Meany. Beck opposed the merger on the grounds that there were many unresolved jurisdictional disputes between the Teamsters and CIO unions.[14] His real concern was that the merger would lead to a 'no-raiding pact' that would prevent the Teamsters from stealing shops away from CIO unions as they had in the past.

Beck's Friend in 'Labor Relations'

Under Beck's leadership, the Teamsters union became an ever more corrupt operation. When Arkansas Senator John L. McClellan's Select Committee on Improper Activities in the Labor or Management Field (better known as the Senate Rackets Committee) began to investigate the Teamsters in the early 1950s, it came out that one of Beck's buddies was Nathan W. Shefferman, the head of Labor Relations Associates of Chicago, Inc.; Shefferman described himself as a 'labor relations consultant'. In fact, Shefferman, who frequently traveled with Beck around the country and overseas, was a professional union buster; Sears, Roebuck & Co. had set Shefferman up in business and remained his main client.

Another of Shefferman's main jobs was to act as the middleman for payoffs from employers to Teamster union officials. George Kamenow, Shefferman's man in Detroit, took payoffs from businessmen to stop Teamster organizing campaigns or strikes. Using employer money, Kamenow took Teamster officials on fishing trips and to baseball and football games, and paid their expenses at union conventions. At times when employers were being organized by some other union, Shefferman would recommend that they instead recognize the Teamsters, which was more 'friendly' and could give them a sweetheart contract, often with wages close to the minimum wage.[15]

Beck and Meany

As the McClellan committee hearings on labor and management racketeering wore on, many union officials, including many Teamsters, were summoned to testify. Beck was asked to appear voluntarily, but declined to do so, setting off a series of events that would lead to the expulsion of the Teamsters from the AFL-CIO.

George Meany, president of the recently merged AFL-CIO, saw McClellan as anti-labor fanatic, but at the same time Meany was well aware that some labor officials were engaged in illegal and unethical activities that could cost the labor movement public support. Nevertheless, Meany was staggered when Robert F. Kennedy, chief counsel for the committee, informed him in early in January 1957 that the committee had the goods on Beck, and that Beck was a thief who had stolen from his union and had taken payoffs from employers. The Teamsters were the largest and most powerful union in the AFL-CIO, and many other unions were dependent on them. Meany did not look forward to a confrontation on the issue of Teamster corruption. On 28 January 1957 Meany introduced a resolution in the AFL-CIO Executive Council calling for cooperation with the McClellan committee. Meany also presented another resolution stating that, while any ordinary individual was entitled to the protection of the Fifth Amendment, a labor leader who invoked it had 'no right to continue to hold office in his union.'[16]

Beck, who had already told all Teamster officials to invoke the Fifth Amendment, was furious. 'I have no use for racketeers', he said, 'but I will be goddamned if I am going to be a party under any conditions with interfering with men's constitutional rights.'[17] Meany argued with Beck, telling him that if they did not cooperate with the government the situation would get even worse for labor. 'You don't know the legislation you will get', he said. 'You will be under government control.'[18] At first, several other union leaders supported Beck, but Meany pushed the argument until at last the motion passed by a vote of twenty-two to one, with only Beck voting against it.

The McClellan Committee Case Against Beck

After the meeting, Beck fled the country to avoid appearing before the committee, claiming that he was sick; he first headed to the West Indies and then to Europe. Meanwhile, the McClellan Committee went after him, calling witnesses and reviewing documents. Robert F. Kennedy summarized the testimony on behalf of the committee.

First, Beck had taken at least $370,000 from the Western Conference of Teamsters; then, in order to pay the money back, he had borrowed $200,000 from the Freuhauf Trailer Company; then to repay Freuhauf he had sold his Seattle mansion to the Teamsters for $163,000, while continuing to live in the house. Second, Beck had given Shefferman $85,000 of Teamster money to buy things for Beck and his family and friends. Third, Beck spent $150,000 in Teamster money on his Seattle mansion to build a swimming pool and another home nearby for his son. Fourth, Beck had many business relationships with employers, such as those in the beer and beverage distribution business.

Perhaps the most disgusting disclosure concerned money contributed by Teamster members and intended for the widow of Beck's friend, Western Conference of Teamsters publicity director Ray Leheney. Cheating the widow, Beck used the money in a real estate deal on which he made several thousand dollars.[19] When Beck finally appeared before the committee on 26 March 1957, he took the Fifth Amendment almost 100 times. Meany then moved against Beck, and in May 1957 Beck was suspended from the AFL-CIO Executive Council. At the same time that the McClellan Committee was investigating Beck, his personal finances and union finances were also being examined by federal investigator Claude J. Watson, assisted by fifty other federal agents. On 12 March 1957 Waston turned in a 445-page report concluding that Beck had not paid taxes on all of his income; a Tacoma grand jury then indicted Beck for tax evasion.

Beck was brought before Judge George Boldt for a trial that lasted several months, though the Teamster leader never testified. In the end, Beck was convicted, and Judge Boldt stated in summary, 'A fair appraisal of the evidence shows beyond the glimmer of a doubt that, as an incident of his tax fraud, Mr. Beck plundered his union, his intimate associates, and in some instances personal friends, most of whom quite readily would have freely given him almost anything he asked.'[20] An appeal failed and Beck was sentenced to five years in federal prison.

How Beck Changed the Teamsters

Dave Beck left the Teamsters a very different organization from the one he had found. Using the techniques of organizing from above he had brought tens of thousands of new members into the union. The IBT had become an industrial union, organizing everyone involved in industries like trucking, warehousing and food processing. To deal with the new industrial organization, Beck had reorganized the union's structure, creating the conferences and trade divisions. The union was no longer the loose federation of locals that it had been in the early days of the Tobin administration.

As a Teamster leader, Beck tried to establish a kind of partnership with the employers aimed at stabilizing the industry, raising profits, and thus raising wages for some of the Teamster members. He opposed other unions that might threaten his relationship to those employers and his position in the labor movement, and the Teamsters became the 'friendly' union that the employers 'could live with'. At the same time, Beck and other Teamster union officials like him came increasingly to identify with the employers and their problems, to share the employers' concerns, to adopt their lifestyles, and ultimately to become businessmen themselves. While not excusing Beck from his crimes against his own members, his dictatorship over the union and his use of union funds, there is much truth to the view that it was the employers who created Dave Beck and his Teamsters union. It was they who wanted a barrier between themselves and more militant labor unions, it was they who wanted sweetheart contracts and special deals. But if the employers were 'a corrupting influence', Beck was only too willing to be corrupted.

Jimmy Hoffa

With Beck in prison, Hoffa made his bid to take over the union, using the base he had built in Michigan and the Midwest during the previous twenty years. In 1940, at the age of twenty-seven, Hoffa had become the Central States Negotiating Chairman, and in 1941 was elected the vice-president of the Central States Council. When he returned to Detroit in 1941, Hoffa found the CIO was attempting recruit the carhaulers out of the Teamsters-AFL, and this led to another war between the conservative Teamsters in the AFL and the more radical CIO. In his *The Hoffa Wars*, Dan Moldea claims that Hoffa defeated the CIO with Mafia muscle provided by Santo Perrone, Angelo Meli, Frank Coppola and other criminal figures.[21] The more important factor in Hoffa's victory was the reluctance of the United Auto Workers union to become involved in the struggle in a big way. When the 1941 convention of the CIO was held in Detroit, John L. Lewis was defeated and the new CIO president, Phillip Murray, called for an end to the raiding of rival labor organizations.

During World War II, Hoffa formed the Michigan Council of Teamsters, made up of all the locals in the state. Hoffa was elected its first chairman, and under his leadership the Michigan Council of Teamsters fought against both recalcitrant employers and local union officials to create a state-wide trucking industry contract. At the end of the war, the union was finally on a solid financial and organizational basis, and Hoffa's organizers fanned out from Detroit throughout the Midwest and into the South. In 1952 the Central States Drivers Council was extended into Ohio, and shortly afterwards into the Southern states. In the 1950s, carriers rarely covered more than a few states and therefore depended on interlines, or trans-shipments between one trucking company and another, to complete a shipment. The union had a stranglehold on a company if it could break the interlines. One way the union could disrupt interlines was for union workers to refuse to move the freight of non-union or struck companies, a practice known as refusing 'hot cargo'. The employers were virtually powerless in the face of the union's strike and boycott strategy.

Another way Hoffa could put pressure on an unorganized trucking company was to get organized companies to refuse to accept interlines from the non-union company. Or Hoffa could put pressure on shippers to refuse to ship with an unorganized company. The main source of pressure on the companies available to Hoffa was the 'open-end grievance procedure'. Unlike most union contracts, which called for arbitration as the final stage of the grievance process, the Teamsters' freight contract at that time gave the union the right to strike over grievances.

In reality, the strike weapon was used not only to solve grievances, but also to pressure trucking companies to boycott interlines as Hoffa demanded. Although Hoffa used boycotts and other forms of pressure, at the center of his strategy was the strike, or the threat of a strike. Secondary and tertiary boycotts, combined with the threat of a strike, succeeded in bringing most carriers into the union.

As a result of the Taft-Hartley Act, the Landrum-Griffin Act and various National Labor Relations Board decisions, the use of 'hot cargo' and other forms of secondary boycott was severely restricted. Hoffa was able to get around this by negotiating common expiration dates for contracts in different areas. If a carrier refused to raise wages in one area, it could be struck in another area because the contract had expired simultaneously, thus evading the charge of a carrying on a secondary boycott. As more and more companies were organized, the web of relationships that Hoffa controlled became ever wider and thicker, and it became more and more difficult for carriers to resist; they capitulated more rapidly as time went on. It was the union's power over Midwestern trucking companies that made it possible to organize the South quickly.

Like Beck, Hoffa changed from organizing from below, by organizing the rank-and-file workers, to organizing from above, by organizing the employers. Although most workers wanted the higher wages, and later the pension and health and welfare benefits that the union won, some of those workers had never had any contact with a union official until they were actually in the union. As result of Hoffa's organizing efforts, tens of thousands of new members were brought into the Teamsters union, the Central States Drivers Council freight contract had been extended to twenty-five states, thirteen of which were in the anti-union Southern states – one of the most successful union organizing campaigns ever carried out in the South. Hoffa's principal goal was to bring about uniform wages and working conditions under all the Teamster freight contracts, and by April 1963 Hoffa announced that the union had achieved '85 percent of uniformity'.[22]

The growing power of the union made it possible to make greater demands on the employer, not only in terms of wages but in benefits as well. During and after World War II, several unions had sought pension benefits for their members, including garment workers, miners and steelworkers. In 1955 Hoffa negotiated the union's first pension plan, covering 100,000 workers in the Midwestern and Southern freight industry. The employers paid only $2.00 per worker per week initially, which amounted, however, to almost $1 million per month. The employer contribution rose to $4.00 in 1960 and to $7.00 in 1964.[23]

The Taft-Hartley Act required that pension funds be governed by equal numbers of union and employer trustees, and this requirement gave Hoffa effective control of the pension funds, given the divisions among the employers. When employer pension fund representatives refused to go along with Hoffa's plan for investing the funds, Hoffa could use the open-end grievance procedure and the threat of a strike to bring them into line.

The benefit funds could have been of tremendous value to the Teamsters and the entire labor movement. They might have financed projects in housing, health care or other programs. But Hoffa instead turned the pension fund over to the mob, bringing in the Union Casualty Company as actuary for the fund – a company with connections to the old Capone mob in Chicago. Unlike other pension funds, which mostly invested in government and corporate bonds and stocks, Hoffa directed the Teamster pension fund loans mostly into mortgages and real estate deals. Many of these loans went to investments in hotels, motels, shopping centers, land development and spe-cial-purpose buildings in Florida and Nevada,[24] including Las Vegas gam-bling casinos with ties to the Mafia. These Teamster loans frequently carried lower interest rates than similar loans from other pension funds, because Hoffa wanted the fund to make friends as well as money.

Loans were given to Teamster employers, Teamster officials and mobsters. For example, John Gottlieb, one of the signers of the first freight contract and a stockholder in a big Illinois trucking company, got a loan of $1,150,000 for a laundry company he owned in Los Angeles. His brother, James Gottlieb, another trucking company owner, got a $5 million loan for the Dunes Hotel, the co-owner of which was Major A. Riddle, another employer with Teamster contracts. Homer 'Dutch' Woxberg, an important Western Teamsters official, received $700,000 from the Central States Pen-sion Fund to set up a taxicab company in Las Vegas. One of the biggest recipients of Teamster loans was syndicate figure Morris 'Moe' Dalitz, who owned the Desert Inn and Stardust hotels; Dalitz also owned laundries in Detroit and was a Teamster employer.

To Hoffa, the union and its pension funds were a business like any other, to be operated for profit even when doing so might hurt labor unions and the workers that belonged to them. For example, Hoffa arranged a loan of $200,000 from union funds to J.W. Thomas Company in Minneapolis, despite the fact that a long and bitter strike by the Retail Clerks International Association was in progress. On another occasion, Hoffa arranged a loan of $2,980,000 from the Teamster Pension Fund to a toy manufacturer, the Auburn Rubber Company in Deming, New Mexico. The Auburn plant in Deming was a runaway shop that had closed its union-organized plant in Indiana and moved to New Mexico to find cheap, non-union labor. The United Rubber Workers Union followed the company to New Mexico and began an organizing drive; in response, Hoffa sent in Teamster organizers to keep the Rubber Workers out.[25]

With the success of his organizing drives and the development of the pension funds, Hoffa's stature and power grew within the union. He received his first International union office in 1943, when he became an International trustee, and in 1952 he was made an International vice-president. Hoffa wanted to be the top Teamster, and his way was cleared by the resignation of Teamster General President Dave Beck.

However, Hoffa was himself a target of the McClellan Committee, and he was called to testify before it on 20 August 1957. He continued to testify before the committee for several days, cross-examination being conducted by committee chief counsel Robert F. Kennedy, the man who had become Hoffa's archenemy. This cross-examination revealed that Hoffa had engaged in a number of unethical and illegal activities, but most damaging were revelations that he, in partnership with Owen Bert Brennan and other Teamster officials, had become the owner of various trucking companies.

Like Beck before him, Hoffa had used his position in the union to build a personal fortune. Trucking company officials and labor consultants were happy to lend Hoffa money, obviously believing that such loans would improve their relations with the Teamsters, even if no quid pro quo was involved. Jack Keeshin, the Chicago trucking company owner with whom the union had originally negotiated the first regional freight contract, lent Hoffa $5,000. Likewise, Jack Bushkin, a labor relations consultant representing companies dealing with the Teamsters, lent Hoffa $5,000.

Hoffa also extracted loans from companies or individuals dependent on the Teamsters union, such as a $25,000 loan at no interest from Harold Mark, the accountant and auditor of the Central States Pension Fund. That loan was apparently a kickback for a $100,000 loan at 6 percent interest made to Mark by Teamster Locals 299 and 337. Another accountant, Herbert L. Grosberg, lent Hoffa $11,500. Hoffa borrowed another $25,000 from Henry Lower, a real estate promotor involved in the Sun Valley, Florida development that was sponsored by the Teamsters union. That loan was apparently a kickback for a loan from a Detroit bank where the Teamsters had large deposits. Hoffa also borrowed $18,000 from Teamster business agents who were dependent upon him for their jobs.

Some of the money Hoffa borrowed was used to set himself up in business, frequently in partnership with trucking company owners or executives. The biggest scandal involved the Test Fleet company. Hoffa and Brennan, in cooperation with Commercial Carriers, created the Test Fleet trucking company and registered it under their wives' names. Commercial Carriers gave Test Fleet money to buy equipment and a contract to transport Cadillac cars. Out of an investment of $4,000 Hoffa and Brennan reaped a profit of $125,000 in 1949 alone. The committee heard evidence that Hoffa did not always fairly represent workers employed by companies with which he was doing business – for example, that he had not fought for the jobs of some workers fired by Commercial Carriers.

Hoffa acquired interests in other trucking companies in Detroit that had contracts with Local 299, sometimes in partnership with Dale Patrick, a nephew of Frank Fitzsimmons. Fitzsimmons was then a business agent in Local 299. Hoffa also bought large blocks of stock in companies with which the Teamsters had contracts, including 400 shares of A.C.F. Wrigley Company, a Michigan supermarket firm; 600 shares of McLean Industries, owner of McLean trucking company; and $25,000 worth of stock in Fruehauf.

As Hoffa himself became a businessman, he treated the union and its pension funds as if they, too, were simply businesses. During Hoffa's tenure in office, union monies were invested, lent, and given away for a variety of corrupt purposes. Sometimes loans went to Teamster insiders, like a $75,000 loan by Teamster Locals 299 and 337 to the Marbery Construction Company, which was jointly owned by Teamster accountant Herbert Grosberg and Teamster attorney George Fitzgerald. Teamster Local 337 lent $50,000 to the Northville Downs Racetrack, where Hoffa's friend Owen Bert Brennan raced his harness horses. Locals 299 and 377 purchased the home of Paul 'The Waiter' Ricca of the Capone gang.

Gradually, the union began to move closer to the Mafia. Hoffa often accused Robert F. Kennedy of attempting to convict him through guilt by association, and claimed that as the head of an important union it was his job to know everyone who might affect the industries in which his members worked. That 'duty' accounted for his contacts with other union officials, employer and mobsters. Hoffa repeatedly denied that the Mafia was involved in the union.

However, those who followed the McClellan hearings could not help but see a pattern emerge, and it was a pattern of deep mutual involvement of the Teamsters union and the Mafia. As Jonathan Kwitny wrote many years later in his book *Vicious Circles*, 'It was during the late 1940s ... that the Syndicate bought its ticket to eventual full control over the Teamsters. The Chicago Mafia, the old Capone organizations, made a deal with a rising young union leader from Detroit – Jimmy Hoffa (by all available evidence, Hoffa was not a Mafia member himself). The Mob would support Hoffa in his campaigns for Teamster power, and he would be their man.'[26]

Early on, Hoffa began to give insurance business from the Michigan Conference of Teamsters to Paul 'Red' Dorfman of the Chicago Capone mob. There had always been Mafia figures in the Teamsters, but during the Hoffa years their role grew in importance. There was Joey Glimco, the head of Chicago Taxicab Local 777, who was part of what had been the Al Capone mob; Anthony 'Tony Pro' Provenzano, New Jersey mobster and Teamster leader; William Presser in Ohio, who was closely associated with Mafia figure Louis 'Babe' Triscaro, for whom Hoffa once organized a testimonial dinner. Presser was the head of the Ohio Teamsters, and Triscaro was second in command in Joint Council 41. Hoffa was also associated with Lou Farrell, a Des Moines, Iowa gangster, supposedly part of the Capone mob, who was also involved in labor relations. Another Hoffa associate was Angelo Meli, a Detroit mob figure whose career had begun during prohibition.

In addition, Hoffa put many gangsters in positions of power in the Teamsters union. For example, there was Eugene 'Jimmie' James, who was accused of stealing almost $1 million from the Laundry Workers International Union Welfare Fund. Hoffa made James the head of Juke Box Local 985 in Detroit and lent him over $2,000 to start up the union; James in return placed Hoffa's and Brennan's wives on the local union's payroll under their maiden names of Poszywak and Johnson. The McClellan hearings also demonstrated that Hoffa had brought many petty criminals into the union, men with records resulting not from arrests on organizing drives or picket lines, but from illegal activities such as robbery.

Hoffa himself became involved in business with the Mafia figures who were mixed up in the Teamster pension funds. For example, he went into business with Allen Dorfman, the son of Capone mobster 'Red' Dorfman and the general agent of the Union Casualty Company, which handled the Teamster insurance fund of which Hoffa was a trustee. Together with Allen Dorfman and his wife, Hoffa bought the Jack O'Lantern Lodge in Wisconsin, also known as Joll Properties. Joll Properties in turn received a loan from an insurance company retained by the Central States Conference of Teamsters. With all of these entanglements between top Teamsters and Mafia godfathers, it was impossible by the end of the Hoffa years to see where one ended and the other began.

The McClellan hearings also revealed that Hoffa had brought into the union more than a dozen local unions controlled by New York gangster Johnny Dio. Dio was associated with the Dorfmans and tied to other mob figures in other unions. He had come to control the United Auto Workers – AFL (not connected with the United Auto Workers union in the CIO, headed in those days by Walter Reuther). Dio's organizations were unions in name only and served no other function than to extort money from employers and workers.

When Hoffa was preparing to run for general president of the Teamsters in 1957, Johnny Dio created seven new Teamster locals to give Hoffa control of the New York delegation. Many of these were 'paper' locals that had no real membership. These revelations of Hoffa's control of the upcoming convention through the phony votes of paper locals led a group of Teamsters to seek an injunction to prevent the convention from taking place. A committee of thirteen Teamsters from New York and New Jersey led by John Cunningham, a dissident milk driver, and represented by attorney Godfrey Schmidt, sought an injunction from Judge F. Dickinson Letts of the District of Columbia to prevent the convention from taking place on the grounds that it was rigged. The judge granted a temporary restraining order, but the Teamsters took the issue to the Court of Appeals, which vacated the injunction: the convention went on as scheduled.

Government Monitors Oversee the Union

The 1957 Teamster convention opened on 20 September in Miami Beach, and the AFL-CIO sent representatives to explain why the Federation was suspending the Teamsters until such time as they could 'eliminate corrupt influences from positions of leadership', but the delegates refused to hear them. Ignoring the McClellan Committee and defying the AFL-CIO, the

AP/Wide World

Jimmy Hoffa (left) and Anthony 'Tony Pro' Provenzano at a New Jersey Teamster conference.

convention then proceeded to elect James R. Hoffa the fourth general president of the Teamsters union. Two months later the AFL-CIO Executive Council expelled the Teamsters.

Meanwhile, on 23 October 1957, Cunningham's committee of thirteen Teamsters sought another injunction from Judge Letts prohibiting Hoffa and other newly elected officials from taking office. Letts granted the injunction, the appeals court upheld it, and a trial on the merits of the petition was set for November. In the meantime, Hoffa would take office as the 'provisional' general president of the Teamsters. Hoffa testified before Judge Letts for twenty-two days, and finally his attorney, Edward Bennett Williams, suggested that Hoffa take office as provisional general president, to be supervised by a board of monitors made up of one person representing the union, one representing the committee of thirteen rank and filers, and one neutral party. The court agreed, and the monitorship was established for one year. The monitors were Martin F. O'Donoghue, appointed by the court, Godfrey P. Schmidt, chosen by the rank-and-file committee, Daniel B. Maher, chosen by the Teamsters.

While Robert Kennedy liked to refer to these men as 'thirteen rank-and-file Teamsters', this was far from a rank-and-file opposition movement. The moving force was the attorney, Schmidt, who had been a labor advisor to Cardinal Spellman in New York and had helped him try to break a strike by gravediggers in Catholic cemeteries. In addition, he was also the president of AWARE, a group that worked to prevent Communist actors from working. Once involved in the Teamster case, Schmidt quickly established close ties to Robert Kennedy, who provided him with information and advice. Not long after that, O'Donoghue, another one of the board of monitors, also established contact with Kennedy. This gave the Robert Kennedy influence over a majority of the board.[27] The board of monitors soon underwent various modifications. Schmidt was forced to resign when it was revealed that he also represented employers who dealt with the Teamsters, and he was replaced by an FBI agent named Terrence McShane, and then by an attorney from Schmidt's law office by the name of Lawrence Smith.[28]

The monitors never succeeded in exerting any appreciable influence over Hoffa or the union, and Hoffa eventually succeeded in winning over John Cunningham, the leader of the rank-and-file committee. Robert Kennedy claimed that Hoffa and the Teamsters union had bought off Cunningham, a charge Hoffa denied.[29] When at the end of one year Schmidt sought to extend the monitorship, the Teamsters argued that the members' democratic rights as guaranteed under the new Landrum-Griffin Act were being violated, and that the monitorship was costing the union $700,000 a year in attorneys' fees and other costs. The Court of Appeals agreed with the Teamsters and rejected the extension of the monitorship, allowing the Teamsters to go ahead with their planned convention. In 1961 Hoffa was reelected general president, winning election again in 1966.

Jonathan Kwitny writes in *Vicious Circles* that 'some revisionist historians in recent years have painted Kennedy's pursuit of Hoffa as persecution. ... It wasn't persecution. Hoffa deserved everything he got. His administration was fundamentally corrupt.'[30] Kwitny, however, misses the point: granted that Hoffa was corrupt, the question is, Did Robert Kennedy in his pursuit of Hoffa go beyond the limits of the law and of good judgement, violating Hoffa's civil rights? Or, if Kennedy simply wanted to convict Hoffa because he was corrupt, is it not possible that others supported Kennedy because they wanted Hoffa's head for other reasons?

Hoffa made the argument that Kennedy wanted to punish the Teamsters for their support of Republican Dwight Eisenhower over Democrat Adlai Stevenson in the 1956 election, while at the same time winning approval from anti-union Southern Democrats. At the same time, Hoffa argued, Robert Kennedy's role in the McClellan hearings and in the pursuit of Hoffa would help to advance his brother John in his pursuit of the presidency of the United States.[31]

Robert Kennedy as counsel for a congressional committee certainly went beyond legal limits and showed poor judgement in his pursuit of Hoffa. Kennedy's attack on the Teamsters and his violation of Hoffa's rights created a precedent dangerous for other unions and labor leaders. Whatever the ambitions of the Kennedy family, certainly some businessmen and some conservatives in Congress found the growing power of the Teamsters union a threat. While the ostensible purpose of the McClellan hearings was to stop corruption, some congressmen wanted the hearings to stop the growth of the labor unions, and above all of the Teamsters. In retrospect, it certainly seems that the government investigations had little impact on corruption but did diminish the stature of the unions and consequently their economic and political power.

In any case, the government's first attempt at a takeover of the Teamsters union had proved to be a fiasco. The idea of government monitorship of the union was flawed from the beginning. It presumed that Congress or a judge could 'fix up' the union by simply changing or controlling the leadership. But the corrupt union bureaucracy was a result of the relationship of those leaders to the workers, and of the union to the employers and the government. It is impossible to 'fix up' a union by simply tinkering with the leadership. Without a change in the rank and file, without action by the rank and file, the genuine reform of the union was impossible.

The only chance for the real reform of the Teamsters lay in a rank-and-file movement for union democracy, but as Hoffa had centralized bargaining power, so he had also centralized political power until most of it lay in the hands of the general president. The growth of the multistate freight agreement and the creation of the pension funds provided Hoffa with economic and political power that his predecessors had never possessed, and that he was prepared to use to keep himself and his associates in power. At the same time, the growth of Mafia influence in the International and in many big cities, and the presence of criminals among the union's business agents, tended to diminish local expressions of dissidence or opposition.

Jimmy Hoffa's great goal was the National Master Freight Agreement, one contract covering all freight workers from coast to coast. There were many benefits to be gained from such a contract: the Teamsters union would effectively regulate the industry, non-union employers could be virtually eliminated, and wages would be taken out of competition. However, to achieve that goal Hoffa had to overcome resistance in areas where there was a strong sense of local autonomy. This was particularly difficult where strong local Teamster organizations had been able to win contracts that were superior to Hoffa's Central States agreement.

The San Francisco Bay Area's Locals 85 and 70 both had contracts superior to that which Hoffa had negotiated, and when he tried to take control of their bargaining in 1960 the Bay Area locals rejected him. Hoffa was furious with the Bay Area Teamsters, and he brought all his power to bear on them. At the 1961 Teamster convention he changed the constitution so that all locals could be forced to bargain together if a majority of them voted to do so. In that way his control over the many small town local unions would allow him to impose his will on San Francisco.

The Bay Area Teamsters held a mass meeting to protest Hoffa's actions, and in Oakland Local 70 2,000 members passed a resolution criticizing 'the actions of James Hoffa and his rubberstamp officials who are blackjacking and intimidating the rank-and-file members of Local 70, so that we will fall in line with his Western States' wage agreement. We condemn and repudiate the dictatorial power of James Hoffa. ... '[32]

However, Hoffa was determined to keep Bay Area Teamsters from negotiating a contract superior to his. He told the employers that in the event of a strike by San Francisco Teamsters he would expect them to continue to operate and that he was prepared to order other locals to go through picket lines. Hoffa even considered bringing in strikebreakers if necessary. And if the employers failed to resist the Bay Area locals, Hoffa was prepared to strike them in the Midwest.

At the same time, Hoffa went to the Bay Area Teamster negotiating committee meetings, mostly made up of rank-and-file Teamsters, and tried to confuse and demoralize the committee by arguing that should they strike, they would be subject to all sorts of legal problems resulting from recent court decisions. And he told other Western Teamster freight locals that the Bay Area Teamsters were selfish, attempting to win an increase for themselves at the expense of their brothers. Eventually Hoffa won.

During the course of the McClellan hearings it became clear that Hoffa was prepared to use all the power of his office and the resources of his union to keep his people in power. When the top officers of Local 614 in Pontiac, Michigan were indicted for extortion in a Michigan highway paving scandal, Hoffa, who was named the trustee of the local, appointed two of those indicted officials to run the union. Similarly, when Floyd C. Webb of Joplin, Missouri's Local 823 was accused of taking union funds and threatening to kill local union members who complained, Hoffa was named trustee and then appointed Webb to run the local. On another occasion, Hoffa wanted to see Edward Crumback reelected the president of Local 107 in Philadelphia; to achieve this he loaned Crumback $5,000 of the dues money of members from Local 299 in Detroit.

But that was not the worst. During the Hoffa years, in mob-dominated Teamster unions like Tony Provenzano's local in New Jersey and in Roy Williams's local in Kansas City, Teamster dissidents were murdered. In many other cities dissident rank-and-file Teamsters were beaten, or threatened, or fired, or blacklisted. These events created a climate of fear and insecurity, so that the Teamster rank and file hesitated to speak out. In many areas, democratic union traditions that had existed were no longer practiced, and were later forgotten. Where things were worst, the members no longer viewed the union as their own. They saw the union as a racket, an organization they had to pay off to keep their jobs.

Although Hoffa had ended the monitorship, his troubles were far from over. Robert Kennedy continued to pursue him. In 1957 and 1958, as a result of issues raised in the McClellan Committee hearings, Hoffa was indicted in a congressional bribery case and in a wiretap conspiracy case. He was acquitted of both charges. In November 1960 he was indicted·again, this time for mail and wire fraud in the promotion of a Sun Valley development in which he had a financial interest. That indictment was eventually dropped.

John F. Kennedy was elected president in 1960 and appointed his brother Robert to be US attorney general; on taking office, Robert Kennedy immediately created a 'get Hoffa squad'. Hoffa claimed that the squad kept him under constant surveillance, tapping his phone, opening his mail, and using the Federal Bureau of Investigation and the Internal Revenue Service to harass him. In 1962 Hoffa was tried in the Test Fleet case for taking illegal payments from an employer, but the jury was hung seven votes to five. However, Hoffa was then charged with jury tampering and in March 1964 convicted and sentenced to eight years in prison. The appeals, which lasted three years, went all the way to the US Supreme Court, but Hoffa finally entered Lewisburg penitentiary in March 1967.

Hoffa's Legacy

As head of the Teamsters Hoffa changed the union in many fundamental ways: he centralized collective bargaining in a number of areas, but particularly in the freight industry, extending uniform wages and benefits to ever larger numbers of workers covered by Teamster contracts, until finally in 1964 he negotiated the first National Master Freight Agreement. Hoffa's control over bargaining and grievances gave him greater political power within the union, control he formalized at Teamster International conventions, where he amended the IBT's constitution to put greater power into the hands of the general pesident.

He also created and developed the Teamster pension funds, which were the source not only of pension benefits for retired Teamsters but also of greater economic and political power for Teamster officials. And finally, Hoffa brought about the corruption of the Teamsters International leadership through direct Mafia involvement in the affairs of the union and its pension funds at the highest levels.

One of the biggest changes in the union was in what might be called its political style. As Hoffa rose to become general president of the Teamsters, the office of general president itself was fundamentally changed. It was not simply that Hoffa centralized power within the union. He gave the office of

Teamster general president a powerful public image. Hoffa captured the public's imagination as his predecessors never had.

In the Midwest, where he had been an organizer, and especially in the South, where the union had gained a huge improvement in wages, Hoffa was admired and respected among the dock workers and truck drivers. Hoffa remembered the faces and names of union members he had not seen in years. He took phone calls from rank-and-file members, discussed their problems, and settled their grievances. He went to the barns and talked to the drivers and dock workers. It would not be going too far to say that, among many of these men, he was loved.

The Teamsters in the freight industry in the 1940s and 1950s identified with Hoffa, and saw themselves in him. They were mostly white men who, like him, had grown up during the Depression. They had known what it was to be evicted because their parents couldn't pay the rent, or to go without supper because the family couldn't get credit at the corner grocery. They had seen the long, bitter struggle in the 1930s to organize industrial unions, even if they had been too young to participate. Little Jimmy Hoffa, muscular and crewcut, wearing his white socks and black shoes, proud and pugnacious, a little guy standing up for little guys, was one of them.

It is true that Hoffa came from a working-class family, knew hardship, worked on the loading docks, led a strike, became an organizer, took his beatings and meted them out, and rose through the ranks to the top of the heap. That was all true. Hoffa was not a phony, and the tough swagger and dare-me pose that he struck were not merely a mask.

But it was also true that he had been recruited to the union by labor radical Sam Calhoun, trained by revolutionary socialist Farrell Dobbs, and for years associated with the backsliding socialist Harold Gibbons. Hoffa, of course, never denied his association with men like Calhoun, Dobbs and Gibbons, and in both his autobiographies he credited Dobbs with being an organizational genius. But what he did deny and ridicule was the importance of their ideas and their idealism. And that was the meaning of Hoffa's tough guy pose; it was a denial of the importance of moral and political principle, and an affirmation that all that counts is power.

While he was a popular and charismatic leader, Hoffa was also a union boss, a dictator who tolerated no opposition. He once screamed in open court that he would kill a man who had testified against him. He crushed local unions that fought for their autonomy and destroyed rank-and-file movements that rose to fight against him. He did it, he said, for their own good. A demogogue who could stir up class hatred without raising class consciousness, Hoffa never helped the Teamster membership to learn to think and act for itself. On the contrary, he imbued in the union membership a sense of dependency. He, Hoffa, took all credit, and shouldered all blame. Hoffa organized the union. Hoffa negotiated the contracts. Hoffa settled the grievances. Hoffa took care of the Teamsters until they could no longer take care of themselves. That was Hoffa's greatest crime, greater than his own enrichment at the expense of the members, greater than involving the Mafia in the union, both of which were terrible evils. But worse still, Hoffa gave the Teamster members the appearance of power and the swagger of self-confidence, while depriving them of the only possible source of real confidence, the control of their own union.

When Hoffa went to prison, he left the affairs of the union in the hands of Frank Fitzsimmons, a man of whom it was frequently said that he was qualified only to go for the coffee. Hoffa expected Fitz to remain his faithful follower. But Fitzsimmons proved to be more daring and more devious than Hoffa had expected, and he arranged the famous deal with Richard Nixon that gave Hoffa his freedom but removed him from union affairs. It was thus that Fitzsimmons came to preside over the 1970 National Master Freight Agreement negotiations, which in turn gave rise to the first national Teamster reform movement.

Business Unionism

So it was that under Tobin, Beck and Hoffa the Teamsters union had become the corrupt, bureaucratic institution it was in 1976 when TDU began, dominated by the Mafia, manipulated by the government and collaborating with the companies. Contrary to myth, the corruption of the Teamsters was not due to the fact that Jimmy Hoffa had invited the Mafia into the union. The union had been perverted from its original purpose because along the way Tobin, Beck and Hoffa had come to accommodate the employers, adapting to the values of the employers, and to the employers' sense of who should run things. Teamster leaders might strike for higher wages, but they accepted absolutely the right of the employers to run their companies, of businessmen in general to dominate the economy, of the corporate elite to control politics, and of the business ethic of competition to pervade society. They conceded to business the right to set the rules of the game and to deal the cards, and labor would be content to play the hand it was dealt, even if it was dealt from the bottom of the deck.

Having accepted the business ethic, the Teamster leaders became completely involved in and completely integrated into the system. If every institution was to be run like a business, they would run their union like a business. If everyone had to compete, they too would compete, and if necessary with other unions and other workers. If the goal was profits, they too would show a profit, even if the union's funds were invested in non-union corporations. If the goal in life was personal enrichment, they too would earn big salaries, put the tab on their expense accounts, and retire with enormous pensions. The business ethic became dominant within the union leadership, from the big Buicks and Cadillacs the officials drove to the country clubs to which they belonged and the employers and politicians with whom they socialized.

Tobin and Beck ignored the fact that the labor movement had a different philosophy. Labor was founded not on competition, but on cooperation between union members. Labor was not based on bettering oneself at the expense of others, but, by cooperating with others, in bettering all workers in the union and all the workers in society. Labor was not interested in profit, but in people, and in enhancing their lives and making those healthier, happier and more worthwhile.

In choosing the philosophy of business unionism, Beck and Tobin had turned their backs on the history of the labor movement. From the very beginning labor had not accepted the right of the individual employer, or of businessmen as a group, to run things but had been engaged in constant conflict with them. The employers had forbidden unions: the workers struck and won recognition. The law had forbidden unions: the workers had organized anyway and forced their legal recognition. The employers refused to relinquish management prerogatives; the unions took over control of hiring through the union shop and hiring hall. The employers said that they made the rules: the union made its own rules, and management recognized them in the form of the contract. Employers denied that society should provide for the workers: the workers fought for and won free public schools, public hospitals, unemployment compensation, workmen's compensation, welfare and social security.

The Teamsters union leadership had been posed a choice between the business ethic and labor ethic, between competition and cooperation, between self-aggrandizement and solidarity. The Teamster leaders had reached out and clasped in solidarity, not the hand of their fellow worker, but the hand of the boss.

If the union officials accepted the philosophy of business unionism, the members could not afford to. They could not afford to let the employer dictate the terms of their employment. They could not let the employer unilaterally control the workplace. The rank-and-file members had to operate on the principles of solidarity if they were to survive. So over and over again the struggle on the shopfloor gave rise to a struggle to reform the union. And now it had given rise to TDU.

Notes

1. Murray Morgan, *Skid Road: An Informal Portrait of Seattle*, New York 1951, p. 256.

2. The Trotskyists had changed their name from the Communist League of America to

the Socialist Workers Party.

3.   Cited in Walter Galenson, *The CIO Challenge to the AFL: A History of the American Labor Movement: 1935–1941*, Cambridge 1960, p. 485.

4.   Dobbs, *Teamster Bureaucracy*, New York 1977, pp. 138–39.

5.   Many years later the Smith Act was ruled unconstitutional.

6.   Dobbs, *Teamster Bureaucracy*, p. 282.

7.   Vicki L. Ruiz, *Cannery Women, Cannery Lives: Mexican Women, Unionization, and the California Food and Processing Industry, 1930–1950*, Albuquerque 1987, p. 104.

8.   Murray Kempton, 'A Spoiled Baby', *New York Post*, 22 June 1951.

9.   J.B. Gillingham, *The Teamsters Union on the West Coast*, Berkeley 1956, p. 33.

10.   The union also employed his sons, Frank L. Tobin and Frederick A. Tobin, who worked at Teamster headquarters in Washington.

11.   Nard Jones, *Seattle*, Garden City, N.Y. 1972, p. 184.

12.   Robert D. Leiter, *The Teamsters Union: A Study of Its Economic Impact*, New York 1957, p. 50.

13.   Donald Garnel, *The Rise of Teamster Power in the West*, Berkeley 1972, p. 74fn.

14.   Einar Mohn, *Einar Mohn: Teamster Leader*. (Interviewer Corinne Lathrop Gilb. Institute of Industrial Relations, University of California, Berkeley, November 1958–July 1965), p. 544.

15.   Lester Velie, *Labor USA*, New York 1959, pp. 155–66.

16.   Joseph C. Goulden, *Meany*, New York 1972, p. 235.

17.   Ibid., p. 236.

18.   Ibid.

19.   Robert F. Kennedy, *The Enemy Within*, New York 1960, pp. 31–35.

20.   Jones, *Seattle*, p. 187.

21.   Dan Moldea, *The Hoffa Wars: Teamsters, Rebels, Politicians and the Mob*, New York 1978, pp. 37–38.

22.   *The Teamster*, May 1962; cited in Frank C. Pierson, *Unions in Postwar America: An Economic Assessment*, New York 1967, p. 105.

23.   Ralph C. James and Estelle Dinerstein James, *Hoffa and the Teamsters: A Study of Union Power*, Princeton, N.J. 1965, p. 216.

24.   Ibid., p. 248.

25.   Ibid., p. 291.

26.   Jonathan Kwitny, *Vicious Circles: The Mafia in the Market Place*, New York 1979, p. 144.

27.   Paul Jacobs, *The State of the Unions*, New York 1963, pp. 75–82.

28.   Ibid., p. 82.

29.   Kennedy, *The Enemy Within*, p. 70; and James R. Hoffa, *The Trials of Jimmy Hoffa: An Autobiography*, Chicago 1970, pp. 16–67.

30.   Kwitny, *Vicious Circles*, pp. 146–47.

31.   Hoffa, *Trials*, pp. 190–99.

32.   Cited in R. and E. James, *Hoffa*, p. 197.

PART III

THE MAKING OF A MOVEMENT

10

Detroit Puts TDU on the Map

Teamsters around the country had rallied to TDC's 'Ready to Strike!' slogan and then joined TDU. But what really gave TDC and the early TDU some recognition was its following in Detroit, where TDU built its first strong chapter, making it a small but significant force in the Teamsters.

In Detroit TDU attracted freight and carhaul Teamsters from Local 299, UPS workers from Local 243, warehouse and grocery Teamsters from Local 337, and construction Teamsters from Local 247. In each of these locals TDU not only recruited members but also leaders who organized contract campaigns, fought for democratic bylaws, ran for office and served on the TDU committees. Scores of Detroit Teamsters contributed money, time and energy to the newly formed group.

Joe Urman

Among the first to join TDU in Detroit was a group of reformers from grocery Local 337 led by a longtime union steward named Joe Urman. Urman was born in 1928 in the town of West Frankfort in southern Illinois. 'That's coal-mining country', he says, 'you know – hard coal. My father worked at the Orient Number One mine and was involved in organizing with the Progressive Mine Workers Union, a leftist type of union down there. He was not particularly a leftist himself, he was just union. They was working a dollar a day, twelve hours a day, and he realized there was no future in that, so he went into the union. That was probably the twenties or thirties. I remember they went on a strike. Four years they was on a strike, and we ended up on a farm when I was that big', he says, holding his hand a couple of feet from the floor. 'Farmin', to live, you know.'

In 1931 there was a wildcat strike at the Orient Mines in West Frankfort, and John L. Lewis, president of the United Mine Workers, came to town to try to end it. 'I remember them talking about when John L. Lewis came, and he stood up on the second floor of the high school with armed guards, talking to the workers. They'd have flat shot the men, so the women was carrying rocks underneath the kids in the baby buggies. The women went up first, and then the men got the rocks and threw them. They was throwing them at John L. Lewis. He was nothing but a dictator. I mean, they're the worst kind.'[1] Later that year the Illinois mine workers left the UMW and formed the Progressive Mine Workers Union.

Urman moved to Houston and then to New Orleans when he was still a teenager. He dropped out of high school, went to night school for a while, and then just quit altogether. Always a big man, he lied about his age, and at fourteen got a job as a truck driver, and then at fifteen worked as a pipefitter in a Navy yard during the war. 'And then I just knocked around, you know, different jobs and that.'

On 7 December 1948, Joe Urman learned that his dad had been killed in a mine accident, just six months before he was due to retire. 'Three of them died and one came out alive, broken legs and that.' His mother moved to Detroit, and Urman joined her there. A few months later, he was hired at Kroger. 'I went into the bakery as general help and then I went on to mixing. And I guess I mixed for, hell, about twenty-nine of the thirty years I was there. I was a sweet dough mixer. It was all done with a big mixer, eight, nine hundred pounds at a time. You had blades in it that mixed it. You dropped the dough in a big trough, about as long as this room, and then the make-up crew would take it from there, and cut it up, roll it out and put the fillings in it, chop it up into sweet rolls, cinnamons, your coffee cake, whatever.

'At that time, at $1.26 an hour, that was a pretty good job. I was used to a lot less down in Texas; the minimum wage was like fifty cents or something. The union was there, but it was just name only. I mean, the leadman was the steward *and* the leadman. He hired and fired as well in those days. Used to give 'em a dime more an hour to squeal on everybody, you know. So this was the system that was there. I mean if they wanted to fire you, they just fired you. And if you complained the business agent come out and he would sit there and agree with the company, and said, "Damn, they should have fired you." I mean, there was no such thing as the union.'

Urman decided to try to change things, and after four years he became the union steward. There were two other fellows, Frank Sowa and 'Red' Bill Zabroski, who also thought some changes should be made, and the three of them 'started raising hell'. In 1955 they led the Kroger bakery workers out on their first strike. 'After that walkout', says Urman, 'we started to build, and it took years of building.' Above all, Joe, Frank and Red worked to break the power of those leadmen. They got the bakery workers to stick together, they organized and isolated the leadmen. They forced them out of the steward positions, putting pressure on the leadmen and gradually undermining their authority.

'About fifty-six or fifty-seven we started breaking their backs', says Joe. 'We broke them down to where they were useless.' And when the Kroger bakery moved to the Detroit suburb of Livonia in the 1960s, the position of leadman, no longer useful to the company, was eliminated. After that, there was the issue of the company-controlled grievance committee. 'They ran it like a little clique for themselves. If you was in with them, you got the better jobs and whatever, and if you wasn't, you didn't get nothing. We ignored 'em, bypassed 'em, and finally they just eliminated it.'

So, says Urman, 'We changed it – but it took about eight to ten years to really build up anything of a union.' Kroger, like many companies, saw the leadership qualities of union stewards and tried to recruit them to be foremen: 'They had several stewards that went into training to be foremen and they turned out to be the biggest pricks you ever saw, mostly.' The plant manager frequently came by and offered Urman a job as a foreman. 'This plant manager says one day, "I ask you all the time, tell me the truth, Joe, why don't you take the foreman's job?" I told him, I says, "Well, I'm sorry enough and lazy enough, but I just can't lie enough." One reason I never wanted to get into management, particularly in the bakery, was because the foreman in that bakery was shit. I mean he got it from us – I gave it to him regularly, daily. And the top management treated 'em like dogs, too.'

Urman stuck it out in the bakery mixing sweet doughs, but mostly fighting the company. Though the workers had a strong shopfloor organization in each area, they were isolated. 'There were several hundred of us, but we were in our own little group. The Teamsters had the knack, you know. They never had meetings for the whole company or the whole division. They used to have a meeting for the warehouse, a meeting for the drivers, a meeting for the bakery, a meeting for the meat plant, and then later, when they built the dairy, you had a meeting for the dairy. But you never all met together. You never had a general meeting anywhere of the local. I guess they were smart enough to know that if everybody ever got together they might turn on them.'

Those years in the late 1950s when Joe Urman was working in the bakery, mixing the sweet dough and fighting the leadmen were the Hoffa years. 'For many years, I was a diehard Hoffa supporter', says Urman. 'I was strictly union, strictly Hoffa. There was one thing about Hoffa that these guys from Fitzsimmons on up didn't have: anytime you went down there and you wanted to see him, his door was always open. He always told you that. And he would remember; maybe you didn't see him for a year, but he'd remember you. And he was a hell of a speech maker, he was a magnetic speech maker. I've listened to him, and you're ready to go out there and tackle a fire.

'Now I know how he stayed in power. Years later, as I got older, I learned. He took care of that certain percentage of the union, like thirty percent or so – that was his power base. He wasn't too concerned about the small shops. He was mostly concerned about the drivers and the over-the-road. As far as the bakeries and the other places, they were just like money coming in.'

So he sees it now, but at the time Urman was a Hoffa man, and because Jimmy Hoffa's old pal Bobby Holmes was the head of Local 337, Joe Urman was also a Holmes man. In 1966 Joe ran on the Holmes slate as an alternate delegate: 'Nobody ran against the delegates, they was automatically elected.'

About then Hoffa went to prison, and, says Urman, the Teamsters union began to go downhill fast. 'Now, I had an argument with my wife over Fitzsimmons. I said, "He's there for only one reason, to hold it till Hoffa gets out." My wife said, "Once he feels that power, he'll never let Hoffa get back." And she was right, and I was wrong. He did get hold of that power and he did not let Hoffa get back. He set up that five-year probation, and I guess when it looked like Hoffa was going to come back, that's when they had to make him disappear, because he would have come back, without a doubt. If Jimmy Hoffa had been able to run, he would have been elected unanimously.

'Basically the weakness started a few years after Hoffa left. The Master Freight contract was going down under Fitzsimmons. Fitzsimmons brought in the weakness.' Increasingly disappointed with Fitzsimmons and the Bobby Holmes administration in Local 337, Joe Urman began to organize. 'We started reform in Local 337 back in seventy and seventy-one with the Rank and File Slate. This was with Joe Dubach – the son of our original business agent – and some of his bunch, Jim Reynolds from A&P, and me and Zabroski and Barney Stafford from Kroger. At first we ran for delegates to the International convention, and then we started running slates against them in the local elections.'

Urman got Bob Janadia from Grosse Pointe Foods involved and pushed him forward to run as a candidate for the Rank and File Slate. Later Janadia became one of TDU's outstanding leaders in Detroit, running first for vice-president and later for president of Local 337, and he came close to beating Bobby Holmes. 'At that time we were already at the beginning of the TDU. Actually I think the main force that came in this area into TDU at that time came out of Kroger's and some of the old reform group that was there, like Joe Dubach and Bob Janadia. And Pete Camarata and that group from the 1976 Master Freight contract. That was the beginning of the forming of TDU here in Detroit.' Joe Urman came to play a key role as a leader of the Detroit Metro TDU chapter and of the TDU reform activities in Local 337.

Eileen Janadia

From the time TDU was first established in Detroit in 1976 one of its key volunteer organizers was Eileen Janadia. Janadia was one of those who made the phone calls, rented the meeting halls, organized the local chapter meetings, put out the leaflets and produced the local rank-and-file newspaper. Without Eileen Janadia and a few others like her, there might have been no Detroit TDU.

One of four children, she was born Eileen Farrell in Detroit, Michigan and grew up on the Southeast side of Detroit. Her parents were factory workers, her father at Chrysler and her mother at Eaton Manufacturing. Eileen was sent to Catholic schools. 'My family wasn't involved in the Church, but they were committed. There was a strong Irish Catholic background', says Janadia. 'I didn't go to college. Like most daughters of working-class people, I went off to work in an office. I bounced around for a while, but the place I worked longest was a chemical manufacturer, Difco Laboratories. I was an office worker. It was interesting because the labs where I worked were organized in the union, and, of course, the office workers weren't. I had absolutely no knowledge of unionism or anything related to it, other than that I'd heard my father say, "Go to union meetings."

'But I noticed that when the union people would go out on strike and negotiate a contract, we would get a little bit of what they got, but not as much. I saw this strength in unity. I was naive, but I had a conscience, and I also liked being respected, so I would stand up to any problems that existed in the workplace, and I would try to get people organized, and I couldn't understand why they didn't fall in behind me. But it was basically because we didn't have a union, and they knew how easily you could get fired. We were having some problems where they were cutting the work force in the office, and I was so naive that I went to management and said that I thought maybe we needed a union, too. They didn't like me much after that, but they tolerated me until they finally found a way to get rid of me.'

Six months later, in 1971, she married Bob Janadia, a truck driver at Grosse Pointe Foods, became the stepmother of his teenage daughter, and a year later had her own son. She was now primarily a housewife and mother, but she also began to take an interest in her husband's union activities in Detroit Local 337. In the early 1970s, Bob Janadia had become part of the Rank and File Slate, the reform group in Local 337 put together by Joe Urman from Kroger Grocery, and after they were married Eileen supported Bob's union reform work. As she explains, 'I was just dabbling in the background of Bob's activity, which was running for office in Local 337. There wasn't really much of a part for me to play. But it really interested me.'

Then in 1976 Urman and Janadia and the rest of the Local 337 reform group joined up with TDU. 'Bob went to the TDU founding convention in

Cleveland and came back and was really enthusiastic about it and very excited. I'd never seen him that emotional over anything.' Not long after that, TDU attorney Ann Thompson invited Eileen to a TDU meeting. 'And it took off right from there. I felt good about it and wanted to offer any services that I could. It certainly wasn't the norm for spouses to become that active in union politics, at least not in anything I'd been exposed to. But TDU gave me the opportunity to play more of a role in something that I had found to be interesting for the past two or three years. And I liked the people involved in it.'

Eileen Janadia found that her role was not to be part of a 'women's auxiliary' but to be an organizer and leader of Teamsters. 'I used to be offended that some people would think that my role was to sell cookies to raise money for the organization. I was real good at going out on picket lines and talking with the women and men, and sitting down with them and sort of structuring them in their lines of thinking about questions like, What do you hope to get out of this? What can you give to it? And let's see if unity is the answer.

'It gave me the opportunity to use my ability as an organizer, so I had this strong need to be a part of TDU. It was just real important to me. I wasn't working, it was so exciting, and I gave it all of my time.' Eileen became one of the people the Teamster activists called to talk about their problems. 'Sometimes they needed motivation, or they needed support. Or they needed to have a network within the city, and being truck drivers, you don't usually have that. You're not really able to have a network because people are out on the road. Most of the people who were active at that point were truck drivers, and I was able to keep the doors of communication open for all of them. And so almost immediately, because I was still at home and wasn't working, I became the contact person for the Detroit area, I and another woman, Gisela Wade.'

This was 1976, the Detroit wildcat strike and the Teamster International convention had just ended, the bylaws campaign was beginning, and Al Ferdnance and Pete Camarata were fighting their expulsion from Local 299. 'It was real easy to pull off meetings on a regular basis to organize people into TDU. People were so enthusiastic and so willing to give up their time, because it was all so new and fresh to them. The whole theme of the organization was so wonderful that people were real eager to become a part of it.'

One of the things the local TDU chapter did was organize strike support for other Teamsters. 'We were driving out on Grossebeck Avenue doing some leafletting or some other activity and we saw a whole group of women picketing, and we swung around and came back and talked to them.' They were workers at the Mirex plant, an auto parts factory, and they were Teamsters.

'It was mostly Black and white women who worked there. They worked with what they called steel that had not been deburred, so it wasn't a smooth finished steel. They would have to handle this with their bare hands, they couldn't wear gloves. It was an awful place to have to work, an awful place. I can't remember all the details now, but it was a real rough time for them. The company was trying to bust the union. It was a real violent strike, and a woman striker was killed, supposedly accidentally, when she was run down by a truck on Grossebeck Avenue.

'We were real supportive of their strike. That's how we started out, just seeing them picketing, and we started to picket with them, and talk with them, and then we started to help them with their contract negotiations. They came to TDU meetings and they were real excited. But then they started getting hassled a lot, not only by the union but by the company. And they were red-baited, which was the normal occurrence – anyone that became active eventually was red-baited – and a lot of them became frigid toward TDU.'

As TDU grew in Locals 337 and 299 and throughout Detroit and all of Michigan, the companies and the union officials became worried, and the red-baiting began. TDU, they said, was Communist. 'I didn't know the history of unionism in the first place', says Janadia, 'and I didn't realize how this was one of the ways to effectively fight any organizing that was going on, so I thought it was funny. And then, when I saw that it affected people and that they became more leery of us, then I realized the seriousness of it. I would just say, 'I think it's a counterattack and I just don't want to spend my time dealing with it. There's other matters that have to be dealt with, and I think you can see for yourself what we're doing.' But it became embarrassing sometimes, you know, when Bob would be running for office and there would be some matters that would be mentioned in the newspapers, and then people would question us, relatives or friends.'

Bob and Eileen Janadia's commitment to TDU and the union reform movement had become all-engrossing. 'Well, we were so involved in what we were doing, we didn't have time for other activities. We kind of let the family matters slide. We would back out on cookouts and birthdays, or whatever, and they became angry about that. ... But I don't regret it at all.' Bob, who ran for president in 1974, trying to knock Bobby Holmes out of the box, was the most prominent leader of TDU in Local 337. Those were the years when there were the shootings and bombings involving the officers in Local 299 in Detroit. There were rumors, and sometimes threats.

'At that time the violence wasn't directed at us', remembers Janadia, 'it was still between officials in the union leadership. You know, there were times when I would start to think about it, that maybe, if we became too powerful, or if we became too vocal, or if we rocked the boat too much, that they might start using violence against us. And I would think about it ... and then I would not allow myself to think about it anymore, because there was a mission ahead to be accomplished, and if you thought about what might happen, you might not want to be involved.' More likely than violence was the possibility that Bob might be fired. 'And it was sort of like, well, we know it's going to happen eventually, it's almost inevitable. But Bob had a lot of seniority where he was, so we thought, as long as he kept his nose clean at work, at Grosse Pointe Foods, things will be okay.'

It was Detroit that put TDU on the map, not just Joe Urman, and Eileen Janadia, but twenty more like them who were prepared to give up virtually everything else and throw themselves into the Teamster reform movement. It would turn out that there were hundreds more across the country who were prepared to do the same thing, and were only waiting to be asked.

Notes

1.   Melvyn Dubofsky and Warren Van Tine, authors of *John L. Lewis: A Biography*, describe the incident that Joe Urman's mother told him about. 'In July 1931, Illinois miners at the Orient mines in West Frankfort began a wildcat strike. When Lewis went there on July 26 to urge the miners to return to work, they greeted their president with catcalls, boos, and hisses, and they stopped him from speaking' (p. 168).

11

Long Beach Throws Out the Thugs

As soon as TDU's founding convention broke up, TDU and UPSurge members returned home to stand as candidates in their local union elections. TDU was involved in local elections in Long Beach, Los Angeles, and San Jose, California; Portland, Oregon; Spokane, Washington; New Hampshire; Johnstown, Pennsylvania; and Rochester, New York. In some areas TDU members ran alone, in other places as part of a broader reform slate. Most of the TDU candidates had never run for or held local office before, and both the candidates and TDU as an organization were inexperienced. In some areas the reform candidates faced incumbents who engaged in unfair election practices. Nonetheless, in most of the local elections the TDU candidates got about one-third of the vote, an indication that there was widespread discontent among Teamster members throughout the country.

One of the most interesting elections TDU participated in that year was in Long Beach Local 692 in the Los Angeles harbor area. Local 692 had a reputation as a pretty rough local, and when TDC and later TDU began organizing, the local leadership responded with violence. Nevertheless, TDU's candidates Bilal Chaka and Sharon Cotrell succeeded in building a movement that led to the ouster of the incumbents.

Sharon Cotrell

Sharon Cotrell, who led the fight to drive the gangsters out of Teamster Local 692, was raised on a farm on the Flathead Indian reservation near St. Ignatius, Montana. Her father, Thomas Lewis Cotrell, was descended from Indians and, Sharon believes, was named after a leader of the Little Shell band of the Cree tribe. 'My mother's people came over on the *Mayflower*, so there's the joke that my dad's people were there to meet them', she says.

'My mother's people included the first governor of Massachusetts, and they were at the founding convention of the United States, and they fought in the Civil War.'

Her parents were dairy farmers. 'But I always say that actually we were manure farmers. The product we sold was milk, but in order to get the milk you have to move many more tons of manure. You're always processing manure. We were very poor, and I was raised as both my dad's daughter and his son. I was the oldest, and he raised me to work like a man, and I suppose that has all in the world to do with why I'd be the first woman on the docks, because of that attitude toward physical work.'

Living there on the 'manure farm' surrounded by the Rockies, Sharon Cotrell felt as if she were cut off from the world. In 1957 her father bought the family's first television set, and she learned about life outside the Flathead Valley. 'You should have seen us milk those cows so we could all get in and watch that one channel.' They watched Saturday night wrestling and its star Gorgeous George, they watched the Christophers, and they watched the news.

'We turned on the news, and Little Rock came on.' In Little Rock, Arkansas, Governor Orval Faubus had called out the National Guard to prevent Black students from attending Central High School, and President Eisenhower had then sent in federal troops to enforce the court-ordered desegregation. Crowds of white people came out on the streets and spit on the Black children as they walked to school, and there it was on t.v.

'I said to my parents, "Why are those adults spitting on those kids?" I couldn't understand it. I asked my parents, "In *our* country do people treat Black people this way? Did you *know* this was going on?" They said yes. And I said, "What have you *done* about it? In civics last year they told us a democracy can't work unless all the citizens are involved, so anything that happens in this country is a responsibility of every citizen – and what have you done?" That's the way my child's mind went.'

That fall Sharon entered high school and met the school librarian, Mrs. Van Haverbeke. 'We always called her Mrs. Van. I owe her a big debt', says Sharon. 'She may have been the only person in that town who had a glimmer of who I was, and in her own way she tried to give me support.' Sharon asked Mrs. Van for books about Negroes, and Mrs. Van got them for her. Sharon read them by the dozen, determined to learn why white adults were spitting on Black children. That's the way she went through school, driven by shock and horror at the things happening beyond the mountains and wanting to find out why, and what could be done about it. Anxious to get out of that valley, at the age of seventeen she entered Lewis and Clark College and then later attended the University of Montana at Missoula, always arguing with the teachers and fighting with the deans, wanting to know how the world had gotten this way and what they had done about it.

Cotrell's parents had moved to Long Beach, California and in 1964 Sharon joined them there. She went to school part-time, supported herself as a waitress, and got involved in the civil rights movement in the Black community in Long Beach. She worked in the welfare rights movement and helped recruit for a government jobs program. In the fall of 1966, while she was doing civil rights work, there was a racial incident at Polytechnic High School in Long Beach. Two boys, one white and one Black, got in a fight, and an instructor intervened, manhandling the Black student and later suspending him while sending the white boy back to school. The police aggravated the situation by repeatedly sending squad cars to the school, while the newspaper sensationalized the story on the front page. The Black students were furious, and parents feared a race riot would break out and their children would be hurt.

Cotrell was also afraid that something terrible was going to happen, and she was the one person who, because of her civil rights work, had contacts on both sides of the color line. So she got on the phone and called peace movement activists, lawyers, ministers, priests and rabbis. She organized a meeting in the Long Beach Community Improvement League hall so that the Blacks and whites could sit down and talk to each other. There was no riot, and out of that meeting came a group called FREE, made up of concerned whites dedicated to supporting Black community organizing. They put together another meeting at the Jewish Community Center and 600 people showed up to hear Black representatives talk about problems in their community. Sharon was hired as FREE's first staffperson, putting together meetings and bringing in speakers.

The civil rights work was exciting but exhausting, and after a while Cotrell put it aside and decided to return once again to school. While she had been working with the local civil rights movement, another movement had been growing on the college campuses. The war in Vietnam had dragged on for years, until there were half a million US troops in Vietnam and tens of thousands of casualties. When an anti-war protest demonstration was called on 15 October 1969, some 2 million people from across the country participated. When Sharon went back to school at Long Beach State College in 1971, the anti-war movement was at its peak, and she became a part of it, joining anti-war demonstrations and participating in civil disobedience actions.

Throughout all of this, however, one of Sharon's biggest concerns was making a living. While working as a volunteer organizer and going to school, Sharon had worked as a waitress, a 'paperboy', a janitor and a 'handyman'. She was tired of long hours at low wages and wanted a better job at better pay. By coincidence she came across a copy of the *Southern California Teamster* magazine with an article about women being hired in Teamster jobs. She applied, and six months later, on 9 January 1974 Sharon Cotrell was hired at Sealand to work loading and unloading trucks. She was, she believes, the first woman in the United States to be employed on the docks.

The men who worked on the docks seemed to Sharon Cottrell angry and afraid, but she didn't understand why until one day a dock worker called her aside to talk to her. Local 692, he explained, was run by Secretary-Treasurer Jake Koenig. There were, he said, several mob figures involved in the union, some of whom controlled job-selling on the better paying banana dock jobs. The local officials, the mobsters, and about fifty goons ran the union. Gunner Hansen, president of the local union and business agent, a physical giant, who was six feet, seven inches tall and weighed 400 pounds, led the union goon squad. Be careful, her coworker told her, and don't ask too many questions.

Cotrell was shocked, not only at the mob control of the local, but also at the fear on the part of the members. 'The union has five thousand members and you're afraid of fifty to seventy-five people?' she asked. 'You outnumber them. You ought to be able to do something', she said. 'No, Sharon', her coworker replied. 'It doesn't work that way.' A few months later Sharon ran into some Teamsters who were starting a Teamster reform group in the Los Angeles area, and, concerned about the situation in her union, Sharon joined them. Soon the group began to put out a rank-and-file Teamster newspaper called *The Grapevine*.

It was a propitious moment to launch a Teamster reform movement. The FBI had begun an investigation into the leadership of Local 692 because of some hijacked trucks, and a grand jury started calling various union officers to testify. Gunner Hansen left Local 692 and went off to work for some other Teamster organization, while the local fired Dominic Scaccia, one of the men allegedly connected to the mob. So, as the reform movement in the harbor developed, Jake Koenig didn't have his usual goons on hand.

At about the same time Jimmy Hoffa disappeared, and John T. Williams, a business agent and union reformer in Local 208, had started a movement called Action for Hoffa. The group demanded that President Ford launch a full-scale investigation into Hoffa's disappearance. As Williams wrote in the text of a letter to the president, 'If Hoffa can disappear in a vacuum of silence, then there is no jurisdiction of safety within our ranks, and anyone who speaks with conviction shall be haunted by a specter of fear.'

Sharon heard about Action for Hoffa and got in touch with John T. Williams. He was planning a meeting for September at the Embassy Auditorium, and he asked Sharon to help organize it. She did, and among the other Teamsters she met were Zack Lopez, a steward at Yellow Freight, and Guy Lizotte, a steward at Cal Cartage, two other members of her local who opposed the Jake Koenig dictatorship. The night of the Action for Hoffa meeting arrived, and at the last moment Williams asked Sharon to chair. About 125 Teamsters turned out for the meeting, and suddenly she became known as a leading Teamster activist in Los Angeles.

Soon after Action for Hoffa was organized, the local reform groups like the one putting out *The Grapevine* in Los Angeles joined together to form Teamsters for a Decent Contract. Jake Koenig did not welcome the reformers. As soon as the TDC group started going to union meetings and making motions, Zack Lopez and Sharon Cotrell were fired from their jobs. Zack got his job back right away, but Sharon's case went to the grievance panels and finally to an arbitrator. In the end she won, making her something of a heroine to her coworkers.

Meanwhile things started getting rough. Jake Koenig and the group that had run the union had never faced an opposition before, and they had no idea how to deal with it, so they turned to violence. On 17 July 1976 as Zack Lopez and Guy Lizotte were leaving a union stewards' meeting, they were attacked and beaten up by two unidentified thugs and one man who was identified as Tom Mazur, a Local 692 member and close friend of Jake Koenig. A few days later, on 21 July, Ron Reed, a Local 692 business agent with a black belt in karate, went to the Consolidated Freightways dock and attacked TDC supporter Alex Morales. Morales was an older man, and Reed gave him quite a beating. Then the company fired Morales, the victim, for fighting.

There was fear and anxiety in Local 692, and no one knew who would be fired or attacked next, and even the reformers just wanted to lay low, to draw back. Sharon Cotrell called everyone, trying to convince them that they had to stand up now, or the violence would get worse and they would never be able to lift their heads again. But people were afraid. 'Then I called Chaka', Sharon Cotrell remembers, 'and he was just leaving the house; he was going to test some fishing poles for his kids, so I said I'd meet him at the beach.'

Bilal Chaka

The man Sharon Cotrell called for help, Bilal Chaka, was born in 1937 in the little town of Ruleville, Mississippi and lived there until he was five years old. His family moved to Memphis, Tennessee in 1941, and then in 1953 to Detroit, where Chaka's father worked at the Firestone Rubber Company and was an activist in the United Rubber Workers.

After graduating from high school in Detroit, Chaka went to Tennessee State College in Nashville and then served in the Army, first at Fort Hood and later in Germany. After leaving the Army in 1959, Bilal and his brother moved to Los Angeles, and he got a job in horticulture and worked at various times for the city, county or state government. More important, he was swept up in the civil rights movement.

Chaka joined a civil rights group in Los Angeles, the Afro-American Association. 'We protested discrimination and demanded employment opportunities for Blacks', he remembers. 'We picketed restaurants, and I remember that in 1962 we picketed Ciro's on the strip.' The group fought discrimination in housing and sometimes organized rent strikes. At the same time they worked with the Black student unions on junior high school and high school campuses, instilling pride in African American heritage and culture.

Like many Blacks in the 1960s, Bilal Chaka wanted justice and was angered at the situation of Blacks in the United States. He evolved from a civil rights activist to become an advocate of Black power and Black nationalism. He even traveled to East Africa, to Kenya, Uganda and Tanzania in the search of a better life for himself and for Black people. Back in L.A., Chaka went to an auto mechanics school sponsored by Teamster Joint Council 42, and when he graduated he applied for a job with ONC Trucking. They had no openings for mechanics, but offered him a job as a dock worker. Chaka took it and became a member of Teamster Local 357.

In 1970 Chaka was laid off and spent two and a half years working out of the hiring hall. Working frequently at Yellow Freight's Pico terminal, Chaka got a 'five-day card' entitling him to work for five days at a time, though still on a casual basis without a permanent position or any seniority rights. Week after week he got his 'five-day card', but he never got a job. Chaka saw that there were 245 people working at the terminal at that time, but only 5 of them were Black. Feeling discriminated against because he was not offered a permanent job, he filed both state and federal Fair Employment Practices complaints against the company. He was hired. Later, in June 1972, Yellow Freight opened a satellite terminal in Gardena, California, and Chaka transferred there, where he has worked ever since.

When Sharon Cotrell organized the first meeting of Teamsters for a Decent Contract back in 1975, Bilal Chaka showed up and joined. Chaka worked hard for TDC, raising money at his barn and helping to organize the meetings, and in 1976 he had gone to the TDU founding convention in Ohio. Now Sharon went to find Bilal down at the beach. 'When I got there I was fighting back crying, and then finally I started crying, and I cried and I cried. I just leveled with him: "Why didn't they come after me? Why did they attack these people with kids?" I told him, "If we don't build a demonstration now it will spread the word that you can't do anything."' Chaka said he would help organize the demonstration and be the spokesperson.

Sharon and Bilal encouraged the TDC chapter to put out a leaflet denouncing the violence and calling for a demonstration to protest the attacks. Then the two of them took that leaflet to every barn and dock in the harbor, talking to the dock workers and drivers, trying to counter the atmosphere of fear and intimidation created by Koenig and his henchmen. They

Jim West

Bilal Chaka speaks at the 1984 TDU convention in Chicago.

asked everyone to join them for a protest demonstration at the local union. They got some help from Monty Ogden, a local union politician who was also an opponent of Jake Koenig, but not a member of TDU.

On Saturday, 24 July 1976, Sharon, Bilal, Zack, Guy and Alex showed up for the protest at the hall and waited to see who else, if anyone, would join them. Slowly the cars began to arrive, and Teamsters got out in ones and twos. Eventually sixty-five rank and filers had the courage to walk the picket line in front of their union hall to protest the violence. It was a turning point for the union – the men who had been afraid had lost their fear and were prepared to stand up to the goons.

Under investigation by the government and under increasing criticism from the rank and file, Jake Koenig decided not to run for president in the December 1976 election, and instead picked his right-hand man Joe San Paulo to run for the top office. Monty Ogden decided to run against San Paulo, while the newly formed TDU group slated two candidates for the office of trustee in one of its first elections: Sharon Cotrell and Bilal Chaka.

'I am committed', Chaka said at the time, 'to fight against goon tactics and for democracy and making our elected officers responsive to the membership who pay their salaries.' Sharon stated in her campaign literature, 'I am proud to be a Teamster and a member of local 692, and I am also proud that the current leadership calls me a troublemaker. ... My personal philosophy is when you've got problems, handle them. Ignoring them makes them worse, and no one else will fight if you won't.'

In the end, Cotrell and Chaka lost the election, though they did well for first-time candidates. But Monty Ogden, who had used the demonstrations organized by TDC to build his own campaign, defeated San Paulo for the office of president, ending the gangster era in Local 692. Ogden took the credit for defeating the Koenig-San Paulo administration, but the people who had really defeated the thug element in Local 692 were the scores of rank-and-file truck drivers and dock workers who had come to the demonstrations to protest the violence, and who had voted the goons out. TDU lost that first round of elections, but already in Long Beach it had made a real contribution to cleaning up the Teamsters union.

Assessing the TDU's first round of Teamster elections, *Convoy* wrote, 'We honestly believe that as a first effort to challenge the IBT officials in elections, TDU and its supporters have nothing to be ashamed of.' TDU took the long view. 'TDU sees elections as a means to an end, not as ends in themselves. The important thing is to build the rank and file organization and strength. Elections are just one way of doing that. ... The election effort was but a step in a long organizing process that started way before the election and will continue long after it. That is what counts!'[1]

TDU had great hopes that it would win an election victory in Detroit Local 299 in the fall of 1977, where Pete Camarata ran for vice-president and Walter Ruff and Dennis Wade for trustee. But TDU was to be sorely disappointed. Incumbent President Robert Lins and his slate were supported by Frank Fitzsimmons and the International union and ran a strong campaign. But the opposition was divided between the Concerned Members, led Pete Karagozian, a popular business agent, and the TDU slate led by Camarata. TDU had tried to reach an agreement with the Concerned Members on a common slate, or at least a noncompetitive slating of candidates, but had failed. As a result, the reform vote was split, and Lins and most of his slate won; only two of the Concerned Members were elected to the executive board and TDU was defeated.

The experience of the 1977 election in Local 299 showed that the International would work hard to prevent TDU from winning office in an important big city freight local. At the same time, it taught the lesson that without compromising its principles TDU would have to do all it could to cooperate with other reform candidates or groups if it was going to be successful in local union elections. Still TDU did win some elections; one of its first in 1977 was an important victory in 3,000-member Green Bay, Wisconsin Local 75. In that local, TDU member Claude Carpenter was nominated for trustee, while three other members, a road driver, a warehouse workers, and a cheese plant employee, were nominated for the top three offices on the same slate.

Local President Donald Tilkens tried to stop the TDU nominations on the grounds that the candidates had not attended 50 percent of the local union meetings, a rule that he admitted would have excluded 99 percent of the union's membership, which was made up mostly of road drivers. With the help of TDU attorney Nola Cross, Carpenter filed an appeal, and Fitzsimmons informed Tilkens that the Supreme Court had already ruled that overly restrictive attendance rules could not be enforced. Tilkens was forced to allow the TDU nominations, and in the January 1978 election all four TDU candidates won by substantial margins.

The Green Bay experience would prove to be typical of TDU's election campaigns over the next several years. It turned out to be easier to win in smaller cities and in general locals (rather than freight locals). Incumbent union officials did not have the same kind of bureaucratic political machine in a town like Green Bay that existed in Detroit, Cleveland or Chicago. There was no strong Joint Council ready to back up the incumbents in a local union when it was challenged by TDU or by other reformers. Green Bay was only the beginning, and in the next few years TDU slates or TDU members running on reform slates were to win office in several locals around the country.

In November 1978, when TDU member Jack Farrell won the presidency of Oklahoma Local 886, TDU organizer Ken Paff used that victory as an occasion to discuss the significance of election victories in *Convoy*. 'Power', wrote Paff, 'is concentrated at the top of our union, and of course in the hands of the employers. The International has many ways to influence and control local officers, and neutralize good ones. All this power is strong pressure against crusading local officers, against democracy, against militant grass-roots unionism. *A local officer who wants to represent the members is going against the stream*. And the stream can be strong.'

Paff pointed out that the International controlled the grievances of the joint committees at the Conference level, and those officers who did not cooperate saw their grievances lost. 'So what's the real guarantee that electing a TDU or reform slate will mean real changes for the members? The best guarantee is a well organized and large TDU chapter in that local', argued Paff. Such a TDU chapter should constantly involve the members and 'be a watchdog, to make sure the new officers don't gradually become too much like the same old story.'[2]

The Fight for Bylaws Reform

During these years TDU was also involved in another sort of election. The TDU founding convention had mandated a campaign to democratize the IBT's bylaws, and two rank and filers had written a booklet entitled 'How to Make Your Local By-Laws More Democratic'. TDU proposed changes that would give the members more control over their union, such as the right to elect union stewards and business agents. The bylaws campaign began in the fall of 1976 in Michigan, where TDU had a growing following, and in Pittsburgh, where TDU had a strong chapter. Bylaws proposals were introduced in Detroit in Local 299 and Local 243, in Flint, Michigan in Local 332, and in Pittsburgh in Locals 249 and 250.

Bob Lins, the president of Detroit Local 299, saw the fight over bylaws reform as a test of power between his executive board and the TDU reformers, and he did everything he could to defeat them. While TDU won in the carhauling and city cartage sections of the local, it lost in half a dozen other sections, getting just under half of the total vote in Local 299. Given that this was TDU's first bylaws campaign, *Convoy* called the result 'a victory of sorts'.[3] In Flint Local 332, TDU actually succeeded in getting three new bylaws passed. One reduced the dues of unemployed members, one loosened the restrictions on eligibility to run as a steward, and another spelled out the election procedures for business agents; the bylaw proposal actually calling for the election of the business agents failed.

The fight for democratic bylaws initiated by TDU in 1977 continued for the next dozen years. Three years later, TDUers in Local 299 won the democratic bylaws fight. And in the late 1970s and early 1980s TDU campaigned successfully in many areas against the International's so-called model bylaws – 'reforms' that would actually have reduced what union democracy still existed. In many locals, TDUers led the fight for bylaw reforms calling for election of stewards and business agents.

The Right to Vote

TDU also carried the fight for democracy to the top of the International. When it looked as if Frank Fitzsimmons might be forced to resign in 1977, TDU began to push for his ouster and for the direct election of Teamster officials. When Fitzsimmons called a 'rally round the chief' on 6 April 1977 and ordered 2,000 IBT officials to join him in Washington, DC, TDU organized a picket line with signs that read 'Fitz Out/Dump the Crooks/TDU'.

'We want the right to vote on our president', TDU declared. 'We want the right to vote on everyone who represents us from steward to business agent and right to the top.'[4] At the same time PROD also organized a picket line and a press conference opposing Fitzsimmons. The demonstration was followed by a national campaign with the slogan 'Let's Dump Fitz! We didn't vote for him. We don't want him.' As *Convoy* explained, 'We want Fitzsimmons out and we want the right to elect our International officers.'[5] The 1977 TDU convention also called for a campaign for the right to vote for all officers.

From the very beginning, TDU had no trust that the union officials would clean house themselves, and no faith that the government would reform the union. TDU believed the rank and file would have to determine its own destiny.

Notes

1. 'What We Think', *Convoy*, no. 14.
2. Ken Paff, 'Convoy Editorial: Can Local Elections Win Reforms?', *Convoy*, no. 32.
3. *Convoy*, no. 18.
4. 'Fitz Flops', *Convoy*, no. 17.
5. 'Let's Dump Fitz!', *Convoy*, no. 18.

12

Pension Reform, the Contract, and the PROD-TDU Merger

No sooner had the 1976 Teamster convention in Las Vegas adjourned than the union and Fitzsimmons were overwhelmed by scandal. Labor Department investigators announced that hundreds of millions of dollars were missing from the Central States Pension Fund, of which Fitzsimmons was a trustee. The $1.4 billion fund, which at the time received $1 million a day from employers for the pensions of some 385,000 members, was legally controlled by equal numbers of employer and union representatives. Those trustees allowed International Vice-President William Presser and insurance executive Allen Dorfman, both of whom had ties to the Mafia, to make most of the important decisions about who got loans. Much of the money was loaned to St. Louis Teamster attorney Morris Shenker. Using Teamster loans, Shenker had borrowed $57 million to build the Rancho La Costa country club in California and had failed to repay over $40 million of it. While the fund lent money to mobsters to build casinos in Vegas, it was notorious for denying pensions to Teamster retirees because of technicalities such as 'breaks in service' or transferring from one local union to another. As a result, many Teamsters who had spent a lifetime in the trucking industry retired on the pittance of social security because they were denied the Teamster pensions they had earned.

One fact exposed by the investigation was that Richard G. Kleindienst, US attorney general during the Nixon administration, had received a $250,000 fee from the pension fund in the spring of 1976 for five hours' work in helping the Old Security Life Insurance Company of Kansas get business from the Teamsters. Old Security was alleged to have cheated the pension fund. The fee, which Kleindienst had split with Thomas Webb, Jr., was for having introduced Old Security to Joseph Hauser, who was the key figure in the schemes to loot the companies that received the Teamster insurance funds. The pension fund asked Kleindienst and Webb to return the money, and, when they failed to do so, sued Kleindienst for $14 million in damages.

The Ford administration threatened to put federal trustees in charge of the Central States Pension Fund in an attempt to get the Teamster leaders to undertake the reform of the fund themselves. Nothing could have been further from their minds. When questioned by Labor Department investigators about the fund, William Presser took the Fifth Amendment, and then resigned as Pension Fund trustee and as International vice-president. Fitzsimmons chose William Presser's son Jackie Presser to replace him on the International Executive Board. To appease the government, it was announced that several pension fund trustees would resign, though Fitzsimmons and Roy Williams would stay on. John Sikorski, research director of PROD, pointed out that the new trustees were beholden to Fitzsimmons and the other old trustees and argued that such an arrangement would prevent any real reform.

After Jimmy Carter became president in 1976, new Secretary of Labor F. Ray Marshall pledged that he, Treasury Secretary Blumenthal and Attorney General Bell would speed up the investigation of the Pension Fund and promised that no deals would be made. As a result, Fitzsimmons and other fund trustees were forced to resign in March 1977, and the Labor Department ended its investigation of the fund. New employer and union trustees were to be chosen, but the fund would run by independent managers.[1] Speaking before the House Oversight subcommittee shortly after the resignation of Fitzsimmons, Central States Pension Fund Director Daniel J. Shannon revealed that, though the fund was not bankrupt, at that moment it was 'unsound' by as much as $5 billion.[2]

TDU Demands Reform of the Funds

At the same time, Teamsters for a Democratic Union carried on its own fight for reform of the Teamster pension funds on several fronts. First, TDU supported a suit brought on 13 October 1976 by ten rank-and-file Teamsters not associated with TDU. They sued fifty-one separate Teamster locals, pension funds and officials for fraud, failure to give fair representation, and failure of fiduciary responsibility. At the center of the suit was John B. Daniel, who was forced to retire because his eyesight was failing and who was told he would receive no pension from Teamster Local 705 because of a three-month layoff that had occurred thirteen years before.

Daniel's attorney, Lawrence Walner, argued that the Teamster pension plans should be covered by the anti-fraud regulations of the Securities and Exchange Commission and that Daniel should have been told that his retirement plan was based on the actuarial assumption that most participants would never work long enough to qualify for benefits. TDU attorney Robert Handelman filed an amicus brief for TDU on the side of Daniel and the other rank and filers and against the Teamsters union. The case was fought through the courts all the way to the top, but on 16 January 1979 the US Supreme Court ruled against Daniel and the other retirees. Daniel himself died that same month without ever having received a pension. His widow, Ellen Daniel, was made an honorary member of TDU by the International Steering Committee.

TDU also initiated its own pension suit. On 1 May 1978, two TDU members, Claude Carpenter and James Adcock, filed a class action suit for the recovery of $7 million taken by a conspiracy involving the trustees of the Central States Health and Welfare Fund, including Fitzsimmons and Kleindienst. The suit called for the removal of the existing trustees, election of new trustees, and a $7 million dollar judgment against the defendants. In 1979 TDU won a major victory when the settlement forced the plaintiffs to return some $3 million to the fund. It also created new procedural guarantees to protect the fund from abuse in the future.

The House Committee on Oversight held hearings on the Central States funds in June 1978, and TDU sent Phyllis Carpenter, the editor of *Scoop*, the Schneider road drivers' newsletter, and Pete Camarata to testify. PROD members also testified, supporting TDU's position calling for rank-and-file trustees. TDU took the pension fight directly to the president of the United States. The 1977 TDU convention voted to launch a postcard campaign directed to President Carter and to Secretary of Labor Marshall demanding that they use their powers under the Pension Reform Act (ERISA) to remove the pension fund trustees. The TDU pension reform campaign was largely successful. Because of the long history of abuse and the resulting public outcry, and partly as a result of TDU's pressure, the Carter administration used the power of the federal government to clean up the Central States Pension Fund, removing the gangsters and stopping the poor investment practices of the past.

Protecting Working Conditions

TDU members returned home from the organization's 1976 founding convention and enthusiastically threw themselves into local contract fights and strike support. On the West Coast, TDU members were active in supporting striking beer truck drivers and grocery warehouse workers. In Los Angeles, TDUer Doug Allan led a strike at Acme Carloading. In the East there was a UPS strike lasting three and a half months. In Pennsylvania, TDU members confronted a productivity drive by management, first at Jones Motor and

Helms and later at almost every other freight company. In the spring of 1977 Helms Express introduced production standards that required each worker to move a certain number of tons of freight per shift. Each worker's production was recorded, and workers with the lowest output were subject to discipline, including firing.

At that time production standards were virtually nonexistent in Teamster-represented shops and were contrary to the provisions of the contract, but they nevertheless had been approved by the grievance panel of the Teamsters Eastern Conference Joint Area Committee. This fight over productivity was at the heart of the contract struggle and was to be one of the central issues for the next decade. With the help of TDU attorneys Paul Boas and Ron Berlin, a Helms worker named Tom Sever (who several years later became the president of Local 30) filed suit in federal district court on behalf of Teamsters at Helms against both Helms and the Eastern Conference of Teamsters. TDU persuaded Larry Chrzan, president of Local 30, to support the case, and together TDU and the local union officials set up a legal defense fund.

In February 1978, while that case was still pending, Helms fired Steve Pawlak, the father of nine children, for low productivity. In response, the Western Pennsylvania TDU chapter and Local 30 president Chrzan organized a protest demonstration of 130 Teamsters, spouses and children at the Helms Express terminal in Irwin, Pennsylvania. This was followed up on 17 June 1978 with another protest by 125 Helms workers, Local 30 members and other Teamsters and their families, this time at Teamster headquarters in Washington, DC. It was Chrzan who called the protest and chartered the buses to take the protestors to Washington, while TDU did much of the organizing. Despite these efforts, in early 1979 the US Third Circuit Court of Appeals ruled that workers could be fired for just cause, and – since the union had approved the introduction of productivity standards – failure to meet the standards was just cause. TDU did not give up on the issue, but launched a new campaign in an attempt to get local unions to pass resolutions against productivity standards. In the next several years TDU continued to battle against productivity standards as employers, with the complicity of the union, introduced them at other trucking companies around the country.

In these same years TDU was involved in other equally important fights over working conditions. In 1976 Dave Gaibis and Chuck Lowery began a long fight over the issue of 'baby-sitting the phone'. The trucking companies demanded that workers who were logged 'off duty' wait at home by the phone for a call from the dispatcher. Gaibis and Lowery thought it only right that time spent waiting by the phone be logged as 'on duty', which would soon force the employers to relinquish this practice. Gaibis, Lowery and TDU took the issue to Teamster grievance panels, the Bureau of Motor

Carrier Safety, and to anyone else who would listen. Again, TDU lost, but it had been on the right side of the issue, and it had carried out a serious fight.

Defending the Integrity of the Contract

The fights over productivity standards and 'baby-sitting the phone' in which TDU was engaged between 1976 and 1979 were only particular examples of a much bigger issue, namely the defense of the integrity of the freight contract. When TDU was born in 1976, the National Master Freight Agreement covered almost 500,000 dock workers, city drivers, road drivers, and clerks. It tended to determine the economic terms of the contracts covering carhaulers, UPS workers, warehouse workers and many others. Those freight workers and other related workers were the economic and organizational backbone of the Teamsters union. When the freight contract was weakened it not only undercut the wages, benefits and working conditions of those Teamsters directly affected, but undermined the contracts of other Teamsters whose agreements were based on it and weakened the organizational structure of the entire union. Beginning in the 1970s, the National Master Freight Agreement came under attack from several directions. First, there were the government's moves to deregulate the trucking industry, which would lead to greater competition tending to drive down wages. Second was the growth of non-union trucking companies, a phenomenon that could be expected to increase if deregulation passed. Third, and closely related to the rise of non-union trucking, was the increased use of truck leasing companies, whose employees were paid below union scale. Fourth was the growth of substandard riders, particularly the exempt commodities rider, which was becoming a sweetheart deal. TDU fought the industry on all these issues.

From the very beginning, TDU, like the Teamsters union itself, opposed the deregulation of the trucking industry that was being pushed through Congress by important senators like Democrat Edward Kennedy of Massachusetts. TDU sent Doug Allan of Los Angeles Local 208 and Norm Rosen of Pittsburgh Local 249 to testify against deregulation before the Senate Subcommittee on Anti-Trust and Monopoly. Rosen told the senators, 'Today the industry is in a state of flux without any form of deregulation. Thousands of drivers and dock workers are being shuffled from company to company, losing seniority and vacation benefits with each move. Many do not find jobs because of age or blacklisting. Mergers, acquisitions and bankruptcies are everyday realities.

'The union is both corrupt and ineffective in fighting for our job security. The companies put profits above human considerations. Deregulation, on top of the problems that already exist, amounts to an untimely hit below the belt. Maybe it's time the government showed a little loyalty to the American worker who pays his taxes and has fought its wars. Does it make sense to establish ERISA [the Pension Reform Act] on the one hand to try to protect our pensions and to institute deregulation on the other and put our very jobs in jeopardy?'[3]

Within the union, TDU argued that the union should mobilize the members to stop deregulation. 'If our officers want to *fight* deregulation, rallying the members is the way to go', wrote *Convoy* in February 1979. 'Our union could very easily put many thousands of Teamsters in Washington by calling a one-day protest strike and chartering busses from locals throughout the East, with smaller delegations from distant locals.'[4] There was a precedent for such political strikes: the Black Lung Association of the United Mine Workers had called such strikes in West Virginia in the 1960s to force the state legislature to pass mine safety and health legislation. However, the use of rank-and-file power was beyond the imagination of the Teamsters leadership.

TDU argued that the union itself could effectively regulate the freight industry if the union would just organize it. But in fact the opposite was taking place. The industry was being deunionized by the growth of non-union carriers. The largest and most important non-union trucking company was Overnite. Based in the South, Overnite began to move north during the 1970s: to Louisville, then to St. Louis, and then to Kansas City. As TDU noted, 'Overnite is the first major non-union threat in freight.'[5]

When the union finally did launch a concerted drive to organize the 5,000 Overnite workers, it lost the representation election by a vote of two to one. In an article in *Convoy*, Ken Paff argued that Overnite workers had voted against the union because of the deterioration of the union's contracts and its failure to represent the members: 'What will organize Overnite, Viking, and hundreds of smaller non-union carriers will be winning better contracts, and gaining the confidence of the rank and file so that they will be proud to sell our union to our fellow drivers. That's the job ahead of us.'[6]

Other companies, encouraged by Overnite, either refused to sign the contract, as did Ringsby United, or busted the union altogether, like Dealers Transit. Some union operations subcontracted work to non-union companies or companies with substandard contracts from nonfreight locals. Grocery companies in the Midwest, for example, laid off union workers and with the approval of the union brought in a substandard outfit called Rentar. The Teamsters leadership, rather than taking on the task of organizing the unorganized, decided that it had to grant concessions to unionized carriers so that they could compete with their non-union rivals. One way to do this was through the expansion of the special commodities divisions of unionized companies. Carriers then diverted freight from their union operations to their non-union special commodities divisions. Thus, special commodities became a loophole in the contract. This undermining of the integrity of the National Master Freight Agreement was to make the fight for a decent contract all the more important in 1979.

The Fight for the 1979 Contract

As the 1979 contracts in freight, carhauling and UPS approached, the Teamster rank and file found that they had three opponents to deal with: the employers, the union and the government. After a split in their ranks, the employers reunited in May 1978 as Trucking Management, Inc. (TMI), made up of thirty-five employer organizations representing 500 to 600 carriers.[7] TMI hired J. Curtis Counts, a former director of the Federal Mediation and Conciliation Service, as its chief negotiator.[8] TMI approached the 1979 contract seeking take-aways in the areas of working conditions, and hoping to hold wage and benefit increases to a minimum. 'This time', wrote *Convoy*, 'it's the *employers* who are looking forward to the new contract. They are on the offensive, and getting their way most of the time. The union isn't standing up to them.'[9]

If the employers were prepared for the negotiations, the union was not. One professor of labor relations wrote, 'In sharp contrast to Hoffa, who – despite his shortcomings – provided clear direction and control and held the complete confidence and allegiance of the membership, Fitzsimmons has decentralized power and control in order to retain the support of important union officials at the conference and local levels and does not have the membership's unquestioning support.'[10] As *Convoy* noted, the freight contract may not have been uppermost in the minds of the union leaders. 'Our top officers are more worried about protecting themselves than protecting us. Their big worry is staying out of jail, not negotiating the freight agreement. Under pressure from the federal government, they may be willing to sell out our contract as part of the deal.'[11]

Like the Republican Nixon administration in the early 1970s, the Democratic Carter administration was trying to hold down workers' wages in order to stop inflation. Nixon had used wage and price controls, while Carter called for 'voluntary participation guidelines'. In an attempt to get the Teamsters union to abide by the guidelines, the Carter administration indicated that it was willing to make a deal with Fitzsimmons. Robert Strauss, the chairman of the Democratic Party and Carter's special counsel on inflation, said, 'He [Fitzsimmons] is desperate for respectability, and I'm not too proud to give him some if he helps me.'[12]

In an open letter to President Carter run on the front page of *Convoy* in January 1979, the TDU International Steering Committee wrote, 'Mr. President, we have concluded that we have already sacrificed enough. Our employers' demands made last month are a list of take-aways of our hard-won rights, our union officials are too willing to give in to them, and your administration is encouraging both of them. So we, the Teamsters for a Democratic Union, have decided to work every minute of every day from now till our contracts expire to prevent us from sacrificing any more, and to win back what we have already lost. We believe this stand is not only in our interest, but in the interest of the millions of other working Americans, whether they are in unions or not. We urge you to reconsider just who you are asking to sacrifice.'[13]

TDU: Unity and Organization

What was to be done in the face of the employers and the government? TDU's response was two-fold: unity and organization. It was necessary to achieve unity because there existed several rank-and-file organizations in the union in addition to TDU: first and most important, the Professional Drivers Council, the health and safety and union reform group; also the Fraternal Association of Steel Haulers, which organized and represented owner-operator steelhaulers; and finally, UPSurge, the reform group among UPS workers.

TDU called for a united front of all of these organizations to fight for decent contracts in 1979. On 29 and 30 July 1978 these groups held what *Convoy* called an 'historic summit conference of rank and file Teamsters'. Out of that meeting came the Majority Contract Coalition. The coalition adopted the slogan 'Draw the Line in '79' and passed a resolution calling for a settlement 'no less than the 39 percent won by the miners'. Perhaps more important, the Majority Contract Coalition called for improved grievance procedures, the defense of working conditions, greater job security and an end to the erosion of the contract. It was TDU that put the most energy and resources into building the Majority Contract Coalition, but the concept of the coalition demonstrated TDU's desire to work with the other organizations for the good of all Teamsters.

Having achieved unity, TDU's second job was organization. TDU had begun its organizing work in April 1978, when some forty-seven carhaulers and their spouses from ten companies and thirteen terminals met to form the Carhaulers Contract Committee (CCC). They counted additional support from carhaulers at five other companies and twelve other terminals nation-wide. In the summer of 1978, TDU organized a subcommittee made up of UPS workers from the East and Midwest because relations with UPSurge had broken down, and the UPSurge organization was no longer giving leadership to UPS workers. A contract network of Kroger workers, one of the few grocery chains that had a master contract, was also revitalized.

(Before the freight contract expired, TDU would lead a movement to reject the Kroger master contract by a three-to-one vote.) And TDU's Green Bay, Wisconsin chapter organized the 1,500 Schneider drivers using the *Scoop* newsletter.

The TDU convention in Windsor, Ontario in October 1978 was attended by 400 rank-and-file Teamsters and provided TDU with an opportunity to bring together its leading activists in freight, carhauling, UPS, grocery and other areas and to strengthen the contract organization. Two PROD staff members also attended the convention and announced PROD's intention to work within the Majority Contract Coalition on a local basis.

TDU Organizer Ken Paff explained in a front-page article in *Convoy*, 'TDU is not out to organize isolated wildcat strikes which could possibly result in victimizations by the companies. We are out to organize enough national pressure that will force a sanctioned strike – and the members will then have a chance to keep the heat on and win a decent contract (and when a strike is called it's majority rule, not two-thirds). Naturally, if wildcats do occur we will do everything we can to help protect people and make them as effective as possible. ... '[14]

Throughout early 1979 TDU was busy organizing to oppose Carter's wage policy, the employers' hard-line negotiating position, and their own union officials' tendency to make concessions. On 24 March 1979, a TDU protest rally was held in Washington, DC, and a rank-and-file truck driver named Bill Slater got up to speak.

Bill Slater

Bill Slater was born in 1924 in Riverside, California and spent the first years of his life in the Riverside and San Bernardino areas. His father left the family when Bill was five, and in 1931, in the dark days of the Depression, his mother was forced to place Bill and his sister in a Catholic orphanage in San Diego because she could not support them.

When he got into his early teens, Bill was expelled from the orphanage. 'I was a hell-raiser even then', Bill remembers, 'and I got a little too big, and I had the kids disobeying law and authority, so they decided to get rid of me.' Thereafter he was a 'ward of the county', living in different foster homes until he was seventeen.

In July 1941 Bill joined the Navy: 'Immediately I went to Pearl Harbor, and they started a war.' He was working as an ammunition handler on a ship's gun on 7 December 1941, the day the Japanese launched their in-famous attack. He spent the next four years on ships involved in the great battles against the Japanese in the Pacific. When the war ended Slater considered staying in the Navy. 'I just was dubious about getting out of the

Bill Slater.

service because it was sort of a home to me. I went in there to get a home, and I didn't have any experience or training of any sort. It took quite a bit, but the guys finally talked me out of the service.' Bill had a girlfriend in San Francisco, and he went up there to be near her. He got a job with the San Francisco municipal railway system, married the girlfriend, they had two children, and, forty-two years later they're still married: 'One of us has got to be tolerant as hell', says Bill, 'and I think it's her.'

After a short while Bill left the railway and went to work for Schlage Lock, joined the Metal Polishers and Platers Union, and was elected steward. 'There is one thing that my generation should be very grateful for. We were fortunate to come back from World War II and enter a labor market that was pretty much dominated by strong, tough, militant unions, and the employers were reluctant to take them on.'

Bill left Schlage in 1954, worked for a year as a taxicab driver in San Francisco, and for the first time became a member of the Teamsters union. A year later he bought a truck and went to work as a carhauler for Insured Transport and became a member of Teamsters Local 70. For most of fifteen years there he served as the steward, and in that role he came to see the shortcomings of the grievance system. 'I knew the variation between the International and the lower troops below the International level. If you were a B.A. and you were representing somebody and you took your grievance down to the panel, well, if you did what the International wanted, why you got your grievance taken care of. If you didn't do what they wanted, you didn't win too many grievances.'

One night in the summer of 1978 another truck driver, John Torbet, stopped by to talk to him. 'John is a hell of a sweet guy', says Slater, 'though rather on the naive side. I always call him Mr. Decency. So he came over to the house one night and presented the package to me. I told John that I'd always hoped that there would be something like TDU come along, because I was not satisfied with the Teamsters and the way it was run at all. But I didn't jump right aboard the TDU bandwagon. They were having the Majority Contract Coalition meeting, and John said he was going back.' Bill attended the Majority Contract Coalition meeting in Cleveland in July 1978, and he was excited about the meeting.

'I was impressed with Ken Paff, and Carole Paff, and Mel Packer. And of course Pete. Pete was my idol. I had read his story in that magazine I'm not too wild about, the *Reader's Digest*. I was quite impressed with Pete's activities in 1976, and I thought anybody that would walk into that den of thieves at the Teamster convention, and do what he did, he had to be worth something, right?'

Bill joined TDU, and a year later traveled to the protest rally in Washington where he was to make his first speech. Bill had little formal education and had had no previous speaking experience, but he had spent weeks tinkering with the speech, sitting in the cab of his truck, and occasionally pulling out his notebook and making some small changes. When he stood up to speak he was nervous, but when he spoke, he spoke from his heart:

> Today there is great use of the word 'reasonable' when one is discussing employer and employee relations. The word is used by a lot of very sincere people. But I wonder how many people realize that not too many years ago when the big business barons were king; when there were huge sweatshops filled with young children who were working for the meagerest of wages; when there were no unions; and when you tried to organize one you were beaten and fired – I wonder how many people would have said that the employers were reasonable in those days?
>
> While I was not aware of it at the time, probably the reason I have been heavily pro-union all my working life is a memory that I have that took place many years ago. It is a picture that is permanently etched in my mind. It is of a woman who is struggling to carry two pails of water from her neighbor's house to her own home in order that she may bathe her children. She is carrying the water because reasonable people have turned the water off to her house. In the evening she works by candlelight and kerosene lamps because reasonable people have turned off the electricity. She cooks over the trashburner section of

an old gas stove because reasonable people turned off the gas. Of course, this situation did not last long because shortly thereafter she had to place her children in an orphanage because she no longer had the means to support them. The lady struggling to carry that water was crippled – this lady was my mother.

The only reason these supposed benevolent bastards are reasonable is because there are unions. The very fact that you are able to walk with pride and dignity on the job is because of the union. Every social benefit that you now enjoy was brought about by unions. Social security, workmen's compensation, disability pay, even the public schools were in large part brought about by unions – by unions that organized and struggled against great odds – who fought pitched battles in the streets of every major city in this nation. They struck for months to secure our future.

I make this pointed opening statement because I want you to understand that we, the members of Teamsters for a Democratic Union, are one hundred percent behind the rank-and-file Teamster movement.

However, we are unalterably opposed to all those people, official and unofficial, who have made our union synonymous with corruption. We are opposed to those people who have abused the power that was entrusted to them. We are opposed to those who have shamed the memory of all those good men who were murdered back in the thirties, and all those who had their heads beat on in order to gain the conditions we now enjoy. We are opposed because these officials have not kept faith with those brave and courageous people. They have abdicated their duty. ...

Just look at a few of the things these people have done. For openers, how about the looting of the Central States Pension Fund? No one knows the amount of money stolen. The last figure I heard was something like eight hundred million dollars. Every one of the former trustees for that fund has a criminal record as long as your arm. How about Tony Provenzano appointing his twenty-one-year-old daughter as secretary-treasurer of a large New Jersey local while he serves a life sentence for the murder of his rival? All this with the approval and blessing of Frank Fitzsimmons. How about Fitzsimmons sending the union's plane from Washington, DC to California to pick up his golf clubs? How about the top five families in the union hierarchy who draw one and one-half million dollars of your money each year? It's little wonder that Jackie Presser, a member of one of those families can gift his wife with a Rolls Royce on her birthday. ...

Finally, we are opposed because we now find that they have committed the ultimate crime and they are now sleeping in the same bed with the employer in order that they may keep their own country club life-style intact. ...

My friends, we at TDU are in business solely to give the rank and file a chance to get their union back. We are not going to tolerate any more of their blatant disregard of the rank and file. We are in business so that we might organize to stop productivity schemes that will make us so many digits on an IBM card to be stuffed into a computer, and when the read-out comes, if you do not measure up to standard, out you go!

We have to organize because only the organized will survive. If you want to utter one word of dissent, you had better organize. If you do not want to become a slave to two masters, you had better organize. ... Go into your workplace and sign up your coworkers and their friends. Explain to them the urgent need to rebuild and put dignity back into our union. ...

It may sound corny, but it is as true now as the day it was first uttered: 'United we will stand, but divided we will fall.' This, then, is TDU's reason for being in business – to organize and rebuild our union and regain the confidence and respect of the American people, and to tell the employers that we will not lie down and become their slaves. We ask your help.

Strikes and Contracts

Under pressure from the rank-and-file movement that TDU and its allies in the Majority Contract Coalition had built, Teamster President Frank Fitzsimmons called a national freight strike on 1 April 1979. TDU had forced Fitzsimmons to call the national strike, and that in itself was a historic achievement. Unfortunately Fitzsimmons had no intention of leading and organizing a militant strike to win back the terrain already lost to the employers. The 1979 strike was less militant than either the 1970 wildcat or the brief 1976 strike, which had been accompanied by wildcats in Detroit. At ll:22 p.m. on 10 April, just thirty-eight minutes before the eleventh day of the strike (at which time the International would have had to pay about \$10 million in strike benefits to its members), Fitzsimmons called an end to the strike.

Examining the tentative agreement Fitzsimmons had made with the companies, TDU found the settlement to be poor, and urged the rank and file 'Send This One Back!' After a ten-day strike, the union had gained little in terms of the cost of living clause over which the strike was called, and had done nothing to improve the grievance procedures or defend working conditions. TDU feared that everything would be sold out through contract supplements and riders.

The 1979 Steelhaulers Strike

The steelhaulers, many of whom were owner-operators, had long-standing grievances against the shippers, carriers and the union, which had not only failed to represent them but had attacked them when they tried to organize themselves. The IBT had called for a 'selective strike' of certain steel-hauling companies, but very few were actually struck, and the union was having no impact whatsoever.

In exasperation, the steelhaulers walked out, first in Canton and Youngstown, Ohio and then throughout the Midwest. The TDU members helped organize mass meetings of hundreds of steelhaulers in Canton and Youngstown to keep the members informed and keep the strike strong, and

TDU helped to spread the strike to Pittsburgh, Detroit, Cleveland, Gary, and other steel centers. When Fitzsimmons called off the freight strike on 10 April, the steelhaulers stayed out. It was the biggest rank-and-file rebellion since the 1976 wildcat. Throughout the heartland, there was massive turnout for Teamster steelhauler meetings: 400 in Pittsburgh on 11 April; 500 in Gary on 16 April. At these meetings the steelhaulers voted to stay out on strike, though the union never gave the strike its official sanction.

After four weeks on strike, most steelhaulers returned to work on 30 April with a new contract giving them higher pay, sickdays, tarping charges and a fuel allowance. They had won all of their demands. However, the National Steel Carriers Association still had not signed, and in Youngstown a meeting of 600 steelhaulers voted to continue the walkout until they did. They stayed out until 4 May, when National Steel Carriers finally capitulated.

Shortly before the strike ended, a meeting of thirty-five steelhaulers from Canton, Youngstown, Pittsburgh, Detroit, Erie and Cleveland met in Youngstown on 24 April and formed 'a new *united* steelhaulers movement – TDU Steel Haulers Organizing Committee (TDU-SHOC).' SHOC was an attempt to turn the steelhaulers rebellion into an ongoing part of the Teamster reform movement. 'The job for the future', wrote *Convoy*, 'is to organize every area as well as Youngstown so we can enforce the contract, stop sellouts, and change our union to fight for us instead of against us. The steelhauler strike of 1979 was a very good beginning.'[15] As the steelhaulers returned to work, the official announcement was made that the freight contract, contrary to TDU's recommendation and its hopes, had been accepted by a vote of 127,872 to 45,577.

The Carhaulers Wildcat of 1979

On 1 June 1979 Frank Fitzsimmons announced he had negotiated his 'greatest contract' for the carhaulers – but apparently the carhaulers themselves didn't think so, for in the automotive centers there were rejection votes at union meetings, protest demonstrations, and at the giant Lordstown terminal in Ohio a strike by 700 carhaulers. Michigan carhaulers, their rigs loaded with new cars, drove in a vast convoy to Lordstown.

When the vote on the carhaulers contract was announced on 3 July the rank and file had rejected the contract by a vote of 6,976 to 6,309. The vote was a tremendous victory for TDU's Carhaulers Contract Committee, which had organized the contract rejection. But Frank Fitzsimmons ignored the vote and imposed the pact on the carhaulers under the union's rules, which at that time required a two-thirds majority to reject a contract.

On 1 June the union also announced that it had reached a tentative agreement on the UPS contract. TDU urged the members to reject this contract as well, but among UPS workers TDU was too weak to lead a rejection vote or to force a strike, and the contract was ratified by a majority. The 1979 contract round had shown that the rank and file, led by TDU, was capable of organizing a majority of workers to oppose the union's contracts, as it had done in carhauling, and of leading powerful official and unofficial strikes, as it had done among the steelhaulers.

The Growth of TDU and Its Relations with FASH and PROD

In the three years between 1975 and 1978 TDU had grown into a small but stable reform organization, and in doing so it had become a pole of attraction for other Teamster dissidents throughout North America. One of the most important developments had come in 1978 when Jack Vlahovic, Norm Wilkinson and Jim Blomfield, the leaders of 10,000-member Teamster Local 213 representing construction workers in British Columbia and the Yukon, the largest construction local in the Teamsters, had joined TDU.

Back in 1975 Wilkinson had been elected as a lone reformer on the Local 213 executive board, and then two years later he was joined on a reform slate by Jack Vlahovic as secretary-treasurer and Jim Blomfield as trustee, and all three were elected in January 1977. This did not sit well with Ed Lawson, who was the former head of Local 213, the head of the Canadian Conference of Teamsters, a Canadian Senator, and an ally of Frank Fitzsimmons.

As soon as the reformers won, Lawson moved to block Vlahovic and his slate from taking power in the local. First, Lawson filed charges against Vlahovic, accusing him of damaging Lawson's image during the union election campaign. Vlahovic was found guilty of the charges and removed from office by Joint Council 36 of British Columbia, which Lawson controlled. The charges were later overturned by the Teamsters General Executive Board, but despite his exoneration, Vlahovic was still ordered removed from office. Then Lawson moved to create a new Local 181 in order to split up and destroy Local 213, which Vlahovic now headed. But Vlahovic had strong membership backing and thwarted Lawson's efforts to carve up Local 213; later Lawson's Local 181 was quietly folded up. TDU did everything it could to support Vlahovic and the others in their fight to regain the offices to which they had been elected.

In early 1978 another Canadian group, this one in Ontario, also affiliated with TDU. Called Teamsters for Teamsters, it had developed a program remarkably similar to TDU's. The affiliation of these two Canadian groups represented an important expansion of TDU throughout the Teamster organization in continental North America, and at the same time gave TDU a truly international character. During this same period TDU also worked with Puerto Rican Teamsters.[16]

As TDU got larger, it could no longer be run from somebody's kitchen table. In the spring of 1978 Ken Paff, a truck driver from Teamster Local 407 in Cleveland, was hired as TDU's full-time organizer, at a substantial cut in pay. Paff had been born in Beaver Falls, Pennsylvania, the son of a steelworker and a housewife, and the youngest of seven children. When he was ten years old his parents divorced and his mother moved to California, where one of her older sons was living, and Paff spent his teenage years in a rather poor section of Santa Ana.

A good student, in 1964 Paff went to the University of California at Berkeley to study physics. Like many other students of that generation he became involved in the local civil rights movement and in the related free speech movement at the university. When he left college he worked for a while as a computer programmer, then as a school teacher, but didn't feel he was cut out for either of those professions. Finally Paff got a job as a truck driver in California and soon thereafter moved with his wife Carole to Cleveland. There Paff got a job as a truck driver for Shipper's Dispatch and became friends with some of the TURF activists, including Lester Williams, who worked at Shipper's. Both Ken and Carole Paff became active in the Teamster reform movement and were founders of TDC, which Ken had served as secretary.

The hiring of Ken Paff as TDU's national organizer made it possible for TDU to begin to set organizing goals and priorities. One of the first decisions, in the fall of 1978, was to move the national office from Cleveland to Detroit, where TDU had one of its largest chapters. As TDU's first full-time organizer, Ken Paff was the principal architect of TDU's organizational structure and played a central role in developing its campaigns. 'We tried from the start', Paff explains, 'to build a national and international movement, but based on local chapters and intiative. We always stressed local action, local organization, local leadership. Our national leadership people have come out of the local struggles, the contract fights, and our solidarity campaigns.'

The growing reputation of TDU in the labor movement enabled Paff and the TDU Steering Committee to gradually assemble a small but very talented professional staff to work for the movement. By the late 1980s that staff had grown to ten, with additional interns and volunteers, working on a shoestring budget of just $400,000. Even in 1978, when the office was established in Detroit and the budget was less than half that figure, bold plans were being made. Educational literature and programs, a sophisticated and ambitious legal program, and computerized data base operations were being put in place by the small, underpaid staff – and sometimes in a better fashion than in some international unions. 'We always emphasized education and leadership training. Early on, in 1979, we published the *Teamster Legal Rights Handbook*, written by Ellis Boal, one of our dedicated attorneys who later became a close friend. That was the first of a number of such publications.'

The work for the TDU movement was not without personal sacrifices for Ken and Carole Paff and their daughter Avonda. 'We lived under constant threat in those days. One of the real victories of TDU has been its ability over the years to create a more open atmosphere. Today union members can speak out. A lot of Teamsters don't know it, but this didn't come easy. It took a decade of work and struggle, and a lot of courageous people. Some of them lost jobs, pensions, suffered injuries, and worse.'

Under Paff's guidance TDU developed an organizing style based on close collaboration between the staff, members of the TDU International Steering Committee, local chapter leaders and other activists. As a result, TDU developed a broad leadership and friendly working relations between leaders and staff. Several veteran staff members went on to work for other unions, and all credited TDU for their training. 'I've been lucky, and privileged, really', says Ken. 'Lucky to find such a wonderful use for any talents and ambitions I've got, and privileged to work with and for many fine people. I've worked with so-called ordinary people who are, in fact, extraordinary people.'

TDU was gradually becoming an important, if still small, force in the Teamsters, but it was not the union's only reform organization. There were two reform groups that TDU had to deal with, the most important of which were the Fraternal Association of Steel Haulers and the Professional Drivers Council. Since it was founded in 1967, FASH, under the leadership of Bill Hill, had created strong chapters in the steel centers of Detroit, Gary and Pittsburgh, and in the early 1970s claimed 11,000 members, probably an exaggerated estimate.[17]

FASH had once intended to reform the Teamsters, but it had faced such repression and violence that it decided to take the owner-operator steel and special commodity haulers out of the union. TDU had explicitly repudiated this strategy in the constitution it had adopted at its founding convention. However, in its relations with FASH members and in *Convoy*, TDU tried to make it clear that while it rejected the secession strategy advocated by FASH, it was sympathetic to the problems of the owner-operator.

When FASH called for a strike on 10 November 1978, TDU issued this statement in the *Convoy*: 'TDU believes that the steelhaulers in our union have for too long been unrepresented or misrepresented. ... TDU is working toward a *united* stand of all Teamsters. ... We call upon the General Executive Board to grant the steelhaulers the right to vote separately on their own contract, and to democratically choose their own Teamster negotiators for their contract.'[18] But *Convoy* explained that 'TDU did not back FASH's major demand – to pull out of the Teamsters Union – as we believe that all Teamster drivers will be stronger fighting in a united way for good contracts and to clean up our union.'[19] Despite its criticisms of the FASH strategy, TDU kept lines of communication open and relations amicable. When TDU called for a coalition effort on the 1979 contract, FASH was invited. However, given the fundamental differences in strategy, it was impossible for FASH and TDU to function much more closely.

TDU's relations with PROD were quite different. Although TDU, with its history of having led wildcat strikes, was seen as the radical wing of the Teamster reform movement, and PROD with its lobbying and legal experience represented the respectable reformers, in reality the two groups were converging. TDU leaders began to realize that the two groups complemented each other in serveral ways. Both groups had members throughout the country, TDU having more members in the Midwest and on the West Coast, while PROD was concentrated on the East Coast and in the South. TDU had more members in big cities and more dock workers and warehouse workers, and more Black members, while PROD had more road drivers and more members in small towns. TDU had more experience with contracts and union elections; PROD had more experience with legislation and litigation.

In early 1977 TDU began to make overtures to PROD, the first of which was a letter sent by TDU to PROD calling for greater cooperation between the two groups. *Convoy* reported, 'PROD has declined the offer. But TDU will continue to offer cooperation on specific projects and other common goals.'[20] The road drivers in PROD were proud of their professionalism, and perhaps a little exclusive in their outlook. 'When the merger was first proposed', says Frank Greco, 'I was one of those who opposed the merger, because I thought it was better to have just the truck drivers with their problems and their resources applied to those problems. I thought it would be much more effective. But it just wasn't working out, the resources just weren't there, and we needed a broader base. I think what we got with TDU is much better, the broad concept of all Teamsters. But it took a while to see that.' Charlie Helton, who worked at Roadway in Chattanooga, approved of the idea of a merger between PROD and TDU, because 'It made it look like a large group, instead of two small groups.'

So the discussion went on within PROD, and gradually opinion shifted. A year later, TDU sent a letter to PROD calling for unity between the two groups in a fight for a decent contract in 1979. 'The key is *unity*', wrote TDU. 'Unity of our strategy, our program and our action. For that reason the TDU National Steering Committee is calling on PROD and other rank and file groups, local officers and members interested in winning a decent contract to join us in a rank-and-file coalition. The stakes are high. Disunity could lead to disaster for the membership.'[21] This time PROD was more receptive to TDU's overtures, taking a positive attitude toward the Majority Contract Coalition formed in late July 1978.

The work together on the contract led to increasing contacts both between PROD and TDU members and staff, and to greater mutual respect, leading to the first steps toward merger in the summer of 1979. In the next few months TDU and PROD members spoke at each others' meetings, and in some areas joint chapter meetings were held. Finally, on 3 November 1979 TDU and PROD were united at the annual TDU convention in Ypsilanti, Michigan. The first steering committee of the new merged organization had twenty-two members, eleven from each organization. The new group had two offices, a national headquarters in Detroit, and a lobbying office in Washington, DC to be staffed by an attorney. The name of the organization was to be Teamsters for a Democratic Union, but the PROD name would be used in association with activities in the area of truck driver health and safety, while the organization's newspaper would be called *Convoy-Dispatch*. Unity of the rank-and-file movement had been achieved.

The End of an Era

In the years between its founding as TDC in 1975 and its merger with PROD at the end of 1979, TDU had operated within the well-established framework of the regulated trucking industry and a largely unionized environment. In 1980, with the simultaneous onset of a depression and introduction of deregulation, TDU entered an entirely new situation.

Notes

1. Teamsters for a Democratic Union blasted the bargain between the Carter administration and Fitzsimmons: 'The entire deal now being arranged through the Labor Department is more a cosmetic rearrangement to make things look good than to effectively change the way the fund works for us. Its main aim appears to be saving face for Teamster officials and keeping them out of the slammer. TDU has said that one of the key pension reforms is rank and file control of the pension funds through elected trustees' ('Fitz Quits Pension Fund', *Convoy*, no. 16, March 1977). In 1989 TDU organizer Ken Paff asserted that TDU had been wrong in its criticism of the Carter administration's cleanup of the fund.
2. Nor was the Central States Pension Fund the only Teamster fund coming under criticism. The Labor Department also sued to remove Robert Knee, Jr. as the administrator and the eight trustees of the Teamsters Ohio Highway Drivers Welfare Fund. Knee was accused of taking hundreds of thousands of dollars in excessive payments from the fund. Among the trustees forced to resign was William Presser, who had dominated the fund.
3. 'Crisis in the Teamsters, Part 4: Deregulation – What It Means to You', *Convoy*, no. 26 (April 1978).
4. 'How to Beat Deregulation', *Convoy*, no. 34 (February 1979).
5. 'Overnite Moving in Scabs – International Sits Back', *Convoy*, no. 20 (October 1978).
6. Ken Paff, 'Why We Lost at Overnite', *Convoy*, no. 29 (August 1978).
7. As the contract expiration approached, a group of California carriers, led by Delta Lines, split from TMI and formed the California Motor Carriers Bargaining Unit. TDU described it as 'a move to break from the master freight agreement and negotiate their own (substandard) contract in California' ('California Carriers Announce Separate Bargaining to Bust NMFA', *Convoy*, no. 33, Jan. 1979). If the carriers signed a separate contract, it would mean a historic reversal of the union's drive for a national contract and the breakdown of the NMFA.

8. Levinson, 'Trucking', in Gerald G. Somers, ed., *Collective Bargaining: Contemporary American Experience*, Madison 1980, pp. 142–44.

9. 'The 1979 Master Freight Agreement', a special supplement in *Convoy*, no. 28 (June–July 1978).

10. Levinson, 'Trucking', p. 145.

11. 'The 1979 Master Freight Agreement', *Convoy*, no. 28 (June-July 1978).

12. 'This Deal Stinks!' *Convoy*, no. 27 (May 1978).

13. 'Open Letter to President Carter', *Convoy*, no. 33 (January 1979).

14. 'Strike Happy?' *Convoy*, no. 35 (March 1979).

15. 'How the Rank & File Won the Steelhaul Strike', *Convoy*, no. 37 (May 1979).

16. In 1978 TDU also extended solidarity to a movement of Puerto Rican Teamsters. Juan Caballero, an organizer for Teamster Local 901 in Puerto Rico, had been murdered on 25 October 1977, and Teamster activists believed he had been killed by special police agents who mistook him for another Teamster organizer named Miguel Cabrera. In response, 15,000 Teamsters and other union members struck for one day in November 1977 in the Puerto Rican capital of San Juan. In early 1978, TDU supported a tour by Miguel Cabrera, who had come to explain the issues in Local 901 to Teamsters and other union members in the United States.

Later Miguel Cabrera was framed on the charge of murdering Alan Randall, a corporate attorney and professional union buster, who was reputed to be associated with the CIA. Then Luis Pagan, the secretary-treasurer of Local 901, fired Cabrera, apparently with the approval of the International. Some 150 Teamsters, including 50 stewards, supported Cabrera and called for the impeachment of Pagan. TDU covered the developments in *Convoy* and gave implicit support to Cabrera in his attempt to fight for his reputation and his job. The Puerto Rican Teamster movement did not directly affiliate with TDU, but TDU's solidarity was greatly appreciated and fraternal relations between the two movements were established.

17. See Dan Moldea, *The Hoffa Wars*, and George Sullivan, 'Working for Survival', in Alice and Staughton Lynd, *Rank and File*, and George Sullivan, 'Rank and File Rebellion in the International Brotherhood of Teamsters', in *Liberation*, May 1971.

18. 'TDU Issues Statement on Steelhaulers Strike Call', *Convoy*, no. 22 (November 1978).

19. 'FASH Strike Ends', *Convoy*, no. 34 (February 1979).

20. 'Unity', *Convoy*, no. 15 (February 1977).

21. 'Unity for the Contract Fight', *Convoy*, no. 34 (February 1979).

13

Red-Baiting and the Attack on TDU

TDC's role in the 1976 contract fight, its presence at the 1976 IBT convention, and TDU's strong showing in the first round of elections and in the votes on bylaws reform made TDU a potential threat to the International Teamster leadership and to the employers. The Teamster employers and the union leadership were both unaccustomed to dealing with opposition groups within the union, and their responses were as clumsy as they were crude: they simply lashed out.

The attack was led by Jackie Presser of the Ohio Teamsters, and his principal weapon was red-baiting: the charge that anyone who opposed him was a Communist. Red-baiting had a long history in the Teamsters, and Dave Beck in particular was notorious for branding his opponents as Bolsheviks. Fitzsimmons and Presser revived this tradition. Presser's *Ohio Teamster* newspaper regularly assailed TDU, and the Ohio Joint Council spent thousands of dollars for full-page advertisements denouncing TDU in newspapers in Cleveland and other major cities. They called TDU 'a socialist conspiracy' and charged TDUers with being 'outsiders', 'student radicals', and 'professional agitators', among other epithets.

The red-baiting attacks were effective at first, in part because there were some socialists involved in TDU. This should hardly have been surprising. As those who have read the history of the labor movement know, it has frequently been socialists who have organized labor unions and later worked to reform them, and TDU was no exception. Over the years, many of the most talented and dedicated labor union organizers were associated with one or another wing of the socialist movement. Mary 'Mother' Jones, organizer of mineworkers; Eugene V. Debs, leader of the American Railway Union; Elizabeth Gurley Flynn, leader of the Lawrence textile workers strike; Big Bill Haywood, head of the Western Federation of Miners; William Z. Foster, organizer of the 1919 steelworkers strike; Farrell Dobbs, organizer of the

Teamster road drivers; Walter Reuther, head of the autoworkers union; Harry Bridges, leader of the longshoremen; and even Teamster vice-president Harold Gibbons were all at one time or another members or supporters of one or another socialist or communist party.

But there has also been strong opposition to socialists in the labor movement from more conservative union leaders, from the employers and from the government. In the notorious Palmer Raids in 1919 and 1920, J. Edgar Hoover and A. Mitchell Palmer rounded up hundreds of immigrants who were then deported simply for their radical beliefs or membership in socialist organizations. Despite such repression, the involvement of socialists in the labor movement was taken for granted until the 1950s, when Senator Joseph McCarthy's anti-Communist witchhunt caused thousands of workers to be fired from their jobs and driven from their unions, nearly destroying radical currents in the American labor movement. However, the civil rights movement of the 1950s and antiwar movement of the 1960s brought about the creation of a new generation of radicals who in the early 1970s began to enter the labor force and the union movement in large numbers.

The new generation of socialists played a small but significant role in the organization of farmworkers, teachers and public employees. They were involved in the reform movement in the United Mine Workers and in the Steel Workers Fight Back movement, which supported Ed Sadlowski's campaign for president of the United Steelworkers. In recent years, labor leaders like the late Jerry Wurf, head of the American Federation of State, County and Municipal Employees, and William Winpisinger, president of the International Association of Machinists, have described themselves as socialists.

Some of young radicals of the 1970s were attracted to a small group called the International Socialists (I.S.), which believed in 'socialism from below', by which they meant that ordinary people needed to become active and involved in the unions and in politics in order to bring about real social change. Mostly idealistic young men and women who had been involved in the civil rights and antiwar movements, these people were far from being Communists. The International Socialists was different from most other socialist organizations in that, while it opposed capitalism, it also opposed the various Communist dictatorships in the Soviet Union, China, Vietnam and Cuba, and I.S. was a fervent supporter of Polish Solidarity when it appeared in 1980. It was a few members of the I.S. who became some of the active organizers of reform movements such as TDC, TDU and UPSurge.

Mike Friedman

One of the socialists in TDU was Mike Friedman. Now in law school, for fourteen years Mike Friedman worked as a truck driver and was an active member of Teamster Local 407. He ran for local office in his union and narrowly lost, later supporting and working closely with the reformers who were elected to lead Local 407 in the mid-1980s. He served as a local leader of TDU in Cleveland and as a member of the TDU International Steering Committee for several years. While his socialist views were certainly in a minority among the TDU leaders and members, he was widely respected for his contributions as an organizer, writer and speaker for the group.

Mike Friedman was born in 1944 in Brooklyn and for the first few years of his life lived with his mother, his uncle and his grandparents, while his father was in the hospital recovering from wounds he had received while serving in France during World War II. While his Jewish family was not particularly religious, there was a strong sense of Jewish culture and tradition. 'We went to temple on high holidays, we kept a kosher household, we went to temple on Shabbat fairly frequently. We always said Kiddush with the candles and blessed the wine before we ate on Friday; that was kind of a family ritual. And I went to Hebrew school and was bar mitzvah. So to that extent I had a fairly traditional religious upbringing.'

When Friedman was six his family moved to Richmond, Virginia and when he was ten to Columbus, Ohio. Settling in Columbus, the family felt something like culture shock, not so much because of religion as because of having different social and political values than the more conservative Columbus community. 'I always felt kind of uncomfortable in Columbus suburbia, and I think a lot of that had to do with my parents feeling uncomfortable in Columbus suburbia. It was not so much around religion, because the Columbus Jewish community is fairly tightknit, and I think my parents found a place in it. But it had to do with coming from the East, which reinforced our sense of political liberalism. It made my parents go out of their way to stress their liberal political values about integration, about Democrats versus Republicans. I had a very clear sense even in junior high school and high school that this is a white bread culture – and we eat rye bread at home. That was important.'

Perhaps it was the constant clash between the liberal values of his home and the conservative values of Columbus that led Mike Friedman to become an activist. While still in high school Friedman and his best friend Donny Ruben decided to do something to show the sincerity of their convictions. 'We did the most radical thing we could think of – we joined the NAACP.' Friedman graduated from Bexley High School in 1961 and went to Columbia University in New York City, and loved it. For the moment he gave up his involvement in politics and immersed himself in his studies. In addition to his studies at Columbia, he did a little social work, tutoring ghetto kids and participating in some of the first demonstrations against the Vietnam War. After graduating from Columbia, Mike went to Trinity College of Cambridge University in England to continue his studies in English literature. He spent two years in England, earned his degree from Cambridge, and returned to the US and got a job teaching during the 1967–68 school year at Knoxville College, a Black college in Knoxville, Tennessee.

At the time Knoxville College had an all-Black student body and only a few white teachers. Mike got involved in local civil rights work, and in April 1968 and he and his students were working in Memphis to build Martin Luther King's Poor People's Campaign march on Washington. On the evening of 4 April they learned that King had been assassinated. 'I determined I was going to take as many students as wanted to go to King's funeral in Memphis. But the dean told me I couldn't go because an accreditation group was coming to the campus, and they had to see me in my classroom. I told him I would see them when I got back. To make a long story short, we did go to Martin Luther King's funeral in Memphis – and I was fired.' The firing had to be approved by the faculty council, and Mike defended himself so eloquently that the faculty overruled the dean and Friedman was reinstated. Nevertheless, the college did not renew his contract for the next year.

'After the funeral, I met a number of the Southern Christian Leadership Conference people. Then I and a number of the students went to Washington, and I ended up spending the entire summer living in Washington in the Poor People's Campaign's Resurrection City and working with the SCLC. I was unpaid staff for Resurrection City through the summer of 1968.

'I was very involved. I sat in meetings with Andy Young and Jesse Jackson where a lot of the planning for Resurrection City took place. Resurrection City was a real national event, and it was exciting living and working with those people.' But Mike needed a job and took one teaching English and developing curriculum for Brooklyn College in New York.

'I was really taking politics much more seriously. I kind of threw myself into the stuff that was going on in the city.' As exciting as New York was, it did not satisfy Mike Friedman. 'To me the question was how to link up some of those progressive ideas with Middle America, with that vast majority of people out there. My sense was that unless they believed these progressive ideas you weren't going to get very far.' The group of radicals with whom Mike was working began to discuss this problem: how to explain their beliefs such as opposition to the Vietnam War and opposition to racism to the American people. 'We were a group of people who had very much the same frustration with the student movement. We realized that if we were going to make the kind of changes that we wanted to make, we had to reach beyond the academic environment, we had to reach beyond campus protest.'

So they decided to go to the people, in Middle America. In late 1970 Mike gave up his teaching career and he and his friends moved to Cleveland. Those in the group were all young men and women, most of them college-educated veterans of the student, civil rights and antiwar movements. They all considered themselves socialists. 'Our idea of socialism', says Friedman,

Jim West

Mike Friedman.

'was more democratic control, control by people who actually do the work in society; a bottom-up approach rather than top-down approach; a sense that you have to have a democratic interplay, that there is no group that has all the answers.'

Mike got a job as a cab driver and became a member of Teamster Local 555, and that was how he came to be at the founding meeting of TURF. 'One day someone called me. I'm not even sure who it was, but I think it was Steve Kindred. He said, "I understand you're in the Teamsters. Well, there's going to be a group of rank-and-file Teamsters in Toledo. Why don't you go?" I said, "Just drive out to Toledo by myself?" And he said, "Yeah, yeah, it will be okay."

'I'll never forget it', says Friedman. 'I walked in to the meeting, and there was this big beefy guy, and he said, "What are you doing here?" It kind of scared me. I said, "I'm a cab driver from Cleveland, I'm a Teamster member." And he reached out his hand and said, "You're a Teamster member? Then welcome, brother." That was Joe DiMaria, who we later elected the secretary-treasurer of Local 407. There was a whole group of people from Cleveland at the meeting, and when they returned they began holding TURF meetings. And I used to attend those and got to meet most of the guys who were active in our local.'

But Friedman didn't pursue his involvement in the Teamsters union at that time. He gave up the cab-driving job and took a better job in a factory. 'I ended up working on the assembly line at Westinghouse as a packer-assembler, making street lights, a job I had for almost three years. It was a union shop, the International Union of Electrical Workers. The plant must have had about 1,000 people in it when we started. I was elected steward, and we started a shopfloor newspaper, which we called *Workers of Westinghouse*. There were union elections while we were there, but I never ran for union office other than steward.'

In addition to labor organizing, the group also did community organizing in the Near West Side of Cleveland. 'One of the things we worked on was starting a neighborhood free health clinic. There was a free health clinic, but it was focused on the East Side and mostly oriented towards the drug problems of university students. And so we helped to start a free clinic for poor folks with health problems, and that clinic was remarkably successful. It went on as a free clinic for a number of years supported through charitable contributions, and then the city took it over and made it part of neighborhood health services as part of the city public health department, and it still exists.'

In about 1974 the group that had moved to Cleveland broke up, and Friedman and some other members of the group joined up with the International Socialists, which then had a few other members in Cleveland. 'I got laid off from the job at Westinghouse in 1974 and was looking around for something to do. I had taken a withdrawal card when I left the Teamsters a few years before, so I thought I'd go to truck driving school. So in August of 1974 I went to a school just out side of Columbus. I got casual work, on and off, but that was just when the recession of 1974 began to get pretty bad. So I must have worked from maybe August through December. I worked the dock at Spector, I drove for Mason-Dixon and Smith Transfer, but things started drying up pretty quickly at that point, and for a while I was unemployed or just did odd jobs. In the summer of 1976 I started working casual again, and after a while I was hired by Boss-Linco Lines.'

It was while working for Boss-Linco that Friedman became active in the Cleveland chapter of TDU. Mike Friedman and the few other socialists involved brought a wealth of experience in other social movements to enrich the struggle for reform in the Teamsters. They were also well educated and had technical skills such as the ability to put out leaflets and newspapers, and they were experienced organizers who had put together meetings and conferences. But perhaps most important, they brought their idealism and dedication to building a grass-roots movement.

Fitzsimmons and Presser seized upon the presence of a few socialists like Friedman in an attempt to discredit TDU. 'When we were organizing TDU', Friedman remembers, 'somebody who was sent in would stand up and say, "They say you're a Communist?" Or, "Isn't it true that you're a Communist?" And I would handle that in a very straightforward way, saying, "Look, TDU is not a Communist or a Socialist organization. It's an organization of Teamsters. I personally may be a socialist, and if you want to talk about my politics, I'll be happy to talk to you *after* this meeting. That's not what this meeting's about, and that's not what we're here to take up." And I would often go up to them afterwards and say, "Do you want to know about my politics?" And they were gone. They did not want to hear that. That was not why they said it. They said it for the purposes of disruption.'

At first the attacks by Presser and other union officials had a damaging impact on TDU. They encouraged some union officials to engage in physical assaults on TDU members, and several such attacks occurred. They encouraged the employers to fire and otherwise victimize TDU activists and other outspoken union members. But worst of all, they frightened some rank-and-file members and kept them from reading TDU literature or coming to TDU meetings. It took a long time for TDU to overcome the red-baiting and win the confidence of the rank and file.

It would have been easier for TDU to have denied the presence of socialists in the organization, or to have excluded certain political groups or beliefs from the organization. But TDU's members were well aware that whatever their political views, and certainly most of them were Democrats and Republicans, they would all be called Communists in any case. The word *Communist* had little or nothing to do with an individual Teamster's political beliefs and was simply intended to stigmatize and isolate the reformers. The TDU leadership also decided that excluding socialists would establish a dangerous precedent, for if socialists had to lie and hide today, some other group might have to lie and hide tomorrow. Moreover, the few socialists in TDU were dedicated members, and were generally respected and trusted by the others. In an editorial in *Convoy* by the National Steering Committee entitled 'Why They Fear the Truth', TDU responded to the attacks: 'TDU would like to set the record straight. As anyone knows who has read our program, TDU is not about socialism or dual unionism. It is about returning our union to the rank and file.' The TDU Steering Committee did not deny 'the presence of a handful of socialists in the TDU membership', but argued that the union officials harping on that issue was 'a repeat of the old company tactic of red-baiting.' The editorial pointed out that 'TDU is open to all Teamsters, and independent of any political organization'. TDU concentrated on the issues of union democracy, union contracts, and the 'big task, reforming the most powerful and autocratic union in the USA.'[1] This forthright way of dealing with criticism was used by TDU's leaders and members in countless conversations with their fellow workers and union members.

Things went beyond mere verbal attacks. The Teamsters leadership also moved to eliminate from the union the two most prominent TDU leaders. In February 1977 Pete Camarata and Al Ferdnance, both leaders of the Detroit TDU chapter, were charged with interfering with the union's responsibility to carry out its contractual obligations – in reality for supporting a strike by carhaulers – and then on 28 March they were expelled from Local 299. The Detroit TDU chapter swung into action to save two of its best-known members. TDU immediately got a temporary restraining order in federal court reinstating Camarata and Ferdnance. As the same time, TDU activists circulated throughout the city distributing leaflets and organizing rallies at the hearings to defend them. With the rank and file putting on the pressure, Local 299 dropped the charges against Ferdnance. Then TDU appealed Camarata's expulsion to Michigan Joint Council 43, where the expulsion was reversed and Camarata was found innocent of all specific charges. Camarata's reinstatement was not simply a legal victory, but a victory for the TDU chapter, which had mobilized in their defense.

Camarata was brought up on union charges once again, this time by International organizer Larry McHenry in March 1979. He was accused of fomenting a wildcat strike and put on 'life-time probation' by officials of Local 299, most of whom were subsequently voted out of office. When TDU attorney Ann Curry Thompson prepared to go to court to challenge the frame-up, the Teamster attorneys persuaded McHenry to drop the charges.

As if the attacks by the Teamster officialdom were not enough, another group got into the act. A group calling itself the US Labor Party began handing out literature at highway offramps and busy intersections in several big cities supporting Frank Fitzsimmons and the Pressers and attacking TDU and PROD. The US Labor Party, headed by Lyndon LaRouche, who has since been convicted of fraud, had a reputation for advocating fascism and using physical violence against welfare rights organizations, labor unions, and political opponents. Alexander E. Barkan, national director of the AFL-CIO's Committee on Political Education (COPE) called LaRouche and his organization 'anti-labor, anti-Catholic, anti-Semitic and anti-minorities.'[2] The United Steel Workers' newspaper, *Steel Labor*, had characterized the group as having 'the makings of a fascist movement.'[3] Nonetheless, several Teamster officials warmly welcomed these neo-Nazis. In his *Lyndon La-Rouche and the New American Fascism*, Dennis King wrote that 'LaRouche emissaries in the late 1970s dealt with Teamster officials on all levels, from the local and joint councils up to the general executive board and the office of then IBT General President Frank Fitzsimmons.'[4]

LaRouche and his followers performed many services for Teamster officialdom, acting as spies for the Teamsters, infiltrating PROD and preparing a 32-page report on the organization for Fitzsimmons. They also produced propaganda pamphlets such as *The Plot to Destroy the Teamsters*, which attacked TDU and PROD with the preposterous claim that the Teamster reformers were part of a conspiracy involving President Carter, the Rockefellers, Ralph Nader, the CIA, the AFL-CIO, and others. One piece of US Labor Party literature claimed that 'Illegal Drug Traffic Finances TDU/PROD'. Jackie Presser increasingly adopted the LaRouche line, and his charges against TDU got wilder and weirder.

In order to convince the rank and file that TDU was Communist, the US Labor Party and Teamster officials produced phony TDU posters, leaflets and letters. One such forgery was a bogus TDU poster inviting Teamsters to a May Day parade to March for Communism. Another was a counterfeit letter supposedly from the anti-union Right to Work Committee endorsing Pete Camarata. LaRouche followers also worked to elect incumbent officers who were challenged by reform candidates. In Local 282 they supported John Cody, a four-time convicted felon and friend of Mafia boss Carlo Gambino, and Harold Gross, a former associate of Murder, Inc. and mob leader Santos Trafficante. In Local 705 they worked for International Vice-President Louis Peick producing smear literature to defeat a reform group.[5]

At the same time, Teamster officials were hospitable to the LaRouche organization. In Local 126 in Fond du Lac, Wisconsin, Secretary-Treasurer Donald F. Wetzel sent out a mailing of US Labor Party literature to union members, while officials of Teamster Local 641 in Jersey City allowed the group to set up a display at a union meeting. Around the country Teamster officials worked closely with LaRouche's fascists.

TDU responded to this new attack by sending a letter to Fitzsimmons demanding that he stop the distribution of US Labor Party literature by Teamster officials. In January 1978 the Teamster General Executive Board adopted a resolution disclaiming any association with the US Labor Party and denying that it had provided any funds to the group. Despite Fitzsimmons's disclaimer, however, the US Labor Party continued to be active in and around the union, turning up in Teamster locals in Long Island, Oklahoma City, Flint, Harrisburg, Denver, Grand Rapids, St. Louis and Kansas City. In some areas US Labor Party members acted as campaign managers for Teamster officials.

Ironically, the involvement of the US Labor Party seemed to harm some of the Teamster officials associated with it and may have actually hurt their election campaigns. And despite the propaganda barrage, it was Fitzsimmons and Presser, the heads of a one-party dictatorship, whom the ranks frequently compared to Communists.

Teamster officials also physically attacked TDU meetings. When TDU held an educational meeting for rank-and-file Teamsters in Grand Rapids, Michigan on 28 March 1981, Michigan Teamster officials mobilized some sixty paid officials including business agents and joint council organizers from all over the state to attempt to disrupt the meeting. Among the leaders of the goon squad was convicted extortionist Roby Smith, a Michigan joint council organizer. The Teamster leadership received help from US Senator Orrin Hatch, who issued a press release alleging that there were subversives in the United Mine Workers, the United Steelworkers and the Teamsters union. Teamster officials assisted by the US Labor Party in turn used the Hatch press release in an attempt to smear TDU. A rumor was also circulated that the Senate Labor and Human Resource Committee, chaired by Hatch, was planning to investigate TDU, and stories to that effect were placed in various Teamster newspapers. The man responsible for the rumor was Richard Leebove, a former candidate of the US Labor Party and employee of Bobby Holmes, Sr., International vice-president and head of Local 337.

When Jackie Presser became Teamster general president in April 1983, he created his own praetorian guard, called BLAST, the Brotherhood of Loyal Americans and Strong Teamsters. BLAST was in fact simply a union goon squad created and funded by Jackie Presser for the sole purpose of attacking TDU. BLAST first appeared at the June 1981 Teamster convention in Las Vegas, where it distributed literature claiming that TDU-PROD was made up of 'subversive-fanatic-terrorists'. Later, when Bobby Holmes, Sr. faced a TDU challenge in elections in Local 337, he brought the BLAST organization to Michigan. Roadway, one of the biggest trucking companies in the country, was so impressed by BLAST's literature that the company circulated it nationwide.

When Presser found that accusing TDU of being Communist was no longer effective he began to accuse TDU of being capitalist. Presser and the Teamster leadership claimed that TDU was supported by big business. The argument was that the financial support TDU had received from charitable foundations was really support from corporations. In reality, TDU received financial support from charitable foundations that also supported other progressive causes such as civil rights groups, women's organizations and other labor unions. The trucking corporations' hatred for TDU was too well known for the charge of corporate support of TDU to be credible.

TDU's biggest problems came not from the antics of the US Labor Party, but from the employers who denied TDU activists the right to distribute literature on company property or use the bulletin boards. They gave TDU members disciplinary letters and suspensions and even fired them because of their union activities. Some companies like Roadway and United Parcel Service were particularly flagrant in the violation of their employees' rights to what the law calls 'protected concerted activities', but many companies engaged in this kind of harassment and intimidation. Frequently, local union officials colluded with the company to victimize TDU members.

The firings had what lawyers call 'a chilling effect'. Teamsters who were attracted to TDU by its ideas and its activities were afraid to join TDU, while many rank and filers became afraid even to exercise their rights as union members, such as filing grievances or attending union meetings. TDU and its attorneys were able to defend successfully many of those who were disciplined or fired, and deterred the companies to some degree by winning some substantial financial settlements. Harold 'Yogi' Baer, for example, was fired by Mason-Dixon Lines on 22 September 1976, supposedly because of wage garnishments. In reality Baer was an active union member who had filed many grievances against the company's attempt to impose a 'combination barn', which would have destroyed the established work rules. He had also fought the union over the issue of the members' right to choose their own steward. Moreover, he was a TDU member.

When Baer was fired, TDU attorney Steve Saltzman filed a complaint on Baer's behalf with the National Labor Relations Board. In his decision, Administrative Law Judge Russell M. King, Jr. found that there was a 'conspiracy between Horta [the Local 407 Business Agent] and Schnellberger [the Mason-Dixon terminal manager] to rid themselves of a troublesome employee and dissident union member. 'I find and conclude', wrote King, 'that the vast majority of the officers and officials of not only Local 407, but the Teamsters as a whole in Ohio were opposed to TDU and its members, supporters and activities.' Consequently, King said, 'I think the deck was stacked against Baer from the beginning. ... In the hearing before the Joint Local Committee, I find little, if any, resemblance of traditional fairness and due process.' On 7 March 1978, after eighteen months off the job, Baer was reinstated with full back pay of approximately $30,000.

'Yogi' Baer's case was one of the biggest NLRB settlements won by TDU during that period, but there were many other victories in which members who had been fired were returned to work, those who had been disciplined had their records cleared, and members' rights to distribute literature and use bulletin boards were successfully defended.

Notes

1. 'Why They Fear the Truth', an editorial statement by the TDU Steering Committee, *Convoy*, no. 13.
2. Dennis King, *Lyndon LaRouche and the New American Fascism*, New York 1989, p. 346.
3. 'Fitz and Presser Find New Friends', *Convoy*, no. 20. The quote is from the June 1975 issue of *Steel Labor*.
4. King, *Lyndon LaRouche*, p. 336.
5. Ibid., p. 339.

PART IV

THE TESTING OF TDU

14

Deregulation and Depression

The years between 1980 and 1983 were among the most difficult in the history of the modern Teamsters union. The Mafia, as it was later learned, controlled union Presidents Frank Fitzsimmons, Roy Williams and Jackie Presser. The deregulation of the trucking industry and the depression of 1980 brought widespread unemployment, employer demands for concessions, and outright union busting.

TDU had warned all along that the Teamsters union, despite its size and apparent strength, was in some ways weak and unsound. This was not only because of the notorious corruption within the union, but more fundamentally because of the union leaders' philosophy of business unionism, which led the Teamster officials to view all problems from the point of view of the employers rather than from that of the workers and union members. TDU had warned that if the employers pushed, the union was not only unwilling, but increasingly unable, to push back. But even the TDU leadership never expected the catastrophe that was to come. The union stood on the brink of a disaster caused by a combination of economic depression and the deregulation of the trucking industry.

Beginning in 1980 the Teamsters union and its members were hit by a devastating attack from both the employers and the government. It was like a war, a lightning attack on an unprepared and undefended country. The employers overran the union's defenses while the sentries slept soundly. Every retreat turned into a rout; every line of defense was deserted. Those who were supposed to stand and fight dropped the flag and ran. The union leadership adopted a policy first of appeasement and then of surrender on one front after another. The casualties of lost jobs and lost union members ran into the tens of thousands and then into the hundreds of thousands.

In the midst of the utter collapse of the union's defenses, TDU stood its ground. TDU and a few exceptional union officials rallied the troops, at every moment fearing that each battle might become the last stand. The union rank and file was reduced to virtual guerrilla warfare, fighting barn by barn, company by company, local by local. But after three years of resistance, defeat, retreat, reorganization and renewed resistance, the members learned how to fight under the new conditions of total war, and inch by inch they began to reclaim the ground they had lost.

The Economic Context

The United States had had no really severe economic problems from 1940 to the 1970s, but in 1974–75 the economy plunged into a depression. There were widespread plant closings and massive layoffs, and unemployment in 1975 reached nearly 9 percent. Only four years later, while millions still remained out of work, a second depression hit with more bankruptcies and plant closings: the average unemployment rate reached 7.1 percent in 1980. These two depressions marked the end of an economic era.

In the new era, the employers no longer accepted the collective bargaining arrangements that had existed since World War II. Employers began to demand take-aways, concessions, but most important, they wanted to do away with the pattern agreements that protected union workers in industry. Since the 1940s, most major American industrial labor unions had negotiated pattern agreements or master contracts that established uniform wages, benefits and conditions for all the workers in a particular industry. The backbone of labor's pattern bargaining was the United Auto Workers master contract covering the big three auto manufacturers. Similarly, the United Steelworkers had a pattern covering basic steel; likewise several other unions and industries. The Teamsters union, of course, had the National Master Freight Agreement covering workers in the trucking industry.

This system of pattern bargaining, which had protected workers' earnings and conditions by preventing competition, began to come undone when in October 1979, the United Auto Workers negotiated a concessionary contract with the Chrysler Corporation as part of the Chrysler bailout. Kim Moody described these concessions in his book *An Injury to All*: 'Beneath all the language about saving jobs, the UAW leadership demonstrated its willingness to make wages, benefits and then working conditions subject to competitive bargaining. The pattern in auto was broken, and the standard that upheld worker solidarity eliminated.'[1]

The UAW's concessions to Chrysler led to the first round of concessionary bargaining by many different unions in the years 1979–82. This was followed by a second round from 1983 to 1985.[2] Concessions produced disaster for American workers: 'Seven years of concessions had eliminated master contracts and pattern bargaining in every major unionized industry.'[3]

Added to the economic situation and the new industrial relations was a new political context. In 1980 Ronald Reagan was elected president heading a conservative Republican administration hostile to labor unions as well as to labor's traditional allies, the Black and women's organizations. The tone of labor relations in the United States for the next decade was set when Ronald Reagan went on television on 3 August 1981, four hours after the Professional Air Traffic Controllers union went on strike and told the controllers to return to work within forty-eight hours or lose their jobs. When the strike continued, he fired all 15,000 striking controllers and destroyed PATCO. This was the situation in which the Teamster rank and file found itself: an economic depression, the weakening of pattern contracts throughout the union movement, and an administration in Washington that was militantly anti-union.

The Crisis of the Industry

The first issue facing the Teamsters in 1980 was the deregulation of the trucking industry being pushed through Congress by Democratic Senator Edward Kennedy. Like the Teamsters union itself, TDU opposed deregulation of the trucking industry. And like the Teamsters union, TDU urged its members to write their representatives and senators to express their opposition to deregulation. But while the Teamsters confined themselves to lobbying (and, it would turn out, bribery), TDU advocated rank-and-file action: 'A real strategy to fight deregulation would rely on our own strength – up to and including possible work stoppage. And it would rely on gaining the backing of the entire labor movement. This would be based on a commitment to mutual support within the labor movement – a big step to rebuilding labor solidarity.'[4] There were precedents – the United Mine Workers had struck in support of health and safety laws in the 1960s.

TDU members presented motions advocating national or regional demonstrations in Cleveland Local 407, Baltimore Local 557, Scranton Local 229 and Davenport Local 371. A couple of local unions passed the resolutions, and Baltimore Local 557 planned to hold a rally, but Frank Fitzsimmons sent word through his special assistant Walter Shea not to hold a rally against deregulation because it would embarrass the union! Unwilling to use the power of the members, Roy Williams worked on the sly to try to bribe US Senator Howard Cannon, but despite those disreputable efforts Congress passed a deregulation bill in July 1980.

With the passage of deregulation in the midst of a depression the industry went into a profound crisis, and old established truck lines began to go bankrupt while new, non-union companies appeared. Even before deregulation there had been significant competition from non-union carriers. 'By

1977', according to a study of the trucking industry by Professor Charles R. Perry of the Wharton School, 'the ranks of non-union carriers had grown to the point where they constituted a serious competitive threat to the survival of many smaller unionized carriers.'[5] With the passage of deregulation, 'the total number of regulated carriers increased from 18,000 in June 1981 to 22,000 in June 1982, and to 30,000 in June 1983.'[6] The increased competition led to rapidly falling freight rates in some sectors of the industry. The same study noted that 'the combination of depressed demand caused by the recession and increased capacity, a result of deregulation, produced an intensification of competition within the industry.'[7] The result was an industry shakeout. By 1982 some 183 carriers had gone out of business and another 51 were in bad financial shape.[8]

The loss of business by union firms, combined with the bankruptcy of unionized companies, led to massive layoffs for Teamster members. 'The industry unemployment rate rose from approximately 6 percent in 1979 to 12 percent in early 1981 before falling to under 9 percent in 1982. The IBT, however, estimated that between 19 and 24 percent of its trucking industry members were unemployed in 1981. ... '[9] A report by Norman A. Weintraub, a Teamster economist, estimated that the number had risen to between 26 and 32 percent by April 1982. These numbers reflected not only the decline of unionized carriers but also the growth of the largest non-union carriers. 'The most obvious change', wrote Perry, 'was the tripling, in both absolute and relative terms, of the number of non-union [Class I] carriers.'[10]

The Disintegration of the Steelhaulers Contract

All of the problems in the Teamsters union showed themselves first among the steelhaulers. In the midst of the 1979 steelhaulers strike, TDU had pulled together the Steel Haulers Organizing Committee, but no sooner had the strike ended than the steelhaulers found themselves on the defensive. At the 1979 TDU convention a meeting of steelhaulers was pulled together, chaired by Les Cadman of Youngstown Local 377, and *Convoy-Dispatch* reported that 'the major focus [of the SHOC meeting] was the various attacks being made on the lease conditions of owner-operators.'[11]

Convoy-Dispatch created a special column for steelhaulers called 'SHOC Waves', and its chronicle of the employer attack on the steelhaulers was truly shocking. One company after another cut rates and wages and imposed new, harsher working conditions: Artim, Brada-Miller, McNicholas, Ryder Ranger, Jones Motor, Hess Cartage. Many of these companies cut drivers' pay to 72 percent instead of the 75 percent that had been negotiated in the contract, an arrangement officially approved by the union on 12 March 1980. *Convoy-Dispatch* reported that 'no Union officials stood up against this rip off'. TDU called upon the union to strike: 'That's the only language the companies understand. But it seems our officials have forgotten how to speak it.'[12]

Another aspect of the attack on the steelhaulers was the union's move to throw Pittsburgh Local 800 into trusteeship. The trusteeship had been called for by Local 800 President Todd, who had lost control of the local to TDU and the rank and file during the steel strike. In early November 1979 Robert Dietrich was appointed the trustee of Local 800. TDU demanded 'that the trusteeship should be ended immediately and an election held to restore democracy.'[13] But the steelhaulers were too demoralized to fight, and TDU lost the struggle to lift the trusteeship from the local. TDU-SHOC attempted to organize resistance to the carriers' attacks. The desperation of the situation was clear from the name they gave their campaign: Operation Survival. In the end, however, TDU-SHOC was too weak to lead a steelhaulers movement, and Operation Survival itself did not survive.

As time went on, there were reports of new substandard deals in steel-hauling at Helms Astro, Mill Transports, Lee Cartage, and other companies. Brada Miller began Chapter 11 bankruptcy proceedings and went non-union. The steelhaulers' situation continued to deteriorate as the companies succeeded in signing separate substandard contracts with various Teamster locals, first in Michigan, and then in Illinois, Indiana, Ohio and Pennsylvania. Where there had been one contract, there were now scores of separate agreements, all different and each new one worse than the last.

In May 1982 Mel Packer of Local 800 in Pittsburgh wrote an article on the steelhaulers: 'Chaos and confusion continue to be the operative words in any description of steelhauling. ... Overall the plight of steelhaulers can only be described as dismal.' The only hope, he argued, was for the steelhaulers to stand up and fight back: 'Until that happens, we will continue to eat the crap being fed to us by that trio of conspirators made up of the companies, corrupt union officials and the federal government.'[14] That Mel Packer, a TDU founder and one of its most dedicated and talented organizers, could become so discouraged and depressed was an indication of the disaster that had befallen the steelhaulers.

The Fight for the Freight Contract

The situation in freight was different from that in steelhauling, which was a part of the industry dominated by owner-operators. In freight the union was stronger, and TDU was stronger within the union. Consequently, it was possible to make a stand against the employers. Under the combined pressures of deregulation and depression, the freight companies began to attack the National Master Freight Agreement, just as they had in steel. They pushed for productivity standards, demanded the flexible workweek in order to eliminate overtime pay for weekends, asked for a two-tier contract with lower wages for new hires, and in countless other ways sought to get from their employees more work for less pay to achieve higher profits.

Productivity

At a meeting of the Industrial Relations Committee of the American Trucking Association from 28 to 31 October 1979, the Teamsters gave the employers approval to implement productivity standards. Robert Flynn, executive assistant to the director of the Eastern Conference of Teamsters, told the employers that the Teamsters were happy that the courts had supported the Eastern Conference in upholding firings at Helms over productivity disputes. The decision, Flynn said, had been 'very important to us'. Walter Shea, executive assistant to Frank Fitzsimmons, told the employers, 'We are not opposed to productivity standards.'[15] The Teamsters had given the employer the go-ahead to use the whip.

Konstantine 'Konny' Petros worked on the dock at the Roadway terminal in Toledo when production standards were first introduced in 1980. Petros had earned a bachelor's degree in secondary education at the University of Toledo and and was looking forward to becoming a school teacher. But his father died just before he finished college. With five sisters and a brother to take care of, he needed a job desperately and Roadway was hiring. 'That was right after that strike in 1970', he recalls, 'and they were making $5.79 an hour, and the working conditions were real good and it paid more than teaching, which would have paid me something like four or five thousand a year to start out, and I remember the first full year at Roadway I made over sixteen thousand dollars working on the dock. Then around 1979 things started to really go downhill. Our working conditions at Roadway Express really started deteriorating. In 1980 Roadway said that the bottom ten percent of the people in production in each terminal were going to get fired – in other words, that they were going to institute production standards, which was against the contract.'

In addition, the companies applied the productivity standards arbitrarily and unfairly. 'If the foreman didn't like you, of course he'd give you the worst trailer, and he'd pull you off a trailer with a lot of boxes and bills (they also counted bills) and put you on something that took a lot longer to do and looked worse on paper.' Petros was concerned because the union was not dealing with the issue. 'I thought maybe the union didn't know what was going on on the dock, that maybe nobody had told them, and that maybe the stewards weren't doing their job and adequately representing to them what was happening there. I thought maybe these guys could be talked to and something could be done.

'So I went down to complain about the harassment and production standards, and I was told flat out by the Les Singer, director of freight, who was also business agent, that I was lazy, and the only reason people were getting the letters was because people were lazy and weren't doing the job properly. I was flabbergasted.'

At about that same time Petros learned about TDU. 'Roadway was telling us what bad employees we were in Toledo, Ohio. They said they were going to move out of town to Columbus or Cincinnati. And then somebody put the *Convoy-Dispatch* up on the dock, and it informed everybody what was really going on, that they were telling the people in Columbus and Cincinnati these same stories, that they were going to move the terminal to Toledo if *they* didn't straighten up. I have to add that I hadn't distributed the first *Convoy* that appeared on the dock – but then I joined TDU and undertook to make sure that the *Convoy* was distributed every month thereafter.'

Despite TDU's efforts, the employers now began to fire workers who did not meet productivity standards. One of the first victims was James F. Langley, who had worked for Pilot Freight Carriers in Winston-Salem, North Carolina for over eleven years with no problems. He grieved the case, and TDU came to Langley's defense. TDU was able to beat some of the productivity firings. For example, Joe Berg, a TDU member, was reinstated in his dock job at Helms Express, where he had worked for twenty-three years, with full back pay. The arbitrator who reinstated Berg noted that Helms's productivity system 'breeds suspicion and favoritism. ... Consideration was not given for the quality of the employee's work but only for the pounds moved', which was exactly what TDU had argued.[16] But the victories were few and far between. The push for productivity was on at all the freight companies, led by Roadway, the biggest of the bunch.

Later Roadway introduced the gimmick of 'production cards', on which dock workers were required to record every piece of freight they loaded or unloaded during their shifts. Workers who had low productivity were 'counseled', that is, intimidated or threatened. The cards were a way to get rid of older employees who were protected by higher seniority and who enjoyed longer vacations, or to build a case against more union-conscious workers and replace them with new workers with no union consciousness.

Keith Gallagher remembers when Roadway first introduced production cards on the dock where he worked back in the early 1980s. 'They introduced it as a turkey contest around Thanksgiving, and the workers on the two shifts with the highest production would get turkeys. People knew immediately what this was all about: it was going to be man against man. We could see the long-term effects of this, and we put out a TDU bulletin on the dock. I can remember a frantic assistant terminal manager coming into the lunch room and actually taking these bulletins out of peoples' hands, ripping them off the table and throwing them away. The position we had taken in the bulletin was that it was nothing but a sham, it was nothing but a production scheme, not very cleverly disguised. We asked which ever two shifts got the turkeys to donate them to the Salvation Army to give away for Thanksgiving. They were extremely upset about that.

'They even got two live turkeys and brought them to the terminal. The Roadway terminal has a continuous drag-line that goes around pulling carts that are loaded up with freight. Well, they got two live turkeys and put them in a cage, and had them riding around the drag-line – until someone called the Society for the Prevention of Cruelty to Animals. Eventually it did escalate into a full-scale production scheme, and it did become man against man. Everybody was always worried about what the other person was doing, because of that silent supervisor that you had with you in the form of a production card. It was always there and always watching.'

TDU organized against the production cards, urging workers in barns where the cards had recently been introduced to file grievances under the contract's 'Maintenance of Standards' clause, which forbade changes in established practices. In several locals TDU members introduced motions calling for strike sanction against Roadway if it did not eliminate the cards. There was overwhelming support for such a strike by the workers affected, but the union did not act.

The Flexible Workweek

The other great fight over working conditions had to do with the issue of the flexible workweek. The flexible workweek meant that the employers would have the right to work employees on Saturday and Sunday or before 8 a.m. or after 5 p.m. on weekdays without paying premium rates for overtime. This gave the employer greater flexibility in the disposition of the workers (thus the name), and it also meant that the companies had to pay less overtime. Companies could start workers at any hour of the day or night, and the five-day workweek could begin and end on any day of the week. This system had two obvious effects: it reduced the workers' wages, and it destroyed their family lives.

In 1976 the union had allowed the companies a clause in the Central States Supplement to the National Master Freight Agreement that permitted the employers to force individual terminals to vote on the flexible workweek. That clause was designed to divide and conquer the Teamster membership. The employers' fight for 'flex', as it was called for short, was also led by Roadway. The flex had been introduced early at the Roadway terminal in Toledo. Konny Petros remembers, 'They told the employees that if we didn't vote for flex, they were going to move this terminal to Lima, Ohio and we would lose our jobs.' That was in 1976, before TDU became active in Toledo: 'The employees back then didn't know anything about the contract, didn't know anything about the union in general, and they voted it in', says

Petros. 'They got scared.' Flex was first introduced at Roadway in Toledo as a 'red circle agreement', a two-tier arrangement under which current employees worked under the old agreement, but new employees had to work the flex. Later the company threw out the 'red circle' agreement and all employees had to work flex.

Another leader in the introduction of flex was Consolidated Freightways, which was soon joined by Roadway, McLean, Yellow Freight, Spector-Red Ball and other companies. At all of these companies, management played off one barn against another and one local against another, telling workers that if they did not vote for flex, work at their terminal would be shifted to another terminal that had accepted flex, and then their barn would be closed or greatly reduced in size, and they would be laid off.

The union gave the workers little leadership, and certainly it did not propose an overall strategy to fight the flexible workweek. The union took the position that each barn and each local could make its own decision about flex; that is, they could vote to compete for jobs with their brothers and sisters at other barns or companies. It was as if there were no union at all. Only TDU, through *Convoy-Dispatch*, kept the rank and file informed and helped them resist being played off one against another. Many barns voted flex down, and in some cases voted it down several times. But frequently management would continue to threaten and blackmail the workers, coming back for vote after vote until the company finally won.

Two-Tier Wages

Wages were, of course, one of the companies' keenest interests. In early 1980 Teamster employers covered by the Central Pennsylvania (or 'Eight Cities') Supplement got Edward Harrington, the head of Local 229 and the Central Pennsylvania area, to give them a 'two-tier' contract with lower wages for 'trainees and new hires'. Under this contract 'trainees and new hires' would get only 70 percent of full wages for the first eighteen months and no benefits (vacations, holidays, sick days, pension, or health and welfare) for six months. Moreover, they would remain probationary employees without the status of permanent employees for those six months. All such programs are, of course, an inducement for employers to fire older, higher seniority workers who receive full wages and benefits and replace them with those earning the lower tier wage.

The Demand for Relief

Two-tier wages, flexible workweeks, and production standards were only a few of the ways in which the companies sought to undermine the contract and force their employees to work longer and harder for less. Around the country union officials signed riders and local agreements for all kinds of deals, or signed nothing and simply let the companies ignore entire clauses and chapters of the contract. As Perry wrote, 'The result was a further proliferation of the under-the-table arrangements of the 1970s, to the point where they were more a rule than an exception among small and/or truckload carriers.'[17]

The company went to the union or to the employees and told them that 'relief' was necessary for the company to stay in business. One such local 'relief' deal was granted to Admiral Merchants in Moline, Illinois by Teamsters Local 371. There the workers were paid only for forty hours straight-time no matter how many hours they worked, the company made no health and welfare or pension payments, and there were no wage or cost of living increases. In Texas, PIE, one of the nation's largest carriers, was paying drivers $8 an hour – a cut in pay of more than 30 percent. At Duff Truck Lines in Ohio, workers 'voluntarily' gave back $20 a week of their wages to the company.

There simply was no end to the companies' demands and no limit to their gall. An all-time low was reached when President Andrew Haak of GMW, a St. Paul, Minnesota–based trucking firm, wrote to each employee explaining that the company had to raise $1.25 million. He then went on to ask each employee to work for free for the last two months of the year and suggested that workers who were unwilling to work for nothing quit so that others who were could take their places. He was, as *Convoy-Dispatch* wrote, asking for 'the ultimate concession' – free labor.

Concessions Don't Save Jobs

The employers, often supported by local union officials, asked the workers to make concessions to save their jobs. Their argument was that lower wages and more flexible working conditions would allow the union companies to compete with the non-union carriers, making it possible for the unionized companies to stay in business and keep the Teamsters working. On the other hand, TDU argued from the beginning of the take-aways in 1979 that concessions would not save jobs. In only a couple of years TDU was proved right in a way that gave it no satisfaction. Cooper Jarrett got relief in the form of a 'loan' from its employees, which was supposed to be repaid out of any profits that the company made in excess of $500,000. The loan amounted to 15 percent of the employees' wages by December 1981, but the company not only failed to make a profit, but went bankrupt and closed almost all its terminals. The employees' loans were not 'secured' loans – that is, they were not backed up by any collateral, so Cooper Jarrett's 1,000 employees found themselves not only unemployed, but also cheated out of the money they had loaned their boss.

TDU argued that, given the depression and deregulation, some companies were bound to go out of business. 'There is little the union can do to stop this from happening', argued TDU in the pages of *Convoy-Dispatch*. 'But the union can work to negotiate a job security clause in our contracts that makes sure that the Teamsters whose companies go out of business are hired in seniority order by those large union carriers that will continue to grow in years ahead. The alternative – just giving the companies what they ask for – doesn't work. Just ask any Cooper Jarrett driver.'[18]

The Fight over the 1982 NMFA

As the expiration of the 1982 National Master Freight Agreement approached, the employers demanded a wage freeze, a weaker cost of living clause, and changes in working conditions along the lines already discussed (greater productivity, flexibility, and so on). The union offered little resistance to the companies' demands.

At TDU's Sixth Annual Rank and File Convention in Detroit from 31 October to 1 November, a meeting of over 100 freight Teamsters came up with a list of rank-and-file contract demands emphasizing the cost of living clause, job security and the preservation of union conditions and work rules. TDU had also begun circulating a Petition Against Concessions, Giveaways and Takeaways in the NMFA.

As word of the tentative contract settlement began to get out, TDU called upon the members to 'Send This One Back!' The tentative agreement, TDU reported, called for a wage freeze, a cut in the cost of living allowance, and a cutback in pension contributions. 'Unlike all previous NMFAs', said TDU, 'this proposed contract contains almost no real gains for the rank and file.' Given the economic depression, the number of Teamsters laid off, and the low level of morale among union members, TDU did *not* call for a strike as it had in 1976 and 1979, but simply called on union members to send back the contract. 'We can make a difference by voting NO and sending it back for renegotiation. A NO vote will cause renegotiation – and there is plenty of time to do it prior to April 1. A NO vote will not cause a strike, it will be a signal to our negotiators that they have misjudged what we will accept.'[19] TDU urged rank-and-file Teamsters to attend the union contract meetings to be held in January and February 1982 and to speak out and demand answers to questions about wages, cost of living allowances, work rules and other important issues.

When complete details of the contract became available, TDU called it the 'Worst Contract Ever', and said, 'The new freight contract is a turning point for the Teamsters Union.' Roy Williams, who had become the new Teamster president in May 1981, after Fitzsimmons died, had flunked his first test, as *Convoy-Dispatch* put it. Thousands of angry union members turned out to vote virtually unanimously against the contract in Cleveland Local 407, Detroit Local 299, Quad Cities Iowa-Illinois Local 371, St. Louis Local 600 and Los Angeles Local 208. In many other locals there was also strong opposition, and many local officials declined to try to sell the contract to their members.

The TDU leadership knew that they did not have the power to stop Teamster President Roy Williams from imposing the freight contract. Ken Paff, TDU national organizer, wrote in *Convoy-Dispatch*, 'They [the companies and union officials] may be able to force this contract on the members, out of fear. Fear, the enemy of unionism.' Nevertheless, pledged Paff, TDU would carry on. 'The fight is on. The fight to save our union. The fight of unionism versus fear tactics. The freight contract will hurt us. But our union was formed when people were hurting, and needed a union badly. That time is back again.'[20]

After the contract had been ratified, TDU wrote, 'Although it has been less than a month since the new freight agreement was signed, one thing is already crystal clear; this contract will do nothing to stem the tidal wave of 'relief' that is sweeping across the trucking industry.'[21] The same article listed a number of new substandard deals, including one at GMW, Inc., a freight company in Illinois, Minnesota and Wisconsin employing 700 workers; it had persuaded those employees to *donate* $3,000 each to the company and to promise to donate another $1,500.

The most disturbing aspect of the freight contract was that even after it was negotiated and supposedly ratified, hundreds of companies had still not signed it, and an entire group of California carriers refused to do so. TDU described the situation surrounding the freight contract as 'a confused mess'. The carriers' refusal to sign, TDU argued, was evidence that 'some employers are clearly out to bust the contract' while 'the union has no plan to save it.' TDU called upon the union to give the companies a deadline, to file notice that the union would strike, but most important, to develop a program of organizing the unorganized. 'We are facing an all-out challenge from the employers', wrote *Convoy-Dispatch*. 'What we do now will determine whether we survive as a union in the trucking industry.'[22]

TDU continued to organize among steelhaulers, helping to put together a meeting of 150 steelhaulers in Pittsburgh on 13 February 1982 to plan strategy for the contract. With steelhaulers, as with freight workers, TDU did not advocate a strike in 1982, but rather asked the question, 'Will steelhaulers walk as they did in 1979?'[23] In the end, they did not.

With United Parcel Service, the situation was altogether different. TDU launched the UPS contract campaign, calling for higher wages and with an emphasis on 'no forced overtime'. TDU argued that UPS should get 'No Concessions in 1982' because, unlike other trucking companies, UPS was quite profitable. Nevertheless, the Teamsters did recommend concessions for UPS, proposing a 37-month wage freeze, a reduction in cost of living increases, diversion of cost of living allowances to pension and health and welfare funds, and significantly lower wages for part-time workers. Above all, there were no improvements in working conditions or language protecting UPS workers from harassment. TDU called the contract 'a complete sellout'.

There was not the same kind of fear among UPS workers that existed among freight workers, and TDU succeeded in organizing a movement to reject the contract. TDU printed 10,000 copies of UPS bulletins, put out 1,500 buttons that said 'Vote No', and hundreds of t-shirts with the slogan 'Harass my –, Vote No'. TDU turned out thousands of UPSers to local union meetings, and there were large votes against the contract in New York, New Jersey, San Francisco, Detroit, Pittsburgh, Cincinnati, Louisville, Philadelphia, Dallas, Toledo and other UPS locals. But again, despite struggle, TDU was not strong enough to win the vote, though it did succeed in producing a 48 percent vote against the contract.

The 1982 Teamster contracts were a disaster for freight workers, steelhaulers and UPS employees. In freight and steel the Teamsters not only accepted concessions, but failed for months to get hundreds of employers and entire carrier groups to actually sign the contract. At UPS, concessions were granted to a company that was both profitable and growing. The union was slowly being destroyed.

Notes

1. Kim Moody, *An Injury to All*, London 1988, p. 176.
2. Ibid., pp. 168-69.
3. Ibid., p. 2.
4. 'Deregulation: Last Chance for Action', *Convoy-Dispatch*, no. 6 (May 1980).
5. Charles R. Perry, *Deregulation and the Decline of the Unionized Trucking Industry*, Industrial Research Unit, The Wharton School, University of Pennsylvania, Philadelphia 1986, p. 67.
6. Perry, *Deregulation*, p. 92.
7. Ibid., p. 83.
8. Ibid., p. 85.
9. Ibid., p. 89.
10. Ibid., p. 103.
11. 'SHOC Sets Organizing Goals', *Convoy-Dispatch*, no. 1 (Nov.–Dec. 1979).
12. 'Shoc Waves', *Convoy-Dispatch*, no. 5 (April 1980). See the 'Shoc Waves' columns and other articles about steelhaulers in the *Convoy-Dispatch,* numbers 1–11.
13. 'TDU Organizes to Fight Local 800 Trusteeship', *Convoy-Dispatch*, no. 1 (Nov.–Dec. 1979).
14. 'Steelhaul Situation: Confusion Continues', Mel Packer, Local 800 Pittsburgh, *Convoy-Dispatch*, no. 26 (May 1982).
15. 'Top IBT Brass OK Productivity', *Convoy-Dispatch*, no. 2 (January 1980).
16. 'TDUer Overturns Productivity Firing', *Convoy-Dispatch*, no. 4 (March 1980).
17. Perry, *Deregulation*, p. 106.

18.   'Relief Fails to Save C.J.', *Convoy-Dispatch*, no. 22 (January 1982).

19.   'Send This One Back!' *Convoy-Dispatch*, no. 22 (January 1982).

20   'What the NMFA Means: "The Fight of Unionism vs. Fear",' Ken Paff, *Convoy-Dispatch*, no. 24 (March 1982).

21.   'New Contract Fails to Stop Relief', *Convoy-Dispatch*, no. 24 (March 1982).

22.   'Employers Aim to Bust Contract: Time for Rank & File Action', *Convoy-Dispatch*, no. 25 (April 1982).

23.   'Local 800 Rejects Contract', *Convoy-Dispatch*, no. 23 (February 1982).

15

UPS: The Totalitarian Workplace

During the early 1980s it became clear that TDU was dealing with a fundamentally new kind of management in the trucking industry. The boards of directors and executive officers of the corporations and conglomerates that now owned the trucking companies demanded higher profits. To achieve them they began to introduce the principles of so-called 'scientific management' developed in the manufacturing industry by Frederick Taylor in the 1890s, and later applied by Henry Ford on the assembly lines in his auto plants. 'Save ten steps a day for each of 12,000 employees', Ford once said, 'and you will have saved fifty miles of wasted motion and misspent energy.' Taylor and Ford believed that the worker should exercise no independent judgement and have no control over the work process, and that management should organize every detail of the work so that not one moment of the employee's time was lost, not one bit of his energy wasted. It was the introduction of 'scientific management' to the labor of dock workers, truck drivers and clerical workers that had given rise to the fight over production in which the Teamster rank and file had been involved.

The pacesetter in the introduction of these methods was the nation's largest trucking company: United Parcel Service. Because of the nature of the freight that UPS handled – mostly small packages – it was easier for UPS to standardize procedures and generalize its methods. Every other trucking company now looks to UPS as the model to emulate. Every Teamster in the trucking industry looks at UPS as a crystal ball in which he or she can read the future – and it is a frightening vision.

In 1982 a worker loading packages on a moving conveyor belt at a UPS facility in Columbus, Ohio suffered a back injury and fell down in the aisle. The conveyor was equipped with safety devices and emergency shut-off switches, but when the worker collapsed, the supervisor did not stop the conveyor belt, and not one of the workers dared to do so for fear of being disciplined or even fired. Some coworkers stopped packages from falling from the moving conveyor belt onto the injured man, who lay in the aisle for twenty minutes. Eventually he was given medical attention. But the belt never stopped rolling, the packages never stopped moving, and production never ceased, not even for a moment.

Less than a year later, on 8 February 1983, James E. Fox, a supervisor employed by United Parcel Service in Charlotte, North Carolina, noticed that a conveyor belt was jammed with packages. Rather than shut off the conveyor belt long enough to break up the jammed boxes, he attempted to unclog the jam on the moving belt with his hand. As he reached in among the packages, the machine caught his hand, dragged him into the belt, trapped him at the end of the belt's roller, and crushed him. Having heard cries for help, a coworker shut off the belt, but it was too late: Fox was already dead.

A UPS package car driver in Portland, Maine (I will call him 'Nathan') had been off work with a back injury for five weeks in 1983. When he returned to work, his productivity was not what UPS management thought it should be. The next time he went out, a manager and a supervisor were assigned to accompany him on his run, supposedly to make suggestions about how he could improve his work methods. That day, while delivering packages under the direction of the supervisors, Nathan collapsed on the sidewalk. Neither the supervisor nor the administrator called for emergency medical service; instead, they called the division manager for orders. A local storeowner saw Nathan lying on the sidewalk and called for an ambulance, which took him for medical care; later he was diagnosed as having suffered a nervous breakdown. Many of his coworkers believed Nathan had been driven over the edge by UPS.

These are, of course, 'horror stories', extreme examples rather than typical experiences. But the typical experience of the UPS worker is itself a horror story of human beings pushed to the limit and driven to extremes of physical and psychological exhaustion. UPS, its ads say, runs 'the tightest ship in the shipping business'. But the United Parcel ship is not just tight, it's very nearly totalitarian.

Much like Japanese companies, UPS has a military discipline; all employees must wear uniforms and must cut their hair short, and men may not wear beards or allow their mustaches to extend below the corners of their mouths. After a pep talk and a report on production begins the long workday in which each worker's every move is monitored, measured and managed. 'UPS maintains rigid control over nearly every aspect of its operations', Kenneth Labich wrote in an article in *Fortune* magazine. 'Each task, from picking or delivering parcels on a route to sorting packages in a central hub, is carefully calibrated according to productivity standards. Workers know precisely what is expected, and deviations are tolerated only rarely.'

In order to better control the workforce, UPS managers and supervisors are taught to use the methods of sociology to study the behavior of employees. A UPS manual, 'Learning to Chart Spheres of Influence', tells supervisors how to make sociograms charting the relationships between employees and identifying 'Informal Group Leaders'. Supervisors are told to find out what the workers do in their off-work hours: 'As a manager or supervisor, listen carefully to your people to know as much as you can about their *own time* contacts.' Supervisors are to learn if workers ride the same bus to work, attend the same church or drink in the same tavern, to find out which workers are friendly, and which antagonistic. Most important, they are to learn to find out who influences whom. Examples in the manual tell supervisors to listen to employees' opinions of union elections.

As the manual explains, 'Instead of trying to influence each of your people individually all the time, you will do a more effective job by getting to know, and working especially closely with, the Informal Group Leaders.' Supervisors are told to 'make new charts at least once a year. Review your charts whenever a man leaves or a new man is hired – the groupings are likely to shift then.' Not only do UPS supervisors observe the employee's every move at work, but UPS hires detectives to spy on UPS employees. A group of UPS workers at a union activity in Detroit were videotaped by detectives hired by UPS. The company has also hired spies to attend UPSurge and TDU meetings. UPS tries to control its employees' behavior and their minds, on the job and off.

UPS, the totalitarian state, began as UPS, the benevolent dictatorship. The company was founded in Seattle in 1907 as the American Messenger Service by a nineteen-year-old messenger boy named James E. Casey. Casey bought a couple of bicycles, hired six drivers, and adopted the slogan 'Best Service – Lowest Rates'; he specialized in delivering department store merchandise to retail customers. The company was so successful that by 1919 it expanded to Oakland, California, and by 1930 it had moved its corporate headquarters to Manhattan. As early as 1916 Jim Casey invited the Teamsters to organize the UPS employees.

Changes in the department store business in the 1950s, particularly the growth of the suburban shopping mall, eliminated much of the need for retail deliveries and forced UPS to become a common carrier, a freight company specializing in small parcels, a move that put UPS in direct competition with the US Post Office. Eventually UPS won the battle, and in 1988 the Post Office delivered 1.4 billion packages, while UPS delivered 2.3 billion. Jim Casey retired in 1962, and the company passed on to younger managers, most of whom had come up through the UPS ranks. But Casey's policies remained, including the company's status as a privately owned partnership, most of whose 20,000 partners are UPS managers and supervisors.

UPS is one of the biggest transportation companies in the country, the biggest trucking company and the biggest Teamster employer. Its 190,000 employees – 130,000 of them Teamsters union members – work in nearly 1,500 terminals and drive tens of thousands of vans and tractor trailers. They deliver packages for some 850,000 customers to fifty states, Puerto Rico, Canada, and West Germany, and the company expects to deliver to all of Western Europe in the 1990s. UPS has a rapidly expanding air freight division with over 100 airplanes serving sixteen European countries and Japan, and not long ago it purchased two computer companies. It has grown to be the dominant package delivery company because of its particular production methods and the psychological hold it has on its employees.

And United Parcel Service is the most profitable transportation corporation in the United States. With their robot-like labor, UPS workers earn the company over $700 million a year in after-tax profits on over $10 billion in revenues. It is those fabulous profits that have made UPS methods the model not only for other package delivery companies, but also for many freight companies.[1]

'It was a smaller company in the 1960s', says UPS worker Gerald Gallagher, 'and a good company to work for back then – if you can believe it. You just went to work, and you did your job, and it was a good place to work.' Gallagher was born in Dearborn, Michigan, the son of Irish immigrants who had settled in the Detroit area in the 1920s. His father was a truck driver, and his mother was a housewife until 1955, when his father died; then she took various jobs to support her family, eventually going to work in the Ford Motor Company cafeteria.

'After high school I worked full-time at a couple of different places', says Gallagher, 'and then I went to Wayne State University for a year. I dropped out of Wayne State, got married and went to work full-time for UPS in 1967.' About 1973 Gallagher became a steward at his barn, in part because conditions at UPS had begun to change for the worse. 'I can only tell you what I think happened at UPS', he says. It was after Jim Casey died that the change began: 'The company went to a more aggressive stance regarding labor-management relations. And it's my view that the accountants took over, and as the wages increased they started demanding increased productivity.' It was then that 'the pusher mentality came into being at UPS'.

'When I first worked in the department', says Gallagher, who is a clerk in a UPS loss prevention office in Detroit, 'if we had a hundred tracers to close in a day, and we got a hundred tracers closed, that was it, that was fine. Today in my department everything we do is stroked on a time card. You stroke each job you do in a little box. If you close a tracer, stroke it in a box. If you have to issue a claim on it, you stroke that in another box. And they really started getting that broken down into minute detail, and scrutinizing every aspect of the job.' The job studies were then used to establish job standards. 'What really became important to management were the standards.' The typical UPS workday is nine and a half hours, but drivers are expected to stay out until the job is done, even if it takes twelve hours, and during the pre–Christmas rush it frequently does. But it's not just the pushing or the long day that characterizes UPS management methods. It's the total control of every aspect of the job from the second that the worker punches in until the second he or she punches out.

'It's very stressful', says San Diego UPS driver Jim Moody. 'You have a lot of time limitations that you must work under. In my case I have anywhere between eighty and one hundred and five delivery stops that I have to complete between 9:20 and 3:00, and then at 3:00 I have fifty-one pickup stops. This is all in a commercial zone, and I have to complete the whole day's work before 5:00. And it takes me twenty minutes to get back to the barn.'

As every UPS employee works, every motion, every step, every turn has been studied, measured and timed. Drivers must work exactly according to UPS methods: enter the truck with the right foot, not the left; carry the package with the left arm, not the right, carry the truck keys on the little finger of the right hand, and on no other finger.[2] 'I began to get so exhausted, coming home tired, irritable, stressed out', says Moody. 'My wife would call me a UPS robot.'

In some parts of the country UPS has implemented an incentive plan. Simply put, the faster you work, the more you get paid. This system increases the tension under which the drivers work. Moody explains: 'If I have a commercial route, every package, everything that I do is broken down into elements by United Parcel Service, and those elements consist of a tenth of a second, or a second, or two minutes for a COD, and there's a computer printout that figures out everything that I do.

'And the day following my work, the computer printout will indicate what my day was worth; I have a computer telling me if I did my job right or did it wrong, and that's what management looks at. That's how they analyze or evaluate a driver's performance, by the computer readout. If the job was worth nine hours, and it took me eight and a half hours to do the job, then I will get paid eight hours straight time, a half hour overtime, and then thirty minutes, if I beat the route by thirty minutes, I get thirty minutes straight time – that's the incentive. The incentive program puts a lot of stress on the drivers to think of themselves as "production animals". They've got to do the route within a certain time frame, and if they don't, they're substandard, they're not doing their job right.'

The top Teamster officials actually encouraged the anti-union incentive plan for many years, though recently pressure from TDU and the rank and file has made them less enthusiastic about it. Naturally, there are physical injuries with such pressure. Cheryl Marquis drives a package car in San Diego. 'You're always going one hundred and ten percent, and I never took a break, I never took lunch, or, if I did, it was for five minutes to eat on the road. And it's because I didn't know any better, and I assumed that's what was expected. I'd say they basically led me to believe that.' Marquis has been hurt twice, once injuring her shoulder and once her knee: 'A lot of the injuries are because people feel like they have to push so hard, and they rush and rush and rush and they don't get time to think.'

But perhaps a greater problem than the physical injuries are the psychological problems, the problems caused by stress. 'Certainly this idea that you just dispatch somebody and they stay out until they get it done must wreak havoc with family life', says Gallagher. Some UPS workers handle the stress of work through drugs and alcohol. 'It's easier to take drugs and work at UPS than it is alcohol' says Don Paddock, a UPS employee for more than twenty years, the vice-president of Teamster Local 542 in San Diego, and a member of TDU. 'You take the alcohol, it's going to show up. You're going to look like you're drinking. You're going to be sluggish. The drugs are easier. They're a little pill. You just take it, and it speeds you up, and that's exactly what they want. I see a lot of people drink coffee and drink Coke to give them at least that caffeine edge, to keep them moving.'

Other UPS employees can't handle it, and while work goes on their families fall apart. 'There's a lot of anxiety toward your family and your friends and relatives', says Paddock. 'You're very upset a lot of the time. They don't understand what you're going through. You can get divorced real quick.' Some UPS workers have told me that the stress of the job has caused them to become unable to perform sexually, and that is not an easy thing for a young man in his twenties to confess.

It is not at all surprising that a company would try to control its workers. What is surprising – and frightening – is the degree to which many workers *internalize* the company's drive for production and profits. Overwhelmed by their initial indoctrination in the company's work ethic, reinforced by frequent pep talks and a barrage of propaganda such as the UPS magazine *The Big Idea*, many UPS workers have come to *demand of themselves* that they meet the company's productivity standards, and come to think of themselves as failures if they do not meet them. Gallagher believes that while the company's prime objective in its strict regimentation of the workplace was to increase productivity, it also had a secondary objective. 'It broke down worker solidarity because they had a tendency to single people out.'

The union contract did not allow workers to be disciplined for failing to meet productivity standards, so to get around the union's objections UPS would discipline workers for failing to follow the company's methods. Gallagher explains: 'They have a philosophy as far as drivers that they work with the "least best driver". That means the driver who runs over what is allowed according to company standards. I believe the standard load is nine and one-half hours. If it takes him ten and one-half hours to do it, that means that he's supposedly one hour over what is allowed. If he's the highest over what is allowed, he's the guy they work with. They'll put a supervisor on the truck with him and ride with him. They'll check his methods all the time.'

By allowing the company to discipline workers for failure to use company methods the union left the workers without protection. And, without backing from the union, says Gallagher, 'People have a tendency to look out for themselves and to lose sight of the big picture. You found the worker solidarity deteriorating when this big push came on, and I think it was by design. The company would isolate people, people that weren't as productive as they would want them to be. Or isolate people that were union activists, or people that were excessively absent and see if they couldn't remove them from the group. And they work with you, and they leave the impression that you have to do this job, and you have to do it our way, and you have to maintain our standards, and if you don't, you're not going to get any help from your union, you're going to be looking at the unemployment line. And it's been successful. There's nobody in the world that works harder than a UPS worker, a UPS driver especially.'

The Fight Against UPS

Faced with this totalitarian nightmare, UPS workers were forced to develop creative techniques to defend themselves. When he became the steward in the mid-1960s, Vince Meredith, the chief steward at UPS in Louisville, Kentucky, started a sick fund, collecting fifty cents or a dollar from each worker for a fund for employees who were sick. The fund was popular with the members, and Vince and his coworkers decided to create other funds to finance their fights with management.

Eventually they created three other funds as well: an employees' fund; a termination fund; and a health and welfare fund. The employees' fund was used for matters related to employment, like sending stewards to the state panel to argue grievances or hiring lawyers if necessary. And it paid for a UPS worker's record book. 'We make up a record book for each employee', explains Vince, 'to show what he's doing – and so we can prove that he didn't do what the supervisor said he done.'

Then they started a termination fund to help defend workers who were unfairly fired. It pays each fired employee $250 a week for each week he's off. Finally, they created a health and welfare fund, which pays the $70 payment into the employer-union health and welfare fund when either the company or the union fails to do so. These four funds, created and managed by the workers themselves, gave them some real tools with which to fight the company.

UPS workers in northern Virginia have developed the MAD days as one way to fight management. UPS management conducts what TDU has called 'overly strict methods audits', where 'the slightest misstep is considered a failure to follow instructions and is used for disciplinary action.' To resist such harassment, TDU members Anthony Smith and Doug Bell of Washington, DC Local 639 have organized Methods Awareness Days, or MAD days. 'On MAD days we hold a parking lot meeting where we stress that drivers should follow the company's methods to the letter – both the very restrictive and the safety-oriented practices', they explain. 'We stress that drivers should not work off the clock before their normal starting time, should take their full lunch, always walk to and from the package car, and use proper lifting techniques.'[3] In order to avoid accusations that they are organizing a slowdown or illegal job action, the TDUers stress that they only follow UPS rules and take nothing additional from the company.

Such work-to-rule campaigns have been used for years by workers in manufacturing plants to defend themselves, and now that factory-style production has come to the trucking industry there is no doubt that they will spread among UPS workers and other transportation industry workers.

Michael Savwoir

TDU has also fought discrimination and racism at UPS. Michael Savwoir, a feeder driver at UPS in Kansas City, has been involved in the Teamster reform movement since the mid-1970s, when he joined UPSurge, the organization of rank-and-file UPS workers. When UPSurge fell apart, he became a member and then a national leader of TDU. He has been active in the fight for a decent UPS contract, and thanks in part to his organizing his local returned a very high number of 'no' votes on recent UPS contracts. As a member of the International Steering Committee, Savwoir has played a leading role in the development of TDU's policies on everything from drug-testing to the RICO suit.

As a Black worker, he has been particularly concerned about racism. In the last couple of years he has turned his attention to the issue of civil rights in the workplace, and has helped to form a minority caucus of UPS workers in Kansas City called Concerned Minorities. It is not really surprising that he should do so, for Savwoir has grown up with the civil rights struggle.

He was born and grew up in Kansas City, Missouri. When he was a just a teenager, his father got involved in the civil rights movement and in local politics, and was one of the original activists of Freedom, Incorporated. 'It was', says Savwoir, 'Kansas City's first Black political organization, because, while there may have been political coalitions before, they were always white-controlled. For years it was the Black political voice of Kansas City. At that time it was a fledgling organization, and my involvement was

Michael Savwoir at the 1988 TDU convention.

Jerry Bliss, TDU candidate in Local 337.

canvassing the neighborhoods to get people to come out to the polls. So I was knocking doors and shaking hands and assisting him in his precinct captain duties as it was. I was probably thirteen or so, and it gave me an interesting experience in neighborhood organizing.'

In addition to going to school and helping out his dad with the Black political movement, from the time he was thirteen Savwoir worked, first as a busboy, and then as a helper on the city street crews cleaning trucks and installing sewer traps. After high school he worked for a while as a draftsman at city hall, transferring city subdivision maps from paper to mylar and microfilm. After graduating from high school in 1966, Michael went to the University of Missouri at Columbia, studying psychology and worked on civil rights issues with the Congress for Racial Equality. 'During that period we were active in many of the local minority concerns, such as housing and voting rights and things of that sort. And of course we're talking 1966 to perhaps 1969, the period that may have been the height of the civil rights movement.' In 1969 Savwoir got married, and he and his wife Ethel started a family. He left school and they returned to Kansas City, where he got a job as a lab technician with Schlitz Brewery. Later that year he got a job at United Parcel Service.

All his life Michael has been concerned about civil rights, particularly in his hometown of Kansas City. 'The atmosphere tends to relegate Blacks to the worst jobs, it tends to deny them promotional opportunity, to discriminate. That's not just at UPS, it's in all aspects of the business community, and it's everywhere in Kansas City. Of course that's changing, but it hasn't changed as much as it has perhaps in other places. What I'm saying here is there's a subtle racism that exists in this part of Missouri.'

It was in order to combat discrimination that in October 1986 Michael Savwoir helped to found Concerned Minorities, a caucus of minority UPS employees in Kansas City. The group is made up of Black, Latino and Native American UPS workers; much of its work so far has been on behalf of Black women. 'We've been active in the area of Black female rights in the workplace and Black career opportunities in the workplace. We've taken up sexual harassment cases. We've been very active in the routine promotional aspects of the job and terminations. And we've had the opportunity to lend our services to other unions, such as the Kansas Turnpike Authority Employees.'

One of the central activities of the group has been to pressure UPS to hire more Black women workers. 'The say they can't find any qualified Black females, so the workplace is relegated to just one Black female in each capacity. And obviously, very blatantly that's discrimination.' When there is discrimination, the Concerned Minorities organization has protested to the company or the union, or has helped workers sue for their rights. 'Neither the company nor the union have really been willing to acknowledge us. Of course they've had to, but they haven't done so willingly. The company would prefer to ignore our correspondence initially, or to treat us as troublemakers, or to try to isolate individuals, rather than treat the problems as a progressive company would', says Savwoir.

And white workers have been suspicious of the group, if only because the Black, Latino and Native American workers have organized separately. But, says Savwoir, he believes that what the group is doing is beneficial not only to minorities, but to all employees. 'It's just a little cog in the network that can hopefully return some control of the workplace to the rank and file. While some of our nonminority employees may have felt it threatening to them, I think our organization has really brought about a better environment for everyone, not just the hourly people, but management as well, because it seeks to improve working conditions for all of us.'

Notes

1. Kenneth Labich, 'Big Changes at Big Brown', *Fortune*, 18 January 1988, pp. 56–64.

2. Jeremy Schlosberg, 'Hell on Wheels', *New England Monthly*, January 1988, pp. 60–64. See also Matthew Maranz, 'Signed, Sealed & Delivered: An Inside Look at the "Tightest Ship in the Shipping Business"', *Worcester Magazine*, 25 November 1987, pp.12–14.

3. Anthony Smith and Doug Bell, 'Virginia Members Get MAD: Work-to-Rule Throws Ball in UPS's Court', *Convoy-Dispatch*, no. 63 (July–August 1986).

16

'Roy Williams, What Are You Afraid of?'

As the Teamster contracts continued to unravel during the presidency of Roy Williams, so the political situation in the Teamsters also worsened. There were TDU members who hoped that their reform movement might be helped by the AFL-CIO, but those illusions disappeared when Lane Kirkland was elected the second president of the Federation to succeed George Meany. In his acceptance speech, Kirkland, called upon those unions outside the Federation to rejoin, although he did not mention the Teamsters by name. Kirkland's offer was prompted by the fact that over the past thirty years the Teamsters had grown while the AFL-CIO's membership and power had declined.

The Teamsters had endorsed Ronald Reagan in the 1980 presidential election, so no help for the rank and file would be coming from that quarter. In December President-elect Reagan appointed Jackie Presser, fifteenth International vice-president of the IBT, as senior adviser to the economic affairs transition group. Reagan's appointment of Presser, who was known for his Mafia ties, was criticized by Representative J.J. Pickle and Senator Sam Nunn, and in an editorial in the *New York Times*. TDU also condemned Reagan's appointment of Presser. But the Reagan administration was impervious to these criticisms, and Presser became a member of Reagan's inaugural committee and a friend of Secretary of Labor Raymond L. Donovan and Attorney General Edwin Meese. Once again it seemed that the government was embracing the mobster-Teamster alliance, which Presser personified.

Teamster President Frank Fitzsimmons died of lung cancer on 6 May 1981, and about a week later the union's General Executive Board chose Roy Williams as interim general president. In less than two weeks after he assumed office, Williams was indicted for conspiring to bribe Nevada Senator Howard Cannon in order to stop the passage of the trucking deregulation bill.

The Teamster conventions, which occurred once every five years, provided TDU with one of its few opportunities to challenge the power of the International directly. TDU nominated Pete Camarata of Detroit Local 299 and Jack Vlahovic of British Columbia Local 213 as candidates for general president and vice-president as rank-and-file alternatives to the corrupt incumbents. TDU also called for changes in the IBT constitution that would institutionalize union democracy, most important among them being proposals for establishing majority rule on contracts and the right to vote on international officers.

The 1981 Teamster convention opened in Las Vegas, as TDU member Bill Slater described it, 'this monument to decadence, situated in a right-to-work state, which no doubt has some of the lowest paid workers and poorest working conditions in this country.'[1] There was also the familiar sight of a Teamsters Union general president defending himself against federal criminal charges, with Williams proclaiming his innocence, as Beck and Hoffa had done before him.

With Williams under indictment, there were calls for a government clean-up of the union, but TDU rejected direct government involvement. A leaflet handed out by TDU to the convention delegates read, 'TDU members and Delegates at this Convention are dead set against letting the Federal Government say who is, and who is not, fit to be our General President. We do not support the government stepping in against Roy Williams. What we do want is to give the membership the right to elect our General President.'[2] Despite ongoing investigations into Mafia involvement in the Teamsters, President Reagan spoke to the convention in a filmed address in which he praised the union and expressed his desire to work with it in dealing with the country's economic problems. And once again Dave Beck, the living symbol of the long history of Teamster depravity, was present to receive the accolades of Teamster officialdom.

TDU felt it was important for the rank-and-file movement to challenge the Teamster leadership head on, and when it came time for the election of the IBT general president, Pete Camarata was nominated. In a rigged convention dominated by flunkies, and with an air of intimidation that kept honest members from expressing their opinions, Camarata received few votes and conceded defeat early in the voting. But several TDU resolutions won the support of nearly 100 delegates, a significant improvement in support by local officials who had the courage to stand up and be counted. And there was a real debate over the issue of strike benefits, with some delegates calling for doubling the benefits and International officials arguing that this would make the members 'too fat'.

Diana Kilmury

The high point of the 1981 convention was a speech by Diana Kilmury, who became an celebrity overnight after she had the temerity stand up to propose that the union create an ethical practices committee. The delegates rose out of their seats in an angry uproar, cursing and clenching their fists. 'What', she asked the delegates, 'are you afraid of?'

She knew, and they knew.

By raising the issue of ethical practices at the Teamster convention, she had broken the Teamsters' most sacred taboo. One of its own, in its own house, had admitted to the world what the union had always denied: that there might be corruption in the union. The crowd went wild, shouting her down and demanding that she stop, rising from their seats with threatening gestures. They might have saved their energy. As they were bellowing, Diana was thinking that if they did attack her, she would land one good blow. 'I might get hit after that, but somebody is going to feel it.' They were not going to silence Diana Kilmury, who not only had the courage of her convictions but had always relished a challenge.

Diana Kilmury attributes her values and her character in large part to her father – and to her struggles against him. Her father, Dr. Kenneth Evelyn, was the son of a poor Jamaican minister, 'and as my mother so delicately puts it, was "not wholly white".' He came to Montreal during the Depression, won a scholarship to college, went to medical school, and became a physician and professor of medicine.

Dr. Evelyn met Diana's mother at a meeting of the Bahai Society. Bahai is a universalist religion that stresses the spiritual unity of the human race, and Kilmury was impressed by her father's ideas as she was growing up. 'My Dad had a very interesting philosophy really', says Kilmury. 'He thought the scrabbling that people do after the almighty dollar was not good for anybody, and that people could much better spend their time in endeavoring to make mankind better. And I got a lot of that from him.' When Diana was seven, the family moved to Vancouver.

In accord with his principles, her father had dedicated his life to better humanity through medical research. But while working in a decompression chamber, he suffered an accident that destroyed many of the glands in his body. As a result he was afflicted with several diseases, including diabetes and the usually fatal Addison's disease. To treat his Addison's disease he was given cortisone, the side effects of which were at that time unknown. It was learned only later that cortisone can cause psychotic behavior. Life with the father she so adored became unbearable.

'I ran off and got married and had kids, then I got divorced. And I was just lost and floundered around for a long time', she says. Her family had been well-to-do. She had lived in upper class neighborhoods and gone to

Diana Kilmury.

private schools. Now she was on her own with three children to support. Kilmury went back to school, got her high school diploma, and then went to college, while she also worked. 'I had the usual assortment of garbage-can jobs, from working in a potato chip factory to being a cocktail waitress and a go-go dancer – not topless. All of these absolutely deplorable jobs that paid no money.'

In about 1969 Kilmury was dating a fellow whose father owned a little trucking company, and one day, more joking than serious, he asked her if she wanted to try truck driving. 'I thought, "Well, this is just fine, now I just have to learn how to drive a proper truck", because automatically you made twice the money.' She learned to drive the little one-ton baby dump, and then worked her way up until she was driving a tractor and tandem trailers hauling gravel and sand. Still looking for a better job, more money and a challenge after four years as a truck driver, Kilmury applied for vocational training as a heavy equipment operator through Canada Manpower, the state employ-ment agency. She was the first woman to take the course in the operation of the huge earth-moving equipment, completing it in 1974.

The day she finished her training, the United Contractors, a big construc-tion company that was building the Upper Levels Highway from Vancouver to Horse Shoe Bay, informed the heavy equipment school that they would take the entire graduating class. Kilmury went over the next day to apply. The men at the company looked at her incredulously. 'Well, you're a woman!' they told her. 'Yeah, well, I know that', said Kilmury. One man took her outside, pointed to a big 35-ton end-dump cat wagon, and told her, 'Well, I'll tell you what, honey, you jump in there and take that load of rock and dump it on fill, and then bring it back and park it between these other two trucks, and you've got yourself a job.'

Though she had driven a truck and gone to heavy equipment school, these big machines were still new to her. With some anxiety she climbed up the side of the unfamiliar machine, got into the cab and looked at the controls. She was surprised to find there was no clutch, because she had never driven an automatic before. She took the load of rock to the fill, and grabbed the dump lever. 'I wasn't sure what would happen if I pulled it. I've got thirty-five tons of rock on the back and I'm about two hundred feet up in the air, and I really don't want to make a wrong move. We'd built a big fill, and I mean you're dumping rock over the side, so if you miscue, say good night, Dick. So anyway, this thing rumbles and snorts and, sure enough, the box goes up, and I munch back down the hill and stick it in between these other two trucks.' She clambered down the side of the truck, and strode back to the supervisor. 'Well, I'll be goddamned', he said, 'you get your ass down to the Teamsters union and you start Monday morning!'

'I went down to the Teamsters union', remembers Kilmury, 'and there was some consternation down there.' They had no women members in heavy construction, and perhaps they were not anxious to acquire their first, but the union had been unable to fill the position within seventy-two hours, so according to the contract the employer could hire whomever he wanted. The union had no choice but to sign her up and put her on the board.

'I was making $3.00 as a non-union tandem dump truck driver, and the day I became a Teamster I made $5.40 an hour, and double on overtime. I was in seventh heaven. I just couldn't hardly believe the money. For the first time in my life, I was really independent and didn't have to scrimp and save.' Diana Kilmury and her union brothers had some difficulties getting along at first, but they worked them out. 'I was really as happy as I'd ever been in my lifetime. I really liked driving a truck, and everyday something new to drive. And the guys really got a bang out of showing me how to run the HIAB, that's a boom. So at lunch time or coffee time I'd say, how about showing me how to run this or how to run that. And they just sort of adopted me. What a wild bunch of fellows they were, too, drank hard, played hard, but really good folks: salt of the earth.'

In 1977 Kilmury took a job at Site One, a big hydroelectric plant project in the northern part of British Columbia. 'This was my first really big construction job. Paving the highways and building the roads you would have maybe thirty or forty trucks, but Site One had 2,000 men and me, and we're building this dam in the middle of the Peace River. They ran twenty-four hours a day, three shifts a day, and just poured concrete till hell wouldn't have it – and it was exciting.' Diana would get up before work to watch the blasting crews at work, and see the sides of mountains go up in clouds of dust in the dawn. 'Real pretty', she says.

It was up at Site One that she first got active in the union. 'Before I was a union member, I always wanted to get into the union. I was the staunchest union supporter from day one. See, number two tries harder. Nobody had to convince me of the value of being a union member – my wages doubled over night, and instead of having to put up with all kinds of harassment and chasing your bouncing paychecks, you had all of this built-in protection. Things were laid out, and you were paid at a certain time, and if you weren't, all hell would break loose. And I really liked that.'

But it wasn't just the money and the protection that drew Kilmury to the union, it was those values she shared with her father. 'I always liked the idea of people sticking together, because I've always thought the world worked really unfairly, and I could see this was a way to correct a lot of these injustices. My mother is always saying I've got a Joan of Arc complex. But I just dislike unfairness.'

At first Kilmury was the union's pet, because she was the union's token female. 'They could point to me and say, "Listen, we're liberated in Local 213. We've only got one woman, but there she is." In 1974 that was still the big deal, that a woman was driving this big truck. They sent the photographers out to get my picture for the union newspaper. The guys would razz me about it unmercifully. I was twenty-seven when I became a Teamster, and I was reasonably good-looking, I guess, and men just treat a woman different than they do men. Generally these union executives would stop by and pat me on my little head, and so I viewed them differently. And of course they could tell me any brand of b.s. that they wanted to. I really didn't know the difference.'

It took her a couple of years in the union to learn the issues and the personalities involved, and by 1976 she had decided that she didn't think so much of the union executives who had been coming around patting her on the head. She was more impressed with a business agent named Jack Vlahovic. 'He'd been my business agent when I worked for this oil company. He was an absolute powerhouse of a guy, and he was excellent. If you asked him anything, none of this "Oh, we'll get back to you." If he didn't know the answer, he was back with the answer in an hour – but there was very little you could ask him that he didn't know right now. Always well prepared, his stuff together.' Moreover, he was a fighter, a reformer and a militant. 'And I thought, "Well, this is the guy to run the union", so I and a lot of other people voted for him.'

In January 1977 Jack Vlahovic was elected to union office by a slim majority of sixty votes – and almost immediately removed from office by Ed Lawson, the head of the Canadian Teamsters. There was a giant confrontation, almost a riot, down at the union hall in Vancouver; the heavy equipment operators occupied the hall, and the police were called in to remove them. There was no big battle up at Site One, but a committee was organized to support Vlahovic, and Kilmury joined. 'It was the first time I'd gotten an indication of how the Teamsters really operates. I'd gone from this pat-pat on the head to all of a sudden a cold shower. When they removed Jack from office, I took a real dim view, because that was my democratic vote that they had taken and dumped into the garbage.'

Kilmury became an organizer of fundraising for Jack Vlahovic's legal defense. Vlahovic and other leaders of Local 213 had meanwhile joined Teamsters for a Democratic Union, and Kilmury was becoming one of the leaders of the reform movement in Local 213. 'So by now', she recalls, 'I'm on the hall's shit list.' She was very active in the movement for a year, and then on 15 December 1978 she and her son Sean were involved in a terrible car accident. Her leg was shattered in four places and several ribs were broken; her son was in a coma. Her leg would never be the same again, and she qualified for the Canada Pension Plan disability. She should also have qualified for the Teamsters disability, but the union refused to grant it to her. 'They decided that with my child in a coma, two other children to support, lying flat on my back half the time, having operations the rest of the time, or hobbling around on crutches, that they would deny me my long-term disability. I mean, I'm really feeling blue, and the last thing I need is for my union, that I've stood up for on every picket line, to strike out at me and my children when I'm injured because they don't like the way I voted. Well, "Hell hath no fury. ... "'

Enraged at the union officials, she went on her crutches to the Local 213 meeting and told Secretary-Treasurer John Donaldson, a former Golden Gloves boxer, '"You're beating up on my three children, and one of them is in a coma. You're no kind of a man." I just absolutely popped every rivet. I was just livid. I stormed out of the place and fifty guys come with me – there wasn't a person left in the hall.' Outside the men asked her, 'Diana, is that right? They're not paying you?' They couldn't believe the union would do it, deny her disability and strike at her family, simply because she was a supporter of Jack Vlahovic.

'I was just fortunate that my parents had some money, otherwise we'd have sat on welfare for the next three years whilst the hospitals put me back together. I mean the stress of this period – this is what I'll never forgive them for.' She was off work for three years, and though she could not operate an earthmover, she could type and keep books and put out leaflets. So once she was able to move around she became the financial secretary of the

British Columbia and Yukon TDU chapter and a member of the TDU International Steering Committee. She also went back to driving heavy equipment as soon as she was able, although her leg still would not bend at the knee as it should. The men with whom she worked respected her for her courage and for being a fighter, and they elected her as a delegate to the 1981 convention, where she stood and asked, 'What are you afraid of?'

In December 1982, not long after the convention, Roy Williams was convicted of attempted bribery of a US senator, but pending appeals remained free and continued to act as Teamster general president. Then in early February 1983 the US Justice Department asked a federal court in Chicago to order that Williams resign his union offices immediately because of his ties to organized crime, and asked that he be forbidden to hold office while he exhausted his appeals. During hearings in federal court, government witness William Quinn linked Williams to the extortion of union funds and to the 1959 shooting of a union dissident named Jake Henderson in Kansas City, Missouri. Most damning was the government presentation of a transcript of a conversation involving Roy Williams, Joseph Lombardo, Allen M. Dorfman and Nicolas Civella, head of the Kansas City Mafia, discussing plans to take back control of the union pension fund. Finally, in mid-April 1983 Roy Williams offered to resign as general president of the Teamsters union in exchange for remaining free on bail while awaiting his appeals.

Notes

1. Bill Slater, 'I Wish Every Member Could Have Seen It', *Convoy-Dispatch*, no. 17 (June–July 1981).

2. 'Editorial: Let the Members Decide', *Convoy-Dispatch*, no. 17 (June–July 1981).

17

Victories, Defeats and Casualties

Under the impact of depression and deregulation, the membership of the Teamsters union was actually declining, and the important freight sector was declining more rapidly than other areas. Yet TDU was growing, precisely because the union's official leaders were failing to provide leadership. In various parts of the country TDU candidates ran in local elections against local and national Teamster leaders, challenging the union's concessionary contracts.

Election Victories Strengthen the Reform Movement

These candidates for local union office ran either on TDU slates or as part of a broader reform slate. Sometimes the local TDU members backed other reform slates where they did not field their own candidates. TDU members usually ran on a platform of union democracy and opposition to concessions. Local 299 in Detroit continued to be an arena of struggle between the Teamster International and TDU and the other reform forces. Given its history as the home local of Hoffa and Fitzsimmons, its importance as a key freight and carhauling local, and TDU's strong following there, it was inevitable that it would be the site of such struggles. TDU had challenged the December 1977 election in Local 299, and subsequently there were allegations that incumbent President Bob Lins had accepted employer contributions. In order to avoid a trial on those issues, Lins and the Labor Department reached a court settlement calling for new elections in Local 299 in May 1980.

TDU slated two candidates for that election: Pete Camarata, well-known leader among freight workers, for vice-president, and Jim Carothers, a steward at Commercial Carriers, Inc. and a leader of TDU's Carhaulers

Coordinating Committee, for recording secretary. An agreement was reached with Pete Karagozian of the Concerned Teamsters reform group not to slate two reformers for the same post so as to avoid dividing the reform vote (which had happened in 1977). In addition to running its own candidates, TDU supported Karagozian for president.

When the ballots were counted at the end of May, reformer Pete Karagozian had won the presidency with 3,705 votes to Bob Lins's 3,311; three other members of Karagozian's slate were elected as well, giving him a majority of the executive board and effective control of the local.[1] The TDU candidates lost, receiving approximately 2,800 votes or 44 percent of the total.

Nevertheless, TDU felt the results of the Local 299 election were a rank and file victory, because Karagozian, while not a TDU member, was a reformer and a militant. 'Defeating the International's chosen candidates in Fitzsimmons' home Local is a tremendous victory for the rank and file everywhere', said Pete Camarata, 'especially when you consider that the huge layoffs in all jurisdictions (over 50% in carhaul) made our job much tougher. … We feel Pete Karagozian's election to President is a big step forward for the Local and we have no wish to challenge the outcome. Now TDU, all Local 299 members, and our new officers face the exciting challenge of making this a strong, democratic Local – one that represents the members and uses the power of the rank and file instead of fearing it.'[2]

There was a very similar situation at the end of 1981 in Cleveland Local 407, whose president, Jim Kinney, was strongly supported by then International Vice-President Jackie Presser. Kinney and his supporters on the executive board were opposed by two reform groups. One reform slate was led by Sam Theodus. There had been a Cleveland TDU chapter for many years, which published a local TDU newspaper called *Speak Out*. The Cleveland TDU chapter slated Mike Friedman its candidate for secretary-treasurer and Gary Lazarowski and Dave Anderson as candidates for trustees. In the end Theodus won the election while Friedman got 1,542 votes or 43 percent of the total. The elections in Detroit and Cleveland showed that even though TDU still could not win many elections in the big city freight locals, it could change the politics in the local union enough so that other reformers could be elected. Both Karagozian and Theodus were far more democratic and militant than the officials they replaced, and thus represented a real advance for the reform movement.

The other big election challenge during this period was in construction Local 213 in British Columbia and the Yukon Territory. Jack Vlahovic had been elected secretary-treasurer of that local in 1977, but he had been removed from office by union officials loyal to Canadian Conference Director Edward Lawson; John Donaldson had been appointed secretary-treasurer in his place. In the 1981 election Vlahovic led a full seven-person TDU Action

Reform Slate challenging Donaldson for leadership of the local. Unfortunately, there was also a third slate called the Unity Slate, headed by Bill Lewis; it appealed to both Donaldson and Vlahovic supporters and split the reform vote. Donaldson won the election with 1,741 votes, while Vlahovic got 1,464 and Lewis received 1,076. The Local 213 election results were a great disappointment, but TDU remained an important force in the local.

In another important race, TDU leader Bob Janadia, at the head of the Rank and File Slate, ran against incumbent local union President and International Vice-President Bobby Holmes, Sr. and his executive board in Detroit Local 337. There were no other slates on the ballot, and it seemed as if TDU had an excellent chance to beat one of the top leaders of the International in a head-to-head contest. But Holmes, seeing the seriousness of the challenge, used every dirty trick in the book to beat the reformers. First, Holmes hired a former associate of neo-Nazi Lyndon LaRouche, a man named Richard Leebove, as a 'communications' aide to organize a vicious red-baiting campaign against TDU, while at the same time spending thousands upon thousands of dollars on his own publicity.[3] On election day uninformed voters or Holmes loyalists were bussed to the polling places and given free food and alcohol, while BLAST goon squads intimidated and harassed oppositionists. In addition, TDU believed there may have been irregularities in the balloting and vote counting itself.

Despite all these shenanigans Holmes defeated Janadia only narrowly, winning with just 51 percent of the vote. And Holmes still suffered a blow to his power and his pride when TDU member Jerry Bliss won 53 percent of the vote, defeating Holmes's son, Bobby, Jr., for secretary-treasurer. The election of Jerry Bliss to the executive board of Local 337 was another milestone in the growth of TDU, as it put a TDU member on the board of one of the union's most powerful locals. Shortly after Bliss's victory in Local 337, Doug Allan was elected a trustee of another important local, Local 208 in Los Angeles.

In a few areas TDU succeeded in electing the top officer and a majority of the local's executive board. For example, in December 1979 a full seven-person slate won election in Spokane Local 690; it was led by Rocky Lattanzio, a long-time reformer who had joined TDU soon after it was founded. The TDU chapter founded in 1977 was elected in 1979, and with virtually the entire chapter holding union office the TDU group disappeared. Once in office, however, and with no chapter to support them, differences developed among the reformers. Bob Wahl, who had been a member of Lattanzio's slate, opposed Lattanzio in the 1982 election, and Lattanzio was defeated. That unfortunate defeat showed how important it was to have a strong TDU chapter – as important as winning union office itself.

Only very rarely did a TDU member elected to union office turn against TDU. Such was the case with Brendan Kaiser, a carhauler for JATCO and a TDU member in Wisconsin Local 579 who decided to run for the local's top office. Shortly before the election he resigned from TDU, and in December 1980 he was elected secretary-treasurer. Kaiser repudiated and attacked TDU, at the same time becoming an advocate of concessionary carhauling contracts. Such turncoats were few and had little impact on TDU. There were many other cases around the country, too numerous to list here, in which TDU members were elected to local union office. Many remained active TDU members; others, under heavy pressure from the union, resigned – though most remained committed reformers even if they were no longer associated with TDU.

Where the incumbents were defeated and TDU members were elected, the local union was generally more democratic and more militant. TDU officials like Jerry Bliss and Doug Allan used their offices and titles to help the movement, speaking out as elected union officials and testifying before legislative bodies. Where enough TDUers had been elected in any one local or region, they began to have an effect on the bodies that dealt with negotiations and grievances. An article in *Convoy-Dispatch* in March 1981 noted that as a result of TDU-CCC organizing and election victories in Michigan, 'For the first time in years cases are being considered and decided on their merits.'[4]All of these improvements in democracy encouraged in turn the growth of TDU and the rank-and-file reform movement.

Eileen Janadia

The economic crisis, the employers' offensive, and the union's opposition to reform had a disastrous effect on many Teamsters, and TDU suffered many casualties. Two of TDU's casualties were Bob and Eileen Janadia, who had been in the forefront of the fight for Teamster reform in Detroit, Bob as candidate for office against Bobby Holmes, Sr. in Local 337, and Eileen as one of the key organizers of the Detroit Metro TDU chapter.

In 1981 Grosse Pointe Foods closed its doors, and Bob Janadia was thrown out of work. 'When Bob's company closed', Eileen Janadia remembers, 'we were left with the breadwinner not having a job, and it happened during the worst time, because it was right at the start of the recession. I had always said, "Well, if Bob loses his job I'll just go to one of the factories and I'll get a job. I'll make equal money to what he's been making." I'm not afraid to go out and do that. But unfortunately the recession had set in and *nobody* could find jobs.

'Our lives changed, our personal lives came to a screeching halt when Bob's company closed, and he couldn't get work. Bob was blacklisted, although we've never been able to go to court and prove it, but it's been very obvious over the years. Every time he would get a Teamster job, once the union officials found out who he was they'd get rid of him. He's never been able to hold a Teamster job for any length of time since then. We ended up having to go on welfare, which was something so foreign to us, but we had no other choice. I didn't feel humiliated by it, but I felt pissed. I was really angry. So in that period of time, I had to quit working for TDU. I went to Macomb College, and I got a degree as a paralegal. And since then I've been going to Wayne State taking general studies to back up the paralegal degree.'

Eileen liked college – because, perhaps for the first time, she didn't feel guilty about sitting down to read a book. 'It was like a real luxury, being able to have time to read. There was this real thirst for knowledge, and it was okay to do it because you were going to get a degree out of it. It wasn't that you were lazy and laying around reading all the time. You could hang out in libraries and look at books, and not be chastised.'

She worked for a while as a paralegal for a bank, but found the atmosphere at that job too conservative. In January 1987 she took a job working as a legal secretary for TDU attorneys Barbara Harvey and Ellis Boal. 'I came here', says Eileen, 'because I knew that they were working on issues that I felt good about, and that I could relate to, and I know a lot of their clients and a lot of the people they associate with and that's been real nice. Sometimes it's real frustrating being a secretary. I imagine I will eventually want to go ahead and be a paralegal – somewhere if there's a niche for me in a job I can feel good about.

'I'm real limited about who I can go work for because of my ideals. You know I don't want to go work for a firm representing the companies, because I just wouldn't feel good about doing that, and there's not a whole lot of plaintiff labor law firms in this area. A lot of paralegals are getting jobs in hospitals now, but I couldn't do that, I can't represent the hospital against the patient. So I'm limited.'

Today, blacklisted from union jobs, Bob Janadia is working as a non-union truck driver, earning $7 a hour with no benefits whatsoever. But, whatever hardships their involvement in TDU caused them, Eileen is glad about what it has given to their son, Bob. 'He's now a teenager, he's pretty opinionated, and he gives us a tough time with his opinions. He has enough of a conscience that he feels good about standing up for people's rights, because he saw people in TDU doing it, and they were neat people, and they seemed to be right in what they were doing. And now I see him doing it at school. He's sensitive enough that he's real nervous about being any kind of a political activist, though he's on the student congress at the high school and he's vocal.

'Kids that are going to college now, are not part of the working class anymore, they're part of middle-class society. But I would hope that at least he's going to have a conscience as a result of what he saw Bob and I being involved in. That maybe someday if he's part of management – God forbid, but it could happen – he will have a conscience. He's going to feel bad about anything he does; and he's going to have a hard time justifying that in his own mind, because he will have been exposed to the struggles of the working-class people.'

The Kroger Bakery Victory

As TDU gathered for its annual convention in the fall of 1982 the situation was extremely bleak. The convention delegates exchanged stories of bankrupt companies, unemployed union members and contract concessions. But when one older lady, a Teamster member from Detroit, came forward, TDU members found they had something to be proud of, something to cheer about.

The story had begun four years earlier. In January 1979 the Kroger Bakery in Detroit had closed and 150 bakers were laid off. Ninety-one of those bakers had over twenty years of service and one, Mary Roback, had worked forty-four years for Kroger. She had started working at Kroger in 1935, the same year that Jimmy Hoffa and Bobby Holmes led the strike at that same Kroger warehouse where they began their careers as union activists. Several other workers also had thirty or forty years of service.

Yet when Kroger closed its doors the bakers were told that they would receive no pension, not a dime. They were denied their pensions because in 1970 they had transferred from the Kroger pension plan into the Central States Pension Fund, and they were all a few months short of the eligibility requirement. Neither the company, the union, nor the Central States Pension Fund trustees offered them any help. In fact, three months after the plant closed, Bobby Holmes, Sr., the head of their local, wrote them to announce, 'There is no further action that this Union can take on your behalf.'

Discouraged, the workers might have simply given up, but one man kept them together, kept them organized, and kept them fighting back. TDU member Joe Urman, who had been the chief steward at Kroger for twenty-five years, had a strong organization in the warehouse. He called a meeting to organize the laid-off Kroger's workers, and the group began picketing at Kroger's grocery stores.

'We were doing informational picketing at Kroger's grocery stores for a couple of hours on Saturday, once a week', Joe Urman remembers. 'We had signs that said "Kroger: Don't Shop Here". One time it was ten below zero, and we were out there picketing, and this poor old woman, I had to force her to sit in the car – she wanted to picket. This went on for about three and a half months. I'd say that at the stores we were hitting we was about fifty to sixty percent effective with our informational picketing, they was beginning to hurt. But we didn't last that long.

'The main point wasn't to hurt Kroger's – primarily it was to solidify the troops, the people. You had a lot of factions, but you had a coming together when they was out there together picketing. They realized, whether I'm Black or I'm a d.p., or I'm a pollack or a hillbilly – we're in the same boat. This guy ain't no different, and I'm no different than he is. We're all the same group. And this was the point, to solidify and to keep them together, and make sure they didn't fall apart till we got the legal stuff going.' *Convoy-Dispatch* periodically reported on their fight and kept the issue before the Teamster membership, while at the same time the bakers' lawyer, TDU attorney Ann Curry Thompson, sued the Central States Pension Fund. The combination of legal action, protest and publicity worked, and a little less than four years later a settlement was reached providing the Kroger bakers with their full pensions and retroactive pension payments, which in some cases amounted to $18,000.

When Mary Roback spoke before the 1982 TDU Rank and File Convention and reported that after forty-four years of work and four years of picketing and protesting she finally had her pension, thanks to TDU, the crowd responded with crying and cheering. The Kroger victory in 1982 not only won the bakers' pensions, it gave TDU hope and encouragement in otherwise dark days.

Notes

1. Susan Brown and Ralph Orr, 'Teamster Reform Slate Wins Local 299 Election', *Detroit Free Press*, 31 May 1980.

2. Pete Camarata, 'Tremendous Victory, Exciting Challenge', *Convoy-Dispatch*, no. 7 (June–July 1980).

3. Dennis King, *Lyndon LaRouche and the New American Fascism*, New York 1989, p. 356.

4. 'New Carhaul Panel', *Convoy-Dispatch*, no. 14 (March 1981).

PART V

FIGHTING BACK

18

'A Slap in the Face for Jackie Presser'

On 21 April 1983 Jackie Presser was chosen by the General Executive Board to serve as general president of the International Brotherhood of Teamsters. It was typical of Presser's rise to power: he had never stood in a contested election before the membership, but had instead risen through family connections, favoritism, and, it would turn out, through Mafia influence.

Whatever their weaknesses, and they were many, Dan Tobin, Dave Beck and Jimmy Hoffa had all known what it was to work. Tobin had driven a team and wagon in Boston, Beck had worked on the laundry trucks in Seattle, and Hoffa had heaved cases in a grocery warehouse in Detroit. All had led strikes. Presser had never worked a day in his life, had never stood for elected office, and had never led a strike. Many years before, Dave Beck had suggested that he saw no reason why union officers should not bequeath their offices to their sons as businessmen did their property, and over time that was how the system came to work. Jackie Presser had inherited union office from his father, William Presser.

William Presser, who had for thirty years been the head of the Ohio Teamsters, had liked to tell the story of how his mother had been beaten while walking the garment workers' picket lines in New York. And perhaps when he began organizing fish and poultry workers in the 1920s Bill had had some vague idea of what unions were all about. But he had forgotten. In the early 1940s he organized a jukebox workers union, the Musical Maintenance Workers Union, which later became Local 442 of the International Brotherhood of Electrical Workers. He also helped the other side organizing the jukebox owners into an employers association, and together the association and the union controlled the jukebox business.

Naturally, Bill Presser could see no reason why he should be left out of such a deal. He opened his own jukebox company in partnership with John Nardi of the Cleveland Mafia. Then the deal got sweeter. In 1951 Presser obtained a charter for Teamster Local 411 and moved the jukebox operation there. Tavern owners now had to install a jukebox from Presser or lose their beer deliveries.

Then Presser joined forces with Louis 'Babe' Triscaro, Mafia don and head of Teamster Local 436. They supported Jimmy Hoffa in his fight for the Teamster presidency, and Presser became Hoffa's man in Ohio. Bill Presser later became president of Cleveland cabdrivers Local 555, head of the Cleveland Joint Council, and the leader of the Ohio Conference of Teamsters. A family man, Bill Presser put three brothers-in-law in union positions.

Life was not without its little ups and downs. In 1953 William Presser was convicted of restraint of trade in his role as head of an employer group, the Tobacco and Candy Jobbers Association. In 1960 he was sent to prison for contempt of Congress for destroying evidence sought by the McClellan Committee in its investigations of union corruption. And in 1971 he pleaded guilty to eight counts of shaking down employers by making them buy ads in joint council newspapers in exchange for labor peace. Presser was fined rather than being sent to prison because it could not be proved that he, rather than the union, had actually received the money.

Nevertheless, despite the minor irritations of appearances in court and a short stay in jail, Presser continued to wield enormous power in the Teamsters union, perhaps second only to Hoffa himself. In 1957 Hoffa put Presser on the board of the Central States Pension Fund, and that position became his main source of power and influence. Presser became second in command after Allen Dorfman, the main Mafia figure in charge of the pension fund. It was Dorfman and Presser who made the bad loans in the 1950s and 1960s, and who were responsible for the policies that denied so many thousands of Teamsters their pensions.

William Presser's son Jackie was born in 1926 in Cleveland. Jackie Presser dropped out of school in the eighth grade, joined the Navy at seventeen, and after serving in World War II got a job through his father's influence as a staff member of Local 10 of the Hotel and Restaurant Employees Union in Cleveland.[1] In three years he became president of Local 10 and then attempted to expand the local rapidly through a series of mergers – but the new members he had recruited threw him out of office.

In 1952, again through his father's influence, Jackie Presser became a Teamster organizer, and with his father's help in 1964 he got a $1.1 million loan from the Central States Pension Fund to build a sports club and restaurant in suburban Cleveland – but the project failed, Jackie Presser defaulted, and the pension fund lost $265,000. A failure as a legitimate businessman, even with the help of a Teamster loan, Presser decided to make a career in the labor movement. In 1966 his father gave him a charter for a new Teamster Local 507, of which he became the president. Under Jackie Presser's leadership, Local 507 grew not by organizing workers but by making sweetheart contracts with employers and taking members from other Teamster locals.[2] Jackie Presser became an important figure in the Ohio Teamsters, and when his father was forced to resign as International vice-president in 1976, the IBT General Executive Board selected his son Jackie to replace him. In a career in the labor movement of almost twenty years, Presser had never faced an opponent in a contested election.

At an inaugural press conference, Presser denied that there was any organized crime influence in the Teamsters union and pledged to run an 'open, honest administration'. But from the moment he was elected IBT president, Presser was under investigation by the government in a union embezzlement case for having spent union money on 'ghost employees' who never really worked for the union. TDU and the rank and file were outraged at the choice of Presser. In an 'Open Letter to Members and Officers', TDU argued that the seventeen-member General Executive Board had 'held every member in contempt because they know Presser was a man no group of Teamsters would freely choose, and who will sell us out for his enrichment and power. And every local officer was held in contempt as well, because the General Executive Board members didn't so much as consult with them, or they would be well aware Presser couldn't win a vote there either.' TDU referred to Presser as 'a man who had turned unionism into its opposite – the pursuit of personal enrichment off the backs of others.'[3] With the election of Presser the Teamsters seemed, from any moral or politically progressive point of view, to have hit rock bottom.

The first indication that something was changing for the better had come somewhat earlier, in the spring of 1982, at a meeting of union officials called by Roy Williams to discuss the United Parcel Service contract. Such meetings had usually been rubber-stamp affairs at which the local union officials gave their approval to the contract presented by the International leadership. But that isn't what happened on 'The Day the Officers Stood Up', as TDU called it.

'How many times have we heard local officers tell us "my hands are tied" when a problem comes up, to pass the buck', wrote *Convoy-Dispatch*. 'On Wednesday, May 5, 1982, a couple of hundred local Teamster officers proved that those excuses are just that – excuses. They stood up for the members, the way they were elected to. And they did it to Teamster Pres. Roy Williams, and to United Parcel Service, the largest Teamster employer there is. On behalf of TDU we salute those officers. ... And then at least some of those officials – not most, but some – took an even more important step. *They went home to their members and they told them the truth.* That the contract is a disgrace to the union and it should be voted down, and Williams should be sent back to the bargaining table.'[4]

This changing attitude among United Parcel Service workers was demonstrated again, in September 1982. Some 5,000 Teamsters in New York and New Jersey walked off the job on 9 and 10 September, and then from 13 to 15 September 3,600 UPS workers from New Jersey Local 177 struck seventeen buildings over the issue of union representation for UPS's air service operation. TDU organizer Ken Paff drew the lesson: 'Will the members participate in the union? You bet they will, if they have leadership. ... The next time you feel like saying that the members are all apathetic, remember this little story. Fifty came to a union meeting, and three days later 500 poured out for a union rally.'[5]

By early 1983, there began to be a more general change in attitude among rank-and-file Teamsters as the economy continued to improve and the national economic situation started to seem somewhat less desperate. For example, *Convoy-Dispatch* reported that many representatives attending a May 1983 meeting of the Central-Southern Carhaul Panel in Atlanta 'feel the time for giveaways is past.'[6] After four years of concessions, this attitude was something new. Both local union officials and union members were tired of take-aways: the tide had turned.

'A Slap in the Face for Jackie Presser'

Presser, however, had not noticed the rising waters. On 6 July 1983 Presser called a National Freight Negotiating Committee meeting in Chicago and proposed what he called the 'Voluntary Laid-Off Employees Rider', which would have resulted in wage cuts of between 18 and 35 percent for many thousands of Teamsters. The heart of Presser's proposal was a two-tier arrangement under which laid-off Teamsters could be recalled to work at lower wages.

The proposed contract rider was supposed to be secret, and all copies were collected before the officials left the room. But TDU had the information about the rider as soon the meeting ended and immediately launched a campaign to defeat it, a 'campaign to save the contract'. At local union meetings held to discuss the rider, the members not only rejected the contract – they rejected the man who had negotiated it. On 20 August 1983 400 members of Columbus Local 413 voted unanimously to request the resignation of Jackie Presser. The next day 500 members of Cleveland Local 407 did the same. Their votes of no confidence in the Teamster leadership were especially telling, coming as they did from Presser's home state. When the final tally was announced on 16 September 1983 TDU had been vindicated and Presser was annihilated: 94,086 members had voted against the rider, and only 13,082 had voted for it. It was a tremendous victory for TDU, and as *Business Week* reported, it was '"A Real Slap in the Face" for Jackie Presser'.[7]

TDU's victory over Presser on the relief rider in September 1983 represented a turning point for the Teamster rank-and-file movement. TDU could no longer be dismissed as a 'small group of dissidents', as it had so often been called. TDU had led the movement to reject the rider, and 88 percent of the members had voted for the position advocated by TDU. While TDU's membership was still only a few thousand, the vote on the rider proved that TDU's influence was far greater than its numbers might have suggested.

The Continuing Decline of the Freight Contract

The ranks had begun to fight back, but unfortunately the movement was not yet strong enough to force the union to deal with the union's central problem – the weakening of the key trucking industry contracts. The continuing breakdown of the freight contract was the result of four specific policies adopted by the freight companies and accepted by the union. The first was 'double breasting', the practice of unionized carriers creating non-union subsidiaries. The second was the employee stock option plan (ESOP), a strategy usually accompanied by wage-cuts. The third was the two-tier contract. The fourth was a tremendous increase in the use of casual workers. In addition to these strategies, many companies maintained a systematic campaign of intimidation and harassment.

Double-Breasting

Deregulation had led to the growth of non-union trucking companies, which the Teamsters union failed to organize, and these non-union firms put increasing pressure on unionized carriers. Some unionized carriers, faced with such competition, took advantage of deregulation and opened their own non-union subsidiaries, a practice known as 'double-breasting'.

One of the first to engage in double-breasting was Branch Motor Express, which opened two non-union divisions in Charlotte, North Carolina in January 1981. The 'Rebel' division hired owner-operators with their own tractor-trailer combinations, while the 'Nomad' division hired drivers who owned tractors to pull company trailers. The company then diverted much of its work from its union company to its new non-union subsidiaries, which had lower wages and benefits.

Ironically, Branch won a 15 percent wage concession from its employees in March 1982, with support from some union officials, to finance the double-breasting operation. In November 1982, Branch asked its employees for voluntary pay cuts of from 5 to 15 percent, and the employees kicked in some $500,000 a year. The money was used to pay for the development of the non-union competitors owned by Branch, not to save jobs at Branch itself.

Leaseway, a trucking, truck leasing and warehousing corporation with more than a dozen subsidiaries that did billions of dollars in business, also created its own non-union subsidiary, called Leaseway Express, operating in the East, South and Midwest. Likewise, Consolidated Freightways opened an entire national system of non-union subsidiaries under the name Con-Way Express Group. Another one of the biggest trucking companies, Roadway, operated two non-union subidiary truck lines, Spartan and Roberts – and later purchased Viking, with thirty-seven terminals in ten states and 2,000 non-union drivers and dock workers. Ryder/PIE, Transcon and Preston also created or purchased non-union subsidiaries.

Article 32 of the Teamster contract clearly stated that work being done by a collective bargaining unit should not 'be subcontracted, transferred, leased, assigned or conveyed in whole or in part' by the employer to 'any other plant, person or non-unit employees.' And it explicitly stated that employers were not permitted to create subsidiary companies to do work covered by the National Master Freight Agreement. But, as usual, the union did nothing about such violations of the contract.

TDU opposed double-breasting from the beginning, and as the problem grew and the union failed to act, a hue and cry went up from the members and local leaders. Cleveland Local 407 passed a resolution in April 1983 asking Presser to make the Conway Express problem one of his priorities. Chuck Mack, president of Oakland Local 70 and an important official in the Western Conference, wrote to the International that Consolidated Freightways should be put on notice that 'we do not intend to stand idly by and watch the work of our members diverted to these new non-union subsidiaries.'[8]

ESOPs: The New Deals

In the late 1970s and early 1980s, trucking companies came up with a new plan to get employees to pay for their capital investment, mergers, and acquisitions. Employee stock ownership plans had many apparently attractive features. Workers would receive stock in the company. The workers would no longer simply take orders, but would have representatives on the board of directors who could vote on the company's policies. As stockholders, the workers would receive not only wages, but also dividends and appreciation in the value of their stock. In exchange for stock in the company, the workers were asked to take a cut in pay, usually 15 percent. The wage cut, it was often argued, would allow the company not only to stay in business, but to make a profit to be shared with the employees. This utopian solution was not all that it appeared.

Interstate Systems, an important freight company with 3,600 employees, created an ESOP in early 1984, accompanied by a 15 percent wage reduction. Dave Blesing of Toledo Local 20 wrote in a letter to the *Convoy-Dispatch,* 'All union members who joined did so believing that Interstate's financial distress was very real and that the ESOP was the last possible chance to preserve their jobs.' Over 85 percent of the employees signed up to participate in the Interstate ESOP.

The company began to expand on the basis of these new financial arrangements. But early in 1982 the company closed over seventy terminals and laid off 2,000 employees. A few weeks later Interstate filed for bankruptcy under Chapter 11 of the federal bankruptcy code, allowing the company to renege on its contract with the union. The value of the employees' stock fell sharply after the company announced its bankruptcy. A month later the company announced that the 'New Interstate System' was cutting wages by 35 percent and would pay newly hired workers $7.00 an hour. Finally, the Teamsters struck the company on 15 May.

The Interstate Systems story was not unique. Branch Motor Express had instituted an ESOP in 1983, and then in the summer of 1984 the company filed for bankruptcy under Chapter 11 and closed its doors: Branch stock became worthless. A similar fate befell thousands of workers at Suburban, Murphy, System 99 and other companies.

But even where the company survived, the situation was far from ideal. Transcon created an ESOP in November 1983, and 91 percent of the 3,500 employees agreed to take a 12 percent pay cut in exchange for stock. 'No one was thrilled about losing the money', wrote Pete Sercombe, a Transcon driver from Sacramento, California, 'but it didn't sound all that bad. We were to end up with 49 percent of the stock after five years, and we'd elect two people to the Board of Trustees. We also got a joint labor-management committee to administer the plan. The 49 percent of stock, combined with stock that we had already bought through our savings plan, would give us a 60 percent share of Transcon. We would own our own company!'

But the deal didn't work out that way, Sercombe explained: 'Right now, we're paying $26 per share through our 12 percent giveback for stock that's currently worth $8 per share. Our joint committee has five people on it, three company lawyers and two workers handpicked by the company. We don't have a chance! One of the two "union" people just quit the committee, [because] she was so disgusted with her lack of say in the company. As for owning our own company, that hasn't worked out so hot either.' The company would accept on the company's board of directors only two representatives appointed by 'the round man in Washington, Jackie Presser'.[9] One of those two representatives appointed by Presser, John Fanning, later told *Business Week,* 'I have never received any instructions from the union and don't even meet with the Teamsters unless it's together with Transcon management.'[10] ESOPs at PIE and at Smith Transfer provided similar stories; Smith was later bought by American Carriers – which subsequently went bankrupt.

At freight terminals across the country, workers were shaken down by the bosses, and gave up their wages for what frequently turned out to be worthless stock in collapsing companies. In early 1988 a group of workers at Advance Transportation in the Chicago area sent a desperate letter to Jackie Presser: 'We are a large group of black and white working men who are employed as drivers, dockmen and yardmen at Advance Transportation Co., Bedford Park, Ill. We have a problem and need help. We feel that Advance is doing something that is not entirely legal.' The letter explained how the workers at Advance had taken first a 5 percent and later a 12 percent pay cut in return for an ESOP. The letter went on: 'A truck driver retired after paying into the plan for nine months. This amounted to a $3,500 contribution to the plan. When he left the company he received a check for $56. Tell us IS THAT FAIR? IS THAT LEGAL?

'Approximately 90 percent of the employees signed the plan for fear of losing their jobs. If you refused to sign up for ESOP, the bosses called you into their office five to ten times harassing you until you gave in and signed. Now that this ESOP plan is almost over, Advance has decided that all this extra cash is too good to pass up. So Advance has come up with yet another plan to get money from their employees for another three years. This new plan is called Employees Wage Contribution and Profit Sharing Plan. They want another 12 percent of our wages. ...

'We as family men are not rich and have a difficult time making ends meet. Some of us have to work two jobs because of ESOP taking away our money. Because of this we see our families less and less in order to just survive. Between the company and the union, they both would like us to work for free, but still pay union dues and contribute in worthless stock plans. We thought that slavery was against the law. ...

'Advance can close its doors for good and lock us out. If that happens, all of America will know what kind of people run our companies and our unions. All we want are decent lives for our families, and Local 710 and Advance want to take that away from us. ... All we want is an answer to our problem. We have only two weeks until the new union contract goes into effect. At that time it will be in our contract. PLEASE HELP US!'[11]

Help from the Teamsters leadership never came.

TDU had opposed ESOPs early on, and three years before the desperate cry from the workers at Advance, TDU National Organizer Ken Paff had written, 'Some Teamsters look down on these brothers and sisters [who accept ESOP's and wage cuts] – but they are dead wrong. They are just Teamsters afraid of losing their jobs, worried about an uncertain future or disgusted at the idea of a new job at 70 percent of union scale. The blame lies elsewhere. …

'The bottom line is that Jackie Presser and the International Union have sold out 200,000 Teamsters under the NMFA and are trying to escape the blame for it. They signed a contract six months ago and told the companies to go ahead with their individual deals right after it. The entire principle of unionism is that no individual can "bargain" on his/her own with giant corporations like ARA or International Utilities. If we could "bargain" as individuals, what on earth would we need a union for?'

TDU called upon rank-and-file members to submit motions in their local unions such as the following: 'This local union calls upon the International Union to end the practice of allowing corporations to bargain with our members individually over ESOPs, and begin to take responsibility for collective bargaining over the job security of our members and the future of our contract.'[12]

Two-Tier Wage Scales

Another tool the employers used to dismantle the Teamsters union was the two-tier contract. The IBT had accepted two-tier wages in the 1982 National Master Freight Agreement and in other contracts in the form of lower pay for new hires, part-time or seasonal workers. An official from the Western Conference of Teamsters noted that such contracts were acceptable to current union members because their wages were not affected: 'This situation is popular with some officers and BAs because the people who vote for us are happy. The "seasonal", "part-time" and the new hires are not voting members in many cases. When the new hires become voting members we worry about it then.'[13]

Two-tier pay scales were pushed by the employers and accepted by union officials and many Teamster members, and such clauses were negotiated into the contracts of freight workers, UPS workers, carhaulers, grocery workers, food processing workers, and many others. In reality, two-tier wages were a particularly invidious development. Wherever they were introduced, resentment and recrimination soon followed. Lower paid workers envied the higher paid workers doing the same job, while higher paid workers sometimes looked down on their lower paid coworkers as being somehow worth less because they were paid less. The lower pay for new hires gave the company an incentive to attempt to phase out, lay-off, or even fire the older, higher seniority workers. Two-tier pay destroyed the fundamental labor principle of equal pay for equal work. Two-tier simply took money from workers and gave it to employers; it lowered the standard of living of working people while increasing the wealth of the corporations. Most important, it undermined solidarity, the glue that holds the union together.

Even though the union rank and file had overwhelmingly rejected two-tier pay in the vote on the relief rider in September 1983, both the International and local union officials continued to make two-tier concessions to demanding employers. TDU continued to fight two-tier pay as it had from the beginning, and would make it the key issue in upcoming contract fights.

Casuals

Beginning in the mid-1970s the companies began to systematically abuse the use of casual workers, turning them into throwaways. The companies hired enormous numbers of casuals, and many workers were kept permanently in casual status without full rights and benefits as workers or union members. With the introduction of two-tier wages, they were paid less in wages and benefits. *Convoy-Dispatch* reported that in 1984 Yellow Freight had employed 22,000 casuals; Ryder/PIE employed 17,000, and Consolidated Freightways some 12,000.[14] Casual workers were underpaid and overworked, sometimes without loyalty to the union – and who could blame them? – and frequently disdained by the permanent workforce; the institutionalization of a permanent casual workforce was a serious threat to the union.

The companies' offensive against the union took its toll, and the contract began to come apart. Charles R. Perry described this process in his analysis of the trucking industry: 'The competitive fragmentation of the regulated trucking industry, which had threatened to undermine industrywide bargaining as early as 1977, had by 1985 progressed to the point that even the Teamsters with all of their power and pragmatism could not hold the system together. By 1984 ... the industry appeared to be a model of instability and chaos. ... '[15]

War on the Worker

While double-breasting, ESOPs, two-tier pay, and the abuse of casuals were destroying the contract and dividing the union, it was war on the worker as the employers continued trying to break the spirit of the individual employee. UPS and Roadway were the pioneers in the development of this repressive style of management, which was soon adopted by other trucking companies. Using the techniques developed by Roadway and UPS, McLean management went on a rampage beginning in late 1983. At one terminal after another workers were harassed, intimidated, threatened. Going beyond the practices at UPS and Roadway, and beyond the limits of the law, workers were even assaulted.

This war on the worker seems to have begun on 28 October 1983 with an incident at the McLean terminal in Cincinnati. Management claimed that there was a work stoppage – though the employees denied it – and the company brought in thirty supervisors to harass the employees while armed guards were stationed in the parking lot. Two or three supervisors were assigned to each trailer to stand like jailers over the dock workers. The supervisors wrote warning letters for the smallest infraction, real or imagined, and four of the workers were fired or suspended, though three of the four were immediately reinstated with the backing of the union.

But the harassment didn't let up. A few months later the company hired members of the Cincinnati Bengals football team, who were assigned to stand guard over a city driver who was being punished by being made to mop the floors. The company began to videotape dock workers and city drivers making their pick-ups and deliveries. In one month management handed out some 300 warning letters. Road drivers recently transferred to Cincinnati were laid off, and several lost their homes.

This harassment was applied throughout the system and led to protests and demonstrations. There was a walkout by workers in Minneapolis, while in Cincinnati and Lebanon, Pennsylvania, the workers' wives began to picket the terminals to protest the persecution of their husbands. Nonetheless, the harassment continued with suspensions and firings in Atlanta; several workers in Cincinnati were hospitalized with physical and psychological problems resulting from management's campaign of abuse.

In January 1985 things went a step further when Nate Rowan, a worker at the Cincinnati terminal, was threatened by two supervisors. 'They backed me into a corner and used the most profane language I have ever heard,' said Rowan. 'They said they were going to bash my head in.' One of the supervisors, who was a very large man, told Rowan he was going 'to tear my head off.'

Rowan escaped from the supervisors, jumped in his car, drove to the police station and filed complaints. A warrant was issued for the arrest of his bosses, and one of them named Doerger was arrested at the terminal. 'I think they are trying to run us off', said Rowan. 'They don't like the union, and they don't like the older workers.'[16] At Doerger's trial on 8 March 1985 one of the other supervisors admitted he had heard Doerger threaten Rowan. Another dock worker, Eli Lilley, testified on behalf of Rowan. Doerger was found guilty of disorderly conduct and fined $25. 'Such action from McLean', stated Rowan, 'cannot and will not be tolerated any longer, and I would hope that all Teamsters will wake up and realize that we have had it, and now want and demand a more respectable place of employment, a place that we can be proud of.'[17]

Nevertheless, despite courageous stands by men like Rowan and Lilley, companies like McLean, Roadway and UPS continued harassment, intimidation, coercion, threats, suspensions and firings. Sometimes the union fought back. Most often it did not.

Presser Organizes the Organized

Jackie Presser had announced in his inaugural statement that he would attempt to organize public employees and high tech workers, but it turned out that what he really had in mind were mostly mergers and raids on other already organized workers. In July 1983 Presser proposed to merge the Teamsters Union with the 75,000-member International Typographical Union (ITU).

Joseph Bingel, the president of the ITU, favored the merger, but many members did not. Robert McMichen, an opponent of merger with the Teamsters, challenged Bingel for president of the ITU. In the ITU election in July 1984 McMichen received 28,167 votes, while Bingel got only 15,296. As TDU argued, it was one of the few times anybody had every had an opportunity to vote on whether they wanted Presser to lead their union – and Presser lost badly. Ralph Kessler, editor of the ITU *Retirees Newsletter* in San Francisco, said, 'It was a tempting thought to merge with the Teamsters. But as we got closer we saw we would be losing our democracy. Also, retirees are first-class members of our union, and we didn't want to lose that.' Heather Dean, a member of the executive board of a large Toronto ITU local asked, 'If Presser will turn his back on the master freight people, why wouldn't he do the same to us?'[18]

TDU's *Convoy-Dispatch* commented, 'Instead of raiding other unions, we should be organizing the unorganized in trucking, warehousing, canneries and other Teamster fields. The effort going into the ITU merger could have gone in this direction.'[19] A little over a year later, on 28 August 1985, a referendum on the merger was conducted among ITU members, and the merger with the Teamsters was defeated by a vote of 34,234 to 17,547, a margin of two to one. The Associated Press referred to this referendum as 'another blow to the prestige of Jackie Presser'.

Defeated by the rank and file of the typographical workers, Presser turned his attention to the farmworkers. In September 1984 Presser announced that the Teamsters would not renew the peace pact signed between the Teamsters and the United Farm Workers by Frank Fitzsimmons back in 1977, but that the Teamsters would again try to organize farmworkers, though the IBT would attempt to avoid confrontations with the UFW. TDU argued that in reality, Presser was 'launching a raid' against the UFW, and that 'confrontation is inevitable in this situation. In the first years of TDU's existence, before the 1977 IBT/UFW pact, we supported farm workers and their unions. We still do', argued a *Convoy-Dispatch* editorial. 'The UFW has its share of weaknesses and problems, but a Teamster intervention in the fields is not the answer to those problems. We are paying for Presser's wars. We are losing membership in the basic Teamster jurisdictions while wasting our organizing money on attacking the whole rest of the labor movement. We say that it is time to stop these policies and put together a real organizing effort to build our union. We say that it is time to stop the raids on the farm workers!'[20] In 1984 Presser spent more than half a million dollars in Ohio competing with public employee unions there, with very little result. And in early 1985 the Western Conference of Teamsters hired a firm to conduct a survey among 10,000 California state highway maintenance workers who were members of the Service Employees International Union, apparently with an eye to another raid.

The central issue for the IBT was the freight industry – the origin and the economic basis of the union's power. Presser's raids on other unions cost a great deal of money, were accompanied by much fanfare, and were ultimately miserable failures.

Notes

1. See Jackie Presser's obituary, 'Teamsters' Jackie Presser Is Dead at 61', *New York Times*, 11 July 1988.

2. See Robert L. Jackson, 'Uncle Testifies to Union Firings, "Sweetheart" Pacts by Presser', *Los Angeles Times*, 4 February 1987.

3. 'Open Letter to Members and Officers', *Convoy-Dispatch*, no. 34 (May 1983).

4. 'The Day the Officers Stood Up', *Convoy-Dispatch*, no. 26 (May 1982).

5. Ken Paff, 'Strikes Hit UPS in N.Y. and N.J.', *Convoy-Dispatch*, no. 29 (October 1982).

6. 'New-Hire Rates Spark Protest', *Convoy-Dispatch*, no. 35 (June 1983).

7. '"A Real Slap in the Face" for Jackie Presser', *Business Week*, 3 October 1983, p. 43.

8. 'CF's Con Game Undermines Contract', *Convoy-Dispatch*, no. 35 (June 1983).

9. Pete Sercombe, 'Scoop on Transcon's ESOP', *Convoy-Dispatch*, no. 55 (Sept. 1985).

10. 'Freight Lines', *Convoy-Dispatch*, no. 75 (January 1988), citing *Business Week*, 14 Dec. 1987.

11. 'Chicagoans Resist Wage Shakedown', *Convoy-Dispatch*, no. 78 (May 1988).

12. 'ESOPS: Put the Blame Where it Belongs', *Convoy-Dispatch*, no. 56 (October 1985).

13. 'License to Steal Jobs', *Convoy-Dispatch*, no. 41 (February 1984).

14. 'Stop the Abuse of Casuals!' *Convoy-Dispatch*, no. 53 (June–July 1985).

15. Charles R. Perry, *Deregulation and the Decline of the Unionized Trucking Industry*, Philadelphia 1986, pp. 108, 111.

16. 'McLean Using Death Threats?' *Convoy-Dispatch*, no. 50 (February 1985).

17. 'McLean Foreman Found Guilty', *Convoy-Dispatch*, no. 51 (March–April 1985).

18. 'Why Presser's ITU Merger Effort Failed', *Convoy-Dispatch*, no. 46 (Sept. 1984).

19. Ibid.

20. 'Stop the Raids – We Need Organizing', *Convoy-Dispatch*, no. 49 (January 1985).

19

Fighting Back in Los Angeles and Denver

When Jackie Presser and the leadership of the Teamsters union declined to stand up to the employers, TDU was called upon to do so. TDU could provide legal help and put workers in touch with other Teamsters working for the same company in other locals. But often TDU was most effective by organizing workers in the trucking barns and warehouses to use direct action such as work-to-rule campaigns to solve their problems.

Over the years *Convoy-Dispatch* reported on many such incidents at a variety of companies, one example of which was the rank-and-file shopfloor organization at the Yellow Freight barns in California, where TDU leader Doug Allan worked for several years. The story began in early 1980 when Glenn Johns, the terminal manager at Yellow Freight in Los Angeles, began to give out warning notices to employees in an attempt to increase productivity.

Fed up with the harassment by Johns, on Monday, 14 April 1980, only five out of twenty-eight drivers showed up for work; the others called in sick. One of them said, 'I don't know about anyone else, but I think I had the Yellow John-Dus.' The company charged the employees with conspiring to carry out a work stoppage and gave them two-week suspensions, in response to which the workers filed grievances. One of the workers commented, 'The union may not have the power to get rid of Glenn Johns, and the company may not have the sense to get rid of him – but the employees will.'[1]

The 'Yellow John-Dus' outbreak continued for months. 'This sickness that the drivers had affected their ability to perform their jobs. The drivers' right foot did not have the strength to push the foot throttle, so the trucks moved very slowly through the streets of L.A. The drivers did not have the ability to deliver freight if there was the slightest inconvenience, such as No Parking, taking freight to the rear of an address, and many other inconveniences. Almost every day drivers were bringing back more freight than they delivered. It seems even the trucks had the sickness; every day there were several trucks that broke down [with] mysterious flat tires, rigging breaking apart, hoses that leaked air. Even the dock workers must have had a touch of the sickness because a lot of the loads were not loaded properly.'

The workers at Yellow argued that 'the best way to cure any sickness is to get rid of the disease that is causing the sickness.' When the Joint Area Committee grievance hearings were held, Yellow agreed to remove Glenn Johns as terminal manager. 'Glenn Johns is wandering the streets of L.A.', reported *Convoy-Dispatch*, 'looking for *bigger and better* things *without a pay check*.'[2]

A few years later, Yellow workers in Los Angeles faced another obnoxious terminal manager, this one by the name of Paul Bopko. Bopko had previously worked for Roadway, the most exploitative and repressive management in the freight industry, and the workers called him a 'Roadway reject'. 'One of the first things he told the stewards was that he was the *Boss* and things were going to be done his way.' Bopko told the workers he wanted them to obey the rules about filling out manifests. 'The stewards and members met and it was decided if it was a war he wanted, it was a war that he would get. It was also pointed out that when you go to war you must expect casualties.'[3] The response of the workers was a strict adherence to the rules. 'Being conscientious workers, the employees at the Yellow downtown Los Angeles terminal are going by the book just as Paul Bopko wants. They are not parking in red zones nor double-parking because they don't want the company to pay fines. They are driving in a very safe manner so as not to have the company pay for repairs. ... All this had led to a lot of freight being returned, and the pick-ups being missed have increased. When will management ever learn that you can get more work out of a worker by asking him rather than blatantly telling him what to do?'[4]

The conflict between Bopko and the workers continued for months until Yellow's top management dubbed the terminal 'Fort Apache'. The workers continued their work-to-rule campaign, and Bopko wrote warning letters and suspended and discharged employees. All of these actions were grieved, and only one firing was upheld. 'But through it all employees pretty much stuck together, and finally, on or about January 25, Bopko resigned from Yellow.' Yellow's management conceded that Bopko was the cause of the problems at the terminal. Despite Bopko's departure, Doug Allan wrote, 'The battle has been won, but the war will go on if necessary.'[5]

Through their solidarity and militancy, the Yellow Freight workers in Los Angeles were able to exercise some control over management rather than letting management completely control them. The same tactics have been used more recently against Yellow in Barstow, California, where TDU has worked to build a chapter that could take back control of the workplace from management. In the 1970s the big freight companies had begun to move their terminals and breakbulks out of the city and into the suburbs or rural areas. The companies found that the cost of land was lower, that rural workers were willing to work for lower wages and were less union-conscious and that the terminals were farther from the downtown union halls. Largely for these reasons, Yellow opened a breakbulk terminal in Barstow employing about 1,000 workers.

In the mid-1980s a particularly tyrannical manager was assigned to the Barstow terminal. 'He abused our seniority rights', says Scott Askey, 'and he was literally abusing us as people. He had quite a number of sexual harassment charges filed against him. And he was alleged to be skimming money off the construction funds.' The workers went to their union, Local 63 in Los Angeles, and explained the problem. 'The local told us that if we had the guts to do something about getting rid of him, they would back us up.'

Then the workers devised a tactic to get rid of the terminal manager. 'We called it a quality control program', says Askey. 'People paid particular attention to all work rules; they did the best professional job that they could do as far as loading, unloading freight, taping boxes that were untaped and that were broken open, adding plywood and cardboard to help secure a load, to make the load ride better, and also to protect the other freight from being damaged. Basically everybody took extra pride in their job – which in turn meant it took longer to do it.

'The quality control program ran almost fifty days. We brought Barstow to their attention, because, as you know, the company deals in facts and figures, and the production in Barstow had dropped drastically and had stayed dropped for like forty-seven or forty-eight days. The company could see that Yellow Freight definitely had problems in Barstow with production and with labor.

'Yellow Freight in Kansas City came down, they fired the terminal manager and his second in command, who was the operations manager. Instead of tranferring them to another terminal, they went ahead and got rid of them from the system altogether. It was a real victory. It brought unity to the High Desert here, where a lot of people weren't aware of what unionism really was, and what it really helped us do here in Barstow was to reorganize a union barn that had been beaten down and abused for years and neglected by Local 63.'

It was Scott Askey and some of the other organizers of the 'quality control program' who began to organize the TDU chapter at the barn, recruiting about 100 of the barn's 1,000 workers. Then the TDU organization at the Yellow Freight Barstow terminal began to organize other barns like the

Roadway terminal in nearby Adelanto. 'Since we organized the TDU chapter up in Barstow', Askey explains. 'We've had people transfer from Barstow to Salt Lake City, to Albuquerque, New Mexico, to Mantica, California and to Phoenix, Arizona. So we've been able to spread out and organize TDU chapters in other parts of the Southwest.'[6]

In other areas the TDU chapters were successful in running for local union office, and reform officers tried to develop a strategy for the local to take on the employers. Such was the case when Linda Gregg won the presidency of Denver Local 435.

Reform Comes to Denver

'I remember the first Teamsters union meeting I went to as a member, and I put my hand up to speak and I was recognized as "George Gregg's wife." Then I stood up and said, "My name is Linda Gregg, and I unload trailers at Safeway, and I'm a member of this union. And I'm not just here because I'm somebody's wife.' Four years later, in December 1984, the 4,100 mostly male truck drivers and warehouse workers of Colorado's biggest Teamsters union, Local 435, elected to the top office of their union the athletic 29-year-old woman who had made that little speech. Linda Gregg, a member of Teamsters for a Democratic Union, became one of only three women to hold the top office in a Teamster local union at that time.[7]

Linda Gregg was born in New Orleans in 1954 and grew up in Fairfield, Connecticut in what she describes as a 'somewhat conservative, mainstream Republican', Catholic family. Her father was an investment adviser and her mother a school teacher. When she graduated from high school she went to Duke University in Durham, North Carolina, first as a pre-law major and later as a political science student. At Duke, she became involved in a union organizing drive among workers at the Duke University Hospital. 'The workers were poorly paid and had no benefits. I saw it wasn't fair and felt obliged to get involved. I remember my professor of Latin American history saying, "If you want change, do something."'

In 1976 she graduated from Duke University with highest honors, and then, intrigued by her organizing experience at Duke, went to work for the summer for a community organization called Carolina Action. 'I worked in two different neighborhoods in Durham, North Carolina', she recalls, 'organizing door-to-door around neighborhood issues and working on a statewide campaign for utility reform.'

When her community organizing job ended, she spent a few months traveling around the West Coast, wondering what to do with her life. After her labor and community organizing experiences Linda Gregg had changed. She no longer wanted to be a lawyer, and white-collar work held no attraction for her. She wanted to be a union activist, a labor union organizer, and she was willing to begin at the bottom. She moved to Denver, Colorado with a couple of women friends, and got a job at a factory that manufactured steel doors as an assembly-line worker earning $3.50 an hour. She was one of only two women in the plant, and the only woman in her department; most of the workers were Latinos, Vietnamese or Laotians. Because of the low pay, the plant had a high turnover rate.

Linda had studied Spanish in school and could communicate with the Latino workers. The other woman in the plant had a husband who had been a language expert in Vietnam, and he could communicate with the Vietnamese and Laotians. They brought together a small group and began to put out leaflets about problems in the plant. 'We had some victories on health and safety issues, and got management to install some safety devices which we felt were necessary', says Gregg. 'And at one point we had a walkout over forced overtime. But there was so much turnover there, that, though we had an organizing committee, we never did successfully organize into a union.'

After almost two years in the steel-door factory, Linda quit to take a better job at the Gates Rubber Company, at that time one of the largest employers in the Denver area with almost 5,000 workers. She was hired as a machine operator making rubber instruments used in slaughter houses: 'chicken fingers' used to pluck chickens and 'hog paddles' used to scrape the hair off pigs. Gates was an organized plant represented by the United Rubber Workers, and Gregg attended the Rubber Workers union meetings. Soon she was elected to the union's education committee, and worked writing leaflets and distributing them to the workers in the plant. But her career in the Rubber Workers was cut short, because in 1979 Gates cut back production dramatically and laid off hundreds of workers, including Linda Gregg.

Nevertheless, she continued to be active in labor union issues, sometimes helping out some struggling union by walking the picket line with striking workers. It was at one such strike that she met her future husband, George Gregg, a steward in the Teamsters union. The were married in 1979. It was not long after that, in July 1980, that Linda Gregg was hired by Safeway, the big grocery chain, in its Denver distribution center. She worked as a trailer unloader in the salvage department, one of about five women in the facility. The huge Safeway warehouse serviced Colorado, Wyoming and parts of New Mexico and even South Dakota, and employed about 700 drivers and warehouse workers, about 500 of them in Teamster Local 435.

Linda became active in the union almost immediately – and only once did a union official refer to her a 'somebody's wife' rather than as a union member in her own right. At the time she joined Teamster Local 435 it was in trouble. Partly because of the diversity of industries it represented, strong centrifugal forces operated on Teamster Local 435. Many of the 4,000 members were grocery warehouse workers and truck drivers at Super Valu, King Soopers, and Kroger's, though the largest single employer organized by the local was United Parcel Service. In addition, there were many drivers for smaller soft drink companies and paper companies, as well as some manufacturing workers. Even with the best union leadership, it is not easy to achieve a strong sense of solidarity among workers at so many jobs with so many employers. The union had not had the best leadership. Shortly before Linda Gregg joined, there had been a political upheaval in the local. The membership had become dissatisfied with the old leadership headed by Vern Snow and Bill Hebdon, and in 1979 the local had voted overwhelmingly for a reform slate headed by a man named Jim Ivey. But once elected, Ivey changed.

Shortly after the election, the country was hit by a severe recession. There were plant closings and big lay-offs, and employers, even profitable employers, began to demand concessions from unions. It was a trend, and by the early 1980s it had become a full-fledged employer drive to take back the gains that workers had won over the years. The pattern at Local 435 was no different: when the employers asked Teamster leader Jim Ivey for givebacks, he gave. Slowly at first and more rapidly later, concession contracts were negotiated and the membership gradually became dissatisfied with the Ivey administration.

It soon became clear to Linda Gregg, her husband George, and a few other activists in the union that there would have to be a new, genuine reform movement in the local to oppose Ivey. They had joined Teamsters for a Democratic Union and now began organizing a local chapter, putting out a local newsletter called *Teamster Talk*. 'The TDU chapter itself was fairly small', says Gregg, 'but our influence was pretty big, and the newsletter was one of the reasons for that.' The chapter soon attracted about a dozen local Teamster activists. 'Not all of those were TDU members. But they were people who would distribute our literature and join with us in different efforts.' When Ivey ran for reelection in 1981, he was opposed by a new reform slate called The Ticket. Running at the top of The Ticket against Secretary-Treasurer Jim Ivey was Tom Bernard, who had been recording secretary on Ivey's original reform slate. Also on the slate was Linda's husband, George Gregg. Linda Gregg, who in the meantime had become pregnant, used her maternity leave to work as Tom Bernard's campaign manager. They worked hard for The Ticket, but they lost. Ivey was reelected, and, says Linda Gregg, 'Things just continued to go downhill.'

For example, in 1982 the Super Valu company acquired the Western Grocers warehouse in Denver. Threatening that it would not operate the warehouse unless it was granted concessions by the union, Super Valu forced Jim Ivey to agree to a long list of givebacks. Most important, Ivey agreed to a two-tier wage scale. Eventually there were 250 employees at Super Valu, with only 50 of them making the top wage and 200 on the bottom tier. 'That should have been projected', says Gregg. 'They didn't move in here just to stay little; they moved in here to grow and compete.' And grow it did, until Super Valu became the nation's biggest grocery wholesaler. 'This created a terrible situation. Not only because the workforce was resentful and this was a problem for the union, but in terms of the entire industry. Super Valu's competitors were just screaming about the huge labor cost advantage that Super Valu had been given by the union.' So not only did the Super Valu contract mean lower wages for the Super Valu workers, but 'the other employers would use that substandard contract at Super Valu to try to ratchet down wages and conditions for the entire industry.' Eventually the wages of all of the grocery workers could be forced down.

Such developments led Linda Gregg and other union activists to become deeply concerned. 'We were in a situation where we were afraid for the future of the local. Our members in grocery had good contracts, good wages, and working conditions and benefits, and those were beginning to be eroded. And it appeared that over a period of time we really stood to lose a lot. And there was no strategy. Part of it was lack of interest and part of it was lack of knowledge, and the union leadership just wasn't going to do anything about it.'

At the same time, says Gregg, the union was becoming less democratic. Ivey kept trying to drive the reformers, including Linda Gregg, out of the union. 'When I was pregnant, Ivey continually kept issuing me withdrawal cards and refused to let me pay union dues and remain active in the union.' In response, she filed internal union charges against Ivey for violating her rights under the local bylaws and constitution, and the International ordered Ivey to accept her dues and return her to good standing.

More serious was the issue of violence in the union. Tom Bernard brought a $5.5 million lawsuit against Jim Ivey and Local 435 in which he alleged that Ivey had hired a hitman to work him over. In fact, a man had been arrested by police on another charge while waiting in front of Bernard's house. 'There was a stifling atmosphere in the local. Members felt too many deals were being cut. There was an air of confusion and uncertainty', Gregg remembers. Faced with both the continuing degeneration of union democracy, and the negotiation of substandard contracts, Linda Gregg decided that she would run against Ivey herself.

'That wasn't really what I had in mind', says Gregg. 'I've always felt real comfortable working in industry, whether it be in the warehouse or when I worked at Gates. I like being active in the union and doing what I can to educate and involve other folks. But I just thought it was crucial that Ivey not be reelected. I felt a responsibility to the members. I had been one of the most vocal critics of Ivey's administration. And I didn't think letting him run unopposed for a third term could be tolerated. So when it was apparent that there really wasn't anybody to run against him, I decided I would do it myself.'

Gregg put together a partial slate with two other Teamsters: Dean Ribaudo, a worker at a small United Parcel Service center, and Steve Hubmer, a warehouseman at Nobel-Sysco, an institutional food distributor. Ribaudo and Gregg were TDU members, and Hubmer was not, but all three were dedicated to reforming the union. When the ballots were counted, Linda Gregg had been elected by forty-seven votes. Unfortunately for the reformers, neither Ribaudo nor Hubmer had been elected, so Linda Gregg had to go it alone. 'I was installed as secretary-treasurer with a completely hostile executive board and staff on January 1, 1985. It was a terrible situation.'

Meanwhile Jim Ivey appealed to the Joint Council on the grounds that the election process, which he had organized, had not given the members adequate time to vote and return their ballots. To its credit, the Joint Council upheld Gregg's victory. Undeterred, however, Ivey appealed to IBT President Jackie Presser, and Presser, a fanatical foe of TDU, overturned Gregg's election. As soon as she heard the news, Linda Gregg flew to Chicago, where Presser was testifying before the President's Commission on Organized Crime. Presser had just taken the Fifth Amendment fifteen times in response to questions about mob influence in the union and goon attacks on TDU when he came out of the meeting and found Linda Gregg standing in his path, demanding to know why he had overturned her election. Presser marched on, surrounded by his flunkies and bodyguards, and did not even deign to answer her.

Linda Gregg returned to Denver and began again to run for office. In June 1985 she was vindicated; she was elected again, this time by a larger margin, 1,190 to 852, and both Ribaudo and Hubmer were elected as well. Finally, six months after the original election, Linda Gregg was able to function as the chief executive officer of Local 435.

The conditions under which she had finally been elected were, however, far from ideal. The majority of the executive board, four out of seven, were Ivey supporters and hostile to her. And without a majority of the executive board, she could not eliminate from the staff incompetent or hostile business agents or other employees. Nevertheless, with the allies she had on the executive board, and her supporters on the staff, Linda began to try to implement her program, to make the union more democratic and more militant. She revitalized the union's elected negotiating committees and had those committees carry out surveys among the members to find out their opinions about contract issues. She and her staff put out frequent bulletins to the members on contract negotiations to keep them informed and stop the rumor mills. Linda and other union officials held frequent meetings with workers in the workplace to discuss the strategy and tactics of pressuring the employers. They carried out these activities even in the smaller workplaces that in the past had frequently been ignored.

The union tried to avoid strikes, given Denver's depressed economy. Instead of striking, they put out petitions, handed out leaflets, and held demonstrations and press conferences. According to Gregg, this menu of alternative tactics 'worked to varying degrees': the local did win a long list of improved wages, benefits, and conditions at more than a dozen companies. 'I feel that we were really able to help a much larger group of union members understand what the union was all about, and make them feel that they were part of the union, and had a stake in it.'

One of the biggest and most successful fights of her administration was to bring the workers at Super Valu back up to standard pay and benefit schedules. The company started the fight by trying to eliminate the union shop at Super Valu. The company's weapon was a Colorado law requiring that 75 percent of the workers vote for the union in an election on the issue of mandatory union membership and dues payment in order to have a union shop. The company believed that with 200 of 250 workers making far below union scale (the result of Ivey's earlier givebacks) the majority of the workers would vote the union shop out. Gregg saw the contest at Super Valu not only as a challenge, but as an opportunity to mobilize the membership. She and one of her supportive business agents organized a group of rank-and-file members at the Super Valu warehouse and conducted meetings in every department and on every shift around the clock to convince the workers of the need for the union.

In a vote held just two weeks before the contract expired, they won the union shop election 222 to 4. 'It sent Super Valu and the rest of the industry a message about the strength of the union, right before the contract negotiations, and it really helped our position', says Gregg. As a result, the union was able to win a contract that eliminated two-tier pay and brought all the Super Valu workers up to scale over a period of five years.

In an interview with the *Denver Post* about a year after she was elected, Gregg explained her philosophy of unionism: 'Companies are controlled by a lot of money and a lot of power. Workers need protection to earn a decent living. Management talks about belt tightening. I don't see people in top management tightening their belts. They do things which benefit themselves and their stockholders, not the public. My concerns are with people. Corporations are concerned with profit, not people. This job is very hard. But when I start feeling overwhelmed or tired, I try to step back and think about why I'm doing it. If it is to save someone's job who was unjustly fired, I remember why. And it's all worth it.'

In addition to these local efforts, the Gregg administration helped the Teamster organizing drive at Coors Brewery and supported the United Food and Commercial Workers strike against King Soopers. Linda Gregg attended the 1986 IBT convention and introduced a resolution opposing two-tier contracts and another calling for increased strike benefits; she also voted for the right of the Teamster membership to elect their International's officers.

Under Gregg's leadership, Teamster Local 435 was becoming more democratic, developing greater solidarity with other locals and other unions, and beginning to stand up to the employers who had been riding roughshod over the union during the Ivey years. These developments led the employers to decide to take on the union before it grew any stronger.

In the mid-1980s eight of the employers represented by Local 435 closed their doors, resulting in 400 Teamsters losing their jobs. The economic depression dampened the militancy of the workers, who feared that if they fought the employers they might find themselves on the unemployment line. In 1985 the Gregg administration faced three contract negotiations, at Coca Cola, Dixon Paper and Air Filter Sales and Service, all of them conducted on behalf of the companies represented by the Mountain States Employers Council, a union-busting firm.

'They pushed concession bargaining', says Gregg, 'even with employers who were operating profitably. And they attempted to provoke labor disputes.' The result was strikes at all three companies. The membership took the strikes hard. 'They weren't prepared for the hardship', says Gregg, 'or, even if they were, they weren't prepared to deal with watching people cross the picket line to take their jobs.' The strikes were unsuccessful, and at Air Filter the National Labor Relations Board conducted a decertification election in which only the scabs were allowed to vote, and the Teamsters union was decertified as the bargaining agent. The employers' strategy was clear: convince the members that a TDU leadership in the union would mean strikes, sacrifices and defeats. Some members, seeing the employers' militancy and the union's defeat, began to back away from the reformers.

Gregg's biggest problem was that she had only a minority on the seven-person executive board, and so could not remove the staff members who opposed her. 'And they spent most of their time working to see that I would be defeated in the next election, or making sure that any programs I wanted did not get through.' As the 1987 elections in Local 435 approached, Linda Gregg found herself in a predicament. Her opponents on the executive board petitioned the International to move the union election up one month so that it would occur during the crucial grocery contract negotiations – negotiations that would necessarily command all Gregg's attention. The International granted the petition.

So Gregg now faced a dilemma: if she dedicated herself to the grocery negotiations, she would be forced to spend little time on her reelection. If she worked on her reelection and gave less time to the grocery contract, she was sure to lose because she would have let down the grocery workers. Linda Gregg decided that she had to work mainly on the grocery negotiations, campaigning when she could. In their campaign literature, she and her slate put forward a Program for the Future, which called for a major organizing drive against non-union companies.

When the votes were counted, Linda Gregg had lost the election in Local 435; the International's people, backed by the employers, had beaten her. There were no jobs for Linda Gregg in Teamster workplaces in Denver, but she continued her commitment to the union movement by taking a job as an organizer for the Service Employees International Union. Despite the election defeat, Linda Gregg, Dean Ribaudo and Steve Hubmer, George Gregg and Tom Bernard had succeeded in stopping the deterioration of the union, which had snowballed during the Ivey administration. They had been able to bring Super Valu up to standard and eliminate two-tier pay there. And they had saved the grocery contracts and the union shop.

Notes

1. 'Rank and File Fight Harassment at LA Yellow', *Convoy-Dispatch*, no. 6 (May 1980).

2. 'Cure for Yellow "John Dus"', *Convoy-Dispatch*, no. 9 (October 1980).

3. 'Workers Win Battle at Fort Apache', *Convoy-Dispatch*, no. 41 (February 1984).

4. 'Roadway Reject Brings Turmoil to Yellow Freight', *Convoy-Dispatch*, no. 31 (January 1983).

5. 'Workers Win Battle at Fort Apache', *Convoy-Dispatch*, no. 41 (February 1984).

6. With strong support in his barn, Scott Askey joined with other TDU members and other union reformers to run a slate for union office in Local 63 in late 1988, and did well as a first-time candidate.

7. In addition to my own interview and TDU publications, I have used as sources the following articles about Linda Gregg: Janet Wiscombe, 'Big Sister of the Brotherhood', *The Sunday Denver Post*, 26 October 1986; Kenneth C. Crowe, 'The Lady and the Teamsters', *Newsday*, 12 August 1985; 'King Soopers Teamsters Approve 5-Year Contract', *Rocky Mountain News*, 19 September 1987.

20

Drugs, Deceit, and Presser Pulls a Fast One

In the late 1980s the labor movement in general and the Teamsters in particular were suddenly faced with a new challenge to workers' rights and union power: the potentially controversial and divisive issue of drug testing. It began about 1984, when some Teamster employers began requiring their employees to take drug tests, and some Teamster organizations accepted the practice; a few had even allowed language calling for drug tests to be put in the contract. Drug testing soon led to abuses. For example, a dock worker at Yellow Freight in Maybrook, New York was forced to take a blood test because he had 'red eyes'. The test found small amounts of THC metabolite in his bloodstream, and he was fired. There was no further testing, no due process, no hearing, no warning, no rehabilitation; he was just fired. Other Teamster jurisdictions around the country were also giving in to employer demands on this issue. Apparently without considering the pitfalls, the Teamsters' West Coast Tanker Division decided to allow companies to send workers for drug-screening tests at the employers' discretion. Denver Local 435 negotiated a contract with Associated Grocers that allowed management to send workers for urinalysis, which, if positive for drugs, would lead to their being fired. There were similar problems in other areas.

The issue was a tricky one. Drug abuse is a national problem, and the use of drugs in connection with driving is deadly. Everyone wants to eliminate drug abuse, but the question is how to do it. TDU feared giving more police power to the employers – many of which already ran the workplace like a police state. The Teamsters union simply ignored the complex scientific questions and the sensitive issue of civil rights. While avoiding the real issues, Jackie Presser joined Sylvester Stallone, star of the film *FIST*, in Nancy Reagan's 'Just Say No' campaign.

The drug issue required TDU to think on its feet, and in developing its response, TDU based itself on two principles: first, the defense of the civil rights and jobs of individual union members, and second, the need to strengthen the union. TDU agreed that 'nobody should permit the use of drugs or alcohol while driving a truck or operating potentially dangerous equipment.' But, argued TDU, medical experts believed many of the tests were not reliable, and, in any case, the tests constituted an intrusion 'on their employees' rights outside of the workplace ... a chilling invasion of privacy which calls for strong action from the union.' Unfortunately, the union was already giving in to the employers.

Late in 1984 the International reached an agreement with Trucking Management, Inc. allowing employers to require drug testing at the time of Department of Transportation physicals and at any other time the employers saw fit. Under the agreement the company needed only 'a reason to believe' that the employee was intoxicated, and no specific evidence was required in order to compel a worker to submit to a test. The order for the test was supposed to be given in the presence of a steward, 'if available'. Refusal to take the test was considered an admission of guilt.

According to the agreement, tests were to adhere to the standards of National Medical Service (NMS) of Willow Grove, Pennsylvania, even though the NMS standards had been criticized by medical experts. Arthur McBay, chief toxicologist for the state of North Carolina, commented that 'the standards used in these tests are for the birds. This laboratory has never proven its ability to positively show marijuana intoxication with these standards.' George Washington, a Detroit attorney who had handled drug-testing cases for labor union members, argued that 'positive tests in a blood or urine test do not necessarily mean that the employee was intoxicated on the job. For all they know, positive results in these tests could mean that the employee was in the same room as someone else smoking marijuana the night before the samples were taken.'

TDU opposed the IBT-TMI drug-testing agreement, arguing that 'this new policy opens up the potential for the violation of freight Teamsters' civil rights.'[1] TDU also argued that 'these tests can be used selectively to harass good union members', and gave the example of a TDU activist who was forced to take an unprofessional test.[2] As TDU pointed out, because of two-tier pay, 'The employers have an incentive to fire long-term employees. After all, for every senior worker fired, they hire a new worker at 70 percent.'[3]

TDU recommended a number of measures that union members could take to protect their rights, including demanding that a union steward be present, getting the number of the seal on the test and the identity of the personnel doing the testing, and having another test done by an independent laboratory. TDU attorney Barbara Harvey recommended that workers who had agreed to be tested could reasonably be asked to sign an authorization, but not to sign a release. She urged workers who felt the tests had violated the agreed-upon procedure to file grievances.

TDU also argued that if a person tested positive he or she should be given the option of rehabilitation, not immediate discharge. As *Convoy-Dispatch* wrote, 'Men and women do make mistakes. So do machines. The margin of error in drug testing laboratories is well documented. ... For those with a problem, they would get a chance to put their lives back together – a noble goal for any union. For those falsely accused through human or technical error, they would at least be able to return to their jobs. ... Human compassion has never nor probably will ever play a role in the business world. Compassion, justice and dignity are not objectives thrown to the wind by hasty decisions. The union should return to some common sense and correct this tragic error, because, after all, it could happen to you.'[4]

For two years TDU continued to defend the civil rights of all workers, and to argue for compassion for those who had drug and alcohol problems, calling upon the union to defend workers from the companies. But the IBT leadership rejected TDU's arguments and supported the employers' demands for drug-testing programs; as a result, many Teamsters were victimized.

Then came the scandal. In 1986 it came to light that Teamster health and safety experts had told Presser to adopt what was substantially the TDU position of civil rights, compassion and union resistance to the employers' demands for drug testing – and that Presser had ignored them. Internal Teamster documents published by TDU showed that Presser had been advised that the testing procedures were questionable, that they resulted in unjust discharges, and that rehabilitation was necessary. In one memo, R.V. Durham, the IBT's director of safety and health, wrote, 'I would recommend that the following be done: suspend the testing until appropriate steps are taken to assure everyone that the National Medical Services, Inc. procedures are being followed without exception. We have a serious problem on our hands and I ... strongly recommend we give this matter priority attention.'

Suzanne Kossan, the IBT's industrial hygienist, also felt that there were problems with testing. She acknowledged that laboratories were not taking prescription drugs into account. In a particularly telling memo, she conceded, 'We have numerous reports from local unions that these procedures are not being followed and may have resulted in unjust discharges.' It was also revealed that in 1984 Durham had recommended to Walter Shea that 'if an individual takes a DOT physical and has a problem, why not provide for him to take a leave of absence and undergo a rehabilitation program?' Despite this advice, Shea and Presser had agreed to immediate discharge on the first offense.[5]

In one instance Presser had gone so far as to introduce a drug-testing clause into a union contract without a vote of the members. TDU leader Joe

Day brought suit in *Day et al.* v. *Presser et al.* to stop the drug testing on the grounds that the members had never had an opportunity to vote on that clause of the contract. In February 1987 a settlement was reached, and employers and top Teamster officials agreed to end drug testing for the approximately 25,000 Teamsters covered by the National Automobile Transporters Agreement. TDU had won an important victory.

Nevertheless, the issue of drug testing did not go away. Throughout 1987 and 1988, TDU continued to be involved in educating union members, challenging employers and the union, and speaking before congressional hearings on bills dealing with drug testing.

Sarah Bequette

One of those who first became active in TDU during the period when drug testing became an important issue was Sarah Bequette. Sarah is a homemaker, a description she takes some pride in. She has not only been the homemaker for her own family, but she is also the president of the 850-member Madison County, Illinois Homemakers Extension Association, which provides educational to children, homemakers and farmers.

Sarah's husband, Delmar Bequette, is an over-the-road driver for PIE, has been a Teamster for over twenty-six years, and was for several years the union steward at his barn. Concerned about the decline of the union, in 1980 he joined TDU and began going to meetings. He invited Sarah to come along, but wasn't until September 1984 that she finally took him up on his offer and accompanied him, and over the next few years the model homemaker became a Teamster activist. 'Dear Dan', Sarah wrote me in January 1988,

> Now that the fog in my brain and the frog in my throat are gone, along with the holidays, I am writing to tell you a little more about my activities with TDU. You couldn't quite imagine why a full-time homemaker would want to become actively involved in an organization like Teamsters for a Democratic Union, so let me tell you. Now where do I start?
>
> My dad was an active Union man; a buffer-polisher for Knapp-Monarch, a small appliance company in St. Louis. He was steward, foreman, leadman and always led the fight to maintain union benefits and shop specifications and safety. I listened to and absorbed much from him about conditions where he worked. He went on strike, was laid-off, filed grievances, went to union meetings, was fired and won his job back and always came home black with grinding compound and exhausted. He died in 1969, age fifty-nine, after fighting serious heart problems for ten years. So, even at an early age, I've tried to take an interest in how the process of 'security' happens and what it takes to maintain it.

Perhaps more and more women are learning to not take the security provided by their husband's income for granted (or anything else, for that matter). When my husband, Delmar, went on the road in 1973, our youngest child was just starting kindergarten. The children and I were on our own about 70% of the time, while he was gone. One learns to cope with all sorts of things, to make spot decisions alone, and 'Mom' virtually raised 5 children and maintained the home until the kids were well out of high school or college and on their own, too. Delmar and I had to nurture what became a part-time, long-distance marriage which, to date, has lasted over 29 years.

Anyway, it was spending so much time carrying the responsibility for the family that I began to appreciate that things do not come easily; they have to be earned. Everyone has a part to play in earning his livelihood, whether or not he or she brings home a paycheck. So, during these years, I learned how to earn mine, and am still doing it.

My last real employment ended in 1959 after two years as a secretary for an insurance agency, when I quit to raise a family. At that time, Delmar worked for a small non-union lumber company as a delivery driver and this is where he got his over-the-road training. He was paid $75 a week, with no benefits except a week's annual vacation and maybe a $50 bonus at Christmas Time. He worked 6 days a week plus overtime, for which he wasn't paid. In 1961, he was fired because he took off a Saturday to attend my sister's wedding. We had a two-year-old daughter and a 6-week-old son. Getting fired was a favor.

Four days later, he went to work for Mi-Lee Trucking, a now defunct drayage company in St. Louis, as a city driver. He worked only 4 or 3 days a week for a while, but some weeks he brought home $100 or so. We were rich! Then, in April 1962, he was hired by PIE (Pacific Intermountain Express – the *REAL* PIE) and joined the union. Believe me, we appreciated Union wages and benefits and I've been listening to shop talk and union talk ever since.

My husband and I enjoy an 'interdependence'. We can stand on our own, but also need each other. Each has separate activities, but we are interested in what the other is doing, as well. When Delmar joined TDU in 1980, I couldn't really understand why, except that there was a chipping away at long-ago earned dignity and just wages, and the working conditions of the employee, while more and more the benefactor of the contract tended to be the employer. Meanwhile most unions and, and specifically the Teamsters, were becoming self-preserving entities.

Delmar tried to interest me in TDU by showing me how they were trying to counteract this trend, so when he invited me to a special TDU meeting in 1984, I went. There I met our then chapter chairman, Cliff Coonley, and his wife Carol, TDU Organizer Ken Paff, and several other TDUers. After the meeting, all of us went out to dinner, and I realized as I became acquainted with these people, that I really had very much in common with them. They were not big-mouthed, militant airheads wearing chain-drive wallets and combat boots, but caring, intelligent human beings who would be leaders and the movers and shakers no matter where they lived or worked.

In October, 1984, we went to our first TDU Convention in Chicago, which we enjoyed very much. There, at Delmar's suggestion, Cliff Coonley asked me to make the chapter a quilted banner, and eventually, I did. Then I found we were corresponding frequently with the staff in Detroit by mail and phone, so by and by, my interest and our involvement grew. I joined TDU in February, 1985, and we attended another convention in October 1985, again in Chicago. Soon after, we learned Cliff Coonley had cancer. Two weeks after the 1986 Convention in Atlanta, he died, and that's when Delmar and I became very active in the chapter. (In March, 1987, we held a dinner in honor of Cliff. We presented a plaque to Cliff's widow, Carol, and each of us told what he most remembered about Cliff. It was our way of saying goodbye to him.)

Delmar had been elected to the TDU International Steering Committee at the '86 Convention. He also became treasurer of the chapter, and I, recording-secretary. We were superbusy during the winter of 86-87. I wrote the chapter constitution and by-laws and began a monthly newsletter. Both of us helped a friend and fellow Teamster and TDUer campaign for the office of Trustee for Local 600 in the December 1986 election. I helped our friend write the campaign flyer, and, though he lost the election, he received a decent number of votes. Because of some election irregularities, we were also involved in a series of protests concerning the Local 600 elections.

The drug issue was 'hot' about this time, so we distributed TDU drug flyers, and designed, printed and distributed drug-record folders to fit the wallet to remind drivers that all drugs, even over-the-counter, had to be reported when they tested for drugs. I believe the use of drugs should be outlawed, but testing was very unreliable, the methods of testing the drivers were being abused, and innocent people were losing their jobs along with the guilty. So, we tried to teach them how to deal with the problem of random testing.

Now, after nearly three years as a TDU member, I serve on the TDU International Steering Committee (ISC). (Would this ever happen in the IBT?) If, as an ISC spouse member, I can encourage more wives to participate in TDU, that will be my goal, primarily. Women generally have a special intuition, a uniquely different perspective than men, in handling problems or handling decisions, but are timid about expressing that opinion. This is especially true if she is the minority in a group of mostly men. Yet, her input is valuable in that it may help to bring about a better solution or plan. It may be the difference, like the difference between biscuits and raised bread, say. A little yeast makes all the difference. The IBT and other like organizations do not have, or even aspire to having, this spousal input. So, we sort of have a 'secret weapon,' don't we?

Why did I become interested in TDU? I don't believe any man has a right to impose unbelievable and degrading conditions on any other human being. It makes me mad. Somebody has to speak out against them. That somebody has to be you, and yes – why not? – me too. It matters to me what we will leave behind for those who follow us, and I believe that in taking something from this life, we should all put something back, too.

I hope this information has given you a little insight into me, the homemaker.

(signed) Sarah Bequette

The 1985 Contract Bargaining Round

As the 1985 contract bargaining round approached, TDU attempted to help create a broad Teamster movement to demand an end to concessions. On 18 August 1984 a meeting was held in Cleveland that included TDUers and several of the outstanding reform leaders in the Teamsters: Sam Theodus, president of Cleveland Local 407; Ron Carey, president of New York UPS Local 804; and Gene Fort, vice-president of Local 371. The Contract Unity Meeting, as TDU called it, was held to discuss the upcoming freight and UPS contracts, and was attended by 125 Teamsters from Cleveland, Toledo, Youngstown, Akron, Columbus and Detroit. But before the ranks could get organized, Presser pulled a fast one.

Presser's 'Sneak Attack' on the UPS Contract

In August 1984, several months before the expiration of the UPS contract, Jackie Presser had begun meeting secretly with UPS management and had quickly agreed to their proposal for a three-year contract extension. As *Convoy-Dispatch* wrote, 'The deal was cut without the knowledge of a single one of the 90,000 Teamsters covered. Before anyone knew negotiations had begun, they were over!'

It was far from a desirable agreement. It called for wage increases of sixty-eight cents, fifty cents, and fifty cents over three years, or 5 percent, 3.5 percent and 3.5 percent, while the cost of living allowance would continue to be diverted to health and welfare and pension plans. Most onerous, the two-tier wage scale remained in place. The inducement for workers to agree to the new contract was a $1,000 bonus ($500 for part-timers), money that would not be figured into the base pay. And since UPS workers had suffered under a wage freeze for two and a half years, the money was naturally welcome.

Vowing he would not 'get burned again' by TDU, as he had on the relief rider, Presser called a meeting of local union officials, and within twelve hours shipped out the secretly prepared contract ratification ballots to the 90,000 UPS workers. Included with the ballot was a glossy promotional flyer with a picture of a fistful of bonus dollars and the words 'Best Contract Ever Negotiated'.

Many local officials and union members did not consider it the best contract ever negotiated, or even an acceptable contract. When workers receive money as a 'bonus' rather than as part of their base salary, they clearly lose out in the long run. There was opposition in Cleveland Local 407, Columbus Local 413, Des Moines Local 90, from locals throughout New England, and from New York Local 804. Supporting this rejection sentiment, TDU distributed 15,000 copies of a contract bulletin on 17 August that went to over l00 locals.

Nevertheless, Presser's 'sneak attack' worked. TDU and local unions that opposed the contract simply had not had time to respond to the secret negotiations and tentative agreement. The members received only Presser's propaganda, the promise of a 'fistful of dollars', and no real evaluation of the contract, much less any opposing viewpoint. The members voted to accept the contract. To prevent such maneuvers in the future, TDU filed a suit, *Bauman* v. *Presser*, and eventually won a decision forbidding the International to negotiate such secret settlements without a vote of the members.

The Freight Contract

The freight companies, which were represented by TMI, were again seeking big concessions from the Teamsters union, including a two-tier wage structure, the introduction of production standards, and the elimination of past practices. As in l982, TDU did not advocate a strike because it recognized the weak position and low morale of the rank and file. Rather, TDU asked, 'Are we, the rank and file, prepared to say NO to the employers?'[6]

When the union reached a tentative agreement, Presser called it 'the best contract ever', but TDU urged the membership 'Vote No'. The contract contained a two-tier clause calling for new hires to receive only 70 percent of the standard wage, 80 percent in their second year, and 90 percent in their third year; they would receive union scale only in their fourth year with the company. In addition, casuals' wages were cut to $ll an hour. There were many other concessions as well. Not only did TDU oppose the contract, but a meeting of officials in Chicago on 3 April to discuss the contract made it clear that many of them would also oppose it in their regions.

TDU still rejected the idea that giving in to company demands would save Teamster jobs. Keith Gallagher, a Roadway dock worker, a member of Local 229 in Stroudsburg, Pennsylvania and a long-time TDU leader, analyzed the givebacks this way: 'Deregulation has left in its wake bankrupt companies, unemployed members, a concessionary contract, and a union unwilling or unable to deal effectively with these problems. The union's strategy in l982 was simply to help the industry in order to save jobs. It was an idealistic approach. But did it help? In the past three years companies have still gone bankrupt, forcing our members into unemployment lines, while the larger companies like Roadway and CF have continued their monopolization of the industry. Those concessions granted in l982 will haunt us for years, possibly decades to come. One thing is clear – in the past three years the rich companies have gotten richer, while the poor just went bankrupt. ... The union's strategy has failed, and it's time to face some cruel facts. It is only a matter of time before the small trucking companies fold. We cannot save them. Further concessions to the giants will only speed the monopolization process.'[7]

That was the message that TDU took to union meetings across the country: concessions don't save jobs, vote no on two-tier pay and low rates for casuals. Nevertheless, despite widespread opposition, the leadership succeeded in selling the contract and winning the vote. TDU again brought suit in court against the union, this time because Presser had denied many casuals the right to vote on the contract. The suit resulted in a consent order signed in June 1985 providing that all dues-paying Teamster casuals would be given the right to vote on their contract, though the judge denied TDU's request to order another vote on that particular contract. While TDU lost the vote to reject the contract, it had won another victory in the fight for the rights of the members.

Joe Day

Carhauling was, perhaps, TDU's area of strongest support, and the carhaulers continued to be one of the most militant groups in the union. TDU had established the Carhaul Coordinating Committee in the 1970s, and it continued to recruit new leaders and activists. One of them was Joe Day, a driver for Anchor Motor Freight and a member of Framingham Local 170, who came to play a central role in the carhaulers organizing campaign and in the TDU leadership.

'My family is from the other side of the fence from where I am now', says Day. 'My family was basically management. My great-grandfather was into real estate, and built an empire in Manhattan, New York City and down in Florida. I grew up all up and down the East Coast, but mostly in Massachusetts. In my growing years my Dad did a lot of work for government contracts, so I lived from Puerto Rico up to New Brunswick.' Joe Day went to the University of Oklahoma for a couple of years, and was then drafted during the Vietnam War. After getting out of the Army, he worked at a variety of jobs, then went into business for himself for a while: 'I owned a couple of bars, a couple of restaurants, and I drove truck non-union.' Finally he went to work as a carhauler.

The carhaulers, Day explains, are different from other Teamsters for a number of reasons. 'The carhaulers are probably the last bastion of real hard core, the way freight used to be years ago. We're still rather a radical group, and historically carhaul has some very active people. There was virtually no unorganized competition in carhaul, and by and large the companies remained profitable, so there was less basis for demands for relief. Consequently, when the union negotiated a carhaul contract with concession language, there was great opposition. Historically we've been 99 percent union.

Now we're starting to see some non-union companies creeping in such as Centurion.

'Carhaul has always had a better deal. The senior men worked for the past thirty years at getting the deal that we got. Years ago everything used to be a one-way haul. You loaded at the terminal or the rail site, and you went out and you delivered, and you then came back and you loaded again. ...We had what they call a one-way haul, so we were getting twice the freight rate, and we still do and this is what the companies are after. A carhauler can make anywhere from twenty thousand up to a few who make one hundred thousand a year depending on his seniority, where he works, and what terminal he works out of. Typically carhaulers who drive over-the-road make around forty or forty-five thousand.

'Now with the petroleum change, fuel charges, the companies have found that they can't afford to do business that way, the shippers aren't allowing them. The shippers are saying, "We don't care how you do it but we're going to cut costs", and so they began the back haul. So now we're hauling both directions. And with that they're attempting to bring us down to the freight rate, what they call "running mile", rather than the way we're paid now, which is "loaded mile" or "one-way haul".'

Joe became more active in the union after a change of management at Anchor. 'A couple of real hard asses that came in and decided that they were going to break us apart. They were going to change our working conditions, they were going to come at us from every front. And that's when I realized that we didn't need one active steward and one active business agent, we needed 250 active people, and I felt that I should pick up my part of the work load, as I felt everybody should.'

One day somebody left off some copies of the *Convoy-Dispatch* in the drivers' room and some flyers announcing a TDU meeting, and Joe Day went to see what it was all about. 'I saw TDU's purpose as the same as mine, in that I saw concessions coming down the road. I saw the companies in the industry becoming more organized, getting their act together, and if we didn't come together and get our act together I felt we were going to be in very serious trouble. I personally was in a local and in a barn that was very organized – we were in good shape – but I saw that around us other locals were not. And I thought it behooved everybody to try to help out the other locals.'

Joe Day and scores of others like him worked with TDU to turn out a no vote on the carhaulers contract. The response was overwhelming. Detroit Local 299 urged its members to vote no. Large numbers of carhaulers in Wilmington Local 326 turned out for the meeting and voted to send a letter to the International rejecting the proposal. Carhaulers in New Jersey Local 560 started a petition to reject the contract. Carhaulers in Kansas City Local 498 voted against the proposal and, incidentally, for the removal of their business agent. The first offer that contained two-tier wages for drivers was rejected by 81 percent of the drivers, and that rejection led to a three-week carhaulers strike.

TDU was concerned not only about the content of the contract, but also about the way the members would vote on it. TDU, as always, called for 'fair votes in the union halls' and demanded that the union notify each member of the meeting, make details of the contract available in writing, and institute safeguards ensure fair voting. The International refused TDU's demand for a vote in the union halls and ordered the membership back to work pending the outcome of a mail ballot referendum. TDU then demanded the right to have material for and against the contract sent out with the ballots. TDU brought suit against the International over these issues, and the Teamsters then claimed that TDU was delaying the vote.

Both the companies and the union put out propaganda urging a yes vote. Brendan Kaiser, secretary-treasurer of Wisconsin Local 579, put out a letter urging a yes vote that was distributed by Teamster employers throughout the country. The members finally approved a second contract, which was considerably better than the one they had rejected. Once again, a contract battle had ended in a defeat for Presser and a victory for the rank and file and TDU.[8]

The Balance of the Contract Fights

During the 1985 contract fights TDU had held its ground and made some progress. Presser had pulled a fast one with the early UPS vote. But despite his success with that tactic, TDU grew faster than ever among UPS workers, expanding its network. At the same time, the substantial vote against the concession freight contract, the 81 percent rejection of the first carhaulers contract, and, most important, the carhaulers strike, showed that many union members were no longer afraid to fight back. This new spirit of resistance was soon to be demonstrated in the great Watsonville strike.

Notes

1.   'Union Agrees to Drug Tests', *Convoy-Dispatch*, no. 49 (January 1985).

2.   'My DOT Physical', *Convoy-Dispatch*, no. 51 (March–April 1985).

3.   'Drug Testing Needs Protections', *Convoy-Dispatch*, no. 63 (July–August 1986).

4.   Ibid.

5.   'Cover-up Exposed; Top IBT Experts Agree with TDU', *Convoy-Dispatch*, no. 66 (December 1986).

6.   'Are You Prepared to Stand Up to the Employers' Contract Demands?' *Convoy-Dispatch*, no. 50 (February 1985).

7.   Keith Gallagher, 'Concessions Don't Save Jobs', *Convoy-Dispatch*, no. 51 (March–April 1985).

8. TDU continued to press for the Teamster members' right to a fair vote on the contract. TDU had asked Presser for the mailing list of carhaulers so that it could give the members its opinion of the tentative agreement. Presser had denied the request, and TDU attorney Paul Levy filed a lawsuit, *Carothers et al.* v. *Presser et al.* demanding the right to an informed vote. On 11 June 1986 TDU appeared to have won a victory in that suit when Judge Oliver Gasch in Washington, DC ruled that the IBT and Jackie Presser had to allow groups of members or local unions the right to mail dissenting views on the contract to the members before the voting could take place; however, the case was later lost on appeal.

21

The Great Watsonville Strike

Esperanza Torres walked out of her house, crossed the street and entered the plant. She went over to the time clock, punched her timecard, said hello to a couple of friends and walked to the line. She put the net on her hair and the plastic apron over her blouse, slipped on her rubber gloves, and picked up her knife: then she waited at her little worktable. When the clock read exactly eight o'clock, the conveyor belt began to move.

Esperanza reached out, picked up a head of broccoli and cut it into pieces. And then she reached out and grabbed another. Sometimes they cut each head of broccoli into six slender pieces, and sometimes they cut it into many small pieces, the cut they called 'floret'. Today they had been told to cut the broccoli into four pieces. It was the peak of the season, and she would be there cutting broccoli for ten hours, as she had every workday for the last four months.

Esperanza Torres had worked in frozen food plants for eight years, and at Watsonville Canning and Frozen Food Company for the last five, and they had always cut fourteen heads of broccoli per minute. That was the understanding that the company had with the union. Today, her supervisor told her, the company was changing the rules. They would no longer cut fourteen heads of broccoli per minute: from now on, they would cut twenty. That was how it began. After that, Torres noticed, everything got worse. The company had hired more supervisors, and the forelady now walked the line with a stopwatch in her hand, stopping beside each worktable where the women cut the broccoli to time and count their production.

In the summer of 1985 Watsonville Canning employed almost 1,000 workers on two shifts, most of them women, and not everyone could keep up with the new pace of twenty heads of broccoli in a minute. In the next few weeks, those who could not keep up were transferred, disciplined or fired. Workers who had twenty or thirty years' seniority with the company were replaced by new workers who had been hired off the street.

Other rules were changed as well – for example, the workers were now forbidden to go to the bathroom between breaks. It was not just a question of production; there was an atmosphere of intimidation. The company fired one woman for stealing because she had eaten a bite of cauliflower. 'We used to say that all they need is a whip, so they could lash those who did not do the work exactly as they were told', says Torres. 'They were really treating us like slaves.'

Then something strange happened. Each of the women who worked on the conveyor belt at Watsonville Canning received a letter from the company and a check for $13. The company informed them that it was returning the monthly union dues deduction that had been withheld from their check, and from now on, they were told, there would be no more Teamsters union at the Watsonville Canning and Frozen Food Company. Now it was all clear – the company was out to break the union.

Teamster Local 912 was not a very good union, as unions go. Local 912 had been chartered in 1952 when Watsonville Canning and other local employers had invited the Teamsters to come in and represent their workers in order to get rid of a popular and militant CIO union. The workers had not wanted the Teamsters union, and had not voted for it; they had been stuck with it. In 1952 Richard King had been a business agent. Early in the local's history he was elected to the executive board, eventually becoming head of the local; thirty years later he was still running it. He owned a building in town, and he rented half of it to the union and had a bar in the other half. Some workers complained that he spent too much of his time in his bar, and not enough in the union hall.

When King first took over the local, most of the workers had been English-speaking men; now most of them were Mexican or Mexican-American women. There were about 5,000 members, and most of them spoke Spanish better than they spoke English, if they spoke English at all. King didn't speak Spanish, but he had a bartender who did, a fellow named Sergio Lopez. So King hired Lopez to be his business agent so that he could communicate with the members. Thereafter King talked to Lopez, and Lopez talked to the workers, and nobody was supposed to talk back.

Though it was a lousy union, it was the only defense against the employer that the Watsonville Canning workers had, and they were not about to give it up. The day the women received the refund for their union dues deduction in the mail, they took the money and went to the union hall, all 500 of them from the day shift, and stood in line waiting to pay their dues to King and Lopez.

Mort Console, the owner of Watsonville Canning, had expected that the women would simply let the union go, but since they had not, he would now have to fall back on an alternative plan. He would force the union into a strike, and then drag the strike out for a few months, but certainly less than a year. After a few months on strike, he thought, the workers would be happy to come back to work at any wage with or without the union. With a substantial cut in wages and benefits, and an end to union work rules, he could lower costs while increasing production through speed-up. Then he could not only beat his competitors, Shaw and Crosetti, but he would make millions more in profits. Even if he took a loss during the strike, he would make it up in the next season or two. It was a good plan, he thought, but it would take money to expand freezer capacity to stockpile some product into the fall, to hire attorneys and guards, and to bring in strikebreakers. He would have to secure a large loan, and to do so he would need the backing of the businessmen who sat on the boards of the local banks. The bankers and big growers who dominated the local economy were behind him, because they would also prosper if the unions were eliminated. Wells Fargo Bank loaned Console the money, a total of $23.5 million.

On a Friday at the beginning of September 1985, Watsonville Canning informed the workers, who were then earning $6.66 an hour – 40 cents below the wage scale paid at other frozen food companies – that the company was going to reduce their wage to $4.25 an hour. Richard Shaw, Inc. frozen foods, employing another 1,000 workers, announced that it was going to cut wages to the same level as those paid at Watsonville.

'In 1977 we earned $4.72 an hour, and we paid only $200 a month in rent', says Esperanza. 'Now in 1985 we're paying $400 a month in rent. How could we possibly accept a lower wage?' The women would not accept the wage cut, and refused to accept the company's attempt to break their union. On that Saturday the great Watsonville strike began. It was going to last a lot longer than Mort Console expected.

If it were only a question of Teamster boss Richard King, sitting there in his bar, Mort Console would have won. But Local 912 was more than Richard King; it was also those women who stood ten hours a day, year after year, cutting broccoli at little tables. They had fortitude and endurance, and for the last few years they also had the rudiments of an organization.

In 1980 a few truck drivers, mechanics and cannery workers had started a chapter of Teamsters for a Democratic Union in Local 912 in Watsonville. The group tried to get workers to go to the local union meetings, but without much success. The workers were pretty skeptical about Richard King and his union. As they saw it, King seemed to own both the bar and the local. TDU didn't make much headway until a year or two later, when Juan Parra decked the foreman. Parra worked at Watsonville Canning, and for months he had been badgered and bullied by one of the foremen. One day he just couldn't take it any more, and he turned on the foreman and hit him over the head with a push broom. The company immediately fired Juan Parra and charged him with assault with a deadly weapon as well.

Parra went to the union to talk to Sergio Lopez, and Lopez talked to King. Well, it was a bad situation, as King saw it, and, as usual, there wasn't much the union could do. King explained that to Lopez, and Lopez explained it to Parra. And that shrug of the official shoulders might have been the end of it. But the local chapter of TDU decided that something could and should be done. The chapter put out leaflets in Spanish and English explaining what had happened and organized meetings involving hundreds of workers to demand that Parra be reinstated, that the charges against him be dropped, and that the foreman be fired. The workers' response was one of support: at one of the meetings, a woman said, 'When Juan hit the foreman, he hit him for all of us.' A petition was circulated in support of Parra, and when all the signatures had been collected, the workers left their little tables by the conveyor belts, and their packing boxes, and their forklifts, and went as a group to take their petition to management. It was in effect a work stoppage, a short strike, and it worked: – Watsonville Canning fired the foreman.

The day that Juan Parra went to court, TDU organized a demonstration of support at the courthouse. However, as the workers were waiting for the trial to begin, agents of the US Immigration and Naturalization Service arrived and began arresting people, including three of Juan Parra's witnesses. No one doubted that Watsonville Canning had called the INS. The community was incensed, and there was a great outcry against the INS for so flagrantly involving itself in the trial on the side of the employer. Embarrassed by the bad publicity, the INS conducted an internal investigation. The judge threw out the charges against Juan Parra. Parra, and TDU, had won. (A few years later, Parra, with the help of a TDU attorney, won a settlement of several thousand dollars as the result of a civil rights case.)

Then there were other issues. At the J.J. Crosetti frozen food company, TDU petitioned management for a lunchroom for the workers, and the company conceded. TDU then took up the issue of union meetings. Local 912 meetings were conducted only in English, a language that most of the union members did not understand well and in which they could not easily express themselves. TDU demanded and won the right to have union meetings conducted in both English and Spanish so that the workers would know what was going on and could participate. Once business was conducted in Spanish as well as English, there was more interest in going to the meetings, and TDU brought a group of at least a dozen to every monthly meeting to ensure that there was a quorum.

It was in the course of these small battles that TDU began to convince the members that Local 912 was theirs, and that they could make the union do something about the situation in the frozen food plants. In small ways the rank and file of Local 912 was beginning to feel that they had some rights, and that their initiatives could make a difference.

In 1982 a TDU member named Frank Bardacke ran against King for the top office in the local, together with a TDU slate for other offices. TDU won 44 percent of the vote, showing that King could be challenged and that there was widespread opposition to his administration. Thus, by the time Watsonville Canning and the Shaw company provoked the strike, Esperanza Torres and the other women who cut and packed the broccoli had more to rely on than Richard King and Sergio Lopez. They had confidence in themselves, they had faith in their coworkers, and they had learned from the TDU chapter how the Teamsters union was supposed to work.

Esperanza Torres was typical of the women who worked in the Watsonville Canning plant and the other frozen food plants in the area. She had been born in the town of Jacoma, in the state of Michoacán, on the West Coast of Mexico; her parents were farmers. She had finished her basic education – in Mexico, the sixth grade – and had then gone to a vocational school for two years. Despite high unemployment she had been fortunate and had found jobs, first for a year as a dispatcher in a bus terminal, and then for two years as a clerk in a clothing store. In the meantime, she married and began to raise a family.

In search of a better life, she and her husband Enrique Torres moved from Mexico to the United States and found their way to Watsonville, 'Frozen Food Capital of the World', a little town only a few miles and a world away from the beach and university town of Santa Cruz, California. They got jobs in the frozen food plants, and eventually both Enrique and Esperanza ended up working at Watsonville Canning: 'The World's Largest Frozen Food Plant'. They had been married now for almost twenty years and had five children.

Esperanza Torres got involved in the union reform movement simply because it seemed to her that it was right. 'I think it's just something that a person carries inside of oneself', says Esperanza, speaking in Spanish. 'I was always bothered by injustice. It bothered me when they treated the workers badly. You see that you are doing your job, and then here comes the foremen, giving everybody a hard time, and demanding more work.' There were a lot of workers who felt as Esperanza did. They wanted to be treated with dignity and respect. They wanted justice.

On the eve of the strike the union called a meeting, and the TDU chapter organized hundreds of workers to come. As usual, at the front of the union hall was Richard King, but King, who had made a career of retreat and surrender, was unprepared to lead a fight. He had no strategy for winning the strike; his only plan was to keep things quiet and to try to end the strike as soon as possible on any terms. King tried to talk, but in the back of the union hall a couple of the women unfurled a banner reading 'On Strike – All Canneries Under One Contract'. The workers turned to the back of the hall, and then the whole group, led by the women with the banner, marched out the door, leaving King standing there alone. The workers marched to a nearby park, and there they held a strike rally, discussed the strategy for the strike, and made picketing assignments: if the union's leaders would not lead a strike, the workers would do it for themselves. On Monday morning the pickets were at their stations.

'Well', says Esperanza, 'it was really a very lovely thing. Here we were, most of us women, and we were all united, we were all strong, and, you know, we were all angry because of the way we had been treated. So we wanted to fight for our rights, to defend our rights as workers. Because, after all, we weren't slaves, we were being paid a wage for our work. We all had children, and we said, we are fighting for their future, because if we let ourselves accept this now, then what can we hope for our children later? There were quite a few married couples working in the cannery, both the man and the woman. And that made it harder from an economic point of view. But at the same time, it was really wonderful, because we were living through this thing together, and both of us had the same ideals, and we were fighting for the same cause.'

Watsonville Canning hired Litler, Mendelson & Tichey, a law firm with a reputation among labor unions as one of the biggest union busters in the West. The lawyers secured an injunction limiting the number of pickets to four at each of the plant's four gates. The police riot squad was sent to swoop down on the picket lines, and over the next several months many strikers were arrested for minor offenses, though the strike was entirely peaceful. A month after the strike began TDU helped organize the first Solidarity Day, inviting labor union activists and supporters from the nearby San Francisco Bay Area to come to Watsonville for one day as a show of solidarity. On that first Solidarity Day in October 1985 there were 3,000 people in the streets, and the crowd was so large that they were able to break the court injunction and hold a solidarity march right through downtown Watsonville.

The Watsonville strike was a rank-and-file workers' movement, but it also became an entire Mexican-American community on strike, a movement of networks of families and church members, of neighbors and compadres. At a mass meeting held some time later, the workers elected a strike committee that coordinated activities throughout the long strike: under rank-and-file pressure, the union hall was opened to the members, picket lines were organized, food distribution was set up, and speakers were dispatched to unions all over Northern California to seek support.

Northern California Teamster Joint Council 7 contributed funds, but did little else. The strike was really worker-controlled, and while the workers had shied away from electing a TDU leadership, neither was the strike committee controlled by Teamster officials. Though they had not chosen TDU to lead them, they had adopted TDU's principles and taken the organization of the strike into their own hands.

As the strike went on Mort Console bought some buses and vans, and began to bring in strikebreakers from other communities. 'The boss even made a barbecue for them in the plant', says Esperanza. 'And he cooked for them, and served them, and, well, it was really surprising, because in all the years we had worked there we had hardly ever even seen his face. We didn't know whether he was doing these things to attract more scabs, or just to make us mad.'

At one point, the Rev. Jesse Jackson came to Watsonville to walk with the strikers. But after the first couple of months, there was little drama and little excitement in the strike. Every two hours, sixteen workers went to picket at the four plant gates, and occasionally there was an arrest. The scabs would roll into the plant in the buses, making obscene gestures at the strikers. The strike became a siege. It went on through 1985, and then into 1986. Then the strike at Shaw was settled, but still the strike at Watsonville Canning went on. The 1,000 striking cannery workers lived on $55 per week in strike benefits from the union, they used up their savings, and then they went to work in the fields picking apples and berries. Some went to work in the electronics industry in the Silicon Valley around San Jose. Many just couldn't make it; they lost their cars and the furniture they were buying on time. Some were forced to move to other towns to live with friends or relatives, and some just moved out of their homes and lived in their pick-up trucks or cars. But still they came to the occasional union meeting and took their turn at picket duty, and though the strike went on for eighteen months, *not one single striker, not one out of a thousand, ever went back to work.*

In the middle of the strike Richard King stepped down as secretary-treasurer and top officer of the local, and Sergio Lopez took his place. Lopez claimed that he was a reasonable and moderate leader, and that TDU was too radical, too militant. There were differences of opinion among the strikers; some supported Lopez, and some were more skeptical about whether his replacing King signified any important change. The strike had gone on a long time now; people were tired, they were losing hope, but they would not give up, and still the strike went on.

Finally at the beginning of March 1987, the union and the employer reached a tentative agreement. The strike had bankrupted Mort Console, the man who had started it all, and Wells Fargo Bank had arranged for a consortium of fourteen growers headed by a rancher named David L. Gill to buy the plant. The new company was called Norcal, and it was with Norcal that the union reached an agreement. Sergio Lopez endorsed the new contract, and Chuck Mack, president of Teamster Joint Council 7, told the press that the contract 'makes labor history. ... In a day and age when organized labor has faced so many reductions', reaching this agreement is a tremendous victory.'

A meeting was called at the union hall, and all strikers showed up to hear the terms of the proposed agreement. Sergio Lopez recommended that the workers accept the proposed contract, which called for a basic hourly wage of $5.85, less than the workers had been making, but more than the cut in pay that Mort Console had originally tried to impose.

The workers were about to accept the contract when a man at the back of the hall raised his hand and began to speak. The union officials at the front of the hall tried to shout down the speaker, but the members demanded that he be given the floor. The speaker was Joe Fahey, a UPS driver and TDU member who had been elected recording secretary and business agent in 1985. Fahey explained that the contract that was being proposed would deny most of the members their medical benefits, and he suggested that, rather than accept or reject the contract, the Watsonville workers simply postpone the vote for a week while the union officers negotiated a better deal. The Watsonville Canning workers were tired, and they wanted to go back to work – but they realized that Fahey was right: after all this time on strike, there was no point in going back to work with no health insurance. So they voted to postpone a ratification vote on the contract, and to continue the strike.

As they left the union hall, Esperanza Torres began to recite the rosary, other women joined her, and then a group started off to St. Patrick's Church, two and a half blocks away. Several of the women fell to their knees and began crawling to the church. Hundreds of workers joined in the march, praying and walking, overcome with emotion. When they arrived, the church was already full of other strikers who gone on ahead. 'And it was really very wonderful', says Esperanza, 'because the strikers had been divided, and this was what united us.'

The Teamster officials were furious that the contract had been rejected, and to punish the workers they closed the union hall and terminated strike benefits. It was as if the strike were starting all over again, only now as an unauthorized strike, a wildcat strike. The workers fell back on their own resources, their own traditions of struggle in the fields of California and the factories of Mexico. Locked out of their own union hall, they moved the strike headquarters to the Torres's house, across the street from the plant. Esperanza and six other women began a hunger strike.

Since the injunction no longer applied, because the union had nothing to do with this unofficial strike, the workers set up a camp in front of the plant gates. There were big picket lines again, as in the first few days of the strike. It was the rank and file against the company, the women workers against the growers and the bankers. Within a few days Gill and Lopez came back with another agreement – and this one included the health benefits. On Wednesday, 11 March the workers voted 543 to 21 to return to work. In the end, they went back to work with a pay cut, and there were still the supervisors and the foremen with their watches, but they had saved their union and they had won their health benefits, and they had done it themselves. Following the strike many of the workers returned to the church and prayed. 'We were giving thanks to God', says Esperanza Torres, 'that after so much work, and so much effort, and so many sacrifices, that we had finally achieved something good.'

Mort Console, Watsonville Canning and Wells Fargo Bank had thought that they could get away with breaking the union and tearing up the contract. They had the money and the lawyers, the guards and the strikebreakers. They had it all figured out – but they hadn't counted on TDU and the women of Watsonville.

'I would say', says Esperanza Torres, 'that we won.'

22

Presser, the Mafia and the FBI

Unfortunately for the union's members, the leaders of the International Brotherhood of Teamsters were not much interested in events like those taking place in Watsonville. The International officers' attention was instead focused on the continuing scandal involving Jackie Presser and Allen Friedman. In November 1983, Allen Friedman, Jackie Presser's uncle, was sentenced to three years in a federal medical facility and fined $10,000 for embezzling some $165,000 from Local 507, which he had accomplished by paying salaries to union employees who never actually did any work for the union. Presser himself came under increasing pressure from the government, and in February 1985 federal authorities in Cleveland recommended that Presser, too, be indicted for his role in a 'ghost employee' scam.

Heat came from another source when in April federal district Judge Gerhard Gesell ordered Presser to testify before the President's Commission on Organized Crime. Presser tried and failed to have a subpoena quashed, and when in late April he did testify, he repeatedly invoked the Fifth Amendment and refused to answer questions about labor racketeering. At those same hearings several witnesses testified that Presser had been responsible for attacks on TDU members at a meeting in a Detroit suburb. The commission later issued a report noting that the Teamsters union 'had been firmly under the influence of organized crime since the 1950s' and that 'at both the international and local levels it continues to suffer from the relationship with organized crime'. The report concluded, 'The systematic use of trusteeships by the courts may be necessary to prevent organized crime from continuing to do business as usual.'

Trusteeship had already been used against one Teamster union, Local 560 in Union City, New Jersey, which had been controlled since the early 1950s by Anthony, Salvatore and Nunzio Provenzano, all three of whom were closely tied to the Vito Genovese crime family. The government brought suit under the Racketeer Influenced and Corrupt Organizations Act (the so-called RICO statute) against the local and its officers, and in 1984 federal Judge Harold Ackerman of Newark found them guilty of violating the civil section of the RICO Act. 'This group of gangsters', wrote Ackerman in his verdict, 'aided and abetted by their relatives and sycophants, engaged in a multi-faceted orgy of criminal activity. Continuously throughout approximately the last quarter of a century, the associates of the Provenzano group have dominated Local 560 through fear and intimidation, extorting the membership's union democracy rights and have exploited it through fraud and corruption.'[1] In mid-1986 Judge Ackerman removed the union's officers and named as trustee Joel Jacobson, a former organizer for the International Ladies Garment Workers Union and the United Auto Workers. The trusteeship of Teamster Local 560 was seen by some observers as a model for trusteeship of the entire International Brotherhood of Teamsters.

It was widely thought that Presser would be indicted in the ghost employee case, but in July 1985 the government strangely seemed to back off. The Department of Justice announced that, after a four-year investigation, it would not prosecute Presser, although it would continue to investigate his other activities. The *New York Times* asked in an editorial if Presser was innocent, too valuable an informant, or too well connected at the White House to be indicted.

The source at the Justice Department then revealed that the department had decided not to prosecute Presser because it had learned that the FBI had approved some of his criminal activities. NBC News reported that for thirteen years Jackie Presser had been giving information to the Federal Bureau of Investigation and the Internal Revenue Service, even though during part of that time federal prosecutors were trying to indict him for embezzlement. TDU argued that the Justice Department's decision not to indict Presser had the appearance of a cover-up, and that whatever the explanation, a disservice had been done to the rank-and-file Teamster members. TDU again demanded that the members have the right to elect their own president: 'We feel Jackie Presser should not be president of the Teamsters Union, but, more importantly, we feel that decision is up to the rank and file, by the right to vote. We intend to launch a campaign to win that right.'[2]

The Senate Permanent Investigations Subcommittee asked the General Accounting Office to undertake an investigation into why the Justice Department decided not to indict Presser, while the FBI's Office of Professional Responsibility began an internal investigation into possible wrongdoing by FBI agents responsible for the Presser investigation. In September 1985 this investigation revealed that FBI agents had authorized Jackie Presser to put ghosts on the union payroll and had reportedly rejected his requests to fire them!

Jackie Presser.

As a result of these disclosures, federal district Judge Samuel Bell granted a new trial to Allen Friedman, who had earlier been convicted in the ghost employee case. The Justice Department then announced that it would rather not try Allen Friedman in order to avoid confirming or denying that Presser had been an FBI informant, and so in October Judge Bell granted a government motion to dismiss the charges against Friedman. Shortly thereafter, Jack Nardi, who had pled guilty in the ghost employee case, retracted his plea, and the government decided to drop the case rather than reveal whether Presser was an informant. Consequently, federal district Judge John Manos dismissed the bribery and embezzlement charges against Nardi as well. The federal government was not only proving itself incapable of cleaning up the Teamsters, it was actually freeing those it had previously convicted.

Williams Drops a Bomb: The Mafia Runs the Teamsters

Roy Williams now dropped a bomb. On 13 October 1985 he agreed to cooperate with the federal investigation of the relations between organized crime and the unions in exchange for a 45-day delay of his date to report to prison. Two weeks later, in a federal case against nine men accused of conspiring to skim gambling receipts from Las Vegas casinos owned by Argent Corporation, Williams gave spectacular testimony confirming what many had for so long believed – that the Mafia controlled the Teamsters leadership.

Williams revealed that mobster Nick Civella paid him $1,500 a month for seven years in return for help in getting $87.75 million in loans from the Central States Pension Fund. 'I make no bones about it', said Williams. 'I was controlled by Nick Civella.' In a videotape played at the trial, Civella said to Williams, 'We're going to do everything we can to get you elected.' The election in question was the election of the IBT's president at the Teamster convention in 1981. 'I think that organized crime was filtered into the Teamsters Union a long time before I came here, and it'll be there a long time after I'm gone', said Williams.[3]

At the beginning of 1986, the controversy surrounding the investigations into Jackie Presser and his role as an informant and the testimony of Roy Williams about the payoffs he had received from Civella led to increasing criticism of the Reagan administration's friendliness towards Presser. In a report to President Reagan in January 1986, the President's Commission on Organized Crime suggested that contacts between the Reagan administration and Jackie Presser risked the appearance of impropriety. At the same time, the *New York Times* suggested that the Reagan administration's contacts with Presser could lead to an 'erosion of public confidence'.

In response to this pressure, Labor Secretary William Brock announced in mid-February that the Department of Labor would investigate the way in which the IBT selected its top officials to determine if that process was illegal. The investigation would also attempt to determine if the way in which the Teamsters selected their officers might have helped organized crime secure influence in the union.

But it was all getting very confusing. In March 1986 William Webster, the director of the Federal Bureau of Investigation, said that the FBI had not hidden information from the Department of Justice about Presser, although a month later a federal grand jury in Washington, DC was trying to determine if FBI agents had lied to Justice Department lawyers about the FBI's ties to Presser and his role as an informer, while yet another grand jury in Cleveland was looking into why the fraud case against Presser had been dropped.

Finally, in mid-May 1986 Presser was indicted on charges ranging from racketeering to embezzling $700,000 in a ghost employee scam. Nevertheless, Presser was released on $50,000 bond and continued to hold office as Teamster general president. Also indicted for making false statements that undermined a Labor Department investigation into the ghost employee fraud scheme was FBI agent Robert Friedrick, who was fired by FBI Director Webster in August 1986. It was revealed in October 1986 that Friedrick had blocked an indictment of Presser and that he had subsequently failed a lie detector test. The government's entire program of using the Teamsters had been a fiasco, with Presser corrupting the very FBI agents assigned to oversee his role as an informant.

TDU Demands the Right to Vote

These scandals gave greater credence to TDU's argument that the only answer to the union's problems was rank-and-file election of the International's top officers. In an Op-Ed article in the *New York Times*, A.H. Raskin criticized the Labor Department's do-nothing response to demands by TDU that all Teamster members be given the right to vote for their union's president. A *New York Times* editorial called upon the Reagan administration to break with the corrupt union leadership by challenging the legality of the IBT constitution's indirect method of voting for International officials.

In the fall of 1985, TDU had launched a National Right to Vote Petition Drive to put pressure both on the government and on forthcoming Teamsters convention. The TDU petition stated that the signers were 'in support of the principle of the right to vote for IBT president and International officers on a basis of one member one vote.'[4] TDU used the petition campaign to mobilize its members, and in the early 1986 sent a team of volunteer organizers on 2,000-mile trip through parts of the Midwest and down the East Coast. As a result of this campaign TDU collected over 100,000 signatures on its petition, which it duly delivered to the Teamster convention in Las Vegas in May.

At the same time, TDU candidates ran on a 'Right to Vote' platform in large local unions where additional convention delegates were to be elected. In Local 213, Canada's largest Teamster local, which had eleven delegates and three alternates, TDU's Right to Vote candidates won eleven of those fourteen positions. Heading the TDU slate were Diana Kilmury and Jack Vlahovic. The election was also a vote of confidence on Ed Lawson, Fifth International Vice-President and Director of the Canadian Conference, who also ran for delegate. Lawson suffered a humiliating defeat, finishing seventeenth and failing election as a delegate. The Canadian Right to Vote delegation was joined by a couple of dozen TDU delegates at the convention in May.

While the petition drive and the election of rank-and-file delegates best expressed the TDU philosophy of union reform, it was also important symbolically that a reformer directly challenge Presser for the presidency of the union. The challenge came from Sam Theodus, the 55-year-old president of Teamster Local 407 in Cleveland. A Teamster for thirty-four years, Theodus was both a reformer and a militant Teamster who had opposed the International's sell-out contracts. The TDU endorsed Theodus's candidacy on 26 April, and his home Local 407 added its endorsement the next day. Once again the reform movement was taking its fight to the floor of the Teamster convention.

Presser chaired the 1986 Teamsters convention, and among the first items on the agenda was an address by Vice-President George Bush, who spoke to the delegates by videotape. Also addressing the convention were Congressmen Tip O'Neil, Jim Wright and Bob Dole, as well as the chairmen of the Democratic and Republican parties. All of them were there looking for political support and Teamster money for the 1988 presidential election, and not one of them said a word about the allegations of corruption and Mafia control.

Because of the ongoing investigations into the Teamsters, it had been suggested that Labor Secretary Bill Brock not attend the convention, but with the approval of the White House he did so anyway. Speaking on the first day, Brock asked the convention, 'Are there locals where ... crime interests reign, are members' interests ignored or trampled? If there are such locals, put them in trusteeship. Are there areas where good people have been silent too long, where it's just plain time to clean house? If so, do it.'[5] The irony, of which Brock was well aware, was that corruption was more prevalent in the International itself than in the locals. In any case, Presser responded negatively to these suggestions by the secretary of labor: 'The government's five-year investigation', said Presser, 'has been a farce. ... It smells like persecution. It smacks of total hypocrisy.'[6]

The 1986 Teamster convention was not like other conventions before it. As *Convoy-Dispatch* reported, 'This time there was the beginning of a real debate, between the forces of Presser and the forces of reform. Even though the Presser forces had the overwhelming majority, they were on the defensive, concentrating on defeating all proposals for democracy and positive new direction.'[7] Sam Theodus introduced a resolution calling for a rank-and-file vote on International officers. This resolution was supported by 100 Teamster officials who had signed an open letter to the convention, another example of TDU's attempt to build a broad network of reform-minded officials within the union, and to begin to create what might be called a 'reform party' within the union.

A TDU resolution intended to control the proliferation of two-tier contracts had broad support, but the International argued that it would 'interfere' with local unions that wanted to sign such agreements. And TDU also introduced a resolution to limit the salaries of officers to $100,000. But it was the TDU resolution to increase strike benefits to between $90 and $110 that had the most support; it was backed by some 200 delegates. Presser claimed that the union could not afford to pay higher strike benefits, and had put a ten-year-long freeze on them at $45 to $55. Interestingly, the General Executive Board's consitutional changes, which were adopted, included a few that were clearly similar to TDU proposals. One example was an article that keeps defeated officers from taking large amounts in severance pay and other benefits when they leave.

The 1986 convention appeared much more democratic than previous Teamster conventions, but although Presser allowed dissenters to speak,

TDU said that 'heavy pressure and intimidation [was] put on local officers behind the scenes to get them to toe the line.' In particular, Presser demanded that local officials vote for him for president. In the end only twenty-four Teamsters voted for Sam Theodus. 'A number of TDU members, along with many more reform-minded officers, felt they had to cast their vote for Presser or put their local at risk.'[8]

In May 1986 Presser pled not guilty to the charge of embezzling money from the union, but nevertheless his troubles continued. In November 1986, Anthony 'Fat Tony' Salerno, convicted boss of the Genovese mob, and his associates Milton Rockman, John 'Peanuts' Tronolone and Vincent Cafaro were charged with arranging the election of Jackie Presser to the office of general president of the Teamsters union, and with influencing Presser's decisions about union business and about management of pension and welfare funds.

But even bigger problems were looming on the horizon for the Teamster leaders. In November 1986 the Department of Justice indicated that it would file a civil suit against the Teamsters under the Racketeer-Influenced and Corrupt Organizations Act to remove the General Executive Board of the International Brotherhood of Teamsters; the Justice Department then proposed to put the union put under a federal trusteeship. It was the first time that the federal government had attempted to take over an entire labor union. .

The Teamster Campaign Against the RICO Case

In response to these prosecutions, the IBT issued a statement claiming that 'organized crime has never, does not today and never will control the international union.' The RICO suit, it said, 'was an insult to the rank-and-file members of this union and will be dealt with accordingly when and if such action is filed.' The proposed suit was 'a political ploy designed to take the pressure of numerous problems off the [Reagan] Administration.'

The Teamster leadership argued that the such a suit would be 'an obviously specious attempt to interfere with the free trade union movement. It is insulting to us that the government would even consider any such litigation. Takeovers of unions are nothing new – communists and fascists have been doing so for decades. However, it is a sad day in the history of the United States and the American labor movement when such tactics are employed.'[9]

Lane Kirkland, president of the AFL-CIO, also opposed the suit. 'It doesn't sound to me like the proper relationship between a government and a private institution in a free society', said Kirkland. The AFL-CIO Executive Council adopted a resolution in August saying, 'If the Justice Department brings suit seeking supervision over an international union, the

AFL-CIO will do whatever is useful and productive in legal circumstances to prevent such supervision.'

Jackie Presser and the entire Teamster leadership launched a major public relations and lobbying campaign to attempt to stop the government from filing the RICO suit. The Teamster campaign was coordinated by general counsel John Climaco and director of communications Duke Zeller, and headed by Barry Feinstein, president of New York Local 237. The choice of Feinstein to lead the fight against the trusteeship was a clever one. Feinstein was a political liberal, a supporter of George McGovern in 1972, Walter Mondale in 1984, and Jesse Jackson in 1988, and more likely to garner support from other union leaders. (Though Feinstein himself had been criticized by a New York State commission for not acting against insurance brokers who had defrauded his local's welfare fund.)[10] In addition to the Teamsters' own effort, an organization was formed in Washington, DC called Americans Against Government Control of Unions. The group was headed by Victor Kamber, a public relations man whose clients were mostly labor unions; William Olwell, vice-president of the United Food and Commercial Workers, acted as its treasurer.[11]

In early September 1987 the Teamsters placed full-page advertisements in newspapers across the country opposing the trusteeship and arguing that it would be no different than the Polish government's suppression of the free trade union movement Solidarity. On 15 September 1987 the union held a rally of 4,000 local union officials in Cincinnati; it was chaired by Jackie Presser and attended by presidents of several other international unions and candidates for the office of president of the United States. The 4,000 Teamsters, wearing buttons reading 'And Justice for All – Even Teamsters', were told by Presser, 'We are going to win this war. You are the soldiers. You and your members must flood your congressional offices with letters, postcards and phone calls ... to get Congress to say, "No, you can't do this." Teamster officials in attendance were given kits explaining how to carry out a letter-writing and phone-call campaign to influence legislators. The union, said Presser, was prepared to spend what was necessary. 'We're going to spend $2 million more, and maybe another $2 million beyond that. The entire labor movement is in jeopardy.'

Four presidential candidates – New York Representative Jack Kemp, former Secretary of State Alexander M. Haig, Jesse Jackson and Illinois Senator Paul Simon – spoke to the rally in opposition to the trusteeship. Jackson was cheered when he alluded to the many members of the Reagan administration who were either under indictment or under investigation for their violations of ethics laws. The union officials supporting the Teamsters included Richard Trumka, president of the United Mine Workers; William Wynn, president of the United Food and Commercial Workers; Lenore Miller, secretary-treasurer of the Retail Workers Union; and Robert Georgine, president of the AFL-CIO's Building and Construction Trades Department.[12]

A month later there was another rally, this one called by Barry Feinstein in New York and attended by 700 union stewards from his 20,000-member Local 237. The rally was entitled 'Trusteeship – Union Democracy or Government Dictatorship', and featured Rep. William L. Clay (Dem., Missouri) and New York defense attorney Barry Slotnick.[13] One had to admire the vigor and energy of this Teamster campaign and wonder what might have been accomplished if the Teamsters had launched such a campaign to fight deregulation of the trucking industry, or to organize Overnite, or to support PATCO and UFCW Local P-9. The Teamsters leadership seemed capable of such vitality only when its own jobs, salaries and freedom from prison were at issue.

TDU's Position on the RICO Suit

Since its inception, TDU had opposed the idea of government takeovers of the union or any of its affiliates, so when in 1987 the government proposed to take over the entire union, TDU did not jump on the bandwagon. Linda Gregg, cochair of TDU, president of Denver Teamster Local 435, and an outspoken critic of Jackie Presser and the International leadership, told the *Los Angeles Times*, 'I worry about the government using a few bad apples as an excuse to launch an attack on all trade unionists in this country.'[14] TDU was somewhat ambivalent about the RICO suit. On the one hand, it definitely did *not* want a trusteeship that would mean a government takeover of the union; on the other hand, it would approve a 'reorganization' in the form of government-supervised direct rank-and-file elections of union officers, if the government could prove its RICO case against the Teamsters. At times TDU emphasized its support for the reorganization of the Teamsters through elections, while at other times it stressed its opposition to a government takeover.

In April 1987, even before the official announcement of the RICO suit against the Teamsters, TDU National Organizer Ken Paff sent a nine-page letter to Stephen Trott, assistant US attorney general, laying out in detail TDU's views at the time: '[W]e strongly urge the government to seek reorganization of the IBT under Section 1964(a) of the RICO Act.' However, TDU suggested that the government combine RICO with principles derived from the Labor Management Reporting and Disclosure Act (LMRDA, also known as the Landrum-Griffin Act), principles intended to insure the rights of rank-and-file union members. Paff also stated that TDU did not want a trusteeship: 'Under a prolonged trusteeship we really would be giving up important democratic rights. Also, under a prolonged trusteeship, the court-appointed monitors would be in a position of running our union and deciding whether to call national strike or organizing drives. Under this kind of "absentee-leadership", our union could falter as an institution.' And, because of the complexity of an International union, such a trusteeship simply 'may not be workable'.

'Indeed', wrote Paff, 'there is only one "reorganization" under RICO that the government can effectively undertake: namely, to direct the IBT to hold direct rank-and-file elections under government supervision for all International officers.' The supervision of these elections would be such as that provided by the Department of Labor, but TDU asked that government supervision continue for three consecutive elections.[15]

The 1987 TDU convention held in Windsor, Ontario tended to emphasize TDU's more negative views of the government suit. The TDU passed a resolution stating in part, 'The Convention reaffirms that in the event of a U.S. Department of Justice suit against the IBT using racketeering statutes, TDU will intervene to strongly oppose a court-appointed trusteeship, and to support a plan that will provide for a supervised one-member, one-vote election for International Union officers.'[16]

Reaffiliation with the AFL-CIO

The Teamsters' fight against the RICO suit led to increasing cooperation between Teamsters officials and officials of labor unions affiliated with the AFL-CIO, as well as with officials of the Federation itself; Kirkland and many other AFL-CIO officials supported the Teamsters. Ironically, it was the Teamster officials' criminal activities that had led to their expulsion from the AFL-CIO in 1957, and their criminal activities that would lead to their reaffiliation thirty years later.

In October 1987 the IBT General Executive Board sought readmission to the AFL-CIO, and on 24 October 1987 the AFL-CIO Executive Council voted unanimously to readmit the Teamsters to membership. 'We're giving them no cover, no insulation whatsoever, from their duty to comply with the law', said Kirkland. 'It is a process of pursuing what I have repeatedly stated is the essence of trade unionism: solidarity.'[17] The truth was that Kirkland and the AFL-CIO were willing to overlook the Teamsters' criminal activities if they could get the Teamsters' numbers, their backing in organizing drives, and their dues, which would make up 15 percent of the AFL-CIO budget. And the Teamsters desperately wanted the support of the AFL-CIO in their fight against the RICO suit.

Two days later Kirkland made good his part of the bargain, telling the press, 'A government-supervised trade union, like an employer-supervised trade union, is a contradiction in terms. If the Justice Department brings suit seeking supervision over an international union, the AFL-CIO will do whatever is useful and productive in the legal circumstances to prevent such supervision.'

On 29 October 1987 Jackie Presser, now a pathetic figure, dying of cancer and visibly suffering the affects of chemotherapy, told the assembled delegates of the AFL-CIO, 'We want to come home.' Presser, under indictment, alleged to be an FBI informant, with his union facing a federal suit for racketeering, but holding in his hands millions of dollars in dues and $10 million in political action committee money, was unanimously voted a member of the AFL-CIO Executive Council.[18]

The Teamsters' reaffiliation with the AFL-CIO was 'an exceptionally savvy move', according to Arthur Fox, the former head of PROD and lawyer for Public Citizen who frequently handles TDU cases. 'They're basically trying to buy the AFL-CIO's support and get them doing their bidding to head off this suit. There will be a massive political campaign, led by the AF of L, and primarily involving the Hill, to pressure the executive branch to pull in its horns.'[19]

TDU, which had for twelve years been fighting to rid itself of the mobsters who dominated the union, was understandably irritated by the cynicism of Kirkland's embrace of Presser. TDU issued a statement critical of both the AFL-CIO and the RICO suit, and insisting that the Federation support TDU's calls for a rank-and-file reform of the union. 'The AFL-CIO rightly condemns the notion of a government-controlled union', read TDU's statement, 'but ignores the existing problems of mob control. We call upon the AFL-CIO leadership and affiliates to support the TDU plan for supervised elections within the Teamsters for our top officials, because only the rank and file can clean up the corruption and begin the process of strengthening and bringing more democracy to our union. The only reason for the AFL-CIO not doing so would be a greater loyalty to protecting the future of Jackie Presser and his friends than the rights of 1.6 million rank and file Teamsters.'[20]

The congressional lobbying campaign that Arthur Fox had predicted soon began in earnest. The Teamster Political Action Committee made larger than usual contributions to congressmen, while Teamster lobbyists worked to line up support among the legislators. More than half the members of the House of Representatives signed a letter urging the Justice Department to reconsider its decision to file a RICO suit against the Teamsters. Not suprisingly, there was a high correlation between those who signed the letter and those who received large Teamster financial contributions.[21]

Two months after the reaffiliation of the Teamsters with the AFL-CIO, Justice Department deputy counsel Richard M. Rogers acknowledged that Teamster President Jackie Presser was indeed an FBI informer. As Presser's ghost employee trial approached, his attorney filed a motion to dismiss the labor racketeering charges against Presser on the grounds that Presser had been a secret informant for the FBI from 1973 to 1983 and had carried out illegal activities at the direction of the FBI.

Among the documents supporting the motion was a memo from Oliver B. Revell, head of the FBI's criminal division, which had been sent to FBI Director William Webster on 10 May 1983; this memo authorized Presser to participate in criminal activities with people under investigation if approved by the FBI in advance. But the memo was ambiguous and also stated that Presser's assistance was to be viewed as 'strictly voluntary and will not exempt him from arrest or prosecution for any violation of law' unless approved by FBI guidelines.[22] The contents of this memo were rather disturbing. Debate had raged about whether the government should take control the Teamsters, but the memo seemed to indicate that one arm of the federal government had been exercising a good deal of control over the Teamsters through the IBT's top official, Jackie Presser.

TDU: From Dissident Minority to Opposition Party

Affilicted with cancer, under indictment, and caught between the Mafia and the FBI, Jackie Presser suffered the reversal of the fortune that had brought him to the top of the International Brotherhood of Teamsters. Meanwhile, his opposition in the union was transforming itself from a dissident minority into the opposition reform party. The biggest indications of the growing power of TDU were the results of the 1987 and 1988 contract votes. Throughout the 1970s and early 1980s, TDU had been a small but significant minority in the union, followed by perhaps a third of the workers under the freight, carhaulers, and UPS contracts. Now the union membership, having suffered through deregulation and depression, having lived under the thumb of one crooked official after another, voted in a majority against Presser and against the International – and mainly against the employers.

It began in 1987, when 53 percent of the Teamsters voted as urged by TDU against the UPS contract proposed by Jackie Presser. Presser nevertheless imposed the contract. Then in May 1988, the freight contract was defeated by a vote of 64,01 to 36,782 (a no vote of 64 percent). Acting General President Weldon Mathis then imposed the contract.[23] By July 1988, when the carhaulers rejected their contract by 9,220 to 3,535, Mathis and his successor McCarthy dared not impose it. It looked, finally, as if the rank and file was in a position to throw off the dictators and parasites who had been living off their dues all these years.

The RICO Suit Is Filed

Despite the campaign by the Teamsters and the AFL-CIO, the Justice Department filed the RICO suit against the Teamsters International union on 28

June 1988, charging that 'the IBT leadership has made a devil's pact with La Cosa Nostra – La Cosa Nostra figures have insured the elections of the IBT's top officers, including the union's last two presidents.' The government claimed that 'organized crime has deprived union members of their rights through a pattern of racketeering that includes 20 murders, a number of shootings, bombings, beatings, a campaign of fear, extortion and theft.'

The suit charged forty-eight defendants, including Jackie Presser, the entire Teamster General Executive Board, the commission of La Cosa Nostra and its ruling council, and twenty-six Cosa Nostra defendants, some of whom were also Teamsters. The government asked that the court appoint monitors to oversee new elections for International officers.

Faced with widespread criticism of the suit, US Attorney Rudolph W. Giuliani asserted, 'We are not seeking to take over the union. We are using the racketeering statute in a surgical way to take back the union from the Mafia.' But John Climaco, the chief counsel of the Teamsters, strongly disagreed: 'It is pure myth that this organization is in any way influenced or controlled by organized crime. I'm shocked and surprised that anyone who had reviewed this case, not in the Soviet Union, not in Poland, but in the United States of America, would take such action. It's totally un-American and wrong.' The AFL-CIO called the suit 'a clear abuse of the Government's prosecutorial power and is based on legal theories which, if sustained, would undermine a free trade union movement.'[24]

Because of his poor health, Presser never came to trial on the charges of labor racketeering. He finally died of a heart attack in the Cleveland suburb of Lakeland in July 1988 while undergoing brain surgery, taking to the grave the real story of his relationship to the Mafia and the FBI. His funeral oration was delivered by Senator Orrin Hatch, an anti-union Republican from Utah who had helped Presser in his campaign of dirty tricks against TDU and the rank-and-file movement.[25]

Notes

1.   'Court Oversees Jersey Union in Test for Possible Takeovers', *New York Times*, 28 March 1987.

2.   'Presser Non-Indictment Raises Crucial Questions', *Convoy-Dispatch*, no. 55 (September 1985).

3.   Arnold H. Lubasch, 'Ex-Teamster Chief Tells Jury Union Is Controlled by Mafia', *New York Times*, 2 June 1987.

4.   'National Right to Vote Petition Drive Launched', *Convoy-Dispatch*, no. 56 (October 1985).

5.   *Proceedings, 23rd Convention: International Brotherhood of Teamsters, Chauffeurs, Warehousemen of America, Las Vegas, Nevada, May 19, 1986*, First Day, p. 55.

6.   *Proceedings*, p. 69.

7.   'Debate on Democracy', *Convoy-Dispatch*, no. 62 (June 1986).

8.   Ibid.

9.   Robert L. Jackson and Ronald J. Ostrow, 'Teamsters Assail Justice Dept. Suit', *Los*

Angeles Times, 11 June 1987.

10. Philip Dine, 'Polished, Urbane Teamster May Get Union's Top Post, *St. Louis Dispatch*, 22 November 1987.

11. Henry Weinstein and Ronald J. Ostrow, 'Teamsters Rally Forces to Battle U.S. Takeover', *Los Angeles Times*, 10 September 1987.

12. Robert L. Jackson, 'Teamsters Press Congress to Avert U.S. Seizure of Union', *Los Angeles Times*, 16 September 1987.

13. Mark A. Uhlig, 'Teamsters Urged to Battle U.S. Bid to Take Over Union', *New York Times*, 18 October 1987.

14. Henry Weinstein, 'U.S. Move Against Teamsters Jolts Labor', *Los Angeles Times*, 14 June 1987.

15. Letter from Ken Paff to Stephen Trott, April 1987.

16. 'Right to Vote Resolution Endorsed at TDU Convention', *Convoy-Dispatch*, no. 74 (November–December 1987).

17. Kenneth R. Noble, 'Teamster Return to AFL-CIO Wins Approval', *New York Times*, 25 October 1987.

18. Kenneth R. Noble, 'Presser Foresees Merger Creating "Political Giant"', *New York Times*, 30 October 1987.

19. Kenneth R. Noble', Teamster Move Is Seen as Harmful to U.S. Suit', *The New York Times*, 24 October 1987.

20. Daniel Forest, 'Are Teamsters Less Corrupt Now?', *The Guardian*, 11 November 1987.

21. Brooks Jackson, 'Congressmen Who Got Teamster Funds Join Effort to Block Suit Against Union', *Wall Street Journal*, 24 December 1987.

22. Don Irwin, 'FBI Memo Describing Presser Role as Informant Told', *Los Angeles Times*, 9 April 1988.

23. TDU National Organizer Ken Paff asserted that the proposed contract may have actually been voted down in a voice vote at the 7 April 1988 meeting of 277 Teamster freight locals' officers. However, Weldon Mathis declined to count a show of hands and declared that the motion to accept had carried.

24. Philip Shenon, 'U.S. Sues to Oust Teamster Chiefs and Have Trustee Run the Union', *New York Times*, 29 June 1988; and Ann Hagedorn, 'Government, in Suit, Seeks to Take Over Teamster Union Leadership Elections', *Wall Street Journal* 29 June 1988.

25. Kenneth R. Noble, 'Hundreds at Funeral for Presser Are Told to Recall His Leadership', *New York Times*, 13 July 1988.

PART VI

TDU: THE PARTY OF REFORM

23

Atlanta TDU: Teamster Reform Comes to the South

Several men are gathered around the box at the front of the room examining the Remington thirty-aught-six deer rifle that the chapter is raffling off. 'She's a beauty', says one of the fellows, looking through the scope and pointing the weapon at some speck on the far wall, 'a real beauty.' It's a warm Saturday night, 2 July 1988, and the Atlanta, Georgia chapter of Teamsters for a Democratic Union is holding its monthly meeting in the community room of Firehouse No. 2 in the suburb of College Park. They are mostly truck drivers, and mostly men, but there are several wives and a few women drivers. Waiting for the meeting to begin, they get a cup of coffee and a donut and discuss the latest developments.

Jackie Presser is still in a hospital somewhere dying of cancer, and Weldon Mathis, known as 'Mr. Clean', has taken over as acting president of the Teamsters– and hopes to make the position permanent. In Local 728 there's great interest in Mathis's career. Weldon, as he is familiarly called, has been the head of the local for as long as anyone can remember. The previous October Weldon's supporters had stuffed the ballot boxes and cheated the TDU reformers out of victory in the local election. Then Weldon split Local 728 in two, creating a new Local 928 and putting his son Lamar Mathis in charge of it.

TDU has protested the irregularities that occurred during the election to the Labor Department, a development that could hurt Weldon's attempt to stay in the Teamsters' top office. In June 1988 the Justice Department named Weldon in a civil lawsuit that it filed under the Racketeer Influenced and Corrupt Organizations Act. The Justice Department asserted that Weldon Mathis had aided and abetted extortion of members' rights, had engaged in mail fraud, had received illegal benefit fund payments and had several times violated the racketeering statutes. 'Mr. Clean', it seemed, might not be as spic-and-span as he made himself out to be. Nevertheless, in July 1988 he continued to fight for the Teamster presidency, and the spotlight had been on Atlanta.

Don Scott, who is presiding at the TDU chapter meeting, asks the group to stand and bow their heads in prayer. 'Lord', he says, 'we ask for your guidance in our struggle to bring democracy to the Teamsters union.' They run a businesslike meeting down here in Atlanta. Joyce Mims reads the minutes of the previous meeting and reports the balance in the TDU account: $180.60. Then Richard Black, a young UPS driver, gives a report on the first meeting of the newly created Local 928. Black is a little nervous about speaking, but he does fine. He explains that Lamar Mathis has promised better representation and better processing of claims for health and welfare. Black says that he has his doubts.

He also reports that he has had some trouble at work. The UPS center manager has tried to stop him from distributing TDU literature in the locker rooms. Black told the supervisor that it was his right to do so under the National Labor Relations Act, but the supervisor still ordered him to stop. Black reports that he has filed a complaint with the National Labor Relations Board and asks the chapter for support.

The next report is from Ron Smith, a driver at ANR, a big national trucking company. The company is paying drivers only $10.33 an hour – about 70 percent of union scale – and has refused to sign the new freight contract. 'We get no representation from Local 728 to correct our situation', says Smith. 'The union says they will not come to represent us until we have a contract.' He's been in contact with ANR barns in other cities. 'They're doing this all over the United States', he reports. The national TDU office is looking into the situation.

Bill Stromatt, a driver from Yellow Freight, reports that he and the drivers he works with have been successful in getting the company to accept a proposal they made concerning company work rules. Stromatt is also in charge of organizing the Atlanta chapter's fund-raising concert, and he lays out his plan for the event, including his hope that he can get Rhubarb Jones to emcee. Expenses for the concert will be a few hundred dollars, but the chapter should make enough money from the affair to cover their union election expenses. Joyce Mims, the real organizer of the chapter, stands to make a motion to endorse the plans for the concert. 'But', she adds, 'when you're called, you're going to have to come out and help.'

The business of the meeting has concluded, and Don Scott reads from a letter that the Labor Department has sent to Teamster President Jackie Presser concerning the irregularities in the Local 728 election. 'Looks like we may get a new election pretty soon', Scott says. The meeting over, the group adjourns to a restaurant around the corner and continues the discussion about Weldon and Lamar, the RICO suit and the Labor Department investigation over plates of buffalo wings and other such tidbits.

On 10 August 1988, a little over a month after I attended that meeting, Teamster Local 728 waived all defense in the government's investigation of the fraudulent October 1987 election. The Department of Labor agreed to supervise a new election in Local 728, and TDU members began preparing to run for office in the next election. However, this settlement fell apart when the TDUers who filed the complaint with the Department of Labor demanded that the split-off Local 928 be reunited in Local 728. The Mathis family refused to accept that proposal, and the issue awaits trial. Weldon Mathis had meanwhile been defeated by William J. McCarthy in the contest for IBT general president.

In the late 1980s TDU continued to expand, and one new area of activity was Atlanta. Just as it had done for over a decade, TDU turned up a remarkable group of rank-and-file union activists who turned Atlanta into a model chapter.

Doug and Joyce Mims

In October 1987 Doug Mims ran for vice-president of Teamster Local 728 in Atlanta as part of the Teamsters for Democracy slate, which was supported by Atlanta TDU. 'My wish', says Doug Mims, 'was simply to get the union back to the people it belongs to – the membership. That's all I've ever wanted. I don't want to hold local office. If these people that's running our local union would get up off their ass and represent the membership, instead of representing the companies, I could go fishin' again, like I did for years when I was getting representation, instead of going to the union meetings.'

Doug Mims was born in 1938 in Dothan, Alabama, but when he was still a small child his parents moved California, where both worked in the aircraft industry during World War II. Later they moved back to the South, and when Doug was only seven years old his father died at the age of forty-six. 'My mother was an old farm girl, and she raised three boys and a girl by herself. My mother supported us on what we drew from my Dad's pension, and she also worked for a drugstore at the time.' Doug grew up on farms and in small towns, and was really a country boy. In his senior year Doug Mims went to a country high school, and there he met Joyce.

Joyce was also born in Dotham, in 1941, and was raised on a farm. 'Dad planted peanuts, cotton, corn, vegetables', says Joyce. 'We raised all of our own food, our vegetables, and cows and pigs and chickens. In the summertime we worked in the fields mostly, and during school we did all the farm chores before morning, and in the afternoon after school we did farm chores as well, such as the peanuts. We worked long hours from the time I was born, but it didn't hurt us any.'

Doug and Joyce married even before they finished high school. 'It was young, too young', says Joyce, 'but I've never regretted it. I worked in a grocery store as a cashier, and Doug also worked in the grocery store in the meat department, and that's how we supported ourselves that first year.'

'I studied basic engineering at Chipola Junior College in Marion, Florida', says Doug, 'and I loved it. I liked it so well that I got into mechanical drawing and blueprinting just a little bit.'

Joyce goes on: 'And then I became pregnant, and Doug did not know if he wanted continue school or what he wanted to do, but then after we found out I was pregnant, that made the decision.' They had a son named Stephen and then a daughter named Darinna, and to support the family Doug held odd jobs.

'And then', says Doug, 'a friend of mine said, "Let's go truck driving." Well, I been driving a truck ever since I was a baby. We had that farm and we had big equipment, and I was just a teenager when I started driving trucks. So I went driving a truck from coast to coast in 1960. And I drove coast to coast for a couple of years.'

Joyce remembers, 'He was gone like five and six weeks at a time, and he would only be home two or three days, and when he would come home for those two or three days our daughter Darinna, who was four, really didn't know him and Stephen didn't know him. So after a year and a half of that, I told him I just didn't feel I could live that way anymore, that I was raising the children by myself, and that I would prefer that he would do something else.'

'I came back and went to work for another parts company', Doug recalls, 'trying to come off the road because of the kids. There's a couple of years when I sold pots and pans door to door; I sold *Encyclopaedia Britannica*. I hocked my tenor saxophone just so I could pay the damn bills, and there's a couple of years where it's just fuzzy.' Then in the early 1960s Doug got a job with Railway Express. 'I was a driver. I drove over the road and in the city, and I worked on the dock.' Doug liked his immediate boss, and the boss liked him, and soon he was promoted to terminal manager and assigned to Athens, Georgia.

'I worked long hours in the office with him', says Joyce, 'in order to try to get all the work done. There wasn't that many employees there, and Doug had the responsibility of selling to the customers, and keeping the customers happy, and doing all the office work, and he didn't have a secretary, so I helped him a lot. But after they wanted him to do some things that were just directly against his principles, he resigned, and came back; we went back to Columbus, and he started work for R.C. Motor Lines.'

'Working for R.C. Motor Lines was a different world', says Doug. 'It was tremendous. When I went to work for them, George Joiner held controlling interest in the company, and his son Jack Joiner was terminal manager in Columbus. He and I were good friends. We were friends before I went to work there. Mr. Joiner knew his drivers, he knew his employees. When he came in a terminal he'd walk around and call every man by his first name. And on your birthday you'd get a birthday card and most of the time you got a telephone call from him. For thanksgiving you got a turkey, and for Christmas you got a ham and maybe a record album. It was just a different type situation – they left you alone, except every once in a while they'd get on somebody's case. It's the kind of company you don't get to work for any more, the kind of company that you bend over backwards to work for.

'Well, just like on Friday night when I first went to work for them in Columbus, which was a textile town. If we got through on Friday night around nine-thirty or ten o'clock the terminal manager would give somebody ten or fifteen dollars to go to the liquor store, or go to the hot dog stand *and* the liquor store, and bring back barbecued ribs and liquor, and everybody'd sit around and just kind of chew the fat and take the edge off. *Now* you don't do anything like that.'

'When we lived in Columbus we were very, very involved in the church', Joyce remembers, 'and we were youth leaders in the MYF, Methodist Youth Fellowship. We did that for a number of years, and while we were living there I was on the board of directors of the church.'

In the 1970s Doug transferred to Columbia, South Carolina, where he got involved in an attempt to change the policies in the Teamsters union there. 'I was one of the main people that forced the local in South Carolina into receivership because of the way it was being handled', says Doug.

Then R.C. Motor Lines was taken over, first by Eastern and then by Consolidated Freightways, and Doug Mims found he was no longer working for a family-run business but for a big corporation. The good times had come to an end. When he arrived at the terminal in Atlanta, his reputation as a union dissident in Columbia had preceded him. 'My first confrontation with management was the first day I went to work in Atlanta. They didn't want me because they had heard I was a troublemaker. Tony Smith, the line-haul supervisor, came out with Leroy Darling, the terminal manager. The first words out of Tony Smith's mouth – I'd never laid eyes on the man – was: "I didn't want you, you're a troublemaker, and I'm going to fire you." Now that really makes a man feel good, when he's got all these years tied up. Of course, he tried several times to do just that, but I'm still hanging tough.'

Doug remembers those days with some bitterness. 'They allowed the company to just starve me to death. They would rail my freight, run city drivers out of Rome, Georgia, and Jacksonville, Florida, round and through me, and leave me sitting home seven or eight days at a time. I guess the company and the union together figured if they could just starve me out I'd go back to South Carolina and leave them holding their little bag, and everything would be fine.

'But I didn't do it. I laid the paperwork on them. Every time they railed a trailer, I filed the paperwork, and a lot of the time I collected on it. And every time they run a city man round through my domicile, I filed the paperwork on it. And I collected several thousand dollars until we got this straightened out that I wasn't going to drop it.'

Working for Consolidated Freightways in Atlanta brought a lot more pressure and a lot more problems, but no support from the union. 'Weldon Mathis, Lamar Mathis and all the business agents haven't represented the membership for twelve, fifteen years', says Doug. 'Up until that time, I would have fought for Weldon Mathis. He was a big union man, a big union leader. He could get more done by making one telephone call to the company than you could by filing three months' paperwork. He was that powerful, that strong, and the companies were afraid of him.

'But then he was appointed vice-president to the International, and he went to Washington, DC, and he allowed Billy Waters and Wayne Shepherd and Al Johnson and all the rest of these people to start running the local union. Al Johnson was there, he would pretty well hold his own. But when Johnson retired it really got rough. And Weldon got up and made this little talk: "Well, y'all do what you have to do, you know, but if you reelect me to office I'll come back down here and I'll run this local from the local level. I'll leave Washington, DC." He made this promise twice, and he didn't keep it either time.

'But it just went from bad to worse. Any time you filed a grievance, the business agent wanted to see what the company had to say about it. I don't pay union dues to the company – I pay union dues to the union. And the union is supposed to settle my grievance. They're not supposed to call my damn supervisor on the damn telephone and ask him what he thinks about me filing a grievance. They're supposed to *tell* him – not *ask* him.'

The problems with the company and the union were eating at Doug, and he wanted to do something about them. 'I started going to union meetings, and I started asking questions. Weldon Mathis never has liked for anybody to ask questions, so if he didn't like the questions I asked, he'd rule me out of order, and if it got bad enough, he'd ask me to leave the union hall. I was trying to do something about my local union by myself.' And it wasn't working. It was at that point that Doug Mims ran into TDU. 'The local TDU chapter had a meeting', he recalls, 'and I was invited by a friend of mine to go to the meeting. Rick Smith and Ken Paff were down here for that meeting, and after being in the meeting probably forty or forty-five minutes, I realized that these people were doing just exactly what I had been trying to do by myself. I had been hardheaded, and I didn't really believe anybody else cared. I mean, I was caught up in my own little world. I filed my own grievances, and I fought my own battles, and I got thrown out of the union hall about monthly.'

Joyce had been out of town that weekend, and when she returned, Doug told her about the TDU meeting. 'He was very impressed, he liked the people, he liked what they had to say, and it fit the goals that he had. He decided he was going to become involved. And I said, okay, fine, whatever he wanted to do I would support him in. When we first started going to the TDU meetings, I felt like he should be the one that had the more active role, and that I would just be in the background and help him and support him.'

Joyce had plenty of other things to do: she had a small business in her home, she was president of her neighborhood pool and recreation club, active in the arts and craft club, and working on organizing a homeowners group. But when Doug was elected to the TDU International Steering Committee, Joyce was elected to the chapter steering committee and has served on it ever since. 'I'm glad I did, and I'm glad I've been involved; I've learned a lot. But sometimes I have to give Doug a little push, because he is the organizer, and he is the one who has the job and is the Teamster. I find that more and more of the responsibility is mine rather than his because he's on the road all the time. I have TDU members that call here, and if Doug's not in town they say, "Well, you know as much as Doug does, I'll just talk to you." And they ask me about their problems.'

In reality Joyce functions as the TDU organizer in Atlanta. 'Basically, I send out notices, and call people about the meeting, and I record the minutes and keep up with the money. I order the literature, and get it out to the membership, and I set up a table and sell literature at the meetings. When we had nominations for the election we were going to have a demonstration in front of the union hall. I wanted to have a wives' demonstration, so I called all the TDU members' wives who were either TDU members themselves or who had attended the meetings. It was pouring rain that day, and we demonstrated in the rain– that was really our first television news coverage. When I first became a member of TDU it would be myself, Milly Grant and Patty Cloward, and that would be the three girls at the meeting, but now a lot of the time we'll be half and half. A lot of them have joined TDU.' Joyce now doesn't have as much time for her crafts business, and Doug can't just go fishing– at least not until things in the union are straightened out.

Waymon Stroud

Another member of the Teamsters for Democracy slate that challenged the Mathis administration was Waymon Stroud, a dockworker at Carolina who had also served a term as chair of the Atlanta TDU chapter. Stroud brought to TDU not only his dozen years' experience in the trucking industry and the Teamsters union and his deep religious convictions, but also the experience of racism that only a Black Teamster can fully appreciate.

In 1980 Waymon Stroud was laid off by Mason-Dixon, where he had been a road driver. With four years' experience in the freight industry on the dock, as a city driver, and then on the road for Mason-Dixon, he had no doubt that he would soon be able to find a job. And so he did, with a private carrier, Owens-Illinois, a glass manufacturer. It was a sleeper-team operation, where two drivers travel together, taking turns driving, one driving while the other sleeps in a bed in the back of the cab. 'I made my first trip with Owens-Illinois in March of 1980', Stroud remembers, 'and while I was in the break room waiting on them to get me my trip pack and everything, one of the men did approach me and began to talk. His words to me was, "I don't know why you want to work here", he said, "because if they put me in a truck with a Black man, I'm not going to drive with him, I'm not going to work."

'And I asked him, what was his problem? Why would he tell me something like that? And he said, "Well, I'm just letting you know that some of us just won't ride with Blacks." I said, "Well, that's your problem, it's not mine." I said, "If I'm assigned with a white man, I'm going to get in the truck. If you get in there that's fine. If you don't, it's still fine."

'And he began to tell me how his father raised him up, hating Blacks. And I told him, "Well, your father didn't care too much about you." I never would get upset. I'm one that if you make me mad, you have really done something. I kept talking with him, and I said, "Well, I just want you to know that if they assign me and you in the same truck together, I'll be there sitting in the driver's seat waiting on you, and if you don't get there, then that's your business. But I'll be there, because as far as I'm concerned, you're just another man."'

Waymon Stroud was born in Atlanta, Georgia in 1953. His father was a truck driver for Alterman Foods and a member of the Teamsters union; his mother was a housewife. Waymon got married just before he graduated from high school and worked at first in several non-union warehouses. Then he worked at the Ciba-Geigy chemical warehouse until the company moved out of town.

He was a boxer back then, in the mid-1970s. 'I was about ready to go to the Golden Glove bouts, and I began to have marital problems. I wasn't saved then, and I couldn't concentrate in the ring. My coach asked me to leave and don't come back till I get my married life together, because he said, "I've seen too many young men hurt by this same thing." And so that kind of ended it there, and I never have gone back to the boxing career.'

Waymon got saved, and saved his marriage. He joined the Pentecostal Assemblies of the World church twelve years ago and eventually became a licensed elder in the church and the pastor of a congregation in Lithonia. 'I do honestly have to tell the men, you can thank God that you met me twelve years later. There was a time that I wouldn't have stood for some of the things that people have done to me. I knew all the little tricks and the little ins and outs about how to get a supervisor, how to call him off down the end of the dock and mistakenly let a box fall on him, or mistakenly push a float out and kick his ankle, all those little tricks. But I couldn't do it because of the life that I live now.'

In 1976 Waymon got his first union job with Campbell's 66. 'I worked there on the dock, and when they informed me that they wanted to put me on regular, I learned how to drive out in the yard. I worked for Campbell's for two years, until I was laid off. Then I went to Mason-Dixon and became a road driver – that was my start on the road. I ran the extra board. I worked for Mason-Dixon until 1980, when I was laid off there, and then I worked for a month for Consolidated Freightways before taking that sleeper-team job with Owens-Illinois.'

Despite that incident with the white driver who would not work with Blacks, Waymon Stroud continued to work at Owens-Illinois until they closed their trucking operation. He then took a job with Carolina, gave up driving over-the-road and went to work on the dock. As a dock worker, Stroud found that Carolina was constantly violating the contract, and he began to file grievances, some for himself, but mostly for other dock workers who were having problems. In the process he became a sort of unofficial steward.

'This started a few problems, because some of the older men, especially the whites, did not like this. They felt that when you filed grievances the company started making it hard for everybody.' At first the union supported Stroud, and he won virtually all the grievances he filed. He was on good terms with Weldon and Lamar Mathis and with the other officials. Lamar Mathis even asked him to become a steward at Carolina. 'I prayed about it and prayed about it, and the Lord just did not lead me to accept it', Waymon explains.

But after a while the union officials changed their attitude and began to regard Stroud and his grievances as a nuisance. The business agents told him to 'lighten up', and suggested that some of the problems could be solved without filing a grievance. 'That', says Stroud, 'is when I began to search for something stronger.' In 1986 Waymon Stroud learned about TDU from a friend. 'And that's when I began to collect all the literature that I could. I collected the TDU bylaws and constitution, and even the history as to how they got started. And I began to read all of that, and I began to meet people like Doug Mims, and I talked with him. I saw what TDU actually stood for, and they stood for the very things that I stand for, and that is democracy and standing up for our rights.'

The union stewards were none too happy that Waymon Stroud had become a TDU member. Stroud asked one of the stewards, Guffin Hurst – known as 'Stuffin' Guffin' because of his election duties – if he objected to

TDU. To which Hurst replied, 'I don't have nothing to do with nobody that's in TDU. They're nothing but a bunch of Canadians. They are against everything the union does. That woman that started it got almost the whole Canadian people in it. It died down, and now they're trying to stir it up again.'

The Local 728 business agents also attempted to discourage Stroud from participating in TDU. 'They asked me at the union hall why I didn't come to them and ask them about TDU before I joined it. And I asked them, "What would you have told me?" And they said, "We would have told you the truth, they're nothing but a bunch of no-good yankees." And I said, "That's why I didn't come and ask you."'

He remembers that on another occasion after he became involved in TDU he went down to the union hall on business. 'And this time one of the Black B.A.s came in, Willie Baker. The secretary, who is also Black, introduced me to him, and he introduced himself and we shook hands. And she said, "Baker, Stroud is a TDU member." And he looked at me and said, "Man, what are you doing in a racist organization like that?" I said, "Well, you had better explain yourself, because I don't understand." He said, "Man, say, ain't nothing in there but a bunch of whites. Whites operate that." And I asked him, "Baker, let me ask you a question. Who operates the Teamsters? Who are your top officials in the Teamsters? So how are you going to tell me that TDU is a white organization, when you've got white officials running basically the top positions in the Teamsters?" And I never did get an answer for that.'

Waymon Stroud's wife, Nellie Stroud, also joined TDU, and they both began to go to TDU meetings. Waymon started talking to the other union members at work and recruiting them to TDU. 'When they would ask me how do I know so much about the union, I would tell them because I've got outside help from members of TDU who believe what I believe in.'

Within TDU, Waymon Stroud worked with the local TDU leadership to attempt to get more Black Teamsters involved. 'I have felt within my heart, being honest, that TDU is actually out to help the person, not the color. There were many meetings where I was the only Black there. But I was voted the chairman last year of Atlanta TDU. I knew that they were trying to push me into office to help to promote Blacks. In fact, Don Scott and Mims both had talked with me, and they were trying to figure some sort of way that they could get Blacks involved. I did try and promote the Black men to come to the meetings, and there were times that we had eight to ten Blacks in a meeting, and they respected me for the stand that I took.'

As chair of the Atlanta chapter, Waymon Stroud also tried to change the way that TDU members conducted themselves. 'I did find a lot of TDU members were troublemakers – they were, honestly. They just went in looking for trouble. And I really tried to change that. I tried to bring peace between Teamsters and TDU here. I tried to get this point over: just because you are a TDU member doesn't mean you are invincible. Just because you are a TDU member does not mean that you're supposed to go in on that job and throw your weight around. You are a TDU member because of the fact that you stand up for democracy. When the union doesn't do things the way that they're supposed to do, that's when you step in and see to it that it's done.'

In 1987 Waymon Stroud ran for secretary-treasurer of Local 728 against Lamar Mathis on the Teamsters for Democracy Slate, which was supported by TDU. Alhough he lost, the Labor Department later overturned the election because it had been rigged by the incumbent officers, including Lamar Mathis. Waymon Stroud is still active in his barn, writing grievances for himself and other workers, keeping an eye on the company's 'Quality Team' meetings to make sure they don't undermine the union. He remains a loyal member of TDU: 'But I am not the chairman of TDU now because of other commitments that I have in the church. My people have asked me as much as possible to kind of come away from that because I'm looking very seriously to go full-time in the ministry within the next very few years.' Nevertheless, Waymon Stroud remains committed to TDU and its principles: 'It's TDU members who are the ones making the union as strong as it is today. Everybody that's a member of the Teamsters ought to be a TDU member. I did explain it like this one time: We shouldn't even have to have a TDU, the Teamsters union should stand for democracy in every way.'

Linda Strom

Linda Strom worked and waited for six years to become a truck driver and a member of the Teamsters union, finally getting a job as a casual at Yellow Freight and becoming a member of Atlanta Local 728. She was proud of her accomplishment and eager to be a good union member, and, wanting to find out her rights and responsibilities, she went down to Local 728's union hall and knocked on the door of the business agent, R.C. Smith.

'I told him', says Linda Strom, '"I've never been a Teamster before, I've never been in a union, so I would like a copy of the contract so I could study it and know it. I'd like to know what to do and what not to do, to keep from stepping on peoples' toes." And you know the remark he made to me – and this is a quote – he says, "The less you know, the better off you'll be and the less trouble you'll get in." That's exactly what he told me.' Not long after, Linda Strom joined the Atlanta TDU chapter.

Linda Strom was born in Batesville, Mississippi in 1946. Her mother was a nurse, and her father was a brickmason and the president of the small brickmason's local union, although as a child she paid no attention to his union activities. 'I was raised in the Baptist Church', says Linda. 'I was a pianist, organist, church choir director, church musician from the time I was in the eighth grade, a Sunday school teacher – you know, the whole bit. I also taught music when I was in high school. I enjoyed it then, but I knew that I did not want to do it for a living, which was the plan my grandmother had for me.'

After she graduated from high school Linda went to Northwest Mississippi Junior College in Senatobia, and then worked for six years for Gulf Oil as an accountant. She was married, had children, was divorced, and like so many women found herself the breadwinner of the household. In the mid-1970s she was working as the assistant manager at the Days Inn in Jackson, Mississippi and moonlighting as an accountant. 'It was at the Days Inn that I met the drivers from Yellow and McLean, because we handled all the drivers that came into Jackson. And my uncle's a driver, too; he drives for Transcon. They were the ones that really influenced me to get started. I liked the money, the insurance and the benefits – that was something that I'd never had. I was working three jobs in Jackson, day and night, trying to support two children by myself, and I wasn't making a fourth of the money they were making driving a truck. I made the decision then to start driving, but I had to work three years over-the-road, cross-country, to get qualified to even apply to a union company for a job.'

It was the old story: she needed a job to get experience, but she needed experience to get a job. 'So I lied to get my first job. I had a friend who worked for a freight company in Jackson, and she wrote me a reference saying that I had worked for her for six months.' With that letter of recommendation Linda could get hired, but she still didn't really know how to drive: 'I was bluffing it all the way.' The first time she made a delivery she had to ask another driver to back the truck to the dock because she didn't know how to do it herself. 'Whatever problems I ran into, the drivers out there were terrific. Like if the truck broke down, they helped me.' Gradually, she taught herself to drive.

'I worked three years for Sam Tanksley out of Cape Girardeau, hauling produce from the West Coast back East, and dry freight back to the West. The whole point of my starting to drive was to go to work for Yellow. But at the time I got my three years in, everybody was laid off, so then I had to wait a few more years for it to pick back up where I could put my application in and be considered.'

For three years she drove trucks, worked in restaurants, and waited for her chance. In June 1985, after six years of working and waiting, Linda Strom was hired by Yellow Freight as a casual. Like many women in what have traditionally been men's occupations, she found that to be a success at the job she had to be able to do everything the men could do, and then some. 'They put me through my paces. During my casual months they put me on anything they thought might go wrong. I mean I bob-tailed in snow and ice. I pulled wrecked trailers back in to the terminal that should not have been pulled at all. There's just a lot of things I did that the regular guys wouldn't do. I had to do them if I wanted to keep working.' And women were always under the scrutiny of the employers and their coworkers, and subject to a different code of ethics than their male counterparts. 'There's a whole double standard for the women, just like in the South there's a double standard for everybody. I don't drink – I may have one or two drinks a year – but if we wanted to go in and sit down in a bar and have a drink, then that automatically labels us as a slut. The guys can go down there to the motel and go drink and go out with women, and they're macho, they're studs. But you let one of the women do it and then your reputation is shot: same old double standard.

'But the guys have to really be proud of women that work with them, and we have to just show exemplary attitude and conduct. I mean, you go in, you get you a sandwich, you go to bed, you get up, and you come back to work. We're not even allowed to relax. We're constantly a Yellow Freight employee representing the company. We have to be Miss Shirley Temple – not that I would want to do anything else, you understand – but I'd just like to be able to relax and not be on guard all the time. You're constantly on your guard, because if you get out there and mess up, then the guys really hold it against you.'

The double standard for women is complicated by white workers' attitudes towards Blacks. 'You have to be very careful about what you say or how you act toward a Black, even though they can be your best friend. There are two or three Black guys that I've known since I worked in Jackson, Mississippi that's been with the company for fifteen years. I feel nothing about sitting down and having breakfast with them. One morning I had got off from work, and went to the Waffle House up there on Windy Hill, and one of the Black guys that I've known for so long came in. He was helping me and my husband fix me a radio box to carry in my truck for my CB and my AM-FM. He sat down with me while I was eating breakfast. He had a cup of coffee and read the newspaper while I finished eating, and then he gave me the list of the parts I needed to get for them to finish the box. Well, somebody came in, though I don't even remember seeing another Yellow Freight driver in there, and later it was discussed in front of dispatch that me and this certain Black driver was over at Waffle House having breakfast. One of my close friends like to got in a fight with a guy right there in the dispatch office. It's ridiculous, you know.

'This one Black friend of ours has been a friend to me in so many ways, for so many years. Once I have come out from a terminal to a satellite where I've been down there swapping-out, dropping trailers and picking up trailers, and I come back out on the highway, and he and another guy were running up I-75 and I came up behind them. And they were talking on the CB, and I didn't butt in. And they were talking about different people, and they were commenting on them, and I had the best feeling about the way he talked about me.

'He said, "You'll never hear her use a cuss word." He said, "She's always a perfect lady." This is what this Black guy was telling a white driver. He said, "I've known this girl for years, and I've never heard her be out of the way or anything but understanding to anybody." I just felt so good all over I could hardly stand it. I finally said something. I said, "Lug Nut, are you my fan club?" just like that. And he said, "Gal, where are you?" But it just made me feel good all over.

'I'm that way with white guys, too. When they've been out of work, I've had a couple of them that's under me on the board, say to me, "Linda, do you have twenty dollars? I don't have running money." I give them twenty, forty, fifty dollars to give them running money till they get a check. I've been there; I know.'

Linda Strom was hired while a concession contract negotiated by Jackie Presser was in force. It provided for lower wages for casuals, and it was one of the main reasons she ended up joining TDU. 'I worked casual for Yellow for ten months. At that time the union had no use for the casuals whatsoever. They didn't care about the casuals, even though they were going to be future Teamsters. They were not concerned about your wants and needs. You just didn't exist.

'Back then, they had the casuals working at 80 percent of full wages for ten months. They put me on regular in April of 1986, when I finished my thirty days. Then, when they put you on regular, due to that contract, they dropped you back to 70 percent of full wages, but at least I got my benefits. I worked for 70 percent for a year, and then I got back up to 80 percent. Then I worked to April of 1988 at 80 percent. It was going to take me three years, to the beginning of the fourth year, to make a l00 percent according to the last contract. I felt like I was very much screwed, if you want to put it plain.

'Here I was doing the same job everybody else was doing and getting only a percentage of the pay. And you had to be qualified to drive for Yellow Freight before they ever put you on. I mean I had five years out there cross-country doing a lot harder job than I'm doing now. I really felt like they had taken me to the cleaners, I really did, and I still do. This is one of the reasons I joined TDU, because ever since I had been in the union it was one thing or another taking money out of my pocket. I had heard about TDU through several of the drivers, but there was a lady driver at Roadway that invited me to go to a meeting. When I went down there, it just so happened Rick Smith, the TDU organizer, was there, and I was very impressed with him, and I decided to join that night, and I did.'

Part of what appealed to Linda was TDU's idealism. 'I think a lot of my ideals and all are basically TDU's ideals, and they go back to the church, and that's fairness according to the Bible. We open the meetings with a prayer, that's something you don't do in union meetings. I feel like every member of TDU has got a lot more moral strength about them. There's this moral strength and moral background that they bring into it, and I think that's a very important part of your life.' Since joining TDU, Linda Strom has been active in the Atlanta chapter and in recruiting new members. 'Matter of fact, I've got a mechanic in the shop down there that wanted literature, and I sent it to him by my son the other day. I gave him the TDU constitution, "Your Rights as a TDU Member", things that I thought would inform him as to exactly what we are. They're saying we're trying to take over the union, we're trying to do this, we're trying to do that, we're Communists, and all this. I wanted him to see exactly what TDU is, and that is a group of Teamsters that are fighting to get a democratic vote in the union and to make the union do what they're supposed to do. That's what it all boils down to.'

24

The Future of the Union:
The Right to Vote

The twenty-first of February 1988 was a typically beautiful San Diego day, rather cool in the morning but becoming downright hot by midday in the suburb of El Cajon. At about 10:30 a.m. the cars began to arrive at the home of UPS worker and union steward Paul Castillo. As people came into the house there was a lot of handshaking, backslapping and catching up with old friends. By noon about fifty men, women and a few children had gathered around the swimming pool in the backyard. The food was cooking on the grill, the beer and soft drinks were cooling on ice, and it might have been the beginning of any backyard barbecue in America.

Someone led the group in the pledge of allegiance. Then Jim Moody welcomed everyone, introduced himself as a UPS package car driver, and explained that he'd be chairing the meeting. He said a few words about the importance of Teamsters for a Democratic Union for UPS workers: 'Remember, we're not production animals, but people.' Then Local 542 Vice-President Don Paddock told the group, 'If you organize, that's when they really listen.' Local 542 President Hal Smith told them: 'TDU is a necessary step, along with your local union.' And he admonished the UPSers: 'Take your lunch and your break like a human being.'

The featured speakers for the day were TDU West Coast Organizer Doug Allan and TDU International Steering Committee member Gail Sullivan. Doug Allan recounted a little of TDU's history, explained the organization's structure, and described some of its victories. At the center of Allan's talk was the need to change the IBT's constitution: 'We want democracy in our union. When we change the constitution to get the right to vote for all offices, we will have succeeded.'

Gail Sullivan's talk was more personal. She told about her experience as a single parent, and as one of the first female UPS package car drivers. She described how the women at UPS organized, how she came to join Teamsters for a Democratic Union, and how she became an elected business agent. Though she was personal and passionate, she also sounded a note of toughness: 'You represent a challenge to the status quo. Informed and educated rank and filers are much less likely to accept the crap. But you can't organize, and you can't change things unless you have a support group. We need a strategy model. It's like a war.' In any case, she said, 'I don't think UPS will ever be a dream job – it just isn't possible. But personally we can find some satisfaction through fighting back.'

The presentations were followed by questions about TDU or about problems that workers were having with the company or the union. Some people just had comments. One rank and filer raised his hand and was called on: 'With all this overtime', he said, 'we take it out on our wives and our kids. We make good money – but if you can't spend it with your family, what good is it? I think the most important thing is that we have backup.' The meeting had been short, less than an hour. Jim Moody brought it to a close: 'If we unite and communicate, we do have strength among ourselves.' Somebody passed a hat and $50 was collected. A few new members joined TDU. Then they broke out the beer and barbecue and sat talking, enjoying the sunshine and the solidarity.

'The best thing TDU can do for us is give us that knowledge, education that our locals don't give us', says local Vice-President Don Paddock. 'My intention is for TDU to recruit more people and have a louder voice in our locals.' Paddock was born in Hereford, Texas in 1944 and grew up working on a farm, hoeing cotton for fifty cents an hour at the age of eleven, and driving a tractor when he was only a few years older. His family later moved to Los Angeles, then to San Diego, and after finishing school he went to work at UPS in 1963 doing a variety of jobs: porter, belt-boy, carwasher, utility driver – 'anything they asked me to do. It was a good job – it was paying top money then, as it is today. We were smaller then and we had a lot more togetherness. His career at UPS was interrupted in 1965 when Don was drafted into the Army, serving two years in Vietnam assigned to transportation duty. He traveled throughout much of South Vietnam and then returned to work at UPS in San Diego.

Don Paddock was concerned about issues at work, so he became the union steward at his barn and served in that position for several years but quit when he felt that the local secretary-treasurer was not doing his job. Disturbed about the failure of the union to deal with management, Paddock decided to run for union office himself. 'I was tired of hearing all the bad things the union leaders were doing – the big bosses like Hoffa and Fitzsimmons and Presser – and I wanted to get more involved. I figured I could change the union, and TDU played its part, too, in helping me understand more about the contracts and the companies I worked with, and giving the moral support you don't get from your local unions.' In December 1986 Don Paddock was elected vice-president of Local 542, taking office in 1987.

Local 542 is a 5,000-member 'utility local' representing workers at FEDCO, Price Club, and many small companies, mostly truck drivers and office workers. The union has problems, Paddock explains, because it lacks enough membership participation. 'There are five thousand people who don't come down to their local meetings, so the secretary-treasurer does exactly what he wants. He spends the money where he wants, he allocates it, he changes the bylaws. He does what he wants. And it's very difficult to get people active in the union because of the bad reputation unions have. We're trying to make our local union more responsive to the members.'

What is happening in San Diego and increasingly throughout the country is a new development for TDU, the affiliation of significant numbers of reform-minded local officers who are not only willing to be publicly identified with TDU, but also willing to help organize and build it. Men and women like these will be the future leaders of the International Brotherhood of Teamsters.

Rivalry Within the IBT Leadership

When Jackie Presser took his leave of absence on 4 May 1988, Weldon Mathis had, in accordance with the union's constitution, become the acting general president. Mathis, a native of Sylvester, Georgia, had gone to work as a Teamster at the age of sixteen at Huber & Huber Motor Express. After serving in the army during World War II, he returned to work at Huber, and then in 1950 became a carhauler for Complete Auto Transit. A year later he was hired as a business agent for Teamster Local 728 in Atlanta and subsequently rose to become its secretary-treasurer in 1953 and president in 1966. Mathis became an organizer for the Southern Conference of Teamsters in 1957, and in 1967 he was made an organizer for the International, serving as Frank Fitzsimmons's executive assistant. In 1972 Mathis became an International vice-president, and in 1977 director of the Teamsters' Building and Construction Division. Mathis had also served as a member of President Nixon's National Pay Board.[1]

Acting General President Mathis called a General Executive Board meeting for 16 May 1988 in Scottsdale, Arizona (near Phoenix, where Presser was undergoing medical treatment at the time), but eight members boycotted the meeting, and the board only had the minimum nine members needed for a quorum. While several who failed to attend the meeting claimed that they were ill, it was evident that a power struggle had broken out among the board members over who would succeed Presser.[2] Soon it became clear that the contest was between Mathis, on the one hand, and a group of East Coast officials, on the other; this latter group included Presser's assistant Walter Shea, International Vice-President William J. McCarthy of Boston, and, most importantly, Joe Trerotola, the head of the Eastern Conference of Teamsters.

Mathis was seen as a relatively clean Teamster leader – despite the fact that he had been accused in the government's RICO suit of racketeering, using influence to get union jobs for relatives, and deriving personal benefit from his control over Teamster health and pension funds.[3] One of the skeletons in Mathis's closet was an association about eleven years earlier with an insurance company executive named Cornelius H. Dillingham. According to the government, Mathis had Teamster-organized companies purchase health insurance for their employees with Dillingham's insurance company, National Administrators. The government alleged that Mathis passed on pay-offs from Dillingham to other Teamster officials, though no criminal charges were ever filed. Funds from Dillingham's company were supposedly used to purchase a Corvette for 'Chuckie' O'Brien, then a Teamster official in Florida and the 'adopted' son of Jimmy Hoffa. O'Brien promised Dillingham that he would get business for him with the Teamsters' pipe-line division, then headed by Weldon Mathis. At the same time, Dillingham employed Weldon Mathis's son, Lamar Mathis, as a salesman for the company.

Weldon Mathis's influence was apparently useful, for eventually some 9,000 Teamsters were covered by Dillingham's company. In 1984 the US Department of Labor filed a lawsuit against Dillingham and his son, C.H. 'Corky' Dillingham III. Judge William O'Kelley ruled that they had illegally used for personal gain union money that had been put into a trust fund, and he fined the Dillinghams $2.5 million.[4] At the time Mathis assumed the acting presidency of the Teamsters, he and his family were taking hundreds of thousands of dollars a year from the IBT's treasury in salaries and allowances. Weldon Mathis was paid $290,000 in 1987, and several of his relatives were also on the payroll. His son Lamar was the secretary-treasurer of Local 728. His son Anthony was a business agent for Local 728, working in Savannah, Georgia. His son Michael was on the payroll of the Teamster political action committee. And his niece, Phyllis Cole, was employed as his secretary. As with so many other Teamster locals, it was 'all in the family'.[5]

Throughout his career Mathis had supported the Teamster's leadership, its undemocratic constitution and its rigged convention; he had, of course, voted against every reform measure proposed by PROD and TDU. He had never been identified with reform-minded Teamster officers like Pete Karagozian in Detroit, Sam Theodus in Cleveland or Ron Carey in New York. Now, however, on the eve of the Executive Board meeting to choose the new general president, Weldon Mathis underwent a startling conversion

– he became a reformer.

First, Mathis indicated that he was going to change the political allegiance of the Teamsters, opening up the Atlanta Teamster halls to Jesse Jackson and later endorsing Michael Dukakis, a move that aligned the Teamsters politically with the AFL-CIO. More important in terms of Teamster internal affairs, Mathis opposed the two-thirds rule. Ironically, he had just invoked the two-thirds rule to impose a freight contract that had been rejected by 64 percent of the members. 'I had no choice, I had to approve the damn thing', he said. 'This rule has to be changed.' Mathis had also voted against TDU's motion for an ethical practices committee at the Teamster convention, but now he called for the creation of such a committee. 'It would be headed by a retired judge or priest, someone who has, if I can use the phrase, high moral standards. My concern is that this organization change its image.' Finally, Mathis called for the direct election of convention delegates and a secret ballot vote for top officers at the convention.[6] But, significantly, he did not call for the right of the rank and file to elect the International's officers.

Mathis must have hoped that his sudden conversion to union reform would win the approval of the Departments of Justice and Labor, thus forestalling government takeover of the union. At the same time, he hoped to undercut the growing power of Teamsters for a Democratic Union by adopting some elements of its reform program. It was a shrewd move – a program for moderate reform from above rather than a more radical reform through rank-and-file rebellion from below. It would take the initiative away from the reform movement and the government by changing the rules of the game. TDU appreciated the cleverness of Mathis's gambit and actually expected him to be elected Teamster general president. The actual vote by the IBT's General Executive Board would prove, however, that the men who ran the Teamsters were both less clever and more wicked than TDU had believed.

William McCarthy

The General Executive Board meeting on 15 July 1988 chose instead William J. McCarthy to be general pesident of the Teamsters. According to various accounts, the real kingmaker on the Executive Board was 'Joe T.' Trerotola; Trerotola was in turn supported by Harold Friedman, Jackie Presser's old partner. In the end the Executive Board voted nine to eight for McCarthy over Mathis. McCarthy's selection was seen as a victory for the Eastern Conference Teamster organization, and for the organized crime figures with which many of its officials were connected; in that sense, William McCarthy represented the continuity of Teamster leadership.[7]

William McCarthy born in the Boston neighborhood of Charlestown in

1919, went to work as a truck driver at the age of seventeen, and became a member of Teamster Local 25. He was working at the M. & M. Trucking Company in 1941 when he was elected union steward. After serving in the army during World War II, he was elected a business agent for Local 25 in 1947, becoming president of the local in 1955. In 1964 McCarthy became the secretary-treasurer of New England Joint Council 10, and in 1968 became its president. McCarthy was originally closely associated with Jimmy Hoffa, though later, during a power struggle in Joint Council 10, he turned against Hoffa and formed an alliance with Frank Fitzsimmons. In 1969 Fitzsimmons rewarded McCarthy for his loyalty by appointing him to the International's General Executive Board.[8]

Asked at his inaugural press conference what he would do about the union's reputation for corruption, McCarthy responded to the reporter, 'The only reason our union has [such a reputation] is because of the likes of you and others.'[9] However, in July the *Los Angeles Times* reported that according to a secret FBI memo, McCarthy had told Presser that he, McCarthy, had to have the approval of New England Mafia leader Raymond L.S. Patriarca in order to run for International secretary-treasurer in 1984. At the same time it was reported that mobsters Anthony 'Fat Tony' Salerno of New York and John 'Peanuts' Tronolone of Cleveland had discussed McCarthy's possible selection as Teamster secretary-treasurer in May 1984 in a conversation overheard by an FBI bug. Tronolone told Salerno, head of the Genovese Mafia family, that he might support McCarthy, though 'you're going to name whoever you want to.' Salerno said that McCarthy was the 'head boss of the East Coast', and friendly with Jimmy Cashin, a former union official of the International Longshoremen's Association, a convicted criminal and a bag man for the mob.[10]

At a meeting of New Jersey Teamsters in Atlantic City in August 1988, McCarthy expressed his gratitude and respect for his supporters, including the three Provenzano brothers, and 'particularly for Salvatore Provenzano', the former president of Union City Local 560, who had served time for defrauding the union's dental plan. 'I told them he [Salvatore Provenzano] is my friend, and he always will be my friend', said McCarthy. All three Provenzano brothers had been convicted on various charges, including taking employer payoffs and murder.

McCarthy also vowed to fight the RICO suit: 'I feel sure we'll beat RICO. We have to win because, if we lose, it will cost the union another $20 million' to pay the costs of the trusteeship. Nevertheless, the reform movement's pressure on McCarthy was evident. At that same Atlantic City meeting, McCarthy announced that there would be no more concessionary bargaining and that relief would be granted only to truly needy firms. And, he said, no company engaged in double-breasting would receive any relief.[11]

McCarthy's idea of union democracy was shown in the way he arrived at the decision to endorse Republican George Bush for president in 1988. Without any organized discussion within the union, the International took a straw poll in which only 21,207 Teamsters, or 1.5 percent of the union membership, responded. The poll found that 50.2 percent of Teamsters wanted to endorse Bush, while 46.4 percent supported Dukakis. Not surprisingly, the poll coincided with McCarthy's own position. When McCarthy called together a meeting of Teamster officials in Chicago on 28 October to tell them that he had decided to endorse Bush, many local and regional union leaders were incensed and some complained.

Once in power, McCarthy immediately purged the union of several opponents or potential rivals. John Climaco, the Teamsters' chief counsel and a close associate of Weldon Mathis, was fired. Bobby Holmes was dumped as director of the 500,000-member Central Conference of Teamsters, and Edward Lawson was thrown out of office as director of the 100,000-member Canadian Conference of Teamsters: both lost their jobs because they had supported Mathis.[12]

McCarthy claimed that some of his changes were intended to clean up the union. On 7 April 1989 he told the US Senate Permanent Subcommitte on Investigations that he had forced IBT Vice-President Maurice Schurr out of office because Schurr had taken payoffs from employers. But McCarthy's claims of reform did not ring true. Only three weeks later McCarthy appointed George Vitale of Detroit Local 283 to the office of International Vice-President. Vitale been convicted in the 1970s both of taking employer payoffs and funds from the union.[13]

TDU's Position on Mathis and McCarthy

TDU did not believe Mathis's claims of being a reformer before the election of the new general president, and did not believe McCarthy's promises after he was chosen, but TDU was nevertheless delighted at the power struggle taking place. As Ken Paff, TDU national organizer, told the *Christian Science Monitor,* 'The political culture of a dictatorship demands that you have a united top; when you have a split up there, this tends to create an opening. ... That's the biggest thing for us.'[14]

Under pressure from the government and the rank-and-file movement, the first actual steps toward reform of the Teamsters were taken on 17 October 1988, when the General Executive Board meeting voted to do away with the rule that had required a two-thirds majority to reject a contract. Henceforth, a simple majority would be sufficient to accept or reject a contract. 'We have been fighting for this steadily for twelve years', said Paff, 'They called us nuts and screwballs, but we finally have majority rule in this union.'[15]

The RICO Settlement

The International Brotherhood of Teamsters entered a new era when on 13 March 1989 the US Department of Justice and the union reached an agreement settling the RICO suit. The agreement, 'influenced by the concerns and platform of ... Teamsters for a Democratic Union', as the *Wall Street Journal* reported, provided for the direct election of all convention delegates and the union's International officers in 1991.[16] TDU proclaimed, 'We can proudly celebrate the biggest victory in the history of the rank-and-file movement. We have won the Right to Vote! ... The Right to Vote has made possible the creation of a union that will be a model of democracy and strength.'[17]

The court order settling the RICO suit, signed by Judge David N. Edelstein, did not provide for a government takeover of the union and did not remove the International officers of the union (though several had already been driven out of office under government pressure).[18] But the settlement did require fundamental changes in the Teamster constitution to democratize the union. At the same time, it provided for government involvement in the affairs of the union for the next several years to ensure that the ties between the union and the mob were broken.

The court would appoint three officers who would be mutually agreed upon by the government and the Teamsters: an independent administrator, an investigations officer, and an election officer. The administrator was given far-reaching powers, 'the same rights and powers as the IBT's General President and/or General Executive Board under the IBT's Constitution', to discipline union officers and employees and to appoint trustees to run local unions. The administrator was also given veto power over any union expenditures, contracts (except collective bargaining agreements), and appointments of officers and employees, in order to stop racketeering.

The investigations officer was also given extensive powers, including the right to examine the union's books and records, to attend meetings, including the meetings of the International's General Executive Board, and the right to bring in independent auditors to examine the books and records of the union. The elections officer will be responsible for supervising the balloting and certifying the results of the 1991 and 1996 union elections.

It was the elections themselves that TDU believed to be the most important feature of the agreement. The IBT's constitution was to be changed so that all delegates to IBT conventions beginning in 1991 will be directly elected by rank-and-file balloting shortly before the convention (not more than six months before, except for those delegates elected during fall 1990 local union elections). This means that local union officers, many of whom have also been union employees, will no longer automatically be delegates.

The nominations for International officers will be made at the convention, with support by 5 percent of the delegates voting by secret ballot necessary to secure nomination. The general president, secretary-treasurer and all sixteen International vice-presidents will be elected within four to six months after the convention. The election will be by direct rank-and-file vote conducted through in-person, ballot-box voting at local unions, or by absentee ballots where necessary. Five vice-presidents will be elected at-large, while eleven are to be elected by members in the respective conferences, with the Canadian Conference receiving one vice-president; the Southern and Western conferences two vice-presidents each; and the Eastern and Central conferences three vice-presidents each.

The government and the Teamster reform movement both felt that this agreement would make it possible to break the stranglehold of the Mafia on the union. 'This agreement', said Attorney General Richard Thornburgh, 'culminated thirty years of efforts by the Department of Justice to remove the influence of organized crime within the Teamsters union.'[19] TDU organizer Ken Paff told the 1 April 1989 meeting of TDU's International Steering Committee that 'the court order was largely shaped by our views. I think we can take enormous pride in steering the settlement away from government trusteeship and toward the right to vote.'

William McCarthy also understood the significance of the government's intervention. He sent a message to all Teamster locals, which stated, 'I have consistently opposed any settlement. ... I reluctantly accept the terms of the consent order.'[20]

Ron Carey, Reform Candidate for President

The settlement of the RICO suit opened up the possibility of a democratic election for the top IBT officers for the first time in decades. The first to take advantage of this opening was Ron Carey, president of New York Local 804. Speaking to a packed meeting of 2,000 members held at Washington Irving High School in Manhattan on 16 September 1989, Carey announced his candidacy for the office of general president of the Teamsters union.

The 53-year-old Carey had been the president of Local 804 for more than twenty years, and had a reputation for militancy. Ron Carey grew up in Queens, graduated from Long Island City High School in 1953, and turned down a swimming scholarship to St. John's University in order to join the Marines. After two years in the Marine Corps, he returned home in 1955 to take a job at UPS, where his father, Joseph Carey, had worked for forty-eight years. Carey became active in the union, and in 1962 and again in 1965 ran unsuccessfully for union office. In 1968 he was finally elected president of Local 804. Most of Local 804's 7,000 members – some 5,000 – work for United Parcel Service in the New York City area. It was as head of this local that Carey won his well-deserved reputation as a militant local union leader.

Ron Carey, reform candidate for IBT general president.

Ken Paff, TDU national organizer.

He led his local in several strikes for higher wages and better conditions, and after Local 804 was brought into the UPS regional and national bargaining, he openly criticized several agreements negotiated by the top Teamster leaders as 'sell-outs'.

When the 1987 UPS contract proposal was brought before the locals, Carey urged his members to vote no and then went on the road to urge other UPS workers to turn down the contract. A majority of UPS workers did vote against the contract, but the union leadership imposed the contract anyway, using the 'two-thirds rule', requiring a two-thirds majority to reject a contract. Carey then sued the International to overturn the two-thirds rule, but the General Executive Board overturned the rule before the case was heard. Because of his opposition to the International, Carey was never allowed to participate in national UPS contract negotiations, even though Local 804 was the largest UPS local in the country.[21]

While other presidents of locals of comparable size often earned salaries over $100,000, Carey earned $45,000 a year. He was fond of pointing out that this was less than the $52,000 earned by Alain Boineau, the chef at Teamster headquarters. However, Carey's own Local 804 was not untainted by corruption. In 1988 John Long, secretary-treasurer of the local, was indicted for taking a $2,000 kickback in exchange for investing $150,000 in union funds. Carey and other Local 804 executive board members forced Long to resign, and later Long was sentenced to twelve years in prison. Carey's cleansing of his own local was far different from the policy of other Teamster leaders, who kept even convicted felons on the union payroll.

Throughout the 1980s Carey's views had been similar to those of TDU in its fight against the UPS contract, and in other ways. But he had never joined TDU. He had limited most of his activities to his own local, or to the affairs of UPS workers, and had not taken up the big issue of reform of the International.

Now with the membership granted the right to vote for the union's top officers, Carey decided that it was time to move. Now he would not content himself with leading a strong and democratic local and fighting for better UPS contracts nationally, but would move to lead the whole union. First he had to look for reform-minded allies throughout the union, and so it was only to be expected that he would turn first toward TDU. In November 1989 Carey went to the TDU Rank and File Convention in Pittsburgh to seek TDU's support for his candidacy. The TDU convention was the largest in its history, attended by 550 participants from 38 US states and Canadian provinces and from 121 local unions. They represented some 10,000 TDU members in scores of chapters throughout North America.

Carey brought the TDU members to their feet in wild applause several times as he spoke. 'We should not tolerate any corruption in our Teamsters Union', he shouted. 'We have to eliminate the fat-cat salaries of our officials. and we have to let employers know that we won't tolerate them breaking our agreements. We need to let them know that we want to be treated with dignity and respect. And we need to let them know that the party is over.'

After his speech, TDU members rose to question the candidates. After all the years that Carey had kept TDU at arms length, there was one question on everybody's mind, and one rank and filer finally asked it: 'Why haven't you joined TDU?' Clearly made uneasy by the question, Carey responded, 'I'm a Teamster who believes in democracy for our union, and I'm here to get the support of other rank-and-file Teamsters.'

After Carey's speech, TDU convention delegates spent more than two hours debating whether TDU should endorse his candidacy and if so when and on what terms. Some members feared that work on Carey's candidacy might distract TDU from its own goals, or sow illusions in salvation from above rather than reform from below. 'Our goal', said Pete Camarata, 'is to run delegates to change the Teamster constitution, not to elect knights on white horses. I'm worried that we'll get strung out on the Carey campaign and not focus on reforms.'

But many others challenged this position, arguing that work on the Carey campaign and continuing to work for a profound reform of the union were not incompatible. TDU National Organizer Ken Paff called upon the TDU membership to endorse Carey and to do so at once. 'I'm glad', said Paff, 'that we have a chance to endorse Carey before he puts together a slate or forms all of his programs. We have the opportunity of not only going along for the ride, but of being in the front seat.'[22] In the end 90 percent of the TDUers present voted to endorse Carey.

William Serrin, the former *New York Times* labor correspondent, attended the TDU convention and later wrote that with the candidacy of Carey and TDU's support, 'It is possible, just possible, that democracy may be about to come to the International Brotherhood of Teamsters.'[23]

'It took twenty-nine years to get the Berlin Wall down', said Frank Greco. 'Somewhere along the line these things prevail because they are right. It has to happen.'[24] By the beginning of 1990 TDU members were hard at work on the Carey campaign, the delegate elections, and the continued recruitment to their own organization and program. 'TDU now has the opportunity to build a movement that can really challenge for power in the delegate elections in the local unions, and in the election for international officers', said Ken Paff. 'We're glad there's a good independent candidate, Ron Carey, that we can endorse for General President, and we're going to need other candidates that will come forward from within the union. Win or lose, we have a chance to transform the union, and we think we can do it.'

In 1986 TDU had only 20 or 30 committed delegates at a Teamster convention made up of 1,800 delegates, and the organization was able to form a block with as many as 100 delegates on specific issues. Nominations at the 1991 Teamster convention will require 5 percent of about 1,800 delegates – that is, 90 delegates. Thus, to play a role in the future of the Teamsters, TDU will have to reach out to other reform-minded union members and officials in order to create a force large enough to play a significant role at the convention – and that level of influence may require 500 or even 1,000 delegates.

Playing power politics in the Teamsters does not mean that TDU will have to water down its principles. On the contrary, TDU's program of democracy within the union and militancy toward the employers can win the support of rank and filers and local officers. If there are enough reform-minded delegates at the 1991 IBT convention to nominate Ron Carey for general president, a tremendously important milestone will have been reached. If Ron Carey should be elected – a long shot but not an impossiblity – the union will have set out on the road to reform. But as TDU has always emphasized, the reform of the Teamsters depends not on any single individual, but rather on the awareness and organization and fighting spirit of the rank and file. Whoever wins the 1991 presidential election, TDU will still have an important role to play in maintaining such a movement for democracy and justice.

TDU and the Government

One of the most important factors in the future of TDU and the Teamster reform movement is obviously the government. Since it was founded in 1976, TDU has frequently initiated legal action. In particular, TDU has relied upon the 1959 Landrum-Griffin Act (the Labor Management Reporting and Disclosure Act) particularly Title I, known as the 'Workers' Bill of Rights'; Title IV, which regulates elections; and Title V, which requires union officers to conduct themselves toward their members as fiduciaries. Over the years, TDU has repeatedly gone to the National Labor Relations Board, to the courts and to the Department of Labor (and to many other government agencies) to seek justice for union members.

Obviously there are dangers in government involvement in unions, as TDU's leaders are among the first to acknowledge. Roosevelt's use of the FBI against the Teamsters in 1941, Eisenhower's anti-labor investigations, Nixon's alliance with Fitzsimmons and Reagan's with Presser are sufficient reasons for distrust of the government. For almost fifty years the Democrats and the Republicans have attempted to subordinate the Teamsters union to their political agenda and have largely succeeded in doing so. Certainly since the Nixon administration the Teamsters union has been dominated not only by the mob but also held hostage by the government.

Until the union is fully democratic and the rights of individual members are completely respected, says Ken Paff, TDU will find it necessary to continue to seek government intervention. 'We don't *rely* on the government or the law. We use the government and the laws, and we *rely* on the rank and file.' The RICO suit has clearly demonstrated that the government is not monolithic and that Teamster reformers can win significant reforms by taking advantage of the openings that present themselves. Nevertheless, the different elements within the government can be expected to continue to try to control the future evolution of the union for their own political purposes. The government is primarily concerned with managing the economy and preventing the emergence of political challenges. Whether led by Democrats or Republicans, over the years the government has demonstrated that it greatly prefers predictability to democracy and labor peace to labor militancy. In the event of a national transportation strike, the Teamsters union would certainly find itself in a direct confrontation with the government. The government usually intervenes in any important strike in any major industry, but it is especially concerned about strikes in the transportation industry because of their immediate economic impact and because of their affect on other unions.

It was no accident that US Attorney General Robert Kennedy pushed his investigations and indictments of Jimmy Hoffa just as Hoffa completed the creation of the National Master Freight Agreement. There had always been crime in the union, but there had not always been a national freight contract. More recently, President Ronald Reagan simply fired all 15,000 members of the Professional Air Traffic Controllers in 1981 when they went on strike, destroying their union. And when striking machinists and pilots at Eastern Airlines threatened to extend their picket lines to other airlines and to the railroads, President George Bush indicated that he would ask Congress to outlaw such sympathy strikes. Given this reality, the Teamster reform movement will probably continue to deal cautiously with the government, attempting to make use of the government to expand the rights of the rank and file and to keep the government from restraining the power of the union movement.

TDU: A Record of Achievement

Today TDU is in a position to transform itself from a dissident minority into an opposition party. Though only a small dissident group, TDU has always acted as 'the opposition' and has provided leadership for the entire union. The bylaws reform movement first initiated by TDU back in 1976 has continued to spread, and by 1989 scores of local unions had won increased democracy through bylaws reform. When the International violated the members' rights to vote on their contract, TDU brought suit. When local union officials denied members their rights, TDU fought in the legal arena and won a number of victories for union democracy, including important victories guaranteeing the members' right to a fair election. In the area of pension reform, TDU had protected the Teamster pension funds and won pensions for those who deserved them. And TDU also won an impressive number of victories in the area of safety.

The most impressive achievement of TDU, however, is the one that has been particularly documented in this book – its ability to attract the most idealistic rank-and-file reformers and organize them into a reform organization. Rank-and-file opposition to the employers, and to union officials who are allied with the employers, is constantly appearing in local unions and in particular companies. However, without the support of a national organization like TDU, many local reform groups would become discouraged and give up the fight for union democracy and justice from the employer. TDU has helped the local rank-and-file groups to survive and to grow. At the same time, TDU has been able to bring those local activists together in local chapters, and in regional and national meetings, so that they could share their experiences and generalize from them. This has helped to overcome the parochialism of workers in different cities or crafts who might not see beyond their own particular experiences to general issues and trends. A national organization with a broader vision of the Teamsters union and the labor movement has also made it possible for local union activists to develop the strength and the courage to take on what might be more controversial issues such as drug testing, ESOPs, and sexual and racial discrimination.

The TDU Rank and File Convention provided an opportunity each year for 500 or so of the most active Teamster reformers to meet together, discuss developments in the union, and attempt to develop a rank-and-file strategy to deal with them. At these conventions, TDU's company and industry networks, such as those among UPS workers and carhaulers, have worked on developing a global strategy to deal with their problems, something that would never be possible through a local union. At the same time, TDU workshops have provided the activists and local leaders with intensive education, so that they return home more effective in their organizing work.

The labor movement has never been effective without the assistance and involvement of professionals, technicians and other intellectuals. TDU has recognized this and has brought to its meetings and conventions labor educators, labor lawyers, occupational safety and health physicians, and labor historians who can give the rank-and-file union members a broader outlook not only on their own union, but also on the place of their union in the labor movement. It is because of this kind of activity over a period of thirteen years that the rank-and-file Teamster has become more sophisticated and more solidarity-conscious. TDU, both locally and nationally, has supported other unions in their struggles, from the Professional Air Traffic Controllers and Greyhound drivers to United Food and Commercial Workers Local P-9 and striking Blue Cross workers. TDU has supported not only Teamsters in Canada and Puerto Rico but also workers in Poland and South Africa in their struggles for union democracy.

In 1976 Frank Fitzsimmons told TDU and the rank-and-file movement to 'go to hell' and Jackie Presser had proclaimed the movement dead in 1986; but in 1989 the TDU movement was a force to be reckoned with in the union. The organization had grown to 10,000 members with a budget of just over $425,000 and a small but dedicated staff at offices in Detroit, Washington, New York and California. The election of TDU members and other reformers to local union office had a cumulative effect, gradually changing the political climate within the union, breaking the power of long-entrenched cliques and making the union more democratic, more tolerant of differences and more open to change at the grass roots.

TDU's members are activists, and its committees of freight workers, carhaulers, UPS workers, Kroger's and Roadway employees, and its local chapters are dynamic groups of volunteer organizers. The TDU newspaper *Convoy-Dispatch* reaches somewhere between 50,000 and 75,000 rank-and-file Teamsters each month, and local TDU chapters produce another twenty-five local newsletters – some simply mimeographed sheets, others tabloid newspapers that reach thousands more. The TDU officers in a score of unions across the country are not merely functionaries; they are opinion makers and shapers of local union policy. For all these reasons TDU has the capacity to grow rapidly and become the decisive factor in determining the future of the union.

The Mafia will attempt to get its hands on the Teamsters union again. Politicians will try to use the union for their own purposes. There will be other Teamster officials, some calling themselves reformers, who will want to make themselves dictators in the union, and the employers will continue to do everything they can to oppose democracy in the union and workers' power on the job. But there's a chance now, thanks to TDU, for the rank and file to run the International Brotherhood of Teamsters.

Notes

1. 'Labor Banquet, Workmen's Circle Annual Awards, Atlanta, Georgia, Weldon Mathis', n. d.

2. Henry Weinstein, 'Interim Teamster Chief Expects Presser to Resume His Post After Medical Leave', *Los Angeles Times*, 17 May 1988.

3. Tom Eblen, 'Struggle Seen for Teamsters Leadership', *Atlanta Constitution*, 11 July 1988.

4. Gail Epstein and Tom Eblen, 'Federal Suit Drags Up Local Teamsters' Past', *Atlanta Journal and Constitution*, 18 July 1988.

5. Tom Eblen, 'U.S. Challenges "Mr. Clean" Image of Teamsters' Weldon Mathis', *Atlanta Journal and Constitution*, 3 July 1988.

6. Aaron Bernstein, 'How Change at the Teamsters Lost by a Whisker', *Business Week*, 1 August 1988.

7. Ibid.

8. See Allan R. Gold, 'Old-Time Labor Chief: William Joseph McCarthy', *New York Times*, 16 July 1988.

9. Kenneth B. Noble, 'Teamsters, Rejecting Acting Chief, Pick New Englander as President', *New York Times*, 16 July 1988.

10. Robert L. Jackson and Ronald J. Ostrow, 'FBI Memo Says Teamster Chief Related Mafia Ties', *Los Angeles Times*, 28 July 1988.

11. Donald Warshaw, 'New Teamsters Leader Vows to Reopen Bargaining on Freight Contract', *The Sunday Star-Ledger*, 28 August 1988.

12. John Lippert, 'Holmes Loses Teamsters Post', *Detroit Free Press*, 3 August 1988; and Sheila Arnott, 'Teamster Boss Lawson Dumped in Power Fight', *Financial Post*, 4 August 1988.

13. 'McCarthy Appoints Vitale as Vice President', *Convoy-Dispatch*, no. 88 (June–July 1989).

14. Laurent Belsie, 'Teamsters See "A Whole Lotta Shakin' Going On" in the Union', *Christian Science Monitor*, 16 August 1988.

15. 'Teamsters Change Rule on Voting', Associated Press, 18 October 1988. See also Keith Naughton, 'Dissident Teamsters Say Struggle Aids Cause', *Detroit News*, 20 October 1988.

16. Ann Hagedorn and Albert R. Karr, 'Racketeering Suit Is Settled by Teamsters', *Wall Street Journal*, 14 March 1989.

17. 'Right to Vote!' *Convoy-Dispatch*, no. 86 (April 1989).

18. *United States of America* v. *International Brotherhood of Teamsters, Chauffeurs, Warehousemen and Helpers of America, AFL-CIO, et al.*, Order SS CIV. 4486 (DNE).

19. William Glaberson, 'U.S. and Teamsters Reach Accord That Avoids a Racketeering Trial', *New York Times*, 14 March 1989.

20. A Titan computer message to all Teamster locals cited in *Convoy-Dispatch*, no. 86 (April 1989).

21. Kenneth C. Crowe, 'Secret Ballot, New Hopes for Union: N.Y. Teamsters Reformer in Uphill Bid for Top Spot', *Newsday*, 17 September 1989.

22. Phill Kwik, 'Teamster Reformers Back Ron Carey in 1991 Election', *Labor Notes*, no. 129 (December 1989).

23. William Serrin, 'Carey Challenges the Porkchoppers', *The Nation*, 8–15 January 1990.

24. Phil Primack, 'Dissident Teamsters Have Presidential Goal', *Boston Herald*, 14 November 1989.

Selected Bibliography

Books About the Teamsters

Ashman, Charles and Rebecca Sobel. *The Strange Disappearance of Jimmy Hoffa: A Special Investigative Report*. New York 1976.

Barker, James M. *One of a Kind*. Boston 1971.

Brill, Steven. *The Teamsters*. New York 1978.

Dobbs, Farrell. *Teamster Rebellion*. New York 1972.

———. *Teamster Power*. New York 1973.

———. *Teamster Politics*. New York 1975.

———. *Teamster Bureaucracy*. New York 1977.

Fox, Arthur L., and John C. Sikorski. *Teamster Democracy and Financial Responsibility: A Factual and Structural Analysis*. Washington, DC 1976.

Franco, Joseph (with Richard Hammer). *Hoffa's Man: The Rise and Fall of Jimmy Hoffa as Witnessed by His Strongest Arm*. New York 1987.

Friedman, Samuel R. *Teamsters Rank and File: Power, Bureaucracy, and Rebellion at Work and in a Union*. Foreward by Douglas J. Allan and Peter J. Camarata, Co-Chairs, Teamsters for a Democratic Union. New York 1982.

Garnel, Donald. *The Rise of Teamster Power in the West*. Berkeley 1972.

Gillingham, J.B. *The Teamsters Union on the West Coast*. Berkeley 1956.

Hass, Eric. *Dave Beck, Labor Merchant: Case History of a Labor Leader*. New York 1955.

Hill, Samuel Ervin. *Teamsters and Transportation: Employee-Employer Relationships in New England*. Washington, DC 1942.

Hoffa, James R. *Hoffa: The Real Story*. New York 1975.

———. *The Trials of Jimmy Hoffa*. Chicago 1970.

James, Ralph C., and Estelle Dinerstein James. *Hoffa and the Teamsters: A Study of Union Power*. Princeton 1965.

Kennedy, Robert F. *The Enemy Within*. New York 1960.

Leiter, Robert David. *The Teamsters Union: A Study of Its Economic Impact*. New York 1957.

Leone, Richard D. *The Negro in the Trucking Industry*. Philadelphia 1970.

Martin, John Bartlow. *Jimmy Hoffa's Hot*. Greenwich, Conn. 1959.

McCallum, John D. *Dave Beck*. Mercer Island, Wash. 1978.

Moldea, Dan E. *The Hoffa Wars: Teamsters, Rebels, Politicians and the Mob*. New York 1978.

Mollenhoff, Clark R. *Tentacles of Power: The Story of Jimmy Hoffa*. New York 1965.

Perry, Charles R. *Deregulation and the Decline of the Unionized Trucking Industry*. Philadelphia 1986.

Ruiz, Vicki L. *Cannery Women – Cannery Lives: Mexican Women, Unionization, and the California Food Processing Industry, 1930–1950*. Albuquerque 1987.

Sheridan, Walter. *The Fall and Rise of Jimmy Hoffa*. New York 1972.

Velie, Lester. *Desperate Bargain: Why Jimmy Hoffa Had to Die*. New York 1977.

Walker, Charles Rumford. *American City: A Rank-and-File History*. New York 1971.

Zagri, Sidney. *Free Press, Fair Trial*. 1966.

Books with a Chapter or Two on the Teamsters

Bardacke, Frank. 'Watsonville: A Mexican Community on Strike', in Mike Davis and Michael Sprinker, *Reshaping the US Left: Popular Struggles in the 1980s. Volume III of The Year Left*. London 1988.

Galenson, Walter. *The CIO Challenge to AFL: A History of the American Labor Movement: 1935–1941*. Cambridge 1960.

Goulden, Joseph C. *Meany*. New York 1972.

Jacobs, Paul. *The State of the Unions*. New York 1963.

James, Estelle. 'Jimmy Hoffa: Labor Hero or Labor's Own Foe', in Melvyn Dubofsky and Warren R. Van Tine, eds, *Labor Leaders in America*. Chicago 1987.

Jones, Nard. *Seattle*. Garden City, N.Y. 1972.

Kwitny, Jonathan. *Vicious Circles: The Mafia in the Marketplace*. New York 1979.

Levinson, Harold M. 'Trucking' in Gerald G. Somers. ed., *Collective Bargaining: Contemporary American Experience*, Madison, Wis. n.d.

Levy, Jacques E. *César Chávez: Autobiography of La Causa*. New York 1975.

Mollenhoff, Clark R. *Game Plan for Disaster: An Ombudsman's Report on the Nixon Years*. New York 1976.

Morgan, Murray. *Skid Road: An Informal Portrait of Seattle*. New York 1951.

Moyers, Bill. *Listening to America: A Traveler Rediscovers His Country*. New York 1971.

Nelson, Gerald B. *Seattle: The Life and Times of an American City*. New York 1977.

Neuberger, Richard L. *Our Promised Land*. New York 1938.

Newell, Barbara Warne. *Chicago and the Labor Movement: Metropolitan Unionism in the 1930s*, Urbana, Ill. 1961.

Pierson, Frank C. *Unions in Postwar America: An Economic Assessment*. New York 1967.

Sale, Roger. *Seattle: Past to Present*. Seattle 1976.

Sullivan, George. 'Working for Survival', in Staughton Lynd and Alice Lynd, *Rank and File: Personal Histories by Working-Class Organizers*. Boston 1973.

Articles

Common, John R. 'Types of American Labor Organization – The Teamsters of Chicago'. *Quarterly Journal of Economics*, vol. 19 (May 1905).

Plott, Steven L. 'The Chicago Teamsters Strike of 1902: A Community Confronts the Beef Trust'. *Labor History*, vol. 26, no. 2, pp. 250–67.

Sullivan, George. 'Rank and File Rebellion in the International Brotherhood of Teamsters'. *Liberation* (May 1971).

Van Tine, Warren R. 'Daniel Joseph Tobin', in *The Dictionary of National Biography, Supplement V*.

Index